AF699063

Collected ABA and TriBar Opinion Reports 2009

Committee on Legal Opinions and the TriBar Opinion Committee

LAW LIBRARY
JUL 08 2009
GOLDEN GATE UNIVERSITY

ABA Section of BUSINESS LAW

AMERICAN BAR ASSOCIATION
Defending Liberty
Pursuing Justice

Cover design by ABA Publishing.

The materials contained herein represent the opinions and views of the authors and/or the editors, and should not be construed to be the views or opinions of the law firms or companies with which such persons are in partnership or associated or by whom such persons are employed, nor of the American Bar Association or the Section of Business Law unless adopted pursuant to the bylaws of the Association.

Nothing contained in this book is to be considered as the rendering of legal advice, either generally or in connection with any specific issue or case. Nor do these materials purport to explain or interpret any specific bond or policy, or any provisions thereof, issued by any particular insurance company, or to render insurance or other professional advice. Readers are responsible for obtaining advice from their own lawyers or other professionals. This book and any forms and agreements herein are intended for educational and informational purposes only.

13 11 10 09 5 4 3 2 1

© 2009 American Bar Association. All rights reserved.
Printed in the United States of America.

Cataloging-in-Publication data is on file with the Library of Congress.
The collected ABA and TriBar opinion reports 2009 / Committee on Legal Opinions and the Tribar Opinion Committee.

Discounts are available for books ordered in bulk. Special consideration is given to state bars, CLE programs, and other bar-related organizations. Inquire at Book Publishing, ABA Publishing, American Bar Association, 321 North Clark Street, Chicago, Illinois 60654.

www.ababooks.org

CONTENTS

FOREWORD

The meaning of legal opinion letters delivered to third parties in business transactions ("closing opinions") and the work lawyers are expected to do to support them are based on the customary practice of lawyers who regularly give, and who regularly advise recipients regarding, opinions of the kind involved. The leading sources of guidance on what constitutes customary practice on a national level are the reports on closing opinions issued by the TriBar Opinion Committee and committees of the ABA Section of Business Law whose reports are included in this volume. Those committees consist of lawyers from across the country whose practices cover a wide range of business transactions and practice settings.

Since 1993, the ABA has published collections of reports prepared by the TriBar Opinion Committee in book form. The 2005 edition added reports of the Committee on Legal Opinions of the ABA Section of Business Law. This edition combines current reports of those committees with other noteworthy ABA section reports on closing opinions.[1] All reports are presented as they appeared in *The Business Lawyer*.

We hope that bringing these important reports together in a single volume will facilitate reference to them and provide lawyers throughout the nation with a ready source of guidance when giving or requesting closing opinions. Special thanks to Carol K. Lucas, the able editor of this edition.

John B. Power, Chair
Committee on Legal Opinions,
ABA Section of Business Law

Donald W. Glazer
Richard R. Howe
Co-chairs
TriBar Opinion Committee

1. Although not closing opinions, audit response letters present many similar issues.

THIRD-PARTY "CLOSING" OPINIONS

* * *

A Report of
The TriBar Opinion Committee

THIRD-PARTY "CLOSING" OPINIONS

A Report of The TriBar Opinion Committee[1]

Introduction

This is a Report about legal opinion letters that lawyers in business transactions render to non-clients. Among the issues covered by this Report are (i) the content of opinion letters, (ii) the procedures opinion givers follow when conducting the factual and legal investigations required to support their opinions, and (iii) the meaning of language often used in opinion letters.

The TriBar Opinion Committee was formed more than twenty years ago, at a time when third-party legal opinion practice was as much folklore as analysis. Drawing its members from the three largest New York bar associations, the Committee consisted of lawyers from throughout New York State, from big firms and small, from larger cities as well as smaller ones. The Committee members began their work by exchanging information about and discussing their own opinion practices. The Committee members came to see that those on both sides of the opinion process—opinion givers and their clients on the one hand and opinion recipients and their counsel on the other—had a need for practical and continuing guidance on customary practices in giving and receiving legal opinions. The various TriBar Reports followed.

This Report is generally consistent with TriBar's prior reports. It reexamines and replaces TriBar's first report (the "1979 Report"), the two Addenda to it and the Committee's Special Report on the Remedies Opinion.[2] This revision considers the nearly two decades of court decisions,

1. Reflecting the broad use of its Reports, the Committee in recent years has expanded its membership beyond New York. The TriBar Opinion Committee ("Committee" or "TriBar") now consists of designees of the following organizations functioning as a single Committee: (i) Special Committee on Legal Opinions in Commercial Transactions, New York County Lawyers' Association; (ii) Corporation Law Committee, The Association of the Bar of the City of New York, and (iii) Special Committee on Legal Opinions of the Business Law Section, New York State Bar Association. Members of the Allegheny County (Pa.), Atlanta, Boston, Chicago, Delaware and Ontario Bar Associations and of the State Bar of Texas are also members of the Committee. The members of the Committee and the Reporters and Editorial Group for this Report are listed in Appendix C.

2. *See Legal Opinions to Third Parties: An Easier Path*, 34 BUS. LAW. 1891 (1979); *An Addendum—Legal Opinions to Third Parties: An Easier Path*, 36 BUS. LAW. 429 (1981); *Second Addendum to Legal*

legal opinion literature,[3] changes in corporate law and practice, and developments in legal opinion practice since the 1979 Report.[4]

The following three TriBar reports, each of which addresses a specialized area, are not affected by this Report:

- *Opinions in the Bankruptcy Context: Rating Agency, Structured Financing, and Chapter 11 Transactions*, 46 BUS. LAW. 717 (1991);
- *Use of the ABA Legal Opinion Accord in Specialized Financing Transactions*, 47 BUS. LAW. 1719 (1992); and
- *U.C.C. Security Interest Opinions*, 49 BUS. LAW. 359 (1993).

A NOTE ON USING THIS REPORT

Article I of this Report addresses matters having general application and thus applies to all subsequent Articles. Users of this Report should read Article I (including the Glossary in Section 1.9) as well as the particular Article they are concerned with to assure that they understand the context of that particular Article.

Article VI comments on specific opinions that are commonly rendered. It uses as a vehicle for discussion four **Illustrative Opinion Letters**, two on a loan (outside and inside counsel) and two on a related securities sale (outside and inside counsel). The opinion letters of inside counsel cover certain matters not covered (but which might have been covered) in the opinion letters of outside counsel.

An **Index of Typical Opinion Letter Features** precedes Article I and provides an alternative way to access materials about particular opinion provisions.

Citations to certain materials frequently referred to in this Report are in note 3 below.

Opinions to Third Parties: An Easier Path, 44 BUS. LAW. 563 (1989); *Special Report of the TriBar Opinion Committee: The Remedies Opinion*, 46 BUS. LAW. 959 (1991).

3. The following are of special relevance and are generally consistent with this Report: RESTATEMENT (THIRD) OF THE LAW GOVERNING LAWYERS §§ 73, 152 (Tentative Draft No. 8, 1997); RESTATEMENT (SECOND) OF TORTS § 552 (1976); and the "Guidelines for the Negotiation and Preparation of Third-Party Legal Opinions" (hereinafter "ABA Guidelines") in *Third-Party Legal Opinion Report, Including the Legal Opinion Accord, of the Section of Business Law, American Bar Association*, 47 BUS. LAW. 167, 224 (1991) [hereinafter "ABA Opinion Report"]. The ABA Guidelines are not limited to opinion letters that adopt the Accord contained in the ABA Opinion Report.

4. This Report has not been approved by the governing body or membership of any of the bar associations whose Committees or members were involved in its preparation. Accordingly, the views expressed are solely those of TriBar. This Report reflects a consensus of the Committee. It does not, however, necessarily reflect the views of individual members or their firms, organizations or associations on any particular point.

INDEX OF TYPICAL OPINION LETTER FEATURES

This index directs the reader to sections of this Report containing explanations of typical opinion letter features.

ARTICLE I GENERAL MATTERS

SECTION 1.9 CONTAINS A GLOSSARY OF CERTAIN TERMS USED IN THIS REPORT AND IS INTEGRAL TO THIS ARTICLE. TERMS DEFINED IN THE GLOSSARY APPEAR IN *BOLD ITALICS* WHEN INITIALLY USED IN ARTICLE I.

1.1 SCOPE OF THIS REPORT

Substantial business transactions often involve the delivery of an ***opinion letter*** to parties to the transaction who are *not* the ***opinion giver's*** client.[5] These opinion letters usually are delivered at a ***closing*** and cover a number of legal and factual issues. This Report focuses on certain ***opinions*** that are often included in opinion letters to non-clients and the procedures lawyers usually follow in preparing them.[6]

A consensus has developed regarding the meaning of language used in third-party opinion letters as well as the factual and legal investigation required to support particular opinions (together referred to as **"*customary practice*"**, *see* Section 1.4). This Report provides guidance on customary practice in giving these opinions.[7]

Adherence to the customary practice described in this Report may not be sufficient to meet all of the rules and practices imposed by government agencies having authority in particular regulated areas (*e.g.*, securities law, taxation and patents). Also, in transnational transactions consideration must be given to the application of cross-border and foreign opinion practices.

1.2 SOME OPINION CHARACTERISTICS

(a) The Opinion Letter Context

An opinion on a legal issue provides the ***opinion recipient*** with the opinion giver's professional judgment[8] about how the highest

5. The discussion in this Report also has implications for opinion letters to clients. The literature on legal opinions is largely devoted to third-party opinions rather than opinions to clients. Opinion letters to clients often follow the form of third-party opinions. However, the obligations of the opinion giver to a client differ from those to a third-party opinion recipient.

6. The Committee's reports on U.C.C. security interest opinions and opinions in the bankruptcy context address opinions that are not discussed in this Report. *See U.C.C. Security Interest Opinions*, 49 BUS. LAW. 359 (1993); *Opinions in the Bankruptcy Context: Rating Agency, Structured Financing, and Chapter 11 Transactions,* 46 BUS. LAW. 717 (1991).

7. The vast majority of closing opinions follow customary practice. To the extent they depart from customary practice, disclosure is required. *See* Section 1.5. The Accord contained in the ABA Opinion Report does not rely on customary practice but rather constitutes an agreement between the parties as to how opinion letters that incorporate it by reference should be interpreted.

8. *See* RESTATEMENT (THIRD) OF THE LAW GOVERNING LAWYERS § 152 cmt. c (Ten-

court[9] of the jurisdiction whose law is being addressed would appropriately resolve the issues covered by the opinion[10] on the date of the opinion letter.[11] The possibility of later developments or changes of ***law*** or fact and other factors (*e.g.*, the possibility that an ***undertaking*** in an ***agreement*** will be invalidated on policy grounds by the courts of a jurisdiction whose law is not covered by the opinion[12]) limit the predictive value of an opinion letter. An opinion is not a guaranty of an outcome, but rather an expression of professional judgment. That professional judgment is necessarily limited by a variety of factors as discussed in this Report.

The opinion giver acts only with the assent of its own client (sometimes referred to in this Report as the ***Company***) in giving an opinion to a non-client. If an opinion is rendered to a non-client, in most jurisdictions the opinion giver thereby takes on an obligation to the opinion recipient to exercise care in preparing the opinion.[13] However, rendering a third-party opinion does not establish a lawyer-client relationship with the opinion recipient. Rendering a third-party opinion is one aspect of counsel's role in representing a client and does not give rise to an ethical conflict between the client and the opinion recipient.[14]

The relevant agreement in a business transaction will often provide for delivery of an opinion letter as a condition of closing. In some cases, such as a loan, the borrower will furnish an opinion letter of its counsel to the lender. In other cases, such as in some mergers, each side will furnish an opinion letter of its counsel to the other side. Opinion letters generally relate to matters involving the opinion giver's client (*e.g.*, corporate status, corporate power and authorization, lack of regulatory approval requirements). If a remedies opinion is rendered on the enforceability of an agreement, it will only cover the extent to which the opinion giver's client is

tative Draft No. 8, 1997) (stating that in rendering opinions the lawyer "does not function as an advocate . . . [His] duty is to provide a fair and objective opinion.").

9. An arbitration will not necessarily produce the same result as a judicial proceeding. Nevertheless, in the experience of the Committee, parties to agreements are no less likely to seek legal opinions because the agreement is subject to arbitration.

10. *See* Sections 1.9(o) and 4.1. The opinion letter, if it contains a remedies opinion, will cover the question whether the law chosen in the agreement (*see* Section 1.9(p)) will be applied by a court. Sometimes the opinion letter will also contain a separate opinion on governing law. *See* Section 4.4.

11. An opinion giver may not properly be asked to foresee changes in then applicable law, whether statutory, regulatory or decisional. Thus, an opinion giver is not expected to seek out information concerning proposed legislation that if adopted would require qualification of the opinion or a different legal conclusion. The opinion giver is responsible, however, for existing law, including legislation that has been adopted but is not yet effective. The significance of that legislation should be noted in the opinion letter if necessary to avoid misleading the opinion recipient. *See* Section 1.4(d).

12. *See* Section 4.5.

13. *See* RESTATEMENT (THIRD) OF THE LAW GOVERNING LAWYERS §§ 73 and 152 (Tentative Draft No. 8, 1997).

14. *See* ABA Model Rules of Professional Conduct Rule 1.3.

bound (based on the assumption that the other parties are bound). Sometimes only counsel for one side will render an opinion that counsel for both could have rendered (*e.g.*, on the application of the usury laws or effectiveness of Uniform Commercial Code ("U.C.C." filings). This kind of division of labor is common.

Opinions are often subject to qualifications, some stated and some not. Each qualification to an opinion is referred to as an ***exception*** (which term includes both a ***limitation*** and an ***exclusion***). Some opinion exceptions are understood to be applicable whether or not stated. *See, e.g.*, Section 3.3.1. These exceptions are referred to as "standard exceptions". Other exceptions are understood to be applicable only when stated. Opinions that are subject to stated exceptions that are not customary in opinions of the type to which they relate are referred to as ***qualified opinions*** (*see* Section 1.9(i)). In some cases opinion letters contain ***reasoned*** (sometimes called ***explained***) ***opinions*** (*see* Section 1.9(j)), which may or may not be qualified.[15] *See* Sections 2.6.1, 6.5.5 and 6.8 as to the use of the phrase "to our knowledge".

Except for opinion letters containing reasoned opinions, opinion letters do not ordinarily identify the reference materials the opinion preparers have consulted, be those materials a case, a treatise or a law review article. By custom opinion preparers take into account all materials they have considered in preparing an opinion letter even when those materials are not described in the opinion letter.

The description of the meaning of particular opinions in this Report assumes that the opinion discussed is only subject to standard exceptions.

(b) No Obligation To Update

An opinion letter to a third-party does not require updating after its delivery, unless it specifies otherwise. By custom, the opinion giver provides a professional judgment at a specific time, ordinarily to facilitate a closing, and has no continuing responsibility to the non-client opinion recipient.

(c) The Bankruptcy (Insolvency) Exception And Equitable Principles Limitation

The bankruptcy exception and equitable principles limitation are standard exceptions to the remedies opinion and are discussed in that context in Section 3.3. However, opinion givers often include language in their opinion letters that purports to make other opinions or the entire opinion letter subject to the bankruptcy exception and equitable principles limitation. They do so because bankruptcy and equitable principles can affect opinions other than the remedies opinion. For example, an opinion that a security interest has been perfected indicates that the interest has achieved that status under the U.C.C. and that the holder of the perfected security

15. Lawyers have sometimes referred to "clean" opinions, by which they mean opinions limited only by standard exceptions. As opinion forms have become more varied in complex commercial transactions, the term has been used less frequently.

interest has the rights accorded by the U.C.C. to such status. However, enforcement of those rights may be limited in bankruptcy.

Application of the bankruptcy exception and equitable principles limitation to the entire opinion letter is technically overbroad. Some opinions, for example, the good standing opinion, are not affected by the bankruptcy exception or equitable principles limitation. Nevertheless, many opinion givers have adopted the all-inclusive form to save the time required to determine which opinions (in addition to the remedies opinion) should be limited by the bankruptcy exception and equitable principles limitation. Whether or not an opinion letter is drafted to apply the bankruptcy exception and equitable principles limitation outside the context of the remedies opinion, those limitations are understood as a matter of customary usage to apply to all opinions that raise the concerns to which they are addressed (but to no others).

(d) Dealing With Factual Material

Factual information that is the subject of an opinion (*e.g.*, no litigation)[16] or that is relied on in giving an opinion must be established in a way that meets the needs of the parties to the transaction. *See* Section 2.2. Rather than establishing certain facts, opinion preparers as a matter of customary practice sometimes rely on factual assumptions. *See* Section 2.3. Under customary practice some assumptions (referred to as "assumptions of general application") are applicable to virtually all opinion letters, whether or not stated. *See* Section 2.3(a) and note 23. Ordinarily, the parties will want the opinion giver to follow customary practice (*see* Section 1.4 and Article II). If the parties follow another approach, it should be described in the opinion letter.

(e) Dealing With Matters Of Law

Opinions involving matters of law are only given with respect to specific bodies of law. Thus, most opinion letters contain a provision limiting the law covered by the opinion letter (*e.g.*,to New York and federal law). *See* Section 1.9(o).

(f) "Performance" And Other Forward Looking Opinions

Some opinions are inherently backward looking and require an examination of historical materials (*e.g.*, the certificate of incorporation and proceedings of incorporators for an opinion that a corporation has been duly incorporated). Other opinions require the opinion preparers to establish the facts as they exist on the date of the opinion letter (*e.g.*, review of a Secretary of State's certificate for an opinion that a corporation is validly existing). Still other opinions are forward looking, addressing as of the date of the opinion letter such matters as the future enforceability of

16. Some opinion givers believe that statements dealing primarily with factual matters should be referred to as "confirmations" rather than opinions. The customary practice for giving an "opinion" and a "confirmation" is the same. *See* Sections 1.9(h) and 6.8. *See also* ABA Guidelines Section I(A)(1).

contractual provisions or the effect on the Company's existing contracts of the performance by the Company after closing of its obligations under the agreement. The inclusion in an opinion of forward looking language—*e.g.*, "enforceable"[17] or "performance"[18]—broadens the matters counsel is required to consider.

(g) Opinions As To Other Entities By Analogy

The opinions discussed in this Report relate to corporations. The application of this Report to other entities may be derived by analogy to the corporate model. Thus, for example, as to a limited partnership, the analog to an officer's certificate might be a certificate of the managing general partner.

1.3 A REALISTIC CONTEXT FOR NEGOTIATING OPINIONS

Third-party opinion letters should deal only with matters of concern to the addressee in the particular transaction. The opinions contained in an opinion letter for one transaction may (and often will) not be appropriate for another transaction. Thus, any standardized opinion requirements of an opinion recipient should be viewed only as an initial reference point and should be reexamined for each transaction in light of the circumstances involved. Requests for opinions that do not fit the transaction at hand impede communication and the conduct of customary opinion practice. *See* Section 1.4.

Similarly, opinion givers should not be rigid in responding to opinion requests. They should be prepared to explain their reasons for declining to give an opinion rather than merely asserting a law firm "no-opinion" policy on the issue. "Boilerplate" opinion forms that are designed to fit all or many opinion situations are only a starting point for discussion.

The opinion recipient may seek to identify potential problems by initially requesting very broad opinions.[19] In doing so, the opinion recipient (or its lawyer) may not appreciate how much work the request will involve. If the opinion preparers conclude that the cost to their client of preparing the opinions requested will be high, the opinion preparers should seek reconsideration of the requested opinions in light of the likely cost and benefit involved. Counsel for the opinion recipient[20] should respond in good faith.

17. The remedies opinion, which uses the term "enforceable", is inherently forward looking. *See* Section 3.1.

18. The term "performance" is sometimes included in the "no breach or default" and "no violation of law" opinions. *See* Sections 6.5.4 and 6.6. An opinion that refers only to "consummation of the transaction" is not understood to cover performance. *See* note 171.

19. In some cases, the opinion recipient may not want the opinion giver to identify in the opinion letter areas that the opinion recipient knows are problems. Consequently, experienced counsel for opinion recipients sometimes exclude from opinion requests matters that will require non-standard exceptions.

20. The opinion recipient (unlike the opinion giver) is not a lawyer, but rather the client of the lawyer on the other side.

No opinion letter should be sought that is so broad that it seeks to make the opinion giver responsible for its client's factual representations or the legal or business risks inherent in the transaction. An opinion recipient, for example, should not seek an unqualified opinion on an uncertain or disputed legal issue.[21] An opinion cannot change the facts or the state of the law.

Opinion exceptions that are not common to opinions of the type to which they are applied often indicate transaction-specific risks. Sometimes a transaction can be restructured to avoid these risks, thus eliminating the need for an exception.

Three simple techniques are particularly helpful in negotiating opinions. *First*, the lawyers negotiating the opinion on behalf of the opinion recipient should consider whether, if they were counsel for the opinion giver's client, they would be prepared to furnish the opinions they have requested (with the assistance of local or specialized counsel, to the extent appropriate). Conscientious application of this "Golden Rule" will reduce requests for overly broad, burdensome or otherwise inappropriate opinions. *Second*, to avoid misunderstanding and last minute delay, the parties should agree early in the negotiation of the transaction documents on the precise wording of any required opinion letter. The need, if any, for local or specialized counsel's opinions should also be established at that time. *See* Article V. *Third*, material not relevant to the transaction should not be included in opinions. To do otherwise obscures the meaning of an opinion.

1.4 CUSTOMARY PRACTICE

(a) Customary Practice As A Starting Point

This Report describes what an opinion giver should consider when preparing an opinion letter. The starting point is customary practice. Opinion givers must of necessity use their own judgment as to their conformity with customary practice in the circumstances they face. The *Restatement (Second) of Torts* and the *Restatement (Third) of the Law Governing Lawyers* indicate that the customary practice of lawyers similarly situated is a key factor in determining liability.[22]

Customary practice establishes the ground rules for rendering and receiving opinions and thus allows the communication of ideas between the opinion giver and counsel for the opinion recipient without lengthy descriptions of the diligence process, detailed definitions of the terms used and laborious recitals of standard, often unstated, assumptions and excep-

21. *See* ABA Guidelines Section I(B)(3).

22. *See* RESTATEMENT (SECOND) OF TORTS § 552 (1976); RESTATEMENT (THIRD) OF THE LAW GOVERNING LAWYERS § 152 cmt. e (Tentative Draft No. 8, 1997) (stating in part that "customary practice will . . . determine the nature and extent of the factual and legal diligence to be employed by the opinion giver in connection with [the] . . . issuance" of a legal opinion.). The ABA Guidelines state that they are "drawn from current custom and practice".

tions.[23] Thus, in opinion practice, customary practice is an important professional tool.

Unless otherwise indicated, an opinion recipient is entitled to assume that the opinion giver has followed customary practice in rendering an opinion. Reciprocally, an opinion giver is entitled to assume that the opinion recipient understands customary practice and recognizes that it has been followed in preparing the opinion letter.[24] Key aspects of customary practice are described in this Section 1.4.[25]

(b) Customary Usage. This aspect of customary practice relates to how words are used in opinion letters. As will be seen in Articles III and VI, certain words and phrases expressing legal concepts are, by custom, understood to have special meanings in the context of specific opinions. Words and phrases are defined by their customary usage in that context and not simply by (i) dictionary meanings or (ii) meanings of the same words or phrases in other contexts. For example, the meaning of the phrase "legal, valid, binding and enforceable" in the context of a remedies opinion is not an aggregate of the dictionary meaning of each of those words. Together or separately, those words are understood in the context of the remedies opinion to be equivalent to the word "enforceable" used alone. *See* Section 3.1.

(c) Customary Diligence. This aspect of customary practice relates to the extent of the factual and legal investigation an opinion giver undertakes to support particular opinions. Customary practice relating to the opinion giver's factual inquiry is described in Article II. As to matters of law, customary diligence requires the opinion giver to conduct such review of applicable ***law*** as lawyers in similar circumstances would normally conduct. Opinion letters often state (immediately before the opinion paragraphs) that the opinions being expressed are based on a review of certain identified documents "and such other investigation as we [the opinion

23. Some opinion givers, out of an abundance of caution, state assumptions of general application and standard exceptions. Stating the obvious tends to impede effective professional communication. Examples include assumptions regarding "the capacity of individuals, the conformity of copies to originals and the authenticity of original documents." Language excluding changes of law or fact subsequent to the date of the opinion letter ordinarily falls into the same category.

24. Parties to transactions in which opinions are rendered normally are advised by counsel as to the scope and acceptability of those opinions. Opinion givers should consider whether an opinion recipient who is not represented by counsel is familiar with customary practice applicable to opinion letters. A sophisticated party that regularly requests opinion letters in the course of its business may ordinarily be assumed to understand customary practice concerning the opinion letters it receives, whether or not it is represented by counsel in connection with the transaction.

25. Customary practice also includes other matters such as the obligations of an opinion giver in relying on opinions of other counsel (*see* Section 5.1) and the appropriateness of rendering an opinion on the law of a jurisdiction in which the opinion preparers are not admitted to practice. *See* Section 5.3.

giver] have deemed appropriate." The term "investigation" is understood to relate to both law and fact. Thus, the "such other investigation" statement merely emphasizes that the opinion letter is given in accordance with customary practice and its omission is not sufficient, by itself, to indicate that customary practice is not being followed.

(d) Avoiding Misleading The Opinion Recipient. Prior to the delivery of the opinion letter, the opinion preparers must ask themselves whether they believe that the opinions they intend to render will, under the circumstances, be misleading to the recipient. An opinion the opinion preparers believe to be misleading should not be delivered until ***disclosures*** are made to cure the problem. *See* Section 1.9(m).

When considering if an opinion to be given will mislead the opinion recipient, opinion preparers must think not only about the opinion itself but also about areas excluded from the opinion. Ordinarily, a non-standard exception[26] indicates to the opinion recipient an area of concern. A non-standard exception is thus likely to be informative, rather than misleading. A stated assumption (other than one of general application—*see* Section 2.3(a)) may also alert the opinion recipient to a problem area.

Common exceptions may mask problems that are different and more serious than the matters they are commonly understood to exclude. Consider the following situation.

> The opinion recipient has agreed to accept a "no litigation" opinion that is limited to claims asserted in writing, a common form. An opinion containing that limitation would be misleading if to the knowledge of the opinion preparers (but not to the opinion recipient) a substantial and apparently serious claim had been made orally in a formal manner (*e.g.*, at a conference involving lawyers for both sides at which a draft complaint was discussed but not delivered).

In this case, the risk of misleading the opinion recipient could be avoided by an appropriate disclosure.

Exclusions from opinions (whether understood without being stated, *e.g.*, insolvency law and local law, or stated in the opinion letter) relate to areas that are left by custom to the opinion recipient and its counsel. The opinion recipient should not assume that the opinion giver does not have significant information about these excluded areas. However, the opinion giver is not expected to disclose any such information to the opinion recipient. Only if the opinion preparers determine that the opinion will, under the circumstances, mislead the opinion recipient will the need for disclosure (or withholding the opinion) arise.

In determining whether an opinion will mislead, the opinion preparers need only consider what the opinion letter (i) states and (ii) omits to state

26. For example, "we express no opinion as to the enforceability of paragraph ______ of the Agreement relating to liquidated damages."

that is relevant to what is stated.[27] Thus, the omission of information not relevant to the opinion given (*e.g.*, information relevant to litigation if no opinion is rendered with respect to the absence of litigation) does not mislead.[28] The question the opinion preparers must consider is whether under the circumstances the opinion will cause the opinion recipient to misevaluate the specific opinion given.

> **NON-OPINION LIABILITY**
> OPINION GIVERS SHOULD CONSIDER WHETHER APART FROM THE OPINION LETTER THEY ARE EXPOSING THEMSELVES TO LIABILITY AS A RESULT OF THEIR INVOLVEMENT IN THE TRANSACTION UNDER THE ANTI-FRAUD RULES OF THE FEDERAL SECURITIES LAWS OR WHETHER CIVIL OR CRIMINAL FRAUD STANDARDS MAY BE APPLICABLE. THIS REPORT ASSUMES THAT THE REQUISITE STATE OF MIND (INTENT OR RECKLESSNESS) REQUIRED FOR CIVIL OR CRIMINAL FRAUD IS NOT PRESENT.

1.5 VARIATIONS FROM CUSTOMARY PRACTICE

The parties may have good reason to depart from customary opinion practice in particular circumstances. A material departure from any aspect of customary practice (including diligence or usage) should be expressly described in the opinion letter. For example, a mere listing in an opinion letter of documents examined is not sufficient to give notice to the recipient that the opinion giver reviewed only the listed documents (rather than the documents required by customary practice).

Since the third-party opinion is a part of the recipient's business diligence, the parties to a transaction may agree that more or less investigation than is customary to support an opinion should be conducted by the opinion giver. In some situations an opinion letter may state that greater than customary diligence was performed with respect to a specific opinion. Similarly in other situations, a stated assumption, exception or description of the less than customary diligence that forms the basis for the opinion will be included.

27. *But cf.* Roberts v. Ball, Hunt, Brown & Baerwitz, 128 Cal. Rptr. 901 (1976).

28. However, action by the opinion giver unrelated to the opinion letter (*e.g.*, in making a representation in behalf of the client) may mislead and thus give rise to liability. For example, in Rubin v. Schottenstein, Zox & Dunn, 110 F.3d 1247 (6th Cir. 1997), *rev'd en banc*, No. 96-3017, 1998 WL 224080 (6th Cir. May 7, 1998), company counsel was held liable to the recipient of its legal opinion letter, but liability was based on misleading oral statements made by counsel and not on the opinion letter.

1.6 OPINION RECIPIENT RELIANCE ON OPINION LETTERS

Customary practice affects not only the conduct of the opinion giver but also that of the opinion recipient. The recipient of a third-party opinion letter is entitled (except in a few jurisdictions) to rely[29] on the opinions expressed without taking any action to verify those opinions.[30] If an opinion is qualified or reasoned (or both), the opinion recipient must decide whether to proceed with the transaction in view of the qualification or reasoning set forth in the opinion letter.

The third-party opinion recipient is entitled to rely only on what is stated in the opinion letter, regardless of what it requested be stated.[31]

As with the opinion giver's right to rely on information used in an opinion letter (*see* Section 2.1.4), the opinion recipient has no right to rely on an opinion if reliance is unreasonable under the circumstances or the opinion is known by the opinion recipient to be false.

1.7 CLIENT CONTROL OVER THIRD-PARTY OPINION LETTERS

The opinion giver has a professional obligation to protect the confidences and secrets of its client.[32] Thus, the client must consent, specifically or by implication, to disclosures about the client before delivery of an opinion letter to a third-party.[33]

29. The opinion recipient's "right to rely" means that a professional duty is owed by the third-party opinion giver to the opinion recipient. As a result, in most jurisdictions, if the opinion is negligently given and results in damage to the opinion recipient, the opinion recipient has a claim against the opinion giver. A few jurisdictions take the position that a professional cannot owe a duty to a non-client and, thus, that a third-party opinion recipient has no standing to sue the opinion giver. Still other jurisdictions extend the liability of opinion givers not only to opinion recipients but also to others to whom harm was foreseeable when a negligently prepared opinion was rendered. *See* TriBar Opinion Committee, Opinions in the Bankruptcy Context: Rating Agency, Structured Financing, and Chapter 11 Transactions, 46 Bus. Law. 717, 735 & nn. 66-68 (1991).

30. *But see* Greyhound Leasing & Fin. Corp. v. Norwest Bank, 854 F.2d 1122, 1125-26 (8th Cir. 1988), which in imposing a duty of investigation on the opinion recipient does not follow customary practice.

31. *See, e.g.*, Prudential Ins. Co. v. Dewey, Ballantine, Bushby, Palmer & Wood, 605 N.E.2d 318 (N.Y. 1992). However, disputes may arise over what particular opinion language is intended to cover. *See* Section 3.5 relating to the ambit of the remedies opinion. *See also* Restatement (Third) of the Law Governing Lawyers § 152 cmt. c (Tentative Draft No. 8, 1997).

32. *See* N.Y. Rules of Court § 1200.19 (McKinney 1998); *see also* Model Rules of Professional Conduct, Rules 1.6, 4.1 & 4.2 (1992).

33. A failure to consent may prevent delivery. *See also* Restatement (Third) of the Law Governing Lawyers § 152 cmt. d (Tentative Draft No. 8, 1997). Ordinarily, consent is obvious from the circumstances of the closing, and the opinion letter need not recite client consent. In one case a court refused to find a duty of care from the opinion giver to the opinion recipient on the ground that the client had not consented to delivery of the opinion letter. The reasoning of the decision is weak, but, even if followed, the case would not affect opinion letters delivered at closing as contemplated by the agreement. *See* United Bank of Kuwait PLC v. Enventure Energy Enhanced Oil Recovery Assocs., 755 F. Supp. 1195, 1203-04 (S.D.N.Y. 1989).

Opinion givers ordinarily do not obligate themselves in advance to deliver opinion letters to non-clients. Indeed, they ordinarily have no obligation of any sort to the opinion recipient prior to delivering an opinion letter. Even if the opinion giver is prepared to render the requested opinions, release of an opinion letter to a third party is ultimately a decision for the client, not the lawyer.[34]

1.8 "OPINION PREPARERS" ACT FOR OPINION GIVER

The term "***opinion preparers***" is used in this Report (in contrast to "opinion giver") to refer to the lawyers in a law firm who take on the responsibility to prepare an opinion letter.[35] This usage permits a more precise discussion of what a law firm and the lawyers in it must do to meet their professional obligations in rendering a legal opinion.

An opinion letter is usually written on a law firm's letterhead and signed in the name of the firm. It thus purports to express the opinion of the firm, not merely that of the opinion preparers. The fact that an opinion letter is signed in the name of a law firm has given rise to confusion over the obligations of a law firm in preparing an opinion letter. A law firm practices law only through the lawyers who work on its behalf. The opinion preparers determine the content of the opinion letter and are responsible to perform the work required to support the opinions being expressed. The law firm fulfills its obligations to the opinion recipient through the performance by the opinion preparers of customary diligence in preparing and delivering the opinion letter. Except to the extent discussed in Section 2.2.2, other lawyers in the firm are not expected to take action in connection with the opinion letter.

1.9 OPINION TERMINOLOGY: A GLOSSARY FOR THIS REPORT

General Terms

(a) **Agreement; Contract; Undertaking.** The terms "contract" and "agreement" are used interchangeably and refer to the document signed by the parties that sets forth the promises of each party to the other. The term "undertaking" is used to refer to a specific promise in the "agreement" and not to the "agreement" itself. Thus, an "agreement" typically contains many "undertakings". Note that a statement that "this agreement shall be governed by the law of the State of New York" is an

34. Any obligation of the client to cause its lawyers to deliver an opinion is a different question and depends, among other things, on the wording of the agreement between the parties.

35. If a particular lawyer takes responsibility only for a specific opinion, for example, a lawyer specializing in ERISA matters with regard to a pension plan opinion, that lawyer is an opinion preparer only as to that opinion and not as to all the other opinions in the opinion letter.

"undertaking" in that it commits each party to the application of New York law. *See* Section 3.1.

(b) Charter; Charter Documents. As to a corporation, the certificate (or articles) of incorporation and by-laws and any related documents, such as restatements, amendments and certificates of designation and merger.

(c) Closing. In most substantial financial transactions the parties enter into a written agreement that specifies (among other things) the conditions upon which the contemplated transaction will be consummated. Delivery of a third-party legal opinion letter is often one of these conditions. The consummation of the transaction (as opposed to the execution and delivery of the agreement) is referred to as the "closing".

(d) Company. This Report refers to the opinion giver's client as the "Company". The Illustrative Opinions identify the Company as a corporation and at various places this Report refers to corporate officers' certificates and board resolutions. For opinions as to other entities, *see* Section 1.2(g).

Participants

(e) Opinion Giver; Opinion Recipient. The term "opinion giver" refers to the lawyer or law firm in whose name the opinion letter is signed. The term "opinion recipient" refers to the addressee of the opinion letter and others, if any, granted permission by the opinion giver to rely on the opinion letter. The opinion recipient ordinarily receives the letter as a participant in a business transaction.

(f) Opinion Preparers. *See* Section 1.8.

Opinion Practice Terms

(g) Customary Practice; Customary Usage and Customary Diligence. *See* Section 1.4.

(h) Opinion; Opinion Letter. At the closing of many business transactions, counsel for one party to the transaction will deliver a letter to the other party expressing its conclusions on various matters of legal concern to that other party. That letter is normally referred to as an "opinion letter". Each separate conclusion it expresses is referred to in this Report as an "opinion". (In practice, the term "opinion" is often also used to refer to the opinion letter, with the context making clear the meaning intended.) "Opinion letters" often contain many "opinions". For types of opinions ("qualified", "reasoned"), *see* Section 1.2(a). Opinions that are primarily factual in nature (*e.g.*, no litigation) are sometimes referred to as "confirmations".

(i) Qualified Opinion; Exception; Exclusion; Limitation. An opinion giver uses an "exception," which term includes both a "limitation" and an "exclusion", to narrow an opinion. An exception is often phrased to indicate that no opinion is given as to a particular provision in the agreement or specific aspect of the matter covered, rather than to provide a negative opinion on that provision or aspect. An opinion is said to be "qualified" if it contains an exception[36] that is not customary in opinions of that type, thereby putting the opinion recipient on notice as to uncertainties and limitations. Thus, a remedies opinion that excludes coverage of an indemnification provision in a supply contract is a qualified opinion, but a remedies opinion containing a "bankruptcy exception" (which is standard for remedies opinions) is not. *See* Section 1.2(a) as to "standard" exceptions. General unspecified "public policy" exceptions are not used because they make the entire opinion unacceptably vague, requiring the opinion recipient to guess at the opinion giver's source of concern.

(j) Reasoned (or Explained) Opinion.[37] A reasoned (or "explained") opinion is typically rendered when, in the view of the opinion giver, the opinion's conclusions should not be stated apart from its underlying reasoning (for example, when the opinion giver reaches a conclusion despite the existence of possibly contradictory authority). By setting forth the reasoning behind the opinion, the opinion giver spells out, for evaluation by the opinion recipient and its counsel, such matters as a lack of judicial authority, the presence of divided authority or contrary but outdated authority. The conclusions expressed in a "reasoned" opinion are sometimes limited by the phrase "while the matter is not free from doubt" or some similar phrase. However, at other times the opinion, although containing reasoning, will not be limited in this way because the opinion giver has concluded that the opinion as "reasoned" needs no further characterization.

(k) Assumptions. *See* Section 2.3.
Assumptions of General Application. *See* Section 2.3(a)

(l) Unreliable Information. *See* Section 2.1.4.

(m) Disclosure. A disclosure is a statement that is intended to prevent the opinion recipient from being misled. *See* Section 1.4(d). A disclosure differs from an exception in that it does not directly limit the opinion. A disclosure may be made to the opinion recipient within or outside an opinion letter.

Opinion Usages of "Law"

(n) Law. "Law" means statutory, decisional and regulatory law at the state or federal, but not the local, level. Thus, an opinion should not be read to cover such matters as local zoning or building codes unless it does so expressly. If an opinion letter does not state that it covers federal law, that law is understood not to be covered unless the context indicates otherwise (*e.g.*, an opinion as to exemption from registration under the

36. A typical opinion exception states that "we express no opinion as to Section ______ of the Agreement."

37. Opinions phrased in terms of "would" or "should" convey the same professional judgment as to the judicial resolution of the issues covered under statutory law and existing legal precedent as applied to the facts on which the opinion is based. Thus, delivery of "would" and "should" opinions is equally appropriate as a matter of customary practice. TriBar Opinion Committee, *Opinions in the Bankruptcy Context: Rating Agency, Structured Financing, and Chapter 11 Transactions*, 46 BUS. LAW. 717, 733 (1991).

Securities Act of 1933). Since an opinion is a professional judgment and not a guaranty, the opinion preparers are only responsible for the areas of law customarily understood to be covered by the opinion given. Within those areas, the opinion preparers are responsible for law that is reasonably available to lawyers generally as well as the law actually known to them. *See* Sections 3.5.1 and 6.6. *See also* note 11.

(o) **Law Covered By The Opinion Letter.** An opinion letter (unless it is limited to a specific statute e.g., whether a particular transfer constitutes a fraudulent transfer within the meaning of Article 10 of the N.Y. Debtor & Creditor Law) will normally recite what law it is intended to cover (*e.g.*, "the opinions expressed herein are limited to the law of the State of New York and to the federal law of the United States"). *See* Section 4.1.

(p) **Chosen-Law; Chosen-Law Provision; Governing Law.** *See* Sections 4.3 and 4.4. Many agreements contain a provision entitled "governing law provision". However described, such provisions are analytically "chosen-law provisions" because such provisions reflect the choice of the parties. That choice is not always respected by the courts. *See* Article IV. The law applicable to the agreement as determined by a court is the "governing law".

ARTICLE II FACTS

2.1 SOME GENERAL OBSERVATIONS ON FACTS

2.1.1 The Legal Opinion—Law Applied To Facts

Legal opinions typically involve the application of law to facts. For example, an opinion that an agreement has been duly authorized requires (i) an understanding of the "law"—the legal requirements for authorizing the agreement, such as shareholder or director approval, and (ii) a determination of the "facts"—that these requirements have been satisfied.

Certificates of corporate officers regarding records maintained by a corporation about itself provide the basis for much of the information relied on in opinions. Certificates of public filing officials as to public records provide the basis for many other opinions. Additional information may be derived from representations in agreements and statements, oral and written, from those with relevant information. *See* Section 2.2.1(d) as to the formality with which facts obtained from others are established. Lawyers also establish facts through their review of documents. Less frequently, they establish facts by actual observance of events. This Article II describes the customary practice lawyers follow in establishing facts. As discussed in Section 2.3, opinions may also be based on factual assumptions.

2.1.2 The Limitless Indicia Of Fact

Because most events relevant to an opinion occur outside the presence of counsel, opinion preparers must usually rely on information provided by others about what has taken place. The steps that might be taken to obtain factual information are, as a theoretical matter, virtually limitless. For example, an opinion that an agreement has been authorized is often based on a certificate signed by the corporate secretary stating that (i) a meeting of the board of directors, at which a quorum was present, was held on a specified date on notice duly given and (ii) at the meeting a resolution authorizing the agreement was adopted by the required vote. The opinion preparers could also (but almost never do) interview the corporate secretary or obtain certificates from one or more participants in the meeting. Even if that were done, those who purported to participate in the meeting might claim that the meeting was held, even though it was not. The falsity of their claim might, in turn, be revealed by some further step—for example, locating witnesses who are aware of what really happened. In almost every situation the possibility that the information certified is not true would remain despite efforts to look beyond the information provided to that point.

2.1.3 The Lawyer's Special Role In Guiding The Flow Of Factual Information

The opinion preparers must thoughtfully guide the process by which information is obtained in an effort to assure that the opinions given are meaningful. No opinion can be better than the factual information on which it is based.

The process for obtaining information in connection with the opinion will likely be inseparable from other diligence related to the transaction itself. This process usually requires a determination by the opinion preparers of: (i) the factual information required; (ii) the source of that information—*e.g.*, the Company records, a Company officer, a public record or public filing official and past opinion letters for the Company and related documents; and (iii) the vehicle by which the factual information is to be provided—*e.g.*, a specially prepared certificate, a representation in the agreement, or even an oral statement.

Opinion preparers typically draft certificates[38] that set forth with precision various key facts. They then customarily review the certificates with those who will be asked to sign them. In the course of that review, the opinion preparers satisfy themselves that the persons providing the factual information understand that the information provided is being relied on in an opinion letter and therefore must be based on knowledge, not on surmise or a willingness to "take the risk" of being wrong.[39] An equivalent process should be followed when reliance is placed on representations in an agreement, oral statements or other information.

38. Public officials usually draft their own certificates.

39. In some cases inside counsel will draft certificates of corporate officers and review the certificates with the officers although outside counsel gives the opinion. The obligation to review the certificate with the signer then falls on inside counsel.

In some situations, the opinion preparers will elect to go beyond customary diligence.[40] In other situations, the opinion recipient will seek more than customary diligence for a specific opinion. In the latter case, the lawyers on both sides should attempt to resolve at an early stage how much more diligence will be required. The cost of any additional diligence may be a significant factor to be considered by the parties to the transaction.

2.1.4 No Reliance On "Unreliable Information"

The opinion preparers may rely on information provided by an appropriate source (*see* Section 2.2.1) unless reliance is unreasonable under the circumstances in which the opinion is rendered[41] or the information is known to the opinion preparers to be false[42] (together "unreliable information"). Some information is false on its face: a meeting of the Board of Directors, for example, could not have been held on February 29, 1997. Other information is so improbable (*e.g.*, a certificate from a corporate officer of the owner of a television station that no business is done in the only jurisdiction in which the company is licensed to operate the station by the FCC) that it would be unreasonable for the opinion preparers to rely on it without further inquiry. Similarly, it would be unreasonable to rely on information that is inconsistent with a representation given in the same transaction or information known to the opinion preparers. If the opinion preparers identify information as "unreliable," they must find other information to establish the facts. Alternatively, they may include an express assumption regarding those facts in order to give the opinion. *See* Section 2.3(b). In some cases disclosure may be required. *See* Section 1.4(d).

2.2 ESTABLISHING FACT

Customary diligence provides norms for establishing fact. These norms accept as fact information provided by persons who appear to be in a position to know the facts. Opinion preparation is not ordinarily an occasion to question factual information provided by apparently reliable sources nor is the opinion letter a vehicle to ferret out fraud. Of course, all relevant information known to the opinion preparers, however obtained, must be considered.

"Establishing" fact means that in accordance with customary practice (i) the opinion preparers have assembled factual information (whether in certificate, representation or other form), (ii) such information is not "un-

40. For example, when giving the no litigation opinion (*see* discussion in Section 6.8) some opinion preparers examine their firm's litigation dockets even though they have received appropriate certificates from their clients as to litigation and claims.

41. The pace of transactions and the complexity of the businesses involved have resulted in a customary practice under which the opinion preparers do not challenge the facts provided by an appropriate source. The demands on counsel's attention are intense and documents typically continue to change until the moment of closing.

42. Even if reasonable opinion preparers would not under the circumstances conclude that reliance on information was unreasonable, the opinion preparers may not rely if they know the information to be false.

reliable" (*see* Section 2.1.4) and (iii) the information so assembled includes the facts customarily required for giving the specific opinion. Once opinion preparers have met the standard of customary diligence in "establishing" facts required to support a specific opinion, they have discharged their professional responsibility and need not gather additional information or undertake verification procedures (unless they have specifically agreed to do so). Thus, comparison of factual material gathered to support an opinion with additional factual material that may otherwise be available (other than the representations made in the specific transaction) is not customary.

2.2.1 Information Obtained From Others

(a) The Need To Go To The Source To Establish Facts

Ordinarily, the client is the best source of information about itself; the keeper of a public record is the best source of information about that record;[43] the other parties to a transaction are the best source of information about themselves. Most corporations and other business entities maintain specific records on many matters characteristically covered by opinions (*e.g.*, minutes of meetings that cover authorization of agreements). However, in some cases a corporation's records may not be an appropriate source. For example, while a corporation's records will indicate whether it has taken action to grant a security interest (and are ordinarily the most reliable source of information on that issue), they are not ordinarily an appropriate source of information concerning the state of the public record relating to the security interest. Ordinarily, the person or entity that searches the public record (as a business or public service) is the most reliable source of that information.

Although lawyers, accountants and investment bankers may have information in their files, that information often will have been provided for another purpose and may not have been updated. To maintain reliability, each time an opinion letter is delivered, opinion preparers as a matter of customary diligence obtain information (or an assurance that the information in hand remains correct) from the source (*e.g.*, a certificate of a corporate officer or public official) regarding matters that might be subject to change.

(b) No Reliance On Statements Of "Ultimate Fact"; Special Rule As To Charter Documents And Public Official Certificates

Opinion preparers rely on certifiers of fact for the factual elements necessary to render legal opinions. However, they may not rely on certifiers of fact for statements that are tantamount to the legal opinions themselves. Thus, an opinion that stock has been validly issued cannot properly be based on a certificate of a corporate officer that the Company has taken

43. Service companies that search public records as part of their business are an alternative source that is equally reliable and often more accessible than an "official" source. *See* Section 6.1.6.

all steps required to issue the stock.[44] Such a statement, often referred to as a statement of "ultimate fact", is in reality a conclusion of law. If the opinion giver could rely on it, the diligence the opinion recipient expects the opinion preparers to perform would be lost.

Customary statements contained in certificates issued by public officials are an exception to the general rule against reliance on statements of "ultimate fact". Public officials are presumed to have established specific procedures to issue such certificates. For example, opinion givers customarily rely on certificates issued by the Secretary of State regarding a corporation's "valid existence",[45] "good standing" and "qualification to do business"[46]. Unlike the corporate officer or other certifier of fact, the public official is assumed to understand (and to have undertaken the appropriate diligence to support) the statement of ultimate fact (conclusion of law) contained in the certificate.

There is an important limitation to this exception. By custom, opinion givers do not rely on public official certificates as to "due incorporation".[47]

(c) The Appropriateness Of The Source In Establishing Fact

Even if the institutional source of information (*e.g.*, the Company) is proper, the opinion preparers are only entitled to rely on information provided by a person they reasonably believe to be an appropriate representative of the institution. An officer with the title "Vice President—Engineering" may in fact be knowledgeable about corporate financial matters. However, the opinion preparers may not be able to verify that knowledge. Ordinarily, only a corporate officer who has responsibility for the subject matter involved (or a more senior officer to whom that officer reports, directly or indirectly) or an officer who has overall responsibility for the Company (*e.g.*, the President) may without further diligence be treated as an appropriate source of information about the Company.

(d) The Formality Of Establishing Facts

(i) *The Formality Of Certificates*

When rendering opinions, opinion preparers seldom rely on information that has been assembled informally. Ordinarily, they prepare certificates that set forth with precision the factual information they need, and then review the certificate with the proposed signer.[48] This process and the requirement of execution by an appropriate officer make the seriousness of the inquiry clear.

44. Instead, the opinion would require the opinion preparers to determine, among other matters, whose approval was required and whether that approval was obtained in accordance with applicable requirements. *See* Section 6.2.2.

45. *See* Section 6.1.3.

46. *See* Sections 6.1.4 and 6.1.6.

47. Public official certificates as to "due incorporation" are generally based on a review of filed documents that by themselves do not establish all of the elements of due incorporation. *See* Section 6.1.1.

48. *But see* note 39.

(ii) Comparison Of Reliance On Representations Made By Opinion Recipient With Those Made By Client

Reliance on representations made by the opinion recipient in an agreement may be necessary as a practical matter. The opinion preparers have only limited access to the opinion recipient, and the recipient should understand that its representations are providing a basis for the opinion that is being rendered to it.[49] In the absence of representations about the opinion recipient necessary for an opinion letter, the opinion preparers, rather than seeking a certificate of a corporate officer of the opinion recipient, will usually state in the opinion letter that certain facts (or even legal conclusions) about the opinion recipient are assumed. *See* Section 2.3(b).

Reliance by the opinion preparers on representations in the agreement made by their client stands on a different footing. The opinion preparers have access to the client and are in a position to inquire whether a representation is based on actual knowledge, on surmise or even on a determination by the client (notwithstanding its lack of knowledge) that it is willing to risk the consequence of being wrong. Opinion preparers should not base a legal opinion on client representations in the agreement that reflect surmise or risk allocation concepts (unless that is disclosed in the opinion letter or is otherwise known to the opinion recipient).

The process of reviewing with appropriate corporate officers the representations in an agreement and the statements in certificates is essentially the same. Nevertheless, seeking information concerning the client through a certificate makes clear to the client that the information is being used for opinion purposes as well as contract purposes. Further, a representation in an agreement is more likely to be cast as a legal conclusion (*e.g.*, "the stock has been validly issued") than a statement of fact in a certificate specifically prepared for use as a basis for a legal opinion. Thus, a certificate is often more effective in eliciting information from a client than representations in an agreement. *See* Section 2.5.4.

(iii) *Discouraging Use Of Oral "Statements"*

Some opinion letters state that as to certain matters of fact the opinion giver has relied on "statements". A "statement" may include information received orally. Because memories fade and oral communications can be imprecise, reliance on oral communications creates a risk of misunderstanding that the opinion preparers ordinarily will want to avoid. When relying on oral information, opinion preparers would be well advised to consider recording in a memorandum what they have been told, when and by whom.

2.2.2 Information From Others In The Opinion Giver Firm

In applying the rule that lawyers may not rely on "unreliable infor-

49. In relying on representations of the opinion recipient, the opinion preparers are not required to make a judgment whether a representation for any reason constitutes unreliable information. *See* Section 2.1.4.

mation" (*see* Section 2.1.4), the question arises whether, in order to rely, the opinion preparers must inquire as to information unknown to them, but known to other lawyers in their firm or contained in the firm's files.

(a) The Opinion Giver Is Not Accountable For Everything Known To All Its Lawyers Or Contained In Its Files

Before delivering an opinion letter, opinion preparers (regardless of the size of the law firm) do not, as a matter of customary practice, circulate[50] a summary of the factual information on which they are relying to every lawyer (or even some lawyers) in the firm or check that information against the firm's client files. Customary practice reflects an appropriate balancing of the costs such a procedure would entail and the benefits it could be expected to produce. If the information to be relied on has been furnished by an appropriate source, is adequate to give the opinion, and is not "unreliable" (*see* Section 2.1.4), the opinion preparers customarily seek no further information. A law firm's files may be voluminous and the number of lawyers who have had some involvement with the client may be large. Whatever the effect in any specific situation, the probability is small that anything of value would be revealed by either a search of those files or a broad inquiry of lawyers who may not be knowledgeable about the details of a transaction.

(b) Opinion Giver Is Accountable For Information Obtained In Informal Consultations Within The Firm

The lawyers in a firm who represent a client in a transaction will ordinarily consider whether they should make general inquiries of others in the firm who are more familiar with the client's affairs in order to facilitate the handling of the transaction. Lawyers working on an accounts receivable financing, for example, may consult with other lawyers who by reason of prior representation of the client may be aware of contractual or other limits on the client's ability to grant a security interest in the receivables. Opinion preparers also may have occasion to make similar inquiries directed to specific issues raised by the opinion, particularly when they are aware that a lawyer in the firm who is not involved in the preparation of the opinion has information obtained through representation of the client in other matters that is likely to have a material bearing on the opinion issue. The timing and content of these inquiries will vary; they will usually be informal. The opinion preparers must take into account the responses to these inquiries in determining the reliability of the information being used to support the opinion. Ordinarily, however, the opinion preparers

50. This contrasts with responses to audit letter inquiries. *See ABA Statement of Policy Regarding Lawyers' Responses to Auditors' Requests for Information*, 31 Bus. Law. 1709 (1976). The diligence required to respond to an audit letter inquiry for a client includes soliciting information from lawyers in the firm who have rendered professional services to the client during the period involved.

will have no reason to make inquiries within the firm with regard to specific information furnished by the client or others that appears regular on its face and that has been obtained from an appropriate source.

(c) Handling Information That Comes From A Lawyer Within The Opinion Preparers' Firm

Lawyers within the opinion preparers' firm may be the source of information relevant to an opinion. Such information is in general subject to the same rules as to reliability as information from third parties. However, the information customarily is put into a memorandum rather than into "certificate" form: one certifies to another, not to oneself.

2.3 USE OF ASSUMPTIONS AS FACT SUBSTITUTES

A factual assumption is a bridge that allows the opinion preparers to render an opinion without establishing the facts being assumed. Opinion preparers are often permitted by the opinion recipient[51] to rely on assumptions when (i) information is not available (or is only available at substantial cost or delay), (ii) the facts being assumed relate to the opinion recipient, or (iii) the cost of establishing the facts exceeds the likely benefit (often because of the improbability that what is assumed would on investigation prove to be untrue).[52]

(a) Assumptions Of General Application—Sometimes Unstated

Some facts are common to transactions generally and are customarily assumed as a matter of course. Thus, opinion preparers almost always assume the legal capacity of individuals, that the copies of documents furnished to them conform to the originals, that the original documents furnished them are authentic and that the signatures on executed documents are genuine. The alternative of requiring the opinion preparers to establish these matters is likely to generate costs that produce no corresponding benefit. Similarly, in giving a remedies opinion, the opinion preparers will usually assume that the agreement is binding on the other parties to it.[53] As a matter of customary practice, assumptions of general application need not be stated in opinion letters.

(b) Other Assumptions—Stated

Opinion preparers also rely on assumptions that are not of general application. Thus, if the opinion preparers have not been involved in all the steps needed to close a transaction, they frequently will be permitted

51. Prior to delivery of an opinion letter, the opinion preparers will want to consult with counsel for the opinion recipient as to the acceptability of stated assumptions. *See* Section 2.3(b). Acceptance by the opinion recipient of an opinion letter constitutes acceptance of its components, including assumptions stated in it.

52. For example, opinion recipients often permit opinion givers to assume the Company's solvency although that fact has not been (and perhaps cannot be) established or is open to question. *See* Section 2.3(c).

53. Such an assumption may be needed to establish mutuality of obligation, a necessary element to contract formation.

to assume that all those steps were completed, *e.g.*, that a document was filed in a governmental office. Assumptions of specific application can reduce the cost of preparing an opinion and sometimes permit opinions to be rendered that would otherwise be impractical or impossible. Assumptions that are not of general application require an express statement in an opinion letter.

(c) Assumption Responsibilities

Opinion preparers should not rely on an unstated assumption if it is unreliable. *See* Section 2.1.4. Because of the nature of most unstated assumptions, this will seldom be the case. By way of contrast, stated assumptions, like opinion exceptions, put the opinion recipient on notice that the opinion preparers have not established the facts being assumed. Stated assumptions, therefore, shift to the opinion recipient the responsibility for confirming the assumed facts for itself or taking the risk that what is assumed might turn out to be untrue. As with opinion exceptions, reliance on a stated assumption is subject to the limitation described in Section 1.4(d) on rendering misleading opinions.

2.4 THE PRESUMPTION OF REGULARITY AND CONTINUITY

It is not unusual for a lawyer conducting a diligence review to find gaps in corporate minutes or records. For example, suppose that the opinion preparers cannot locate a shareholder resolution believed to have been adopted 30 years earlier approving an amendment to the certificate of incorporation increasing the Company's authorized stock. The minutes of shareholder meetings have been consistently maintained, but the minute book is missing for the period of the amendment. Later minutes indicate that the amendment has been consistently treated as having been effective and available corporate records cast no doubt on the shareholder authorization of it. May the opinion preparers in reliance on the presumption of regularity assume that a satisfactory resolution was set forth in the missing minutes without disclosing such reliance in the opinion letter?

Many lawyers would regard disclosure of that reliance as unnecessary because (i) the missing minutes are not recent, (ii) the minutes that have been preserved in the minute book reflect care on the part of the Company to observe formalities and (iii) subsequent minutes treat the amendment as having been properly authorized.[54] The presumption is frequently relied on without disclosure. The Committee believes that reliance on the presumption without disclosure is justified if, in light of other available facts, the gap in corporate records is unlikely to be significant.

54. The ABA Guidelines in Section II(B) indicate that reliance on this presumption should always be disclosed. However, that approach deprives the presumption of any value to the opinion giver: to require disclosure in every case is to treat use of the presumption as the equivalent to taking an exception.

2.5 OFFICERS' AND OTHER CERTIFICATES

2.5.1 Widespread Reliance On Officers' Certificates In Opinions

In establishing the factual bases for their opinions, opinion preparers customarily rely on officers' certificates. Many lawyers mention reliance on such certificates in the opinion letter, often using language such as that set forth in the Illustrative Opinion Letters. Because nearly every opinion letter relies on certificates, that reliance should be understood, whether or not stated.[55] See Section 2.1.3 as to the preparation of officers' certificates.

2.5.2 Officers' Certificates Are Seldom A Substitute For Certificates Of Public Officials

The opinion preparers look to a certificate of a public official (*e.g.*, as to U.C.C. financing statements filed) when that official is the appointed custodian of the information and has the duty to provide information in writing as to the status of the public record. A service company is an acceptable substitute (and often is more accessible than an "official" source) because it makes a business of examining the records on file. *See* Section 2.2.1(a). On the other hand, a certificate of a corporate officer, even if it recites a search of public files, involves an interested party undertaking a less than familiar task. Sometimes an officer's certificate is used to confirm that the client has executed no financing statements and received no notice of lien since the last available public official or service company certificate. Except in that limited situation, an officer's certificate is not ordinarily regarded as an acceptable substitute for the certificate of a public official or service company.

2.5.3 No Responsibility To Review Certificate Back-Up Materials

Sometimes an opinion will be based on a certificate regarding financial, appraisal, engineering or other matters that contains (or to which have been attached) complex, technical or lengthy materials explaining or justifying the conclusory factual content of the certificate, *e.g.*, computational, diagrammatic or computer file "print-out" materials. As a matter of customary practice, the opinion giver may properly rely on conclusory material in the certificate without attempting to understand or even to examine the supporting materials.[56] In part, this practice relates to competence. In part, it relates to the time required to review and understand the supporting materials. If the opinion recipient wishes to review such materials (which may be technical and best reviewed by those with a technical background), it may require that the certificate and any related materials be provided to it, either as a condition of the agreement or in

55. The closing conditions in agreements will usually specify which certificates are to be presented at closing. Ordinarily, certificates of public officials are presented at closing. Practice varies on the presentation of officers' certificates at closing.

56. *See* ABA Guidelines Section I(A)(1), which state that opinions requiring interpretation of such matters should not be requested.

connection with acceptance of the opinion letter. If the opinion recipient wishes the opinion giver to review these materials (and the opinion giver is willing to do so), the fact that such a review was conducted should be noted in the opinion letter if the opinion recipient intends to rely on the review.

2.5.4 Usual Certificate Style Is By Individual

An officer's certificate usually begins by identifying the signer as an officer of the Company but is executed by the signer as an individual (whether the signature line indicates the officer's title or not) rather than on behalf of the Company. This practice is followed because a certificate by the Company would merely restate a Company representation made in the agreement or another transaction document. By signing as an individual, the officer takes personal responsibility for the representations made in the certificate.

2.6 STATEMENTS IN OPINION LETTERS REGARDING COUNSEL'S RESPONSIBILITY FOR ESTABLISHING FACTS

The opinion recipient is entitled to assume that the opinion preparers have satisfied the standard of customary diligence described in this Report. *See* Section 1.4. To emphasize the nature and scope of the procedures conducted by the opinion preparers in establishing the facts on which the opinion letter is based, opinion givers sometimes include in their opinion letters a statement along the following lines:

> As to certain matters of fact material to the opinions expressed herein we have relied on the representations made in the Agreement and certificates of public officials and officers of the Company [and others].[57] We have not independently established the facts so relied on.

Any such statement should be regarded as included solely as a matter of emphasis since that reliance is customary without any express statement.

2.6.1 "To Our Knowledge"; Defining "Knowledge"

Many lawyers include the phrase "to our knowledge" (or some variant of it)[58] in the "no breach or default" and "no litigation" opinions (dis-

57. It is often proper to rely on certificates from others, such as service companies that deal with U.C.C. filing status.

58. Among the usages are "to the best of our knowledge"; "we do not know of"; "we have no knowledge"; "known to us"; "to our knowledge after due inquiry"; and "to our knowledge after appropriate diligence". The Committee believes that these phrases are largely indistinguishable. Some lawyers define "knowledge" in the opinion letter. To date, no one definition has gained broad acceptance among those who define knowledge.

Opinion letters sometimes use the phrase "nothing has come to our attention" as a way of communicating what lawyers have learned during the course of a diligence process that is unrelated to the preparation of the opinion letter and goes well beyond the diligence that lawyers ordinarily conduct to support an opinion letter. That phrase is principally used in the context of a public offering of securities and appears in a separate paragraph or separate letter containing the so-called 10b-5 opinion or confirmation, which is typically lengthy and establishes the context in which the phrase is to be understood.

cussed in Sections 6.5.5 and 6.8 of this Report) and sometimes in other opinions as well.[59] Those who include the phrase do so to make clear that the opinion should not be read literally but rather in the context of customary practice. By doing so, they do not limit the customary diligence lawyers undertake to support the opinion, and the meaning of the opinion is the same whether or not the phrase is used.

The obligation of the opinion preparers to exercise customary diligence in establishing the factual basis for an opinion is implicit in every opinion letter. An opinion giver can limit or disclaim that obligation by including in the opinion letter an express statement describing the factual investigation it conducted on a particular point and making clear that no other investigation was conducted. Often, this is done simply by adding the phrase "without investigation". Inclusion of the phrase "to our knowledge" in an opinion does not by itself (i) label the factual material involved as unreliable (*see* Section 2.1.4) or (ii) state a limitation on the investigation required by customary diligence.

ARTICLE III THE REMEDIES/ENFORCEABILITY OPINION

3.1 FORM AND SCOPE OF THE OPINION

A remedies opinion deals with the question whether the provisions of an agreement will be given effect by the courts. A typical remedies opinion reads as follows:

> The Agreement is a valid and binding obligation of the Company enforceable against the Company in accordance with its terms.

The remedies opinion may take a number of forms without any difference in meaning. Some remedies opinions, for example, include the word "legal" (usually before the word "valid"). Others omit one or both of the words "valid" or "binding". Still others omit the word "enforceable". Neither the inclusion of "legal" nor any of these omissions expands or limits the generally understood meaning of the remedies opinion. Even an opinion that omits the entire phrase "enforceable against the Company in accordance with its terms"[60], as well as the bankruptcy exception and equitable principles limitation, or merely states that the "Agreement is enforceable against the Company" or that it is "binding on the Company"

59. The "to our knowledge" limitation deals with facts. This limitation should not be used with respect to matters of law.

60. The word "enforceable" or the phrase "enforceable in accordance with its terms" does not mean that a court will specifically enforce the terms of a contract. Specific enforcement is an equitable remedy, the availability of which depends on a variety of factors, including the conduct of the party seeking specific enforcement.

is understood to have the same meaning[61] as the typical remedies opinion quoted above.

As a matter of customary usage, the remedies opinion is not analyzed word by word. Although it may be expressed in a variety of ways, the opinion is understood to have the same meaning so long as it contains one of the operative words, "binding" or "enforceable".

A remedies opinion deals with the present but is also forward-looking. For example, an exception is required if a remedy specified in the agreement will not be made available by the courts in the circumstances contemplated, even though on the date of the opinion letter the event required to trigger the remedy (usually a default) has not occurred and may never occur.

The remedies opinion covers three related matters. First, it confirms that an agreement has been formed.[62] Second, it confirms that the remedies provided by the agreement will be given effect by the courts (requiring an exception if (i) under applicable law the opinion recipient will not have a remedy for a breach of any "undertaking" by the other party to the agreement[63] or (ii) a remedy specified in the agreement will not be given effect under the circumstances contemplated).[64] Third, the opinion describes the extent to which the courts will enforce[65] the provisions of the agreement that are unrelated to the concept of breach[66] (requiring an exception if any of these provisions will not be given effect by the courts).

The broad reach of the remedies opinion can best be understood by analyzing the various undertakings to which it relates.

(a) Some provisions in an agreement obligate the Company to perform an affirmative act but say nothing about what will happen if the Company

61. Some lawyers refer to the opinion as the "enforceability" opinion; others refer to it as the "remedies" opinion. The two terms are synonymous. For simplicity, this Report refers to the opinion as the "remedies opinion." The remedies opinion in its usual form is subject to the bankruptcy exception and equitable principles limitation. The discussion that follows assumes those exceptions are applicable.

62. An opinion that an agreement has been formed is seldom sought as a separate opinion.

63. Frequently, an agreement is entered into before the "closing," and an opinion letter is required to be delivered only if the transaction closes. Thus, if the transaction does not close, no opinion will have been given on the enforceability of undertakings—such as those allocating expenses—that are intended to continue in effect even if the transaction does not close.

64. Some agreements state that they will be specifically enforced against a party. A remedies opinion as to such an agreement is understood to mean that the remedy specified will be available, subject to the bankruptcy exception and the equitable principles limitation. As a practical matter, therefore, all the opinion means is that a court will consider whether to provide specific performance as a remedy. *See* Section 3.3.4.

65. Representations are not undertakings and, therefore, are not covered by the remedies opinion. The opinion does cover, however, any remedies specified in the agreement for a false representation or warranty.

66. For example, chosen-law provisions. *See* Section 1.9(p).

fails to perform. For example, the agreement may require the Company to pay interest and principal on a note, to issue stock, or to obtain an annual audit of its financial statements. For these provisions, the opinion means that a court will either require the Company to fulfill its undertakings as written or grant damages or some other remedy in the event of a breach.

(b) Some agreements specify a remedy if the Company fails to perform particular undertakings. Remedies provisions may be couched as affirmative undertakings (for example, a requirement to pay liquidated damages). More often they take the form of a grant to the other party of a right to take action (for example, to accelerate the maturity of a loan, to enter the Company's premises and recover specified assets, or to reduce the interest of a defaulting partner in a partnership). For those provisions, the remedies opinion means that a court will give effect to the specified remedies as written.[67]

(c) Another type of provision establishes the ground rules for interpreting or administering the agreement and settling disputes under it. These provisions may choose the law by which the agreement is to be governed, indicate how the agreement is to be amended (for example, by a writing signed by all parties), designate the forum in which disputes are to be resolved (for example, arbitration by a specified organization or the courts of a particular state), or waive certain rights (such as the right to a jury trial). While this type of provision is cast as a statement, it constitutes an undertaking[68] of each party to the other. Unless excepted from the opinion, these provisions are covered by the remedies opinion, which is understood to mean that a court will give effect to the provision as written and require the Company to abide by its terms.

The remedies opinion should be read to cover each undertaking by the Company in the agreement. Any narrower reading would invite lengthy negotiations to determine which provisions of the agreement are being opined on and which are not.[69]

67. *See* note 64. An agreement may specify a remedy that the courts in the governing law jurisdiction will never enforce (*e.g.*, entry to the debtor's premises to recover assets without judicial order). In such a case an exception to the remedies opinion should be taken. In other cases, the courts will enforce a stated remedy, but enforcement will be subject to equitable principles in which circumstance no stated exception need be taken. *See* Section 3.3.4 for a discussion of the equitable principles limitation.

68. *See* definition in Section 1.9(a).

69. TriBar's 1979 Report offered a comprehensive definition of the scope of the remedies opinion based on New York custom and practice. Under that definition the opinion applies to each and every undertaking of the Company under the agreement. This approach has received broad acceptance not only in New York but across the country. Its acceptance, however, has not been universal. For example, a committee of the Business Law Section of the State Bar of California issued a report in 1990 endorsing a narrower definition of the scope of the remedies opinion, one that interprets the opinion to cover not all the provisions of an agreement but only those that are material. *1989 Report of the Committee on Corporations*

3.2 NARROWING THE SCOPE OF THE OPINION

Customary practice requires that any limit on the remedies opinion be explicit and not by way of omission of characteristic language. If an opinion giver wishes to render a remedies opinion that does not cover every undertaking of the Company in the agreement, the opinion letter should describe with particularity the limitations the opinion giver intends to impose. For example, if the opinion preparers conclude that a remedy specified in the agreement, such as an indemnification provision, is unlikely to be given legal effect, they should include an exception in the opinion.[70] *See* definition of "exception" in Section 1.9(i). The task of reviewing an agreement to identify the exceptions to be taken is an important part of the opinion process. The exceptions taken should be carefully tailored to the specific undertakings covered by the opinion.[71]

3.3 BANKRUPTCY AND EQUITABLE PRINCIPLES

3.3.1 The Remedies Opinion Does Not Cover Bankruptcy And Equitable Principles Questions

Two uniformly accepted qualifications to the remedies opinion are the bankruptcy exception[72] and the equitable principles limitation. When

of the Business Law Section of the State Bar of California Regarding Legal Opinions in Business Transactions, 45 BUS. LAW. 2169 (1990). A materiality test has superficial appeal: an immaterial provision is by definition unlikely to be of any real interest to the opinion recipient and thus including it within the coverage of the opinion would appear to serve no useful purpose. On analysis, however, a materiality test reveals itself to be unworkable. An opinion giver is in no position to judge whether a provision is, in fact, unimportant to the opinion recipient, who is not the opinion giver's client. From the standpoint of an opinion giver, reliance on an undefined materiality standard therefore invites miscommunication. From the standpoint of the opinion recipient, an undefined materiality standard is equally unacceptable. By restricting the coverage of the opinion without identifying which provisions are omitted, such a standard leaves the opinion recipient unable to determine whether provisions it regards as valuable may later be found not to have been covered by the opinion. Thus, an undefined materiality test creates risk for the opinion giver while significantly undercutting the precision of an opinion and thus reducing its value to the opinion recipient. Its widespread adoption could complicate the opinion process by forcing opinion recipients to ask opinion givers to identify all provisions the opinion giver has deemed to be immaterial.

70. *See, e.g.*, Globus v. Law Research Serv., Inc., 418 F.2d 1276, 1287-89 (2d Cir. 1969), *cert. denied*, 397 U.S. 913 (1970).

71. For example, when considering the enforceability of an acquisition agreement, lawyers give special attention to "lock-up" options and "no shop" and "non-competition" clauses, among others, as well as provisions relating to the resolution of disputes (such as choice of forum, forum *non conveniens* and provisions on subject matter jurisdiction). When foreign obligors are involved, some lawyers add an exception for possible judicial deference by state or federal courts to acts of foreign sovereign states. Whether "comity" is viewed as an integral part of United States law or deference to the law of others, it is of general application and broadly understood. Concepts such as comity that are so broadly comprehended do not ordinarily require a specific exception. *See* SCOTT FITZGIBBON & DONALD W. GLAZER, FITZGIBBON & GLAZER ON LEGAL OPINIONS: WHAT OPINIONS IN FINANCIAL TRANSACTIONS SAY AND WHAT THEY MEAN, § 9.10.2 (Little, Brown & Co. 1992).

72. The bankruptcy exception excludes the effect of bankruptcy law on the remedies

stated, they often follow immediately after the affirmative statement of the remedies opinion and are typically phrased substantially as follows:

> . . . except as may be limited by[73] bankruptcy, insolvency or other similar laws affecting the rights and remedies of creditors generally and general principles of equity.[74]

As in the Illustrative Opinion Letters these qualifications are sometimes stated as being generally applicable to all opinions. *See* Section 1.2(c). These qualifications are understood to be applicable to the remedies opinion even if they are not expressly stated.

Sometimes the language quoted above begins with the words "except as enforcement may be limited by bankruptcy, insolvency. . .". Use of the word "enforcement" is not intended, and should not be construed, to restrict the bankruptcy exception and equitable principles limitation to matters relating to enforcement of contract provisions. Any narrowing of the bankruptcy exception or equitable principles limitation requires clear language rather than reliance on a single word such as "enforcement". *See* second paragraph of Section 3.1.

3.3.2 Bankruptcy Exception Relates To A Body Of Law Rather Than The Bankruptcy Of Particular Parties

The bankruptcy exception is more aptly an "insolvency law exception" in that it covers not only the federal Bankruptcy Code but also any other similar insolvency laws (state or federal) of general application.[75] The

opinion. *See* TriBar Opinion Committee, *Opinions in the Bankruptcy Context: Rating Agency, Structured Financing, and Chapter 11 Transactions*, 46 BUS. LAW. 717 (1991). The opinions discussed in that report (*e.g.*, non-consolidation of entities, fraudulent conveyances, and preferences) do not address the enforceability of an agreement, but rather the applicability of particular principles of bankruptcy law, the effect of which are excluded from consideration by the bankruptcy exception.

73. The language quoted above sometimes begins with the words "subject to the effect of" instead of "except as may be limited by". These usages are understood to be synonymous.

74. The equitable principles limitation takes many forms. For example, the words "whether applied by a court of law or equity" are sometimes added after the word "equity." The meaning of the limitation is now so well established that an opinion letter no longer needs to point out that the limitation applies even if a court is not sitting under local practice as a court of equity. Sometimes the equitable principles limitation will include language (often after the word "equity") along the following lines: "including (without limitation) concepts of materiality, reasonableness, good faith and fair dealing." Language such as this merely illustrates the breadth of the equitable principles limitation. It does not add to or subtract from the limitation.

75. The use of the word "similar" makes clear that the exception does not comprehend those laws that affect creditors' rights generally but are unrelated to laws grounded in insolvency, *e.g.*, usury laws. However, the Committee believes that omission of the word "similar" should not be construed to broaden the scope of the exception: clearer language is required to do that. Some lawyers expressly include in the bankruptcy exception references to "reorganization" and "moratorium" laws. "Moratorium" laws refer to the type of emergency economic legislation enacted during the Great Depression as a means of halting foreclosure of certain classes of property, *e.g.*, farms. Both moratorium and "reorganization" (a term that

"bankruptcy exception" tells the opinion recipient that a specific body of law has been excluded from the opinion. The exception refers to all situations—whether involving insolvency proceedings or not—to which insolvency principles apply. Fraudulent conveyance (or transfer) laws are included in the laws covered by the exception. Sometimes the exception refers to those laws expressly (often after the word "insolvency"). If not, they are included *sub silentio* in the phrase "other similar laws".

The bankruptcy exception relates to a body of law rather than to a proceeding relating to a particular person or entity. Thus, the exception will have application, for example, to a fraudulent transfer, even if the company never becomes subject to a bankruptcy proceeding. Further, the bankruptcy of another person or entity may affect the position of the Company. For example, the Bankruptcy Court may not permit the enforcement of a guaranty against the manager of a bankrupt company if that will disrupt the bankruptcy proceedings.

3.3.3 Whether Bankruptcy Exception Excludes All State Insolvency Law Is Unclear

Read literally, the bankruptcy exception excludes from the opinion (and therefore eliminates the need for the opinion giver to disclose by specific exception) all federal and state insolvency laws. However, the federal Bankruptcy Code specifically excludes domestic banks and insurance companies and certain others from coverage (11 U.S.C. § 109) (1994 & Supp. II 1996), relegating their insolvency to other applicable federal or state law. The opinion giver is entitled to assume that the opinion recipient's lawyer knows federal law and is aware that state law applies to certain bank and insurance company insolvencies not covered by federal law. However, it seems unrealistic (particularly if opinions are submitted to opinion recipients whose lawyers do not customarily practice in the particular state) to assume that counsel for the opinion recipient will be familiar with the coverage of state laws (other than those applicable to banks and insurance companies) that apply to specific types of debtors.[76] As a result, and despite the broad language of the bankruptcy exception, the Committee believes that it is the better practice for the opinion giver not to rely on the bankruptcy exception to exclude from opinion coverage state insolvency laws applicable to specific types of debtors other than banks and insurance companies. Because current practice is unclear, if any question exists whether the Company may be in a class protected by state insolvency law, lawyers representing opinion recipients may wish to make at least an informal inquiry of the opinion giver as to state law.

is integral to the Bankruptcy Code) are within the scope of the bankruptcy exception, even if not expressly mentioned.

76. For example, under the Bankruptcy Code municipalities may be forbidden by state law from filing as a debtor; under the Bankruptcy Code an involuntary proceeding may not be commenced against a farmer. In each case state law can therefore provide a moratorium, if the state chooses to do so. The question is whether state law in fact does so.

3.3.4 Equitable Principles Limitation—The Attempt To Define Equity

Opinion preparers may conclude that particular provisions of an agreement are binding and yet envision that, under certain circumstances, those provisions may not be given effect by a court. The equitable principles limitation relates to those principles courts apply when, in light of facts or events that occur after the effectiveness of an agreement, they decline in the interest of equity to give effect to particular provisions in the agreement.[77] For example, under the circumstances of a particular case, a court may determine that a notice provision is too short or the withholding of a consent is unreasonable. When such court determinations are grounded in the belief that to enforce the contract literally would be inequitable in the context in which the dispute has arisen, the equitable principles limitation would apply. However, if the notice provision would in all circumstances be held to be too short or if the withholding of consent would in all circumstances be improper, the equitable principles limitation would not apply. Relief would be denied because of the invalidity of the provision, rather than because of the application of equitable principles.

What then is covered by the equitable principles limitation? It covers not only the availability of traditional equitable remedies (such as specific performance or injunctive relief) but also defenses rooted in equity that result from the enforcing party's lack of good faith and fair dealing, unreasonableness of conduct,[78] or undue delay (*e.g.*, laches). In addition, the limitation covers those situations in which a court may decline to give effect to a contractual provision because the enforcing party has not been significantly harmed as where an alleged breach is not material and has not resulted in any meaningful damage to the party seeking enforcement.

Because the courts have an interest in justice (as well as predictability) and concepts relating to fair dealing provide broad discretion, any attempt to define with precision the limits of the equitable principles limitation is unlikely to succeed. Thus, opinion letter language purporting to narrow the equitable principles limitation is rarely requested or provided. Even an opinion that a specific remedy will be available is ordinarily subject to the equitable principles limitation.

77. The equitable principles limitation applies to the enforcement of an agreement, not to its formation. If before rendering the remedies opinion the opinion preparers believe that coercion, duress or similar inequitable conduct has prevented the formation of the agreement in question, they should not render the opinion (or should disclose their concerns, if the client consents). Unless they have knowledge to the contrary, the opinion preparers are entitled to assume the absence of conduct so egregious as to preclude formation of an agreement (without so stating and subject to the usual rules governing use of assumptions—*see* Section 2.3).

78. Lack of good faith and fair dealing and unreasonableness of conduct cover concepts such as coercion, duress, unconscionability, undue influence, and in some cases, estoppel.

3.4 PRACTICAL REALIZATION

3.4.1 "Practical Realization"—A Limitation On Stated Remedies Along With A Limited Assurance

While exceptions ordinarily identify with specificity the provisions of the agreement to which they apply, the "practical realization" qualification takes an entirely different approach. One common example of the qualification is as follows:

> Certain of the [remedial][79] provisions in the Agreement may be further limited or rendered unenforceable by applicable law, but in our opinion such law does not make the remedies afforded by the Agreement inadequate for the practical realization of the principal benefits intended to be provided.

Opinion givers use "practical realization" language of the sort quoted above as a way of opining on agreements (most often seen in lease and certain secured financing transactions) that contain many specific remedies, some of which may be unenforceable exactly as written or may be mutually inconsistent but are stated to be nonexclusive. By use of a "practical realization" qualification, opinion givers seek to avoid the time and cost of analyzing each remedial provision and its relationship with the other provisions and of taking numerous, specific opinion exceptions. Some experienced opinion recipients are receptive to this opinion "shortcut". Others view it as depriving them of appropriate guidance concerning the availability to them of particular remedies. Despite its inherent ambiguity, the "practical realization" language quoted above has been encrusted with tradition and become an aspect of customary practice. The Committee believes that its continued use should be confined to its historical context of lease and secured financing transactions.

When the "practical realization" qualification is used, the remedies opinion should be understood to mean that, where inconsistent or legally defective remedies are set forth in an agreement, the remedial provisions available taken as a whole will nevertheless provide the opinion recipient, in the event of a default by the Company, the benefit of its bargained-for ability to realize upon security or leased property and pursue a claim for damages.[80] Like the remedies opinion itself, a reference to practical realization should always be understood to be subject to the bankruptcy exception and equitable principles limitation and to any other specifically stated opinion exceptions.

79. An often-used version of this exception omits the word "remedial," thereby seemingly making the qualification applicable to the entire agreement. The opinion giver thus avoids any risk of controversy over whether a provision is a "remedy." The Committee prefers omitting the word "remedial" for this reason.

80. "The practical realization" conclusion should not be understood to cover benefits conferred by a legal status, *e.g.*, whether a lease is a "true lease," who holds title to property, or whether the lessor is the "tax owner" of leased equipment. Opinions on these issues, if desired, should be requested as separate opinions.

The risk for both opinion givers and opinion recipients is that each will understand "practical realization" to mean something different. Attempts to define the "principal benefits" of the agreement have been unsuccessful.

3.4.2 Broad Practical Realization As A Reassurance Is Inappropriate

Sometimes an opinion recipient, faced with myriad opinion exceptions, will request that the practical realization language quoted in Section 3.4.1 be modified to read substantially as follows:

> Notwithstanding the exceptions noted above, [lender] will achieve the practical realization of the benefits intended to be conferred by the Agreement.

This broad "practical realization" language is qualitatively different from the more limited version described in Section 3.4.1. Unlike the more limited version, which is subject to all the standard and specifically stated exceptions, this version overrides all those exceptions, requiring the opinion giver to conclude that those exceptions collectively will not prevent the opinion recipient from enjoying the "benefits" of the agreement. Sometimes availability of the benefits depends on the value of the security involved because a lender may have no recourse against the borrower. In addition, this language is undesirable because of the possibility of its being confused with the narrower and more frequently seen practical realization form described in Section 3.4.1. In the view of the Committee this form of opinion is inappropriate and should not be requested or rendered.

3.5 AMBIT OF THE REMEDIES OPINION

3.5.1 Other Limits

Besides contract law, other bodies of law also bear on the effectiveness of the provisions of an agreement. These include, for example, usury laws, the antitrust laws, the Securities Act of 1933, the Securities Exchange Act of 1934, statutory shareholder approval requirements and requirements for approval of related-party transactions. Which bodies of law are covered by the remedies opinion depends on customary practice.

Customary practice requires the opinion preparers to take account of law that lawyers who render legal opinions of the type involved would reasonably recognize as being applicable (i) to transactions of the type covered by the agreement and (ii) to the role of the Company (but not other parties to the agreement) in the transaction. The analysis involved is a complex one. It is made more complex by the exclusion of laws that lawyers would recognize as being applicable to the transaction, but that are customarily not covered unless specifically addressed. *See* Section 3.5.2(c). The practicalities of opinion recipient need and the amount of work required to support an opinion have defined customary practice. Opinion preparers do not customarily seek (nor are they requested to seek) guidance from experts in every specialized field of law that might be implicated by the undertakings in an agreement. Such an effort would seldom be cost-justified even in very large transactions.

Under customary practice, an issue is deemed to be covered by the remedies opinion only when it is both (i) essential to the particular conclusion expressed and (ii) reasonable under the circumstances for the opinion recipient to conclude that it was intended to be covered. The remedies opinion does not cover laws that do not affect enforceability of the agreement but merely create an adverse legal consequence (*e.g.*, a fine) for a party to an agreement.

3.5.2 Specific Examples Of Remedies Opinion Limits

(a) Coverage Of Remedies Opinion Where Regulatory System Voids Certain Obligations

(i) *Regulatory Issues Involving The Client's Status Or Activities Are Covered*

The nature of the business conducted by the Company will affect the scope of the opinion. The opinion giver can fairly be charged with the responsibility to advise whether its client has complied with regulatory statutes applicable to it because of the nature of its business if non-compliance impairs enforceability. Thus, in a state such as New York, where a purchase of shares of a telephone corporation by another telephone corporation requires prior New York Public Service Commission approval, a remedies opinion rendered by purchaser's counsel is understood as a matter of customary practice to cover the effect of the Public Service Law on the purchase agreement's enforceability against its client. Similarly, the opinion preparers should consider the effect of the Investment Company Act of 1940 when preparing an opinion on the binding effect of an agreement on a registered investment company.[81]

(ii) *Regulatory Issues Involving Other Parties Are Not Covered*

On the other hand, a remedies opinion is not as a matter of customary practice normally read to cover regulatory statutes applicable solely to the opinion recipient. Thus, in rendering a remedies opinion on a bank loan, borrower's counsel is not passing on whether the loan violates the bank's lending limit or whether the bank obtained any required governmental approvals.

(iii) *Regulatory Issues Involving Both Parties Are Sometimes Covered*

Some statutes affect both the opinion recipient and the opinion giver's client. For example, usury laws, which limit a lender's interest charges, affect the enforceability of the borrower's interest payment obligation. A remedies opinion by borrower's counsel as a matter of customary usage covers usury laws that affect enforceability of the borrower's obligations although those laws also apply to the other party to the transaction, the lender.

A more difficult case is presented by the Federal Reserve Board's margin

81. The opinion preparers should also consider the application of the Act if they recognize that the Company's activities may make it an inadvertent investment company.

regulations, which also contain provisions applicable both to the lender and to the borrower. Unlike coverage of the usury laws, custom is not clear here. Not all experienced counsel believe that compliance with the margin regulations by both parties to a financing transaction is within the scope of the remedies opinion of borrower's counsel, although a violation of the regulations may void a loan. Therefore, many lenders require a separate opinion addressing this question. In light of the unusually complex issues the margin regulations may present concerning a particular transaction structure or a particular borrower, the Committee believes that a separate opinion on the effect of these regulations is the better practice, if such an opinion is desired.

(b) Coverage Of Remedies Opinion As To Disclosure And Discharge Of Fiduciary Obligation—Issues Affecting Authorization

Opinion preparers will routinely obtain certificates or other evidence of various approvals (*e.g.*, approval by the board of directors or shareholders) that are required to give an opinion. The certificate or other evidence is to the effect that the required vote has been obtained and, if necessary, that a meeting was held and appropriate notice was given. Because of the essentially legal nature of these matters (*see* Section 2.2.1(b)), such a certificate is understood as not covering the questions (i) whether those voting were sufficiently informed about the matter on which they voted and (ii) whether those voting were doing so inappropriately because, for example, they had not disclosed an interest in the transaction or had violated a fiduciary obligation. As for the first of those questions, the opinion preparers may assume without disclosure and without investigation (subject to the customary limits on unstated assumptions) that the information required to be presented to obtain an effective approval has been provided. Any assessment of the adequacy of factual disclosure (for example, in proxy statements) is a significant task and one that is customarily not undertaken in order to render a remedies opinion. Similarly, the opinion preparers are not required as a matter of customary diligence to inquire into whether those approving the transaction have violated their fiduciary obligations or have an interest they have failed to disclose, unless the opinion expressly covers those issues. The remedies opinion is based on the assumption, usually unstated, that those who have approved an agreement have satisfied their fiduciary obligations and appropriately disclosed any interest.[82]

(c) Coverage Of Remedies Opinion—Specific Laws: Tax, Antitrust and Securities Excluded By Custom

The remedies opinion addresses enforceability questions. Thus, it calls on the opinion preparers to consider whether provisions of the agreement

82. Some lawyers see these issues as excluded from the opinion rather than being the subject of an assumption. *See* note 148. As a practical matter differences in these approaches are not significant.

would be given effect by a court on the date of the opinion letter and whether they would be given effect in the future in various circumstances. For example, a "floating rate" loan might not be usurious at closing, but if it contains no cap on the interest rate, at some point the loan might be unenforceable in part or whole, thus requiring that an exception be taken to a remedies opinion given at closing. While the emphasis is on corporate and other everyday commercial laws (*e.g.*, N.Y. General Obligations Law), a broad range of other laws may have some affect on the enforceability of an agreement. The antitrust laws might void a joint venture deemed anti-competitive. A transfer of technology to a non-American might be deemed to be subject to the Exon-Florio amendment to the Defense Production Act of 1952. There are many other examples. Which of these statutes should be considered in giving a remedies opinion, and which not? Custom is that (in the absence of language indicating the contrary) the opinion does not cover the tax laws, insolvency laws, antitrust laws, securities laws (except as contemplated by note 81 and the accompanying text) and the Exon-Florio amendment.

3.5.3 Absence Of Custom

The Committee believes that, as to the many areas where custom is unclear, the opinion recipient should request opinions on the matters it wishes to have covered. The Committee also believes that it would ordinarily be counterproductive for opinion givers to try to identify in opinion letters each area that is not covered. First, the list of exclusions will never be complete, yet any list may suggest that it is complete. Second, lists of exclusions in opinion letters are likely to provide a new area for negotiations that will impede rather then facilitate the opinion process.

3.6 REMEDIES OPINIONS AND ARBITRATION

3.6.1 Opinion That Dispute Is Arbitrable Is Inherent In Remedies Opinion

An arbitration provision in an agreement constitutes an "undertaking," a promise by each party to the other, concerning the forum for resolution of disputes. The remedies opinion covers arbitration provisions just as it covers others undertakings in the agreement. Remedies opinions on agreements containing arbitration clauses do not customarily indicate when disputes arising under the agreement are subject to arbitration, nor do they attempt to describe the differences between the resolution of disputes through litigation and arbitration.[83]

83. In arbitration, no appellate court is available to correct a mistake of law. Often the parties will not even be able to determine whether the arbitrators (some or all of whom may not be lawyers) have properly understood and applied the law. Under the rules governing many arbitrations, no explanation of how the tribunal reached its decision is provided; only a statement of the decision is given. Differences may also exist in the discovery that is permissible, the remedies available and other matters.

Public policy sometimes requires that a dispute be resolved in a judicial forum instead of in arbitration. Public policy may also preclude the submission to arbitration of certain issues. For example, some courts will not give effect to an arbitration clause that provides that arbitration can only be commenced by one party to an agreement. However, in recent years a pronounced judicial trend has developed toward narrowing the areas in which public policy will preclude arbitration. If opinion preparers are unable to conclude that the arbitration provision will be given effect in all respects, they should include in the opinion letter an exception to the remedies opinion, for example, as follows:

> We express no opinion with respect to the provision in the agreement requiring arbitration as to matters of _____.

3.6.2 Rules Of Arbitral Tribunals Not Covered By Remedies Opinion

Agreements that contain arbitration provisions usually incorporate by reference the rules of an arbitral tribunal (*e.g.*, "any dispute is to be determined in accordance with the Commercial Arbitration Rules of the American Arbitration Association"). While the remedies opinion addresses the enforceability of the arbitration provision, as a matter of customary usage the remedies opinion is understood not to address the enforceability of these rules.

ARTICLE IV LAW COVERED BY THE OPINION LETTER

4.1 SETTING LIMITS ON THE LAW OPINION LETTERS COVER

Opinion letters customarily include a statement that limits their coverage to the law of a specific state or states.[84] Sometimes the limiting statement relates to a particular area of state law or even a single statute, *e.g.*, the Delaware General Corporation Law.[85] Opinion letters also often state that they cover federal law. If in identifying the law covered an opinion letter does not state that it covers federal law (or the law of a particular state), that law is understood, as a matter of customary usage, not to be covered except to the extent that it is expressly addressed by specific opinions in the letter.

When, as discussed in Article V, opinion preparers are relying on opinions of other counsel with regard to the law of particular states, they

84. Such a statement is not necessary when an opinion letter is directed to a particular statute, such as the Securities Act of 1933, and its coverage is apparent from the specific opinion or opinions being rendered.

85. Many lawyers who do not practice in Delaware regard themselves as competent to render opinions on various matters covered by the Delaware General Corporation Law, such as corporate status. *See* Section 6.1.

typically will include in the statement specifying the law covered by the opinion letter a reference to the law of those other states. In doing so, many lawyers take care to avoid broadening the coverage of the opinion letter beyond what they intend by limiting the reference to the law of other states to the specific opinion paragraphs they intend that law to cover. A statement along the following lines might be used:

> The opinions expressed herein are limited to the law of the State of New York, the Delaware General Corporation Law, the federal law of the United States and, as to the opinion given in paragraph _____, the law of the Commonwealth of Massachusetts and, as to the opinion given in paragraph _____, the law of the State of Connecticut.

In deciding what laws to cover, opinion preparers will consider the competence of their firm in the applicable areas of law as well as other relevant factors. However, even if their firm has the requisite competence, opinion preparers may decline to give an opinion for a variety of reasons. For example, other lawyers available to render the opinion may be more knowledgeable as to the particular subject matter or the opinion preparers may not have done the diligence required to give the opinion.

4.2 EVALUATING PROPOSED LIMITS ON THE LAW COVERED

Once the law to be covered in an opinion letter is tentatively set, the opinion recipient's counsel will need to consider the consequences of the proposed limits. Assume that the Company is a Delaware corporation, based in Massachusetts, represented by Delaware counsel. The transaction involved is a loan by a New York bank secured by accounts receivable and New York law is the chosen-law in the loan agreement and in the security agreement. The opinion letter states that it is limited to the law of Delaware and to federal law. It contains what purports to be a remedies opinion.

The limitation on the laws covered (which, by not specifically including New York as a jurisdiction whose law is covered, excludes New York law) is by custom read to limit the meaning of the opinions given.[86] The No Violation of Law and Approvals and Filings opinions, limited to Delaware and federal law, may be insufficient in the mind of the opinion recipient, given the lack of borrower activity in Delaware. In such a case the opinion recipient may require opinions or other diligence from counsel familiar with New York law and the law of the states in which the borrower's principal operations are conducted. *See* Section 4.6. Creation of a security interest in the accounts receivable will be governed by New York law, but perfection will be governed by Massachusetts law.[87]

86. This is more fully discussed at Section 4.6.
87. U.C.C. §§ 1-103, 9-203, 9-401(d) (1995).

4.3 DETERMINING THE LAW APPLICABLE TO THE AGREEMENT

Agreements often specify the law intended to govern their interpretation (the "chosen-law") using a provision along the following lines:[88]

> This agreement shall be governed by the law of the State of New York.[89]

If a chosen-law is specified in an agreement[90] the court that hears a contract dispute, if required to determine the law applicable to the agreement (the "governing law"), will ordinarily treat the chosen-law as the governing law *if* at least one of the parties or the transaction bears a "reasonable relationship" to the state whose law is the chosen-law.[91]

New York and Delaware,[92] by statute, authorize parties to agreements involving larger monetary amounts to adopt their law as the chosen-law, even if neither the transaction nor any of the parties to the agreement has any relationship to them.[93]

88. *See* definition of chosen-law in Section 1.9(p). If a chosen-law is not specified, a court will ordinarily apply the law of the state that bears the "most significant relationship" to the transaction and the parties. *See* RESTATEMENT (SECOND) OF CONFLICTS OF LAWS § 188 (1971). The result of the analysis of "contacts" made by courts to determine the most significant relationship may be unpredictable. Also, separate agreements forming a part of the same transaction may be subjected to different governing law as a result of such an analysis.

89. Although the authority is to the contrary (*see, e.g*,. Siegelman v. Cunard White Star Ltd., 221 F.2d 189, 194 (2d Cir. 1955)), some lawyers are concerned that courts may construe a clause such as the one quoted in the text to authorize the application of the choice-of-law rules as well as the substantive law of the state whose law has been selected as the chosen-law. Because of this concern, they use a chosen-law provision along the following lines:

> This agreement shall be governed by the law of the State of New York, excluding, however, its choice-of-law rules.

The Committee believes that both chosen-law provisions mean the same thing. Neither provision can be intended to exclude N.Y. GEN. OBLIG. LAW § 5-1401 (McKinney 1989 & Supp. 1998) or any similar statute, nor can it be interpreted (and an opinion as to its enforceability cannot be read) to exclude mandatory choice-of-law rules. *See* Section 4.5.

90. *See* RESTATEMENT (SECOND) OF CONFLICTS OF LAWS § 187 (1971).

91. While chosen-law provisions in agreements usually specify only the law of a state, relevant federal law will apply to the agreement as well. However, as a matter of customary usage an opinion letter is not understood to cover federal law unless the opinion letter indicates that it does. *See* Section 4.1.

Revisions of U.C.C. Article 1 (§ 1-302 replacing current § 1-105) now proposed would require deference to chosen-law provisions in transactions governed by the U.C.C., even when the transaction bears no reasonable relationship to the chosen-law state.

92. N.Y. GEN. OBLIG. LAW § 5-1401 (McKinney 1989 & Supp. 1998); DEL. CODE ANN. tit. 6 § 2708 (1993). Texas takes a different approach in TEX. BUS. & COM. CODE ANN. § 35.51 (1987 & Supp. 1998); that statute permits a choice, but only among jurisdictions to which the transaction bears a reasonable relationship.

93. Those who adopt the law of a state (pursuant to statute like that of New York) in a transaction that may not meet the "reasonable relationship" test will ordinarily provide in

4.4 "CHOSEN-LAW PROVISION" COVERED BY REMEDIES OPINION

The chosen-law provision of an agreement constitutes an undertaking by each party to the other regarding the choice of law that is to govern their obligations. Accordingly, like all other undertakings of the parties in the agreement, the effectiveness of the chosen-law provision is covered by the remedies opinion. Sometimes opinion letters contain a separate opinion that specifically addresses the effectiveness of the chosen-law provision. These opinions are included merely as a matter of emphasis if the opinion letter also contains a remedies opinion.

4.5 INHERENT LIMITATIONS ON CHOSEN-LAW

Even if the chosen-law is determined by a court to be the law generally governing the agreement, it will not necessarily govern every aspect of the agreement. Some aspects will be governed by mandatory choice-of-law rules. Consider a loan agreement granting a lender a mortgage on real estate and a security interest in accounts receivable. The law of the situs governs real estate conveyances and the choice-of-law rules specified in the Uniform Commercial Code govern the perfection of a security interest in accounts receivable. Similarly, the law of the state of incorporation governs the "internal affairs" of a corporation. As a matter of customary usage, these inherent limitations are not ordinarily stated in opinion letters.

As with other opinions, an opinion on the enforceability of an agreement covers only the law of the jurisdictions specifically identified for coverage in the opinion letter. The enforceability opinion (assuming that it covers the chosen-law jurisdiction, as it normally will) considers (among other things) whether the courts in the chosen-law jurisdiction will, in applying the law of that jurisdiction, give effect to the chosen-law provision. The opinion does not address whether the courts outside the chosen-law jurisdiction will give effect to the chosen-law provision. Even if a court outside the chosen law jurisdiction generally were to give effect to such a provision, it might apply the law of some other jurisdiction to particular provisions of the agreement if it determined that (i) another jurisdiction had a "paramount interest"[94] or (ii) the application of the chosen-law offended the public policy[95] of the forum state in some substantial way.

the agreement that any litigation is to be heard only in the courts of the state whose governing law has been chosen. This, too, has been authorized by statute. *See, e.g.*, N.Y. GEN. OBLIG. LAW § 5-1402 (McKinney 1989 & Supp. 1998). Note that the New York statute addresses adoption only of the law of that state and the Delaware statute only of Delaware law.

94. In the following cases, one involving a franchise and the other a distributorship, the chosen-law was rejected as the governing law and statutory safeguards under the law of the forum were applied: Electrical & Magneto Serv. Co. v. AMBAC Internat'l Corp., 941 F.2d 660, 662 (8th Cir. 1991) (Missouri interest overrides provision choosing South Carolina law as governing law); Soloman Distributors, Inc. v. Brown-Forman Corp., 888 F.2d 170, 172 (1st Cir. 1989) (Maine interest overrides provision choosing California law as governing law).

95. The public policy of a forum state is a part of its "law".

4.6 ALTERNATIVES WHEN CHOSEN-LAW PROVISION IN AGREEMENT SPECIFIES LAW OF A STATE NOT COVERED BY OPINION LETTER

In many transactions the Company and its counsel will be located in one state and the other party to the agreement and its counsel will be located in another. In such transactions, the other party to the agreement, for example, a New York bank lending to a borrower headquartered in Massachusetts and incorporated in Delaware, often will require that the law of its state (New York) be the chosen-law. Because borrower's counsel in this example is typically not willing to render an opinion under the chosen-law, a question will naturally arise regarding the adequacy of its opinion (if limited to Massachusetts law) on the loan agreement.

One alternative is for the opinion recipient to require the borrower to retain special counsel to render a remedies opinion under the chosen-law. This is the traditional approach and it is adhered to in many transactions. However, the borrower may object to the additional expense of bringing in another law firm and argue that the bank's counsel, who drafted the agreement, should be the one the bank looks to for an opinion on the loan agreement's enforceability. In some situations (particularly if the loan is small and the cost of preparing the opinion is large in relation to the loan), a lender may forgo a remedies opinion from the borrower's counsel.

Another alternative, and one that has received growing acceptance, is for the opinion recipient not to receive an opinion from borrower's counsel on the enforceability of the agreement under the chosen-law (New York). Instead, the opinion recipient obtains opinions from borrower's counsel[96] that (i) the chosen-law provision in the agreement will be given effect by the courts of the headquarters state (Massachusetts),[97] but (ii) if the law of the headquarters state were nevertheless held to be applicable to the loan agreement,[98] the agreement would be a binding obligation of the Company enforceable in accordance with its terms under the law of the headquarters state. Since the headquarters state is a likely place for a suit to be brought to enforce the agreement, the opinion recipient has reason to be concerned about the effectiveness of the chosen-law provision under that state's law and, more generally, the enforceability under that law of key provisions in the agreement.

96. This assumes, as will usually be the case, that borrower's counsel is in a position to render an opinion on the law of the headquarters state.

97. In some states the applicable conflict-of-laws rules may make such an opinion difficult to give. In those circumstances, opinion recipients will often be satisfied solely with the opinions described in subparagraph (ii).

98. An alternative to the opinion described in subparagraph (ii) that has also gained wide acceptance is for borrower's counsel to render a remedies opinion as if the agreement selected the law of the headquarters state as the chosen-law. Both alternatives are preferable to an opinion based on an assumption that the chosen-law is the same as the law of the headquarters state because it avoids the imprecision inherent in that assumption.

An approach the Committee recommends be avoided is for borrower's counsel to render a remedies opinion without specifying how it is affected by the statement in the opinion letter excluding coverage of the chosen-law. To do so risks misunderstanding between the opinion giver and the opinion recipient's counsel over the coverage of the opinion. Some lawyers have argued that when the chosen-law is different from the law covered by the opinion letter, the remedies opinion should be understood to mean that the chosen-law provision in the agreement is effective under the law of the state covered by the opinion letter—but nothing more. Such an approach lacks general acceptance. The Committee recommends that opinion preparers discuss with counsel for the opinion recipient what the opinion should cover and, once an understanding is reached, reflect that understanding expressly in the opinion letter.

4.7 GOVERNING LAW AND OTHER COMMON OPINIONS

(a) "No Litigation" Opinion

The "No Litigation" Opinion (Section 6.8) is primarily factual in nature. Thus, the determination of governing law is irrelevant.

(b) "No Breach Or Default" Opinion

The "No Breach or Default" opinion will often relate to agreements governed by the law of jurisdictions whose law is not covered by the opinion letter. Nevertheless, the agreements are covered by the opinion. For a discussion of how the opinion is interpreted, *see* Section 6.5.6.

(c) "No Violation Of Law" And "Approvals And Filings" Opinions

The "No Violation of Law" (Section 6.6) and "Approvals and Filings" (Section 6.7) opinions are usually not intended to cover the law of all the jurisdictions in which the Company carries on its operations. This limitation on coverage is accomplished either by (i) the opinion letter provision regarding the law covered by the opinion letter or (ii) the language of the specific opinion (which may contain a limitation beyond that applicable to the opinion letter generally).

ARTICLE V OPINIONS BEYOND THE EXPERTISE OF THE OPINION GIVER

5.1 THE UMBRELLA OPINION

Most complex financial transactions involve the laws of more than one state. For example, assume that a Delaware corporation headquartered in Massachusetts produces a patented item. A New York bank has agreed to lend to the Company on the security of its accounts receivable and its patent, using documentation that designates New York law as the chosen-law. The law of Delaware, Massachusetts and New York as well as federal patent law are involved. The Company's counsel (referred to as the "primary opinion giver" here) is a New York law firm with some expertise in

Delaware corporate law. The primary opinion giver is not willing to provide an opinion on either patent law or Massachusetts law.

Many lenders will prefer to receive a single opinion letter from the primary opinion giver containing all opinions. If the primary opinion giver is agreeable to this approach, it will obtain opinion letters from other lawyers ("other counsel") covering the opinions not within its expertise (here Massachusetts law and patent matters) and will include in its opinion letter (the "primary opinion letter") opinions on those matters in reliance on other counsel's opinions. It will render the New York and Delaware law opinions based on its own expertise. The primary opinion giver will incorporate the conclusions of the other counsel in its opinion *in haec verba* (or by reference) including all applicable opinion limitations. The primary opinion letter will state that the Massachusetts opinions and the patent opinions are given in reliance on opinions of the other counsel (who will be identified by name), and the primary opinion giver will deliver to the opinion recipient copies of the opinion letters of other counsel that it is relying on. The primary opinion letter will state that it covers New York, Massachusetts, Delaware and federal law. Since the opinion (in the primary opinion letter) on Delaware law will be limited to such matters as corporate status, authority to enter into the agreement and good standing, the primary opinion letter often will state that it is limited to the Delaware General Corporation Law, rather than to Delaware law generally. Similarly, the reference in the opinion letter to Massachusetts law will be limited to the specific paragraphs of the primary opinion letter that are based on the opinion of Massachusetts counsel. The primary opinion giver may also wish to rely (in the primary opinion letter) on an opinion of inside counsel regarding litigation and claims since inside counsel is often in a better position than the primary opinion giver to know about these matters.

In relying on opinions of other counsel, an opinion giver takes on the responsibilities described in the following paragraph with respect to those opinions. These responsibilities flow from its statement of reliance rather than from any undertaking in the primary opinion letter or elsewhere. However, many opinion letters, in addition to stating the fact of reliance, state that the opinion recipient (or opinion giver) is "justified" in relying on the other counsel opinions or that those opinions are "satisfactory in form and scope". Such language does no more than state expressly the responsibility of any primary opinion giver who relies on opinions of other counsel and as a matter of customary usage is understood not to broaden that responsibility. By contrast, statements that the opinion is "satisfactory in form and substance" or that the opinion giver "concurs" are understood to go farther.[99]

99. "Concurs" and "satisfactory in form and substance" require not only that the opinion preparers satisfy themselves that reliance is reasonable as described in the next paragraph of

By stating reliance on the opinion of a local or specialized law firm or inside counsel (other than counsel for the opinion recipient), the primary opinion giver indicates that such reliance is in its professional judgment reasonable. To establish that reasonableness, the preparers of the primary opinion must ascertain the reputation of counsel relied on for competence in matters of the kind involved.[100] Such a determination is ordinarily made as a part of the process of engaging that other counsel to render the required opinion. In addition, the preparers of the primary opinion must determine that the opinion of other counsel responds to the needs of the primary opinion giver in its opinion. Since the primary opinion giver's opinion normally will mirror that of other counsel, that burden is not a substantial one.

5.2 UNBUNDLING OPINIONS

Opinion recipients are far more willing today to accept separate opinions of counsel than they were even a decade ago. Thus, in the example above, the primary opinion giver may limit its opinion letter to New York law and the Delaware General Corporation Law, and the opinion recipient will rely on separate opinion letters of other counsel on Massachusetts and patent law. Opinion recipients recognize that the burden of reviewing several separate opinion letters to establish their overall coverage is often not a substantial one. Sometimes the opinion recipient's counsel will prefer to deal directly with one or more of the law firms rendering the separate opinions on behalf of the borrower. For example, counsel for the lender might find an informal discussion with patent counsel informative.

5.3 OPINIONS, EXPERTISE AND ADMISSIONS

In the example in Section 5.1, the opinion giver renders a Delaware corporate law opinion, although none of its lawyers is admitted to practice law in Delaware. The opinion is rendered because the opinion preparers

the text but also that they make some independent investigation of the law involved. While "concurrence" represents the greater responsibility, the diligence these formulations require the opinion preparers to perform is not clearly established by customary practice. In the unusual situations in which these formulations are required, the opinion preparers should consider describing the diligence done rather than using terms that may give rise to misunderstanding as to the responsibility undertaken. In most cases, other counsel is engaged because the opinion giver lacks relevant expertise. Thus, whatever responsibility the opinion giver may undertake in giving a concurrence or similar opinion, that responsibility is by necessity limited by this lack of expertise. Given this context, many lawyers resist "concurrence" and "satisfactory in form and substance" opinions as being inappropriate in most situations. *See* ABA Guidelines Section I(C)(3).

100. If the opinion letter states that it relies on the opinion of counsel for the opinion recipient, such reliance is equivalent to reliance on a stated assumption. *See* Section 2.3. In accordance with customary practice, the opinion preparers are not required to make a judgment as to the reputation of the opinion recipient's counsel. *See also* note 49.

believe they are competent to render it.[101] Customary practice permits the rendering of such an opinion. Had the opinion preparers determined that they lacked competence (or were otherwise unwilling to give the opinion), the Company would have had to engage Delaware counsel as well, unless the opinion recipient was willing to modify its opinion request.

5.4 RELIANCE ON AN OPINION LETTER OF OTHER COUNSEL

An opinion giver who relies on an opinion letter of other counsel customarily obtains permission from the other counsel to do so. Typically, that permission is granted by making the primary opinion giver the addressee of the opinion letter of other counsel or by including permission for use in the other counsel's opinion letter or in some other document. For example, the opinion letter of other counsel might state that:

> The undersigned agrees that [the primary opinion giver firm] may rely on the opinions set forth in paragraphs 1, 2 and 3 of this letter in rendering its opinion furnished pursuant to Section _____ of the Credit Agreement.

The opinion recipient may also obtain permission to rely on the other counsel opinion letter in the same way.[102] Permission to rely is one key element in any malpractice claim against the other counsel. Without it, the claimant may have difficulty showing that its reliance was justified, a necessary part of the claim.

Ordinarily the opinion letter of other counsel to be relied on is prepared for the specific transaction at hand. An opinion letter on the same issue in a previous or even contemporaneous related transaction for the same client normally is not intended for use in other transactions.

On occasion, an opinion giver will rely (with permission) on an opinion of counsel for the opinion recipient. (*See* note 100). More commonly, opinion givers expressly assume the conclusions set forth in the opinion letter of counsel for the opinion recipient (*see* Section 5.5). The responsibility undertaken by the opinion giver is the same, whichever approach is taken.

5.5 ASSUMPTIONS RATHER THAN RELIANCE

In recent years, the business community has increasingly and properly asserted its authority to determine the extent of diligence done and the source of the diligence. This makes transactions more cost-effective. At

101. Even if a lawyer in the opinion giver firm is admitted to practice in the jurisdiction whose law is to be covered, the firm may not feel competent to provide the opinion requested. Mere admission to practice does not establish competency. In any case, the opinion recipient often will not be willing to accept an opinion letter except from counsel known to it to be experienced in the area involved.

102. The opinion letter might state: "In addition to the addressee, _____ may rely on this opinion letter as if it were addressed to and delivered to it on the date hereof." The addressee is the primary opinion giver.

the same time, it presents new questions for opinion givers who are asked to provide full opinions with a different and sometimes less than customary diligence mix. For example, sometimes the client permits other counsel to be chosen by the opinion recipient; sometimes the other counsel is chosen by the client or is inside counsel. The opinion giver may be concerned about relying on an unknown lawyer or one thought to be unfamiliar with the issues. One answer is to unbundle the opinions. *See* Section 5.2. Another is to give the full opinion but to rely on express assumptions for the matters covered by the opinions of other counsel instead of relying on the other counsel's opinions themselves. Still another is for the primary opinion giver to become comfortable enough to rely on the other counsel, after working with it and checking its reputation with lawyers who are knowledgeable about the other counsel.

If the assumption approach is followed and other counsel opinion letters are obtained, the assumptions need not merely "mirror" the conclusions expressed in the relevant opinion letters but may properly go beyond them. For example, an opinion of other counsel might be based on a review of specified documents; the parallel assumption by the primary opinion giver would not ordinarily be limited by the documents reviewed by other counsel.[103]

ARTICLE VI SPECIFIC OPINIONS

Opinion recipients customarily seek information from counsel for the Company regarding the Company, the transaction and the relevant agreement. An opinion recipient typically wants to know, for example, whether the entity it is dealing with is a *de jure* corporation, whether that entity has the corporate power to enter into the transaction and has taken the steps required to authorize it (including obtaining any necessary regulatory approvals), whether the transaction violates applicable law or will result in a breach of other agreements to which the Company is a party, and whether the agreement will be given legal effect in the courts. The Illustrative Opinion Letters at the end of this Report include opinions that are commonly requested and rendered in debt and equity financings. This Article discusses those opinions (except for the remedies opinion, which is discussed in Article III).

The comments in this Article regarding the meaning of an opinion and the work the opinion preparers are expected to do to support it are based on customary usage and customary diligence, which, as discussed in Section 1.4, are key aspects of customary practice. In particular transactions

103. For example, an assumption may be made that the transaction will not result in a breach or default under "other agreements" although inside counsel who came to that conclusion only reviewed agreements identified in his opinion as material. If inside counsel's opinion contains an exception as to specific provisions, the assumption will ordinarily contain the same exception. *See* Section 1.4(d).

the opinion giver and counsel for the opinion recipient may choose to depart from customary practice. Departures from customary practice are appropriate provided the opinion letter clearly specifies any material departures. *See* Section 1.5.

The opinions discussed in the following sections tend to be expressed in much the same way from firm to firm and from transaction to transaction. An opinion giver who wishes to limit the meaning of an opinion framed in customary terms needs to make its intentions clear, ordinarily by means of an express statement in the opinion letter. *See* Section 1.5. If an opinion giver has concerns, for example, about a corporation's existence or the authorization of a class of stock, its omission of the adverb "validly" from the "validly existing" opinion[104] or the adverb "duly" from the "duly authorized" opinion[105] would not adequately communicate those concerns. The comments in the following sections apply not only to the formulation used in the Illustrative Opinion Letters but to all the standard formulations of the opinions discussed.

The following sections refer at various points to the Company's charter. "Charter" is defined in Section 1.9(b).

6.1 CORPORATE STATUS

When lenders or purchasers of stock or other parties to a significant financial transaction enter into an agreement with an entity that purports to be a corporation, they ordinarily request an opinion from counsel to that entity regarding its status as a corporation[106] under the law of its jurisdiction of incorporation. (*See* Paragraph 1 of the Illustrative Opinion Letters).[107] The corporate status opinion appears as the first opinion in most opinion letters. In identifying the Company's form of business organization and the law governing its internal affairs, the opinion serves as a cornerstone for many of the opinions that follow. The corporate status opinion passes on the Company's *de jure* status as a corporation. Thus, it could not be rendered in standard form if the Company is only a *de facto* corporation or corporation-by-estoppel.

How the corporate status opinion is expressed determines the inquiry the opinion preparers customarily conduct to support it. As discussed in Sections 6.1.1 and 6.1.2, both the opinion that the Company has been "duly incorporated" and the opinion that it has been "duly organized"

104. *See* Section 6.1.3.

105. *See* Section 6.2.1.

106. Although the discussion in this Section 6.1 is directed to the status of the Company as a corporation, it may by analogy be applicable to opinions on the status of non-corporate entities, such as limited partnerships and limited liability companies. *See* definition of "Company" in Section 1.9(d).

107. The Illustrative Opinion Letters express the opinion as follows: "The Company is a corporation [duly incorporated and] validly existing under the law of the State of Delaware." The bracketed language appears in the Illustrative Opinion Letters in Appendices B-1 and B-2.

address compliance with applicable incorporation requirements in effect at the time the Company was incorporated. The duly organized opinion also addresses any post-incorporation matters that may be required to complete the organizational process, such as the initial election or selection of directors and officers. As discussed in Section 6.1.3(b), in many transactions opinion recipients have become comfortable in recent years accepting an opinion (a "stand-alone" validly existing opinion) that simply addresses the Company's current status as a corporation as reflected on the public record.

The corporate status opinion is directed to the existence of the Company as a corporation. It does not address the potential liability of stockholders for a corporation's obligations, for example under a piercing-the-corporate-veil theory or pursuant to a statute relating to employee compensation or other matters.

6.1.1 Duly Incorporated

An opinion that the Company has been "duly incorporated" means that the steps taken by the incorporators to incorporate the Company complied with statutory requirements in effect at the time of incorporation. Those steps typically include execution by an appropriate person or persons of a charter in the statutorily prescribed form and the filing of the charter with the proper state officials.[108] The duly incorporated opinion requires that the opinion preparers satisfy themselves that these requirements were met. In doing so, the opinion preparers will be entitled to disregard defects in the incorporation process that the courts of the applicable jurisdiction would deem inconsequential for determining corporate status. In addition, when the record is incomplete, the opinion preparers may be able to rely on the presumption of regularity and continuity.[109]

In rendering a duly incorporated opinion, the opinion preparers customarily rely on (i) a confirmation from the Secretary of State that the charter was filed, (ii) a list prepared by the Secretary of State of all amendments that have been filed to the charter and (iii) copies certified by the Secretary of State of the charter and all amendments.[110] They then ex-

108. Depending on where and when an entity was incorporated, those steps may also include approval by a specified number of qualified incorporators of prescribed matters at a meeting (or by written consent) and execution by incorporators of statutorily mandated documents. Massachusetts, for example, at one time required the incorporators to execute an "agreement of association" and to hold a meeting before signing and filing articles of organization with the Secretary of State. Determining the requirements that were applicable when an entity was incorporated can be a daunting task if the incorporation took place long ago under a corporation statute that is no longer in effect.

109. *See* Section 2.4.

110. A duly incorporated opinion would not seem to require an examination of charter amendments because those amendments relate to a corporation's on-going existence, not its incorporation. However, a duly incorporated opinion is almost always accompanied by a valid existence opinion since an incorporation opinion ordinarily has meaning only if the

amine those documents to confirm that the entity covered by the opinion is the entity to which the documents relate[111] and that the documents do not contain a provision (for example, a limitation on corporate existence to a term of years) that has resulted in its dissolution as a corporation.[112]

6.1.2 Duly Organized

An opinion that the Company has been "duly organized" is a more expansive version of the duly incorporated opinion. In addition to the matters covered by "duly incorporated," it also covers any matters that under the law of the state of incorporation are necessary to complete the organizational process but take place only after the incorporation process is completed. Thus, it typically addresses such matters as the adoption of by-laws, the election or selection of directors and officers, the issuance of stock and the satisfaction of minimum capital requirements, if any. Like the steps required for incorporation, the steps required to complete a corporation's organization are governed by the law in effect when the corporation was organized, not the law at the time the opinion is given.

An inquiry into organizational matters following incorporation can be onerous or even impossible if the actions were taken long ago. Thus, opinions on due organization are rendered most often when a corporation has been recently organized or is being formed specifically for the transaction addressed by the opinion. An opinion giver may also routinely render the opinion when it has rendered it before—*e.g.*, when the corporation was initially organized.

6.1.3 Validly Existing

The due incorporation and due organization opinions look to the past. The validly existing opinion looks to the present, addressing the Company's existence as a corporation on the date of the opinion letter.[113]

corporation continues to exist. *See* Section 6.1.3(a). Therefore, opinion preparers have customarily examined both the original charter and charter amendments without distinguishing whether they do so to support the incorporation opinion or the valid existence opinion.

111. This may not be as straightforward as it seems at first glance. For example, sometimes corporations in an affiliated group have similar names, with the only difference being the use of "Inc." or "Corp."

112. The opinion preparers are not required to address charter provisions that will result in termination of the Company's existence as a corporation following the date of the opinion letter. Nevertheless, if the opinion preparers are aware of a provision that would cause the Company's corporate status to terminate during the term of the agreement to which the opinion letter relates, they will need to consider whether, to avoid misleading the opinion recipient, they should bring the provision to the opinion recipient's attention. *See* Section 1.4(d).

113. As in the Illustrative Opinion Letters, the most common formulation of this opinion states that the Company is "validly existing." Sometimes, the opinion omits the adverb "validly." As a matter of customary usage, that omission is understood not to change the meaning of the opinion.

In New York, the certificate issued by the Secretary of State regarding an entity's current status as a corporation uses the word "subsisting" instead of "existing." The two words are understood to be synonymous.

(a) As A Supplement To An Incorporation Opinion

When supplementing a due incorporation or due organization opinion, the validly existing opinion is based as a matter of customary practice solely on a certificate of the Secretary of State confirming the Company's status as a corporation as of a recent date. Because that date may precede the closing date, opinion preparers often also obtain a confirmation (over the telephone or electronically) from the Secretary of State updating the certificate to the closing date or a certificate of a corporate officer stating that as of the date of the opinion letter no action has been taken by the Company or notice received from a government official looking to the Company's dissolution as a corporation.

(b) As A Substitute For An Incorporation Opinion

In many transactions opinion recipients in recent years have been willing to accept (in lieu of an incorporation opinion) a stand-alone opinion that simply states that the Company is "validly existing as a corporation under the law of" the jurisdiction in which it was incorporated, without also referring to "incorporation" or "organization". The growing acceptance of this opinion reflects a recognition that in many transactions[114] reconstructing and interpreting the corporation statute as it existed at the time the Company was incorporated and reviewing old corporate records are likely to be of limited value relative to the cost and trouble involved. Challenges to corporate status based on a failure to comply with statutory incorporation requirements are extremely rare. Indeed, in many states filing of the charter with the Secretary of State by itself will be effective to discourage such challenges.[115]

When a corporate status opinion states that the Company is validly existing as a corporation without also addressing incorporation or orga-

114. Opinions on recently organized corporations are an exception (because of the ease with which due incorporation and due organization opinions can be given). In addition, while the practice may be changing, purchasers of equity securities still often request a "duly incorporated" or "duly organized" opinion out of concern that if a defect in the incorporation process were later identified, it could result in the Company's ceasing to be recognized as a corporation, thus affecting their rights as stockholders or their status as stockholders (rather than partners) for liability purposes under the applicable corporation law. Lenders, by way of contrast, have less concern about those issues since their rights derive principally from contract law, which is a subject addressed by the remedies opinion, and their status as creditors does not depend on a Company's incorporation. Nevertheless, lenders may also have concerns about the nature of the entity with which they are dealing, for example when they are seeking to comply with legal investment statutes or usury statutes that contain an exemption for loans to corporations.

115. In Delaware, for example, a certificate of incorporation, certified by the Secretary of State, constitutes *prima facie* evidence of the observance and performance of all acts and conditions necessary for the certificate of incorporation's becoming effective. DEL. CODE ANN. tit. 8, § 105 (1991 & Supp. 1997). New York provides that the certificate as filed is "conclusive evidence . . . that the corporation has been formed . . . except in an action . . . brought by the attorney general." N.Y. BUS. CORP. LAW § 403 (McKinney 1986 & Supp. 1998).

nization, the opinion customarily is based on an examination by the opinion preparers (as described in the second paragraph of Section 6.1.1) of the Company's charter (a copy of which normally is certified by the Secretary of State), and a current certificate from the Secretary of State confirming the Company's existence as a corporation (updated to the closing date as described in Section 6.1.3(a)). The opinion does not require a review of the corporate record books. To eliminate any risk of misunderstanding, some opinion letters describe the limited inquiry the opinion preparers conducted to support the opinion. The Committee believes that the limited basis for this opinion is sufficiently well understood that this disclosure is not necessary.

6.1.4 Good Standing Opinions

The corporate status opinion often concludes with a statement regarding the Company's "good standing" in its state of incorporation. What good standing means varies from state to state. In many states it covers the filing of reports with the Secretary of State and the filing of franchise or income tax returns with state tax authorities.[116] That, however, is not so in every jurisdiction. In some jurisdictions, for example, certificates from tax officials are not readily available, and lawyers customarily render good standing opinions based solely on a certificate from the Secretary of State.[117] When used in an opinion, the term "good standing" is understood as a matter of customary usage to cover the matters addressed by the certificates of government officials that lawyers in the jurisdiction in question customarily obtain to support the opinion.

Good standing opinions have been said to provide the opinion recipient comfort that a corporation's charter is not subject to revocation for a failure to keep its state filings current. That comfort, however, is likely to be small. Tax and other filings are usually required at least annually, and thus, depending on when the transaction takes place, key filings may be due not long after the closing.

Good standing opinions customarily are based solely on certificates of government officials, updated, when a certificate is dated prior to the closing date, by a representation of an officer of the Company regarding the matters covered by the certificate (for example, the filing of tax returns and payment of taxes due during the period between the date of the certificate and the closing).

Because opinion preparers customarily do nothing more than rely on certificates of government officials (which normally are presented at closing), good standing opinions usually add little of value analytically. How-

116. This is the case in New York. To render this opinion on a New York corporation, opinion preparers customarily obtain two certificates, one from the Secretary of State and the other from the Department of Taxation and Finance. *See* Section 2.5.2.

117. In Massachusetts, for example, opinion givers customarily render an opinion on "corporate" good standing in reliance solely on a certificate regarding filings with the Secretary of State. *See* MASS. GEN. LAWS ANN. ch. 156B, § 116 (West 1992).

ever, good standing opinions do provide comfort that the opinion preparers do not know the certificates to be unreliable and do place on them the responsibility for confirming that appropriate certificates have been obtained from the proper officials. In situations in which the benefits of good standing opinions are marginal, the Committee believes that the opinion process could be streamlined if opinion recipients were to refrain from requesting them and relied on the certificates alone.

6.1.5 Treatment Of Subsidiaries

When the Company has subsidiaries, the opinion recipient may request opinions on their corporate status as well as that of the parent. At the outset of the transaction thought should be given to which subsidiaries are sufficiently important to warrant a corporate status opinion. When the Company has many subsidiaries, the opinion recipient will usually be willing to limit the subsidiaries on which opinions are rendered to those it views as significant to the Company's consolidated operations or to the particular transaction at issue.

6.1.6 Foreign Qualification And Foreign Good Standing

When the Company's business activities extend beyond its state of incorporation, opinion recipients often seek an opinion on the Company's qualification and good standing as a foreign corporation in the other states in which it conducts business. This opinion provides the recipient comfort that in the states named in the opinion[118] the Company has completed the steps required to qualify as a foreign corporation and, therefore, is not exposed to fines, penalties or administrative sanctions for a failure to qualify.[119]

Although at one time foreign qualification opinions sometimes stated that the Company was qualified in all states in which a failure to qualify would have a material adverse effect on its financial condition, the opinion now usually refers simply to the states in which the Company has qualified. The older form of opinion called for an inquiry by the opinion preparers that was often impractical if not impossible.[120]

Foreign qualification opinions customarily are based solely on certificates of state officials. Although different states use different wording, opinions normally recite that the Company "is qualified" or "is duly qualified" without identifying minor differences in the language used in certificates of particular states.

118. The decision as to which states, if any, are to be covered should be made at the outset of the transaction and typically will depend on the nature and breadth of the Company's activities as well as the type and size of the transaction.

119. A corporation that has failed to qualify will under most circumstances be able to enforce its contracts if it later qualifies. *See* What Constitutes Doing Business, CT Corporation System (1995). Thus, concerns about the Company's standing to bring a legal action usually are not the motivating force behind the opinion.

120. *See* ABA Guidelines Sections I(B)(4) and I(C)(2).

The opinion paragraph on foreign qualification also usually addresses the Company's good standing in the states in which it has qualified. Like the opinion on the Company's good standing in its state of incorporation, good standing in this context customarily is understood to have whatever meaning is ascribed to it in the certificates on which the opinion preparers are relying.[121]

Depending on the state, good standing certificates may be available from the Secretary of State and/or state tax authorities. Because opinion preparers ordinarily do not have a state-by-state knowledge of what certificates are available, as a matter of customary diligence they normally have an experienced corporate service company obtain for them the good standing certificates customarily obtained in the particular states involved and then rely on those certificates without further inquiry into what other certificates might have been obtained.

Opinion letters ordinarily identify by name the jurisdictions whose laws they are intended to cover, thereby excluding any opinion on the laws of other jurisdictions.[122] Many opinion letters (such as the one quoted in Section 4.1) name as covered jurisdictions the jurisdictions addressed by the foreign qualification and foreign good standing opinions, expressly limiting the coverage of those jurisdictions to those particular opinions. However, even if the jurisdictions addressed by the foreign qualification and foreign good standing opinions are not so named the limitation on the laws covered is not read to exclude them. This is contrary to the normal rule. *See* Section 4.2. As a matter of customary usage, the foreign qualification and foreign good standing opinions are understood to cover the jurisdictions to which they expressly refer even if that coverage is inconsistent with standard language appearing elsewhere in the opinion letter regarding the jurisdictions whose law the opinion letter is intended to cover.

Because opinion preparers customarily base foreign qualification and foreign good standing opinions solely on certificates of government officials, which normally are presented at closing, those opinions usually add little (if anything) of value other than confirming that the opinion preparers do not know the certificates on which the opinions are based to be unreliable. The Committee believes that the opinion process could be streamlined without any meaningful detriment to opinion recipients if absent special circumstances the practice of rendering foreign qualification and foreign good standing opinions were discontinued and opinion recipients were to rely directly on the certificates themselves.[123]

121. *See* Section 6.1.4.
122. *See* Sections 4.1 and 1.9(o).
123. *See* ABA Guidelines Section I(C)(2).

6.2 STOCK

When an underwriter in a public offering, a purchaser in a private placement or some other investor agrees to acquire stock from a corporation, it usually requires as a condition of closing an opinion from counsel for the Company regarding the shares it is acquiring. (*See* Paragraph 2 of the Illustrative Opinion Letter in Appendix B-l.)[124] Regulatory agencies also often require such opinions (for example the Securities and Exchange Commission in connection with the registration of shares) as do stock exchanges when a corporation lists its shares on the exchange.

The opinion on the Company's stock typically addresses the authorization of the stock in the Company's charter, the issuance of shares of that stock, the receipt by the Company of payment for those shares and the nonassessable nature of the shares in the hands of stockholders.

6.2.1 Duly Authorized

The first part of the opinion, the phrase "duly authorized," addresses the creation (either in the Company's charter or in the manner provided in the charter) of the class of stock in question and the authority of the Company to issue shares of that class.[125] The opinion means that, under the corporation law[126] of the state in which the Company was organized and the Company's charter, the shares to which the opinion relates (the "Shares") were (or will be) immediately prior to their issuance included within the shares that the Company had the authority to issue. The opinion covers such matters as whether (i) the applicable state corporation law permits shares having the characteristics of the Shares, (ii) the provisions of the Company's charter relating to the Shares comply with that law and (iii) sufficient authorized shares of the class of which the Shares are a part were available when the Shares were issued. If the Shares were authorized subsequent to the Company's incorporation, the opinion also covers whether the resolution approving their authorization received the required vote and was otherwise properly adopted under applicable state corporation law and whether the charter amendments contained required information and were in proper form. In addition, when the Shares are part of a class or series created by the directors pursuant to authority granted to them in the charter, the opinion covers whether the directors acted pursuant to their authority in a manner consistent with the charter, bylaws and applicable state corporation law.

124. The Illustrative Opinion Letter expresses the opinion as follows: "The Shares have been duly authorized and validly issued and are fully paid and nonassessable."

125. The first part of the opinion (the phrase "duly authorized") is directed to creation of the shares in the charter documents not their issuance—even though the issuance of shares commonly is referred to as having been "authorized" by the directors. As discussed in Section 6.2.2, the steps required to approve a particular stock issuance are covered by the second part of the opinion, the phrase "validly issued."

126. Some state constitutions contain requirements relating to the issuance of stock. Those requirements are regarded as part of the corporation law and thus are covered by the opinion.

The duly authorized opinion does not cover compliance with disclosure and other requirements of state or federal securities laws. Those requirements raise complex and intensely factual issues[127] and, when covered at all, customarily are addressed in a separate paragraph or letter containing broad disclaimers and carefully qualified terms.

6.2.2 Validly Issued

The opinion that Shares have been "validly issued" means that the stockholders, board of directors and/or a board committee[128] properly took all action required by applicable state corporation law to approve the issuance of the Shares and that the Shares were issued in compliance with the requirements of that law,[129] the Company's charter and by-laws and the resolution approving their issuance. The opinion covers such matters as whether (i) the body (or bodies)[130] whose approval is required by applicable state corporation law and the Company's charter and by-laws acted on the resolution approving the issuance, (ii) it (or they) acted at a properly called and held meeting (or by an appropriate written consent), (iii) the resolution received the required vote and (iv) the Company received legally sufficient consideration for the Shares. In addition, if action was taken by a committee, the opinion covers whether the committee had the requisite authority to approve the issuance. An opinion that shares have been "validly issued" could not be rendered if the shares were not "duly authorized."

Shares would not be validly issued if their issuance violated preemptive rights requirements of the applicable state corporation law or the Company's charter.[131] Shares may, however, be validly issued even though their issuance resulted in a breach of or default under another contract to which the Company is a party. The absence of such breaches and defaults is customarily the subject of a separate opinion (*see* Section 6.5).

127. Ordinarily, lawyers address disclosure requirements only with regard to prospectuses for underwritten offerings of securities. Of course, if the opinion preparers are aware of a disclosure problem that may affect the authorization of the shares, they should consider whether they would be misleading the opinion recipient if they were to deliver the opinion letter without bringing the problem to the opinion recipient's attention. *See* Section 1.4(d).

128. In many states, a committee of directors may be granted the power to approve issuances of stock.

129. The opinion does not address state or federal securities law requirements (disclosure or registration) applicable to sales of securities. Compliance with those requirements, if addressed at all, is dealt with separately as a matter of customary practice.

130. Stockholder approval usually is not required unless the charter otherwise provides. *See, e.g.*, DEL. CODE ANN. tit. 8 § 153(a) (1991). *But see, e.g.*, N.Y. BUS. CORP. LAW § 505(d) (McKinney 1996 & Supp. 1998) (stockholder approval required for grants to directors, officers or employees of rights or options to purchase stock). Although not covered by the opinion, stockholder approval nonetheless may in some cases be required by stock exchange rules.

131. Sometimes corporations obtain waivers from stockholders of their preemptive rights. An opinion may be based on a valid waiver as well as on compliance with the procedures specified in the statute or charter for affording stockholders preemptive rights.

The validly issued opinion rests on an assumption, customarily unstated (*see* Section 2.3(a)), that fiduciary duty requirements relating to the issuance have been satisfied.[132] If this assumption is unreliable, the opinion preparers should not render the opinion without stating the assumption or otherwise making appropriate disclosure.

In some states businesses in regulated industries (such as public utilities) are required to incorporate under special statutes that call for approval of issuances of stock by a regulatory authority (for example, a public utilities commission). An opinion that stock of corporations organized under such statutes has been validly issued covers receipt of those approvals. In other states businesses in regulated industries are required to incorporate under the general business corporation statute but also are subject to a separate statute requiring regulatory approval of stock issuances.[133] In those states, even though the requirement for regulatory approval is not contained in the corporation statute, as a matter of customary usage the opinion also is understood to cover receipt of those approvals.[134] If the validly issued opinion were interpreted to cover only regulatory approvals required by the statute under which an entity was incorporated, the coverage of the opinion would turn not on a matter of substance but of form, *i.e.*, on the happenstance of where the approval requirement was located in the statutory scheme of a particular jurisdiction.

Once shares have been validly issued, they do not lose their validly issued character even if they are subsequently repurchased or reacquired by a corporation, unless the shares are restored to authorized but unissued status. Validly issued shares that have been reacquired, commonly called "treasury shares," typically may be resold by a corporation without complying with the requirements of state corporation law for an initial issuance.[135]

6.2.3 Fully Paid

The opinion that Shares have been "fully paid" means that the consideration required by the resolution or other corporate action authorizing their issuance has been received in full by the Company[136] and that the consideration received satisfied the requirements of state corporation law[137] and the requirements, if any, in the Company's charter and bylaws.

132. This issue may arise, for example, when in an effort to prevent a hostile takeover the board of directors approves an issuance of shares to a Company retirement plan or other friendly party. For reliance on an assumption regarding compliance with fiduciary duty requirements in Delaware, *see* note 148.

133. This is also covered by the approvals and filings opinion. *See* Section 6.7.

134. As noted above, approvals under the securities laws are not covered. *See* note 129.

135. *See, e.g.*, N.Y. BUS. CORP. LAW § 504(e) (McKinney 1986 & Supp. 1998).

136. As a matter of customary diligence, opinion preparers normally base this aspect of the opinion on an officer's certificate. *See* Section 2.5.

137. This requirement may be contained in the state constitution. *See, e.g.*, DEL. CONST., art. IX, § 3.

The sufficiency of the consideration received for shares is tested both quantitatively and qualitatively. State corporation law often requires that consideration not only be in the correct amount but also be of an acceptable nature. In some states, for example, a promise to pay or to render services in the future does not constitute adequate consideration. Generally, shares having par value must be issued for consideration worth at least par value. When non-cash consideration is involved, the opinion preparers may rely on a determination by the board of directors regarding the value of that consideration.

Opinions covering shares issued or to be issued as stock dividends can present special problems. For example, Section 173 of the Delaware General Corporation Law requires the board of directors to "direct that there be designated as capital" from surplus "an amount which is not less than the aggregate par value of par value shares being declared as a dividend . . .". An opinion may be based on board action to that effect. If, however, the opinion preparers know that the Company did not have sufficient surplus to transfer to stated capital, they should not render the opinion notwithstanding the action of the board.

6.2.4 Nonassessable

The opinion that the Shares are nonassessable means that once the original purchase price has been paid (which is the subject of the "fully paid" opinion) holders of the Shares will not as a result of their ownership be subject to assessments by the Company under the corporation law of the state in which the Company was incorporated. The opinion relates to assessment statutes of a type that were once common (and that may still sometimes be in effect for banks and other specialized businesses) that authorize corporations under certain circumstances to assess stockholders on a per share basis for an additional amount even though their Shares have been fully paid. The opinion does not mean that stockholders will not be subject to other types of liability: for example, liability to the Company for receipt of an unlawful dividend or liability for obligations of the Company under a piercing-the-corporate-veil theory.

Section 630 of the New York Business Corporation Law imposes liability for unpaid wages on the ten largest stockholders of New York corporations (other than registered investment companies) whose shares are not listed on a stock exchange or regularly quoted in an over-the-counter market. Although Section 630 is not strictly an assessment statute (since it does not impose liability on a per share basis on all stockholders), many lawyers make express reference to it in opinions on the nonassessability of stock of privately-held New York corporations.

6.2.5 Coverage Of All Outstanding Shares

Sometimes opinion recipients, for example underwriters in a corporation's first public offering or stock exchanges in connection with an initial listing of shares, will request an opinion covering not only the due authorization and valid issuance of the Shares (as is done in the Illustrative

Opinion Letter in Appendix B-1) but also of all of the corporation's outstanding shares. This opinion addresses the concern of opinion recipients that, if all of the Company's outstanding shares were not validly issued, their existence might adversely affect trading in the Shares or preclude subsequent listing of the Shares on a stock exchange. If, however, the Company has had many stock issuances over many years, this opinion can require an extraordinary expenditure of time and effort on the part of the opinion preparers. In some cases opinion recipients, when alerted to the problem, will be willing to withdraw their request for the opinion, particularly when reputable counsel have previously rendered opinions covering past issuances. If opinions have not been rendered in the past, the parties should consider whether the benefit to the opinion recipient (particularly in view of the assumptions that will be required) is justified in terms of the cost and time involved.

Sometimes opinion recipients will ask the opinion giver to supplement an opinion on the due authorization and valid issuance of outstanding shares with an opinion on the number of outstanding shares of each authorized class of stock. When the Company's stock is publicly traded, an opinion on the number of outstanding shares adds nothing to what is set forth in a transfer agent's certificate (which normally provides the only basis for the opinion). Accordingly, the Committee believes that the opinion process could be streamlined, without meaningful detriment to opinion recipients, if absent special circumstances the practice of rendering such opinions were discontinued and opinion recipients were to rely directly on the transfer agent's certificate. When the Company's stock is closely held, the opinion preparers may, depending on the condition of the Company's records, have no difficulty ascertaining the number of outstanding shares from a review of the stock transfer book and a certificate of a corporate officer. If that can be done readily, the opinion preparers often will render the opinion, even though, because the opinion is principally factual in nature, an officer's certificate alone might have sufficed.

6.3 CORPORATE POWER

Opinion recipients often request an opinion that the Company has the corporate power[138] to execute, deliver and perform the agreement.[139] (*See*

138. Although the adjective "corporate" helps clarify the coverage of the opinion, as a matter of customary usage its omission does not change the meaning of the opinion.

The phrase "corporate power and authority" is also often used. Because as a matter of customary usage the phrases "corporate power" and "corporate power and authority" are understood to have the same meaning, the words "and authority" have been omitted from the discussion in this section and from the Illustrative Opinion Letters.

Opinion recipients sometimes request a "full power" opinion. The phrase "full power" has no generally accepted meaning, and its use, therefore, should be avoided.

139. The discussion in Section 6.5.4 of the coverage of obligations to be performed in the future also applies to the corporate power opinion to the extent the opinion covers future performance.

Paragraphs 2 and 3, respectively, of the Illustrative Opinion Letters in Appendices A-1 and B-1).[140] A corporate power opinion means that the Company has the power to take the specified actions under its charter and by-laws and applicable corporation law.[141]

The corporate power opinion relates to the Company's power under *corporation* law. As such, it addresses the question whether the actions the Company is taking are *ultra vires*. The opinion does not address whether those actions are restricted by other laws, such as those requiring the receipt of licenses or permits.

The corporate power opinion also does not cover provisions in the corporation statute that have collateral consequences, such as the imposition of liability on directors who vote to approve a loan to a director when the loan is not also approved by disinterested directors or stockholders.[142] It does, however, cover statutory, charter and by-law provisions and judge-made doctrines that deny a corporation the power to engage in a specified activity. For example, a corporation organized under a general corporation statute may lack the power to engage in activities, such as accepting interest bearing deposits or writing insurance, that generally are reserved to corporations organized under special statutes.[143] Similarly, in many states a subsidiary may lack the power under the applicable corporation statute or a judge-made doctrine to guarantee the obligations of its corporate parent if the guarantee is not in furtherance of the subsidiary's purposes.[144]

6.4 CORPORATE ACTION

Opinion letters almost always contain an opinion on the Company's authorization, execution and delivery of the agreement (or agreements) governing the transaction into which the parties are entering. (*See* Paragraphs 2 and 3, respectively, of the Illustrative Opinion Letters in Appendices A-1 and B-1).[145] This opinion is intended to respond to the under-

140. The Illustrative Opinion Letters express the opinion as follows: "The Company . . . has the corporate power to execute, deliver and perform the [Agreement]."

141. The opinion presupposes, therefore, that the Company exists as a corporation under the applicable corporation law. That issue typically is addressed in the valid existence opinion discussed in Section 6.1.3.

142. *See, e.g.*, N.Y. BUS. CORP. LAW § 714 (McKinney 1986 & Supp. 1998).

143. Some state statutes permit the exercise of specific powers only if they are expressly set forth in the corporation's charter. *See, e.g.*, MASS. GEN. LAWS ANN. ch. 156B, § 9A (West 1992 & Supp. 1998) (power to act as a partner).

144. *But see* DEL. CODE ANN. tit. 8, § 122(13) (1991 & Supp. 1996). Although the issue of fraudulent conveyance is not covered by the corporate power opinion, such guarantees may also be subject to challenge as fraudulent conveyances.

145. The Illustrative Opinion Letters express the opinion as follows in two subsections of the same paragraph: "The Company . . . (b) has taken all corporate action necessary to authorize the execution, delivery and performance of the . . . Agreement, . . . and (c) has duly executed and delivered the . . . Agreement." Many lawyers include this opinion in the opinion paragraph containing the remedies opinion. Others include it in a separate paragraph or, as in the case of the Illustrative Opinion Letters, in the paragraph containing the corporate power opinion.

standable concern of the opinion recipient that those who executed the agreement had actual and not merely apparent authority to act on the Company's behalf. The opinion means that the agreement was approved (or its execution and delivery were authorized), in a manner consistent with the applicable corporation statute and the Company's charter and by-laws, by the proper body or bodies—*e.g.*, the stockholders, directors (or board committee) or both—by the required vote at a properly called and held meeting (or by an appropriate written consent).[146] The opinion also means that the persons identified in the agreement as signatories had actual authority to execute the agreement on behalf of the Company, that all required signatures were obtained[147] and that the Company delivered the executed agreement (or caused it to be delivered) in a manner permitted by applicable law.

Opinion preparers customarily base the opinion on an assumption, ordinarily unstated (*see* Section 2.3(a)), that those who approved the agreement did not violate the fiduciary duty requirements, such as those governing transactions between a corporation and its directors, imposed on them by the corporation law of the Company's state of incorporation.[148] As with assumptions generally, opinion preparers ordinarily rely on that assumption without making an independent determination that fiduciary duty requirements were met. If, however, the assumption is not reliable, the opinion preparers should not render the opinion without stating the assumption or otherwise making appropriate disclosure.

6.5 NO BREACH OR DEFAULT

Opinion recipients often seek opinions that the execution and delivery by the Company of the agreement do not, and performance by the Company of its obligations under the agreement will not,[149] result in (i) a

146. Approval need not always take the form of a resolution specifically addressing the agreement. Officers may be able to rely on a general resolution granting them authority within appropriate limits to bind the Company.

147. The opinion preparers are entitled to assume, without so stating, that the signatures are genuine. *See* Section 2.3(a).

148. In Delaware a merger requiring stockholder approval has been held to be valid even though the directors violated their fiduciary duty of disclosure by failing to inform stockholders of all material facts. Arnold v. Society for Sav. Bancorp, Inc., 678 A.2d 533, 536-37 (Del. 1996). The court pointed out that the corporation "complied with all of the express statutory requirements for the merger" and concluded that so long as the directors acted in good faith that was enough. *Id.* at 536. The implication of *Arnold*, not only for mergers but possibly also for other transactions subject to express statutory requirements, is that in the case of Delaware corporations reliance on an assumption regarding compliance with fiduciary duty requirements may not be necessary. However, since a requirement of good faith on the part of the directors applies even in Delaware, *Arnold* probably has little practical significance for the opinion process.

149. Opinions sometimes refer simply to "consummation of the transaction" rather than "performance". *See* note 171 for the meaning of that opinion. If an opinion does not use the word "performance" expressly, it is understood as a matter of customary usage not to cover performance. *See also* Section 1.2(f).

violation of the Company's charter or by-laws, (ii) a breach of or default under other contracts to which the Company is a party, or (iii) a violation of any court order to which the Company is a party. (*See* Paragraphs 4 and 5, respectively, of the Illustrative Opinion Letters in Appendices A-1 and B-1 and Paragraph 2 of the Illustrative Opinion Letters in Appendices A-2 and B-2.)[150]

6.5.1 Purpose Of Opinion

The opinion on the charter and by-laws adds nothing to the corporate power and remedies opinions (which could not be given if the agreement violated the charter or by-laws). Nevertheless, the practice of drafting the opinion to cover those documents is well established and, while some members of the Committee think the practice should be changed to avoid redundancy, the Committee regards either approach as acceptable.

As it relates to other contracts (which include instruments for purposes of the discussion that follows) and courts orders, the no breach or default opinion provides the opinion recipient information regarding the effect of the transaction on the Company's other legally binding obligations, thus permitting the recipient to evaluate whether the commitments the Company is making in the agreement will expose the Company to the risk of creating inconsistent legal obligations. The opinion as it relates to other contracts provides the recipient comfort that the transaction will not be subject to attack because it violates restrictions in another contract and will not expose the recipient to a possible claim by a third-party, for example for tortious interference with existing contractual relationships. This opinion is different from the remedies opinion in that, depending on the circumstances,[151] the remedies opinion could be rendered even though performance of the agreement might result in a violation of another contract.[152]

150. Although the no breach or default opinion does not appear in its entirety in any one of the Illustrative Opinion Letters, the Illustrative Opinion Letters collectively express the opinion as follows:

> The execution and delivery by the Company of the . . . Agreement [does] not, and the performance by the Company of its obligations thereunder will not,
>
> [(a)] result in a violation of the Certificate of Incorporation or By-laws of the Company[,] . . .
>
> [(b)] breach or result in a default under any agreement or instruments listed on Schedule [ ] . . . hereto [or result in the acceleration of (or entitle any party to accelerate) any obligation of the Company thereunder], or
>
> [(c)] result in a violation of any court order listed on Schedule [ ] hereto.

151. For example, the ability of the opinion recipient to enforce the agreement may depend on whether it has actual knowledge that it violates another contract. RESTATEMENT (SECOND) OF CONTRACTS § 194 (1979). As a matter of customary practice, opinion preparers assume, without so stating in the opinion letter, that the recipient has no such knowledge so long as they do not know that assumption to be unreliable.

152. In some circumstances, a corporation may choose to bind itself to two legally enforceable contracts even though performance of one will violate the other. For example, a corporation might decide to enter into a merger agreement even though consummation of

The opinion as it relates to court orders permits the opinion recipient to avoid involvement in a violation of a judicial decree.

6.5.2 "No Violation" And "No Breach Or Default" Are Preferred Because They Are More Precise Than "No Conflict"

Historically, the "no breach or default" opinion addressed "conflicts" with the Company's charter and by-laws, other contracts and court orders. In recent years, however, prompted by a growing concern about the imprecision of the word "conflict," a trend has developed of replacing the word "conflicts" with "violations" when the opinion refers to the charter, by-laws and court orders and with "breaches" and "defaults" when it refers to other contracts. The Committee supports this trend and in this Report refers to the opinion as the "no breach or default" rather than the "no conflict" opinion.[153] However, if an opinion uses "no conflict" language without definition, as a matter of customary usage it should be read as if it used "no violation" and "no breach or default" instead.

6.5.3 Adverse Consequences Not Addressed

The no breach or default opinion is *not* an opinion that no adverse consequences will result from the Company's entering into (and, if covered, performing its obligations under) the agreement. The opinion only addresses breaches and defaults. Adverse consequences that do not result from a breach or default (and that therefore are not covered by the opinion) may include, for example, termination of a credit commitment, a change in the manner in which a royalty is computed, an increase in the interest rate payable on outstanding debt, creation of a lien on the Company's properties, a requirement to provide additional collateral to secured lenders, or, in the event of a change of control, creation of "puts" to the Company by existing equity holders or rights to accelerate or require prepayment by existing debt holders.

The concept of adverse consequences is inherently subjective. For that reason a lawyer is not in a position to render an opinion that a transaction will not have any adverse consequences for the Company. Lawyers do, however, often render opinions on whether the transaction will have specific consequences that have been identified to them by opinion recipients as being of particular concern. The no breach or default opinion, for example, could be supplemented with language that deals expressly with the acceleration, and the creation of rights of other parties to accelerate

the merger will result in a breach by the corporation of an existing credit agreement. In making its decision, the corporation may expect to receive a waiver from the lender and, if it does not, to pay off the credit agreement with funds provided by its merger partner. If the opinion recipient did not know that the merger would breach the credit agreement (*see* note 151), the remedies opinion might be rendered while the no breach or default opinion could not. By requesting a no breach or default opinion, the opinion recipient obtains information that might not be provided by the remedies opinion.

153. For convenience this Report uses "no breach or default" to refer to the entire opinion, including the opinions on the charter, by-laws and court orders.

or require the prepayment or purchase by the Company, of outstanding indebtedness and the creation of liens on the Company's property.[154] In the context of a particular transaction, opinion recipients may wish to consider whether to request such language or other language that addresses with specificity consequences that are of substantial concern to them but that do not stem from a breach of or default under another contract.

6.5.4 Coverage Of Obligations To Be Performed In The Future

The no breach or default opinion covers not only breaches and defaults that occur as a result of the Company's entering into the agreement but also, to the extent it refers to "performance," breaches or defaults that could occur as a result of the Company's performance in the future of its obligations under the agreement.

When the opinion is drafted to cover performance, it addresses the performance by the Company of its obligations under the agreement after the closing. Suppose, for example, the Company is entering into a common stock purchase agreement with an investor that grants the investor a right to put its shares to the Company if the Company is still private after a specified period and the opportunity to piggyback its shares in any registration statements filed by the Company after an initial public offering. An opinion that performance by the Company of its obligations under the common stock purchase agreement will not breach or result in a default under existing contracts of the Company covered by the opinion would require an exception if one of those existing contracts was with a venture capitalist and prohibited the Company from repurchasing its stock prior to an initial public offering or granted the venture capitalist exclusive piggyback registration rights once the Company was public. The opinion by its terms addresses the *obligations* of the Company under the agreement. Thus, if the common stock purchase agreement, instead of granting the investor a put, gave the Company a right to call the investor's shares, the opinion would not require an exception, even though repurchases are prohibited by an existing contract, because the opinion covers performance by the Company of its obligations not the exercise by the Company of its rights under the agreement.

Provisions in existing contracts that will be breached or result in a default only if specified events have (or have not) occurred or specified circumstances exist (or do not exist) at the time the Company is called on to perform its obligations under the agreement are beyond the scope of the no breach or default opinion since the opinion preparers have no way to determine on the date of the opinion letter what the effect of those pro-

154. The Illustrative Opinion Letters contain bracketed language that addresses these issues as follows: "or result in the acceleration of (or entitle any party to accelerate) any obligation of the Company thereunder."

visions will be when performance by the Company is required to occur.[155] For example, in the case of the common stock purchase agreement and the Company's grant of a put, the opinion preparers are not required to take into account a negative covenant in an existing loan agreement if the covenant only prohibits stock repurchases if specified financial ratios are not met at the time a particular repurchase is to be effected.[156] By way of contrast, the opinion preparers are required to take into account provisions in existing contracts whose future application is not subject to a contingency. Thus, to use the example of the common stock purchase agreement and the grant by the Company of a put, the opinion preparers would be required to take an exception if the negative covenant flatly prohibited stock repurchases.

Historically, the opinion often has been cast in the present tense—*i.e.*, "execution, delivery and performance of the Agreement do not. . . ." Recently, the practice has developed of drafting the portion of the opinion relating to performance in the future tense. As a matter of customary usage the meaning of the opinion is the same regardless of which tense is used. The Committee believes, however, that in the case of performance the future tense better expresses what the opinion is intended to convey. Thus, the Committee suggests that the clearest way to phrase the opinion is to state that the "execution and delivery by the Company of the Agreement do not, and the performance by the Company of its obligations thereunder will not, breach or result in a default under. . . ".

6.5.5 Identifying Which Contracts And Court Orders Are Covered

Unless the Company is very small or newly formed, the opinion preparers are unlikely to have personal knowledge of every contract and court order to which the opinion might conceivably apply. Therefore, preferably early in the negotiation of the opinion, the parties should agree on a method for identifying the contracts and court orders the opinion preparers will be expected to review.

In the case of contracts, one commonly used approach is to limit the opinion to the contracts listed in an exhibit to the agreement, in a filing by the Company with the Securities and Exchange Commission or in an

155. If the opinion preparers are aware of specific facts that they know would cause the Company, in performing a future obligation under the agreement, to breach an existing contract, they should not render the opinion if to do so would be misleading to the opinion recipient. For example, depending on the knowledge of the opinion recipient, delivery of the opinion might be misleading if under the new agreement one of the obligations to be performed by the Company is to repurchase shares of its stock a few months after the closing and the opinion preparers are aware that the Company is planning a writedown of inventory that will cause the repurchase to breach a net worth covenant in an existing loan agreement. *See* Section 1.4(d).

156. As in the loan agreement example, the future circumstances will often be of a financial nature. However, they need not be. For example, they could involve a specific event such as a change in control of the Company.

attachment to the opinion. Another is to draft the opinion to cover only specified types of contracts—*e.g.*, agreements for money borrowed—or contracts that meet a specified standard of materiality such as a particular dollar amount and to state, as discussed below, that the contracts covered include only those of which the opinion preparers have knowledge. If the contracts are not specifically identified, the opinion preparers often will obtain a certificate from an appropriate officer of the Company[157] listing all the contracts that fall within the specified category. Whatever approach is used, it should be described in the opinion letter.

The practice for court orders is similar. The court orders covered by the opinion often are listed in a schedule referred to specifically in the opinion. Alternatively, the opinion may be drafted to refer to court orders known to the opinion preparers, in which case the opinion ordinarily will be based on a certificate of an appropriate officer of the Company identifying all the relevant court orders.

When an opinion is not limited to a specific list of contracts or court orders, opinion recipients will sometimes request that it be drafted to cover not only contracts and court orders to which the Company is a party but also those to which the Company is otherwise subject. In the case of contracts, inclusion of the phrase extends coverage of the opinion to contracts that the Company did not affirmatively enter into but by which it became bound in some other way. The Company, for example, may have become subject to a collective bargaining agreement to which it is not a party if it acquired substantially all the assets of a corporation that was bound by such an agreement. Similarly, property of the Company may be subject to a mortgage lien (even though the Company did not grant the mortgage) if, when the property was acquired, it was subject to a mortgage previously granted by the seller (and the obligation of the seller was not discharged when the property was acquired by the Company). In the case of court orders, the phrase "otherwise subject" extends coverage of the opinion to proceedings that are applicable to the Company but in which it has not been joined as a named party, such as an *ex parte* proceeding or an industry-wide court order (*e.g.*, an antitrust decree prohibiting specified business practices of all members of an industry group).

Despite the interest opinion recipients may have in contracts and court orders to which the Company is otherwise subject, coverage of those contracts and court orders can raise troublesome diligence problems because their existence may be unknown not only to the opinion preparers but also to the officer on whose certificate the opinion is based. Thus, thought should be given to the implications of including the phrase "otherwise subject" (at least without limitation) before the opinion preparers agree to add it to the opinion.

157. *See* Section 2.5.

Many lawyers include in the no breach or default opinion the phrase "to our knowledge" when referring to the contracts and court orders covered by the opinion. Lawyers include the phrase out of concern that the opinion might otherwise be susceptible to being read as covering every contract and court order to which the Company is a party, whether known to the opinion preparers or not. *See* Section 2.6.1.

When the opinion refers specifically to a list of contracts and court orders, the opinion on its face is clear as to what contracts and orders are covered. In that case, the phrase "to our knowledge" serves no purpose and should not be used.

When the opinion does not refer specifically to a list of contracts and court orders, inclusion of the phrase "to our knowledge" underscores what the opinion as a matter of customary usage is understood to cover. Inclusion (or omission) of the phrase does not, however, change the customary diligence required to support the opinion. *See* Sections 2.2 and 2.6.1.

Opinion preparers increasingly are including a definition of "to our knowledge" in opinion letters. When "to our knowledge" is defined, the definition used in the opinion letter will control.

Customary diligence may be varied by agreement between the opinion preparers and the opinion recipient (or its counsel).[158] Opinion recipients sometimes seek more diligence. Alternatively, the opinion recipient (or its counsel) may agree that less diligence than is customary is appropriate. Ordinarily, whatever agreement is reached will be described in the opinion letter.

Inside counsel is often more knowledgeable about contracts and court orders binding on the Company than outside counsel handling a particular transaction for the Company. Thus, opinion recipients often accept (and may prefer receiving) the no breach or default opinion from inside counsel, even if other opinions are provided by outside counsel.[159]

6.5.6 Interpretation Of Contracts Governed By The Law Of Other States

Contracts covered by the no breach or default opinion may be governed (because of chosen-law provisions[160] in those contracts or other reasons) by the law of jurisdictions that are not specified for coverage in the opinion letter. In that event the opinion preparers are entitled to assume, without so stating in the opinion letter, that those contracts would be interpreted in accordance with their plain meaning[161] (unless the opinion preparers

158. *See* Section 1.5.

159. Outside counsel not only may lack general familiarity with court orders to which the Company is a party but may have no knowledge of court orders to which the Company is not a party but is otherwise subject.

160. *See* Section 1.9(p).

161. In the case of technical terms, their meaning would be what lawyers generally understand them to mean in the jurisdiction (or principal jurisdiction if more than one) whose law is specified for coverage in the opinion letter.

identify a possible problem, in which event they may want to obtain an opinion from local counsel).

6.6 NO VIOLATION OF LAW

Opinion recipients often seek an opinion that the execution and delivery of the agreement[162] do not, and performance by the Company of its obligations under the agreement will not,[163] violate applicable provisions of law.[164] (*See* Paragraphs 5 and 6, respectively, of the Illustrative Opinion Letters in Appendices A-1 and B-1.) This opinion complements the remedies opinion by addressing legal consequences of the transaction, such as fines or government sanctions, that would not prevent the opinion giver from rendering an unqualified opinion on the agreement's enforceability but that may be significant to the opinion recipient. A corporation, for example, could enter into an agreement on which an unqualified remedies opinion could be rendered to sell the assets of a division, but, if the corporation is in the pharmaceutical business and the assets it is selling include controlled substances, the sale could under certain circumstances expose it (and the buyer) to serious sanctions if it does not satisfy government requirements governing the sale of narcotics.

Despite its apparent breadth, the no violation of law opinion does not cover all law. As with other opinions, the no violation of law opinion addresses only the law (including published rules and regulations of government agencies) of jurisdictions that are specified for coverage in the opinion letter. In addition, the opinion is understood to exclude local law, such as city ordinances and county zoning regulations, that are adopted by political subdivisions below the state level.[165]

162. Although some opinions are drafted to cover "related transactions" or transactions "contemplated by" the agreement, those terms are imprecise and may be misleading. If other transactions are to be covered, the Committee recommends that they be identified expressly in the opinion. In addition, opinion givers should not be asked to render an opinion that covers compliance by the Company with laws generally. *See* ABA Guidelines Section I(B)(5). Such an opinion would require a detailed understanding of a Company's business activities and could almost never be rendered (assuming it could be rendered at all) without great expense.

163. The Illustrative Opinion Letters express this opinion as follows: "The execution and delivery by the Company of the [Agreement] do not, and the performance by the Company of its obligations thereunder will not, result in any violation of any law of the United States or the State of New York, or any rule or regulation issued thereunder." In the Illustrative Opinion Letter the word "published" has not been included before "rule or regulation." As a matter of customary practice, the opinion is understood to cover only published rules and regulations whether the word "published" is used or not. For opinions that refer to consummation of the transaction instead of performance, *see* note 171.

164. For purposes of this opinion the term "law" is understood as a matter of customary usage to include published rules and regulations of government agencies even if the opinion does not refer to those rules and regulations expressly. *See* definition of "Law" and "Law Covered by the Opinion Letter" in Sections 1.9(n) and (o).

165. *See* note 170.

Because of the great number and variety of statutes, rules and regulations, no lawyer or firm, no matter how diligent, can reasonably be expected to be familiar with every law, rule and regulation (even within the jurisdiction whose law is covered by the opinion letter) that might possibly apply to the Company and the transaction. For example, depending on the circumstances, counsel for the borrower in a loan for construction of a manufacturing facility might not be expected, even after exercising customary diligence, to recognize that the borrower, because it intends to sell the timber cut when clearing the land on which the facility is to be built, is subject to a statute governing companies engaged in the timber business. As in the case of the remedies opinion (*see* Section 3.5.1), the no violation of law opinion is understood as a matter of customary practice to cover only law (including published rules and regulations) that, given the nature of the transaction and the parties to it, a lawyer in the relevant jurisdiction exercising customary diligence would reasonably recognize as being applicable.

Even when the applicability of a statute or published rule or regulation is readily apparent, counsel as a matter of customary practice might still not be expected to address it.[166] As in the case of the remedies opinion (*see* Section 3.5.2(c)), among the laws the opinion is understood as a matter of customary usage not to cover are tax, insolvency, antitrust and securities laws (except as contemplated by note 81 and the accompanying text) and the Exon-Florio amendment.

To the extent the no violation of law opinion addresses performance of the agreement, the same analysis regarding future performance applies as is set forth in Section 6.5.4 with respect to the no breach or default opinion. In addition, the opinion covers only those laws (including published rules and regulations) in effect on the date of the opinion letter and laws and published rules and regulations adopted on that date that by their terms are to take effect while the Company is performing its obligations under the agreement.[167]

6.7 APPROVALS AND FILINGS

Opinion recipients often seek an opinion that the Company is not required, except as set forth in the opinion, to obtain any approvals from or make any filings with governmental bodies in connection with its execution and delivery of the agreement and, in many cases, the performance of its obligations under the agreement. (*See* Paragraph 6 of the Illustrative Opinion Letter in Appendix B-1).[168] The approvals and filings opinion provides

166. For example, the opinion is understood as a matter of customary practice not to cover compliance with fiduciary duty requirements even when those requirements are statutory in nature. *See* second paragraph of Section 6.4 and note 148.

167. *See* note 11.

168. The Illustrative Opinion Letter in Appendix B-1 expresses this opinion as follows: "The execution and delivery by the Company of the . . . Agreement do not, and the per-

information to the opinion recipient regarding the Company's compliance with legal and regulatory requirements applicable to the transaction. As such, it overlaps to a considerable extent the remedies and no violation of law opinions.[169]

The approvals and filings opinion only addresses approvals and filings that are required by the law of the jurisdictions that are specified for coverage in the opinion letter. As a matter of customary usage, the opinion is understood not to cover requirements of local law unless the opinion letter refers to local law expressly.[170] In some transactions, for example in project financings involving real estate or sales of businesses involving transfers of city or county permits such as liquor licenses or taxi medallions, local law will be important, and opinion recipients may appropriately request specific opinions on approvals and filings required by local law.

As with the no breach or default and no violation of law opinions, the approvals and filings opinion often is drafted to cover not only approvals and filings required for the Company to enter into the agreement but also those required for it to perform its obligations under the agreement.[171] Future performance is discussed in Section 6.5.4. Even though performance will take place after the closing, the opinion only addresses approvals and filings that are required under the laws in effect on the date of the opinion letter and laws adopted on that date that by their terms are to take effect while the Company is performing its obligations under the agreement. The opinion does not (and could not) cover requirements that do not exist when the opinion letter is delivered.

6.8 NO LITIGATION

Opinion recipients sometimes seek an opinion (referred to by some lawyers as a "confirmation"[172] because of its factual nature) concerning pending and threatened actions and proceedings (and sometimes government investigations) against the Company that may affect the transaction. The opinion also often covers actions and proceedings (and investigations) not

formance by the Company of its obligations thereunder will not, . . . require approval from or any filings with any government authority under any law of the United States or the State of New York, or any rule or regulation thereunder." *See* notes 162 and 163.

169. As in the case of the remedies and no violation of law opinions, the opinion is understood as a matter of customary usage not to cover every law, rule and regulation that conceivably might be applicable. For a discussion of which laws, rules and regulations are covered, *see* Sections 3.5, 6.6 and 1.9(n).

170. Local law includes laws, rules, ordinances and the like adopted by political subdivisions below the state level. Ordinarily, local law materials are not available in a way that allows a lawyer to do more than review specific ordinances or regulations. *See* Section 1.9(n).

171. If the opinion does not refer expressly to performance of the agreement but only to consummation of the transaction, the opinion as a matter of customary usage is understood to cover only approvals and filings required for the Company to enter into the agreement and close the transaction and not those that are required for it to perform its obligations under the agreement after the closing. *See* note 149.

172. *See* Section 1.9(h).

relating to the transaction that nonetheless may have a materially adverse effect on the Company. (*See* Paragraph 3 of the Illustrative Opinion Letters in Appendices A-2 and B-2.)[173] When the Company has inside counsel, that counsel often renders the no litigation opinion even when outside counsel is rendering the other standard opinions.

The no litigation opinion does not pass on the merits of particular actions or predict their likely outcome. If the opinion recipient requests the opinion giver's evaluation of a specific matter, the opinion preparers should look for guidance to the ABA Statement of Policy Regarding Lawyers' Responses to Auditors' Requests for Information.[174]

The no litigation opinion is intended to elicit information regarding the *existence* of pending and threatened actions and proceedings ("litigation" for purposes of the following discussion) that might be of concern to the opinion recipient. Thus, the opinion often takes the form of a statement that the Company is not a party to any litigation known to the opinion preparers[175] that may have an adverse effect on the transaction or a material adverse effect on the Company and that is not identified in a schedule to the agreement, an officer's certificate or some other list of litigation referred to in the opinion letter. The presence or absence of the phrase "to our knowledge" does not change the meaning of the opinion. With or without "to our knowledge," the opinion does nothing more than provide comfort to the opinion recipient that the opinion preparers do not know the list of litigation referred to in the opinion letter to be incomplete or unreliable. As a matter of customary diligence the opinion does not require that the opinion preparers check court or other public records or review the firm's files (and an express disclaimer to that effect in the opinion letter is not necessary). *See* Section 2.2.2(a). Nevertheless, the opinion preparers may check the firm's litigation docket (if one exists) and, if they are not themselves familiar with the litigation the firm is handling for the Company, may seek the advice of a litigator or other lawyer in the firm who is. *See* Section 2.2.2(b).

As it relates to litigation affecting the transaction, the no litigation opinion does not ordinarily raise difficult questions. The portion of the opinion, however, that covers litigation generally affecting the Company can be quite challenging. It normally will require the opinion preparers and counsel for the opinion recipient to work out an objective definition of mate-

173. The Illustrative Opinion Letter expresses the opinion as follows: "Except as listed on Schedule [ ] hereto, the Company is not a party to any pending [or overtly threatened in writing] action or proceeding known to me that may adversely affect the transactions contemplated by the . . . Agreement or that may have a material adverse effect on the Company."

174. 31 Bus. Law. 1709 (1976). In most cases the opinion preparers, in applying the ABA Statement, will conclude that an evaluation is not appropriate.

175. *See* Sections 2.2.2(b) and 2.6.1.

riality, such as a specific dollar amount.[176] That definition ordinarily will be set forth in the opinion letter.

As a matter of customary usage the opinion is usually limited to pending and threatened actions and proceedings against the Company to which it is a party.[177] Moreover, because of the difficulty of evaluating the seriousness of oral threats (as well as lawyer-client privilege considerations), opinion preparers often seek to limit the opinion to legal proceedings "overtly threatened in writing."[178]

The no litigation opinion is largely based on information furnished by the Company or a Company officer. Thus, the Committee believes that in most cases the no litigation opinion could be omitted with no real loss to opinion recipients if opinion recipients were instead to rely directly on the Company or its officers for information regarding litigation affecting the transaction and the Company.

CONCLUSION

The formal study of third-party opinion practice began with James Fuld's seminal 1973 article.[179] TriBar's 1979 Report (itself inspired by Fuld) gave rise to a spate of state bar reports, articles and treatises. More recently, the 1991 Third-Party Opinion Report of the ABA Section of Business Law (cited at note 3) provided valuable insights into opinion practice, including brief "Guidelines" for the negotiation and preparation of third-party legal opinions, and the Legal Opinion Committee of the ABA Section of Business Law is currently preparing "Principles" for Third-Party Opinions. The American Law Institute in its Restatement (Third) of the Law Governing Lawyers (cited at note 3) deals with the practices and responsibilities of third-party opinion givers, albeit very briefly. The work of all these groups has clarified the Bar consensus as to what is customary in giving third-party "closing" opinions.

176. One purpose of an objective definition is to avoid the need for the opinion preparers to make subjective judgments regarding the significance of litigation not identified in the referenced schedule or list. Another is to keep the list from becoming overly long by permitting the omission of litigation that would clearly be of no interest to the opinion recipient. Use of a specific dollar amount, however, may not be a complete solution since some complaints may not specify the damages being sought and others may seek a non-monetary form of relief, for example an injunction. Consideration might also be given, therefore, to excluding specific types of actions, such as routine slip-and-fall cases against a retailer, or adopting some other technique for keeping the list within reasonable bounds.

177. Opinion recipients sometimes request that the opinion also be drafted to cover litigation to which the Company is not a party but is otherwise subject. *See* Section 6.5.5. This opinion can raise a variety of problems for the opinion giver and, when given at all, normally should be given only by inside counsel (or by outside counsel who performs a similar function).

178. *But see* Section 1.4(d).

179. James J. Fuld, *Legal Opinions in Business Transactions—An Attempt to Bring Some Order Out of Some Chaos*, 28 Bus. Law. 915 (1973). The 1979 Report and this Report use a number of Mr. Fuld's ideas, including the "golden rule" described in Section 1.3.

Custom is a dynamic concept. TriBar's mission is to describe the current consensus on customary practice and to provide guidance as to how to proceed in those areas where custom remains unclear.

Opinions can be extraordinary teaching and learning devices. While an opinion letter is primarily for the benefit of the opinion recipient, the process of preparing an opinion letter often provides a useful focus for the lawyers on both sides of a transaction. Indeed, at its best, the opinion preparation process can serve to clarify and improve transactions. Yet, to glorify the opinion process would be a mistake. Many opinion letters are drafted in haste; many are delivered in transactions too small to justify the attention they require. Too often recipients view opinions as solutions rather than predictive expressions of professional judgment that, of necessity, are limited in scope to certain jurisdictions and circumstances.

Most transactional lawyers do not see themselves as opinion experts, nor should they. Lawyers should be able to render opinions without extraordinary effort. To assist them, TriBar continues in its efforts to clarify and simplify.

AN INVITATION TO COMMENT ON THIS REPORT

TriBar intends to continue to comment on important opinion issues from time to time. TriBar members learn from each other and importantly from those who read this Report and send comments on it. Please write to: Chair, TriBar Opinion Committee, c/o New York County Lawyers' Association, 14 Vesey Street, New York, N.Y. 10007.

January 13, 1998
All Rights Reserved
TriBar Opinion Committee
Copyright (c) 1998
Reprinted With Permission

APPENDIX A-1
ILLUSTRATIVE OPINION LETTER

(Outside Counsel -
Loan Agreement)

[Law Firm Letterhead]

[DATE]

The Lenders listed on Schedule I hereto
parties to the Credit Agreement referred
to below and World Wide Bank,
as Agent
Ten World Trade Center
New York, New York 10048
re: Macromoney Corporation
Credit Agreement dated as of ___________

Ladies and Gentlemen:

We have acted as counsel for Macromoney Corporation, a Delaware corporation (the "Company"), in connection with the preparation, execution and delivery of, and borrowing under, the Credit Agreement, dated as of _____, among the Lenders, the Agent and the Company (the "Credit Agreement"). This opinion letter is delivered to you pursuant to Section _____ of the Credit Agreement.[180] Terms defined in the Credit Agreement are used herein as therein defined.

For purposes of this opinion letter we have reviewed such documents and made such other investigation as we have deemed appropriate.[181] As to certain matters of fact material to the opinions expressed herein, we have relied on the representations made in the Credit Agreement and certificates of public officials and officers of the Company [and others].[182] We have not independently established the facts so relied on.[183]

Based on the foregoing and subject to the other paragraphs hereof, we express the following opinions.

1. The Company is a corporation validly existing under the law of the State of Delaware.[184]

180. Note: This form of opinion letter is for illustrative purposes. It is intended only to provide a context for the Report of which it is a part.

It is not ordinarily necessary to state that the opinion letter is being delivered at the request of the client. This normally is implicit. *See* note 33.

181. *See* Section 1.4(c).

182. *See* Sections 2.1 and 2.2 regarding the appropriateness of reliance in general, Section 2.2.1(d)(ii) regarding reliance on representations, Section 2.3 regarding reliance on assumptions (many of which customarily are not stated; *see* note 23 and Section 2.3(a)) and Section 2.5 regarding reliance on officers' certificates.

183. *See* Section 2.6

184. *See* Section 6.1.

2. The Company
   (a) has the corporate power to execute, deliver and perform the Credit Agreement and the Note,[185]
   (b) has taken all corporate action necessary to authorize the execution, delivery and performance of the Credit Agreement and the Note,[186] and
   (c) has duly executed and delivered the Credit Agreement and the Note.[187]
3. The Credit Agreement and the Note are valid and binding obligations of the Company enforceable against the Company in accordance with their terms.[188]
4. The execution and delivery by the Company of the Credit Agreement and the Note do not, and the performance by the Company of its obligations thereunder will not, result in a violation of the Certificate of Incorporation[189] or By-Laws of the Company.[190]
5. The execution and delivery by the Company of the Credit Agreement and the Note do not, and the performance by the Company of its obligations thereunder will not, result in any violation of any law of the United States or the State of New York, or any rule or regulation thereunder.

[Insert any other opinions.]

Our opinions above are subject to bankruptcy, insolvency and other similar laws affecting the rights and remedies of creditors generally and general principles of equity.[191]

[Insert any other exceptions, stated assumptions, etc.][192]

The opinions expressed herein are limited to the federal law of the United States, the law of the State of New York, and the Delaware General Corporation Law.[193]

This opinion letter is being delivered to you in connection with the above described transaction and may not be relied on by you for any other purpose. This opinion letter may not be relied on by or furnished to any other Person without our prior written consent.

Very truly yours,

Attachment—Schedule I

185. *See* Section 6.3.
186. *See* Section 6.4.
187. *See* Section 6.4.
188. *See* Section 3.1.
189. This is an example of the use of a defined term in the Agreement.
190. *See* Section 6.5.
191. *See* Sections 1.2(c) and 3.3.
192. *See, e.g.*, Sections 2.3, 3.1, 3.2, 3.4, 3.5, 4.6 and 5.5.
193. *See* Section 4.1.

APPENDIX A-2
ILLUSTRATIVE OPINION LETTER

(Inside Counsel -
Loan Agreement)

[Letterhead of [General] Counsel]

[DATE]

The Lenders listed on Schedule I hereto
parties to the Credit Agreement referred
to below and World Wide Bank,
as Agent
Ten World Trade Center
New York, New York 10048
re: Macromoney Corporation
Credit Agreement dated as of ________

Ladies and Gentlemen:

I am [general] counsel of Macromoney Corporation, a Delaware corporation (the "Company"). This opinion letter is delivered to you pursuant to Section ____ of the Credit Agreement, dated as of ____ among the Lenders, the Agent and the Company (the "Credit Agreement").[194] [Describe participation, or lack thereof, in transaction.] Terms defined in the Credit Agreement are used herein as therein defined.

For purposes of this opinion letter, I have reviewed such documents and made such other investigations as I have deemed appropriate.[195] As to certain matters of fact material to the opinions expressed herein, I have relied on the representations made in the Credit Agreement and certificates of public officials and officers of the Company [and others].[196] I have not independently established the facts so relied on.[197]

Based on the foregoing and subject to the other paragraphs hereof, I express the following opinions.

1. The Company is a corporation validly existing under the law of the State of Delaware.[198]
2. The execution and delivery by the Company of the Credit Agree-

194. Note: This form of opinion letter is for illustrative purposes. It is intended only to provide a context for the Report of which it is a part.

It is not ordinarily necessary to state that the opinion letter is being delivered at the request of the Company. This normally is implicit. *See* note 33.

195. *See* Section 1.4(c).

196. *See* Sections 2.1 and 2.2 regarding the appropriateness of reliance in general, Section 2.2.1(d)(ii) regarding reliance on representations, Section 2.3 regarding reliance on assumptions (many of which are not stated; *see* note 23 and Section 2.3(a)) and Section 2.5 regarding reliance on officers' certificates.

197. *See* Section 2.6.

198. *See* Section 6.1. If this opinion is not included, ordinarily it will have to be assumed. See first paragraph of Section 6.1.

ment and the Note do not, and the performance by the Company of its obligations thereunder will not,

(a) breach or result in a default under any agreement or instruments listed on Schedule II hereto[199] [or result in the acceleration of (or entitle any party to accelerate) any obligation of the Company thereunder],[200] or

(b) result in a violation of any court order listed on Schedule III hereto.[201,202,203]

3. Except as listed on Schedule IV hereto,[204] the Company is not a party to any pending [or overtly threatened in writing] action or proceeding known to me that may adversely affect the transactions contemplated by the Credit Agreement or that may have a material adverse effect on the Company.[205,206]

[Insert any other opinions.]

The opinions expressed herein are limited to the federal law of the United States, the law of the State of New York, and the Delaware General Corporation Law.[207]

This opinion letter is being delivered to you in connection with the above described transactions and may not be relied on by you for any other purpose. This opinion letter may not be relied on by or furnished to any other Person[208] without my prior written consent.

Very truly yours,

Attachments—Schedule I
Schedule II
Schedule III
Schedule IV

199. If there is no schedule, the specific items to which the opinion relates should be otherwise identified.

200. *See* Section 6.5.

201. If there is no schedule, the specific items to which the opinion relates should be otherwise identified.

202. *See* Section 6.5.

203. If inside counsel does not give the opinions in Paragraph 2, outside counsel may be requested to give "no breach or default" and "no violation" opinions.

204. Reference to Schedule IV may be omitted if there are no exceptions.

205. If inside counsel does not give the opinions in Paragraph 3, outside counsel may be requested to give a litigation opinion.

206. *See* Section 6.8, in general, and note 176, regarding the need for a definition of materiality.

207. *See* Section 4.1.

208. This is an example of the use of a defined term in the Agreement.

APPENDIX B-1
ILLUSTRATIVE OPINION LETTER

(Outside Counsel -
Stock Purchase Agreement)

[Law Firm Letterhead]
[DATE]

World Wide Ventures L.P.
Ten World Trade Center
New York, New York 10048
re: Macromoney Corporation
Sale of Stock Under Stock Purchase Agreement
dated as of ___________

Ladies and Gentlemen:

We have acted as counsel for Macromoney Corporation, a Delaware corporation (the "Company"), in connection with the preparation, execution and delivery of, and sale of stock under, the Stock Purchase Agreement, dated as of ____, between you and the Company (the "Stock Purchase Agreement"). This opinion letter is delivered to you pursuant to Section _____ of the Stock Purchase Agreement.[209] Terms defined in the Stock Purchase Agreement are used herein as therein defined.

For purposes of this opinion letter we have reviewed such documents and made such other investigation as we have deemed appropriate.[210] As to certain matters of fact material to the opinions expressed herein, we have relied on the representations made in the Stock Purchase Agreement and certificates of public officials and officers of the Company [and others].[211] We have not independently established the facts so relied on.[212]

Based on the foregoing and subject to the other paragraphs hereof, we express the following opinions.

1. The Company is a corporation [duly incorporated and] validly existing under the law of the State of Delaware.[213]
2. The Shares have been duly authorized and validly issued and are fully paid and nonassessable.[214]

209. Note: This form of opinion letter is for illustrative purposes. It is intended only to provide a context for the Report of which it is a part.

It is not ordinarily necessary to state that the opinion letter is being delivered at the request of the client. This normally is implicit. *See* note 33.

210. *See* Section 1.4(c).

211. *See* Sections 2.1 and 2.2 regarding the appropriateness of reliance in general, Section 2.2.1(d)(ii) regarding reliance on representations, Section 2.3 regarding reliance on assumptions (many of which customarily are not stated; *see* note 23 and Section 2.3(a)) and Section 2.5 regarding reliance on officers' certificates.

212. *See* Section 2.6.

213. *See* Section 6.1.

214. *See* Section 6.2.

3. The Company
   (a) has the corporate power to execute, deliver and perform the Stock Purchase Agreement,[215]
   (b) has taken all necessary corporate action to authorize the execution, delivery and performance of the Stock Purchase Agreement,[216] and
   (c) has duly executed and delivered the Stock Purchase Agreement.[217]
4. The Stock Purchase Agreement is a valid and binding obligation of the Company enforceable against the Company in accordance with its terms.[218]
5. The execution and delivery by the Company of the Stock Purchase Agreement do not, and the performance by the Company of its obligations thereunder will not, result in a violation of the Certificate of Incorporation[219] or By-Laws of the Company.[220]
6. The execution and delivery by the Company of the Stock Purchase Agreement do not, and the performance by the Company of its obligations thereunder will not,
   (a) result in any violation of any law of the United States or the State of New York, or any rule or regulation thereunder,[221] or
   (b) require approval from or any filings with any governmental authority under any law of the United States or the State of New York, or any rule or regulation thereunder.[222]

[Insert any other opinions.]

Our opinions above are subject to bankruptcy, insolvency and other similar laws affecting the rights and remedies of creditors generally and general principles of equity.[223]

[Insert any other exceptions, stated assumptions, etc.[224]]

The opinions expressed herein are limited to the federal law of the United States, the law of the State of New York, and the Delaware General Corporation Law.[225]

This opinion letter is being delivered to you in connection with the above described transaction and may not be relied on by you for any other purpose. This opinion letter may not be relied on by or furnished to any other Person without our prior written consent.

Very truly yours,

215. *See* Section 6.3.
216. *See* Section 6.4
217. *See* Section 6.4.
218. *See* Section 3.1.
219. This is an example of the use of a defined term in the Agreement.
220. *See* Section 6.5.
221. *See* Section 6.6.
222. *See* Section 6.7.
223. *See* Sections 1.2(c) and 3.3.
224. *See, e.g.*, Sections 2.3, 3.1, 3.2, 3.4, 3.5, 4.6 and 5.5.
225. *See* Section 4.1.

APPENDEX B-2
ILLUSTRATIVE OPINION LETTER

(Inside Counsel -
Stock Purchase Agreement)

[Letterhead of [General] Counsel]
[DATE]

World Wide Ventures L.P.
Ten World Trade Center
New York, New York 10048

re: Macromoney Corporation
Sale of Stock Under Stock Purchase Agreement
dated as of ___________

Ladies and Gentlemen:

I am [general] counsel of Macromoney Corporation, a Delaware corporation (the "Company"). This opinion letter is delivered to you pursuant to Section ____ of the Stock Purchase Agreement, dated as of ____, between you and the Company (the "Stock Purchase Agreement").[226] [Describe participation, or lack thereof, in transaction.] Terms defined in the Stock Purchase Agreement are used herein as therein defined.

For purposes of this opinion letter, I have reviewed such documents and made such other investigation as I have deemed appropriate.[227] As to certain matters of fact material to the opinions expressed herein, I have relied on the representations made in the Stock Purchase Agreement and certificates of public officials and officers of the Company (and others][228]. I have not independently established the facts so relied on.[229]

Based on the foregoing and subject to the other paragraphs hereof, I express the following opinions.

1. The Company is a corporation [duly incorporated and] validly existing under the law of the State of Delaware.[230]
2. The execution and delivery by the Company of the Stock Purchase Agreement do not, and the performance by the Company of its obligations thereunder will not,

226. Note: This form of opinion letter is for illustrative purposes. It is intended only to provide a context for the Report of which it is a part.

It is not necessary to state that the opinion letter is being delivered at the request of the Company. This normally is implicit. *See* note 33.

227. *See* Section 1.4(c).

228. *See* Sections 2.1 and 2.2 regarding the appropriateness of reliance in general, Section 2.2.1(d)(ii) regarding reliance on representations, Section 2.3 regarding reliance on assumptions (many of which customarily are not stated; *see* note 23 and Section 2.3(a)) and Section 2.5 regarding reliance on officers' certificates.

229. *See* Section 2.6.

230. *See* Section 6.1. If this opinion is not included, ordinarily it will have to be assumed. See first paragraph of Section 6.1.

(a) breach or result in a default under any agreement or instruments listed on Schedule I hereto[231] [or result in the acceleration of (or entitle any party to accelerate) any obligation of the Company thereunder],[232] or

(b) result in a violation of any court order listed on Schedule II hereto.[233,234,235]

3. Except as listed on Schedule III hereto,[236] the Company is not a party to any pending [or overtly threatened in writing] action or proceeding known to me that may adversely affect the transactions contemplated by the Stock Purchase Agreement or that may have a material adverse effect on the Company.[237,238]

[Insert any other opinions.]

The opinions expressed herein are limited to the federal law of the United States, the law of the State of New York, and the Delaware General Corporation Law.[239]

This opinion letter is being delivered to you in connection with the above described transaction and may not be relied on by you for any other purpose. This opinion letter may not be relied on by or furnished to any other Person[240] without my prior written consent.

Very truly yours,

Attachments—Schedule I
Schedule II
Schedule III

231. If there is no schedule, the specific items to which the opinion relates should be otherwise identified.

232. *See* Section 6.5.

233. If there is no schedule, the specific items to which the opinion relates should be otherwise identified.

234. *See* Section 6.5.

235. If inside counsel does not give the opinion in Paragraph 2, outside counsel may be requested to give "no breach or default" and "no violation" opinions.

236. Reference to Schedule III may be omitted if there are no exceptions.

237. If inside counsel does not give the opinions in Paragraph 3, outside counsel may be requested to give a litigation opinion.

238. *See* Section 6.8, in general, and note 176, regarding the need for a definition of materiality.

239. *See* Section 4.1.

240. This is an example of the use of a defined term in the Agreement.

APPENDIX C

MEMBERS OF THE TRIBAR OPINION COMMITTEE

New York County Lawyers Association
Myer (Mike) O. Sigal, Jr.* (Chair)
Donald S. Bernstein
David L. Bleich
Sol Neil Corbin
Arthur Norman Field**
Edward H. Fleischman
Joseph W. Halliday
A. Sidney Holderness, Jr.*
Morton Moskin*
Charles Niemeth
John B. Tehan
Judith R. Thoyer

The Association of the Bar of the City of New York
Franci J. Blassberg
Rita M. Bolger
Philip E. Coviello
Karl B. Holtzschue
Jerome E. Hyman*
Howard N. Lefkowitz*
Vincent Monte-Sano
Joel I. Papernik
Robert Rosenman
Brian L. Schorr

Allegheny County (Pa.) Bar Association
David A. Murdoch

New York State Bar Association
Frederick G. Attea
J. Truman Bidwell, Jr.
Ronald F. Daitz
Daniel Gersen
Arthur J. Heath
Professor Joseph Hinsey, IV
Richard R. Howe*
Christian G. Koelbl, III
Richard T. McDermott
B. W. Nimkin*
John R. Tyler
Richard L. Veron
Monte E. Wetzler

Atlanta Bar Association
Jeffrey M. Stein

Boston Bar Association
Donald W. Glazer***
Stanley Keller

Chicago Bar Association
Robin Heiss

Delaware State Bar Association
Thomas L. Ambro*

Toronto Bar Association
Wilfred M. Estey

State Bar of Texas
Roderick A. Goyne

* Editorial Group
** Reporter
*** Co-Reporter

TABLE OF CONTENTS

Legal Opinion Principles

*By the Committee on Legal Opinions**

In the Committee's 1991 *Third Party Legal Opinion Report*[1] the Committee undertook to monitor developments respecting the *Report* and the *Legal Opinion Accord* contained in the *Report.* It also undertook in due course to take such further action as might seem appropriate. These *Legal Opinion Principles* are a product of those undertakings.

The *Report* and the *Accord* have made an important contribution to the learning on legal opinions. While the *Accord* has not gained the national acceptance the Committee had hoped, the *Guidelines* in the *Report* are frequently looked to for guidance regarding customary legal opinion practice. In Section 152 of the recently adopted *Restatement (Third) of the Law Governing Lawyers*, the American Law Institute affirmed the importance of customary practice in the preparation and interpretation of legal opinions. The Committee has prepared these *Principles* to provide further guidance regarding the application of customary practice to third-party "closing" opinions that do not adopt the *Accord.* The Committee hopes that these *Principles* will prove useful both to lawyers and their clients and to courts that from time to time are called upon to address legal opinion issues.

The Committee intends to consider the possible extension of these *Principles* to issues they do not now address. The Committee would welcome the assistance of all who are interested in participating in that effort.

*Thomas L. Ambro, Chair. Donald W. Glazer and Steven O. Weise, Co-Reporters.

1. Committee on Legal Opinions, *Third-Party Legal Opinion Report, Including the Legal Opinion Accord, of the Section of Business Law, American Bar Association*, 47 BUS. LAW. 167 (1991).

LEGAL OPINION PRINCIPLES

I. GENERAL

A. At the closing of many business transactions legal counsel for one party delivers legal opinion letter(s) to one or more other parties. Those opinion letters, often referred to as third party opinion letters, are the subject of these *Legal Opinion Principles*.

B. The matters usually addressed in opinion letters, the meaning of the language normally used, and the scope and nature of the work counsel is expected to perform are based (whether or not so stated) on the customary practice of lawyers who regularly give, and lawyers who regularly advise opinion recipients regarding, opinions of the kind involved. These *Legal Opinion Principles* are intended to provide a ready reference to selected aspects of customary practice.

C. An opinion giver may vary the customary meaning of an opinion or the scope and nature of the work customarily required to support it by including an express statement in the opinion letter or by reaching an express understanding with the opinion recipient or its counsel.

D. The opinions contained in an opinion letter are expressions of professional judgment regarding the legal matters addressed and not guarantees that a court will reach any particular result.

E. In accepting an opinion letter, an opinion recipient ordinarily need not take any action to verify the opinions it contains.

F. The lawyer or lawyers preparing an opinion letter and the opinion recipient and its legal counsel are each entitled to assume that the others are acting in good faith with respect to the opinion letter.

II. LAW

A. Opinion letters customarily specify the jurisdiction(s) whose law they are intended to cover and sometimes limit their coverage to specified statutes or regulations of the named jurisdiction(s). When that is done, an opinion letter should not be read to cover the substance or effect of the law of other jurisdiction(s) or other statutes or regulations.

B. An opinion letter covers only law that a lawyer in the jurisdiction(s) whose law is being covered by the opinion letter (*see* II.A.) exercising customary professional diligence would reasonably be expected to recognize as being applicable to the entity, transaction, or agreement to which the opinion letter relates.

C. An opinion letter should not be read to cover municipal or other local laws unless it does so expressly.

D. Even when they are generally recognized as being directly applicable, some laws (such as securities, tax, and insolvency laws) are understood as a matter of customary practice to be covered only when an opinion refers to them expressly.

III. FACTS

A. The lawyers who are responsible for preparing an opinion letter do not ordinarily have personal knowledge of all of the factual information needed to support the opinions it contains. Thus, those lawyers necessarily rely in large measure on factual information obtained from others, particularly company officials. Customary practice permits such reliance unless the factual information on which the lawyers preparing the opinion letter are relying appears irregular on its face or has been provided by an inappropriate source.

B. As a matter of customary practice the lawyers preparing an opinion letter are not expected to conduct a factual inquiry of the other lawyers in their firm or a review of the firm's files, except to the extent the lawyers preparing the opinion letter have identified a particular lawyer or file as being reasonably likely to have or contain information not otherwise known to them that they need to support an opinion.

C. An opinion should not be based on a factual representation that is tantamount to the legal conclusion being expressed. An opinion ordinarily may be based, however, on legal conclusions contained in a certificate of a government official.

D. Opinions customarily are based in part on factual assumptions. Some factual assumptions need to be stated expressly. Others ordinarily do not. Examples of factual assumptions that ordinarily do not need to be stated expressly are assumptions of general application that apply regardless of the type of transaction or the nature of the parties. These include assumptions that copies of documents are identical to the originals, signatures are genuine and the parties other than the opinion giver's client have the power to enter into the transaction.

IV. DATE

An opinion letter speaks as of its date. An opinion giver has no obligation to update an opinion letter for subsequent events or legal developments.

Guidelines for the Preparation of Closing Opinions

*By The Committee on Legal Opinions**

The Section of Business Law of the American Bar Association has adopted the following *Guidelines* for preparing legal opinions delivered at the closing of a business transaction by counsel for one party to another party (or parties) ("closing opinions").[1] These *Guidelines* replace the *Guidelines* included in the Section's 1991 *Third-Party Legal Opinion Report*[2] and reflect developments in customary practice in the decade since 1991.[3] These *Guidelines* complement and are intended to be read and applied with the Section's *Legal Opinion Principles*[4] adopted in 1998 for closing opinions that do not adopt the *Legal Opinion Accord* included in the Section's 1991 *Report.*[5] Like the *Legal Opinion Principles*, these *Guidelines* provide guidance[6] regarding closing opinions whether or not referred to in an opinion letter.

1. Purpose, Scope, and Reliance

1.1 Purpose

The agreement for a business transaction will often condition a party's obligation to close on its receipt of a closing opinion covering specified legal matters from counsel for another party. When received, the closing opinion serves as a part of the recipient's diligence, providing the recipient with the opinion giver's professional judgment on legal issues concerning the opinion giver's client, the transaction, or both, that the recipient has determined to be important in connection with the transaction.

* Donald W. Glazer, Chair. Steven O. Weise, Reporter. These *Guidelines* were first printed in the November 2001 issue. This printing contains corrections to footnotes 1, 2, and 20 that accurately represent the intent of the authors.

1. These Guidelines use "closing opinion" and "opinion letter" interchangeably. "Opinion" refers to a legal conclusion expressed in a closing opinion.

2. Committee on Legal Opinions, *Third-Party Legal Opinion Report, Including the Legal Opinion Accord, of the Section of Business Law, American Bar Association*, 47 Bus. Law. 167 (1991).

3. *See, e.g.*, Restatement (Third) of the Law Governing Lawyers §§ 51(2), 95 (2000) [hereinafter Restatement]; TriBar Opinion Committee, *Third-Party "Closing" Opinions*, 53 Bus. Law. 591 (1998) [hereinafter 1998 TriBar Report].

4. Committee on Legal Opinions, *Legal Opinion Principles*, 53 Bus. Law. 831 (1998). A copy of the *Legal Opinion Principles* is included with these *Guidelines* as Appendix A.

5. These *Guidelines* also apply to opinions that adopt the *Accord*. In the event of any inconsistencies between these *Guidelines* and the *Accord*, the *Accord* controls for opinions that adopt it. The adoption of the *Legal Opinion Principles* and these *Guidelines* is not intended to discourage use of the *Accord*.

6. In appropriate circumstances opinion givers and opinion recipients (or their counsel) may together decide not to follow these *Guidelines* in particular respects.

1.2 Coverage

The opinions included in a closing opinion should be limited to reasonably specific and determinable matters that involve the exercise of professional judgment by the opinion giver. The benefit of an opinion to the recipient should warrant the time and expense required to prepare it.[7]

1.3 Relevance

Opinion requests should be limited to matters that are reasonably related to the transaction. Closing opinions should not include assumptions, exceptions, and limitations that do not relate to the transaction and the opinions given.

1.4 Professional Competence

Opinion givers should not be asked for opinions that are beyond the professional competence of lawyers. To the extent a matter such as financial statement analysis, economic forecasting, or valuation is relevant to an opinion, an opinion giver may properly rely on a factual certificate or assumption.

1.5 Misleading Opinions

An opinion giver should not render an opinion that the opinion giver recognizes will mislead the recipient with regard to the matters addressed by the opinions given.[8]

1.6 "Market" Opinions

An assertion that a specific opinion is "market"—i.e., that lawyers are rendering it in other transactions—does not make it appropriate to request or render such an opinion if it is inconsistent with these *Guidelines*.

1.7 Reliance

An opinion giver is entitled to assume, without so stating, that in relying on a closing opinion the opinion recipient (alone or with its counsel) is familiar with customary practice concerning the preparation and interpretation of closing opinions. On occasion, a closing opinion expressly authorizes persons to whom it is not addressed (for example, assignees of notes) to rely on it. Those persons are

7. When the benefit of an opinion to the recipient is not sufficient, depending on the circumstances, the scope of the particular opinion could be limited (e.g., the opinion on an agreement could be limited to due authorization, execution and delivery) or the opinion could be omitted entirely (*see infra* § 4.2 (opinion on all of a company's outstanding equity securities may not be cost justified)).

8. For a general discussion of this subject (including the role of disclosure), see 1998 TriBar Report, *supra* note 3 at 602-03, 607. This *Guideline* does not preclude limiting the matters addressed by an opinion through the use of specific language if the limitation itself will not mislead the recipient. *See Legal Opinion Principles* §§ I.B, I.C. For an opinion giver's ethical obligations to its client, see *infra* § 2.4.

permitted to rely on the closing opinion to the same extent as—but to no greater extent than—the addressee.

2. Process

2.1 Opinion Request and Response

Early in the negotiation of the transaction documents, counsel for the opinion recipient should specify the opinions the opinion recipient wishes to receive. The opinion giver should respond promptly with any concerns or proposed exceptions, providing, to the extent practicable, the form of its proposed opinions. Both sides should work in good faith to agree on a final form of opinion letter. Discussion of opinion issues while the transaction documents are being prepared can produce constructive adjustments in the documents and the transaction structure and help to avoid delays in closing the transaction. Should a problem be identified that might prevent delivery of an opinion in the form discussed, the opinion giver should promptly alert counsel for the opinion recipient.

2.2 Other Counsel's Opinion

When the opinion giver lacks the legal expertise to render a requested opinion, consideration should be given to whether that opinion should be sought from other counsel. An opinion of other counsel should be sought by the opinion recipient only when the opinion's benefits justify its costs. A primary opinion giver normally should not be asked to express its concurrence in the substance of an opinion of other counsel.

2.3 Financial Interest in or Other Relationship with Client

Lawyers preparing a closing opinion do not normally attempt to determine whether others in their firm have a financial interest (including an equity or prospective equity interest) in, or other relationship with, the client nor do they ordinarily disclose in an opinion letter any such interest or relationship that they or others in the firm may have. Although some lawyers may choose to make such disclosures, disclosure does not excuse those preparing a closing opinion from considering whether a financial interest in, or relationship with, the client that is known to them will compromise their professional judgment in delivering the closing opinion.

2.4 Client Consent and Confidential Information

When the client's consent to the delivery of a closing opinion is required by applicable rules of professional conduct, that consent normally may be inferred from a provision in the agreement that makes delivery of a closing opinion a condition to closing. The opinions contained in a closing opinion ordinarily do not disclose information the client would wish to keep confidential. If, however, an opinion would require disclosure of information that the lawyers preparing the opinion are aware the client would wish to keep confidential, the implications should be discussed with the client and the opinion should not be rendered unless the client consents to the disclosure.

3. Content

3.1 Golden Rule

An opinion giver should not be asked to render an opinion that counsel for the opinion recipient would not render if it were the opinion giver and possessed the requisite expertise. Similarly, an opinion giver should not refuse to render an opinion that lawyers experienced in the matters under consideration would commonly render in comparable situations, assuming that the requested opinion is otherwise consistent with these *Guidelines* and the opinion giver has the requisite expertise and in its professional judgment is able to render the opinion. Opinion givers and counsel for opinion recipients should be guided by a sense of professionalism and not treat opinions simply as if they were terms in a business negotiation.

3.2 Materiality

When possible, an opinion giver should avoid use of a materiality standard by using objective criteria (for example, a particular dollar amount, a specific category, or inclusion on a specified list) when limiting the matters addressed by an opinion.

3.3 Presumption of Regularity

An opinion giver may rely upon the presumption of regularity[9] for matters relating to its client, such as actions taken at meetings during the period covered by a missing minute book, that are not verifiable from the client's records (assuming the matters are not inconsistent with those records). Opinion givers ordinarily need not disclose their reliance on the presumption.[10]

3.4 Use of the Phrase "To Our Knowledge"

Certain factually-oriented opinions, such as the opinions on the existence of legal proceedings,[11] ordinarily are expressed as being to the opinion giver's knowl-

9. *See* Rogers v. Hill, 289 U.S. 582, 591 (1933).

10. An exception is when, based on the available facts, the lawyers preparing the opinion conclude that the deficiency in company records is likely to be significant.

11. Because these opinions lack legal analysis, some lawyers prefer to refer to them as "confirmations."

edge.[12] To avoid a possible misunderstanding over the meaning of "knowledge," the opinion preparers should consider describing in the opinion letter the factual inquiry they have conducted (for example, by stating what they intend "to our knowledge" to mean or by indicating that they are rendering the opinion based solely on their personal knowledge without making any inquiry).[13]

3.5 Explained Opinions; "Would/Should"

Although closing opinions ordinarily do not set forth any legal analysis, opinion givers may include their legal analysis in an opinion when they believe it involves a difficult or uncertain question of professional judgment and have decided that the conclusions expressed should not be stated without setting forth the underlying reasoning. Such an opinion, which is commonly referred to as an "explained" or "reasoned" opinion, may be unqualified or qualified (i.e., subject to exceptions that are not customary for opinions of the type involved).

Opinions have the same meaning whether stated as "would" or "should."[14] Either way they express the opinion giver's professional judgment in the circumstances.

4. Specific Opinions

4.1 Foreign Qualification and Good Standing

An opinion giver should not be asked for an opinion that the opinion giver's client is qualified to do business as a foreign corporation in all jurisdictions in which its property or activities require qualification or in which the failure to qualify would have a material adverse effect on the client. Analysis of the "doing business" requirements of each jurisdiction in which the client has property or conducts activities would require an extensive factual inquiry and a review of the law of jurisdictions as to which the opinion giver cannot reasonably be expected to have expertise. This analysis rarely would be cost-justified.

Because an opinion on qualification to do business or good standing in foreign jurisdictions is based solely on certificates of public officials, delivery of those certificates without an opinion ordinarily should be sufficient to satisfy the needs of the opinion recipient.

12. "To our knowledge" is also sometimes used in opinions that address other factual matters, such as the no breach or default opinion. The trend today in many types of transactions is away from using "to our knowledge" to limit the scope of the opinion. Instead, for example, when giving a no breach or default opinion, lawyers often prefer to identify the contracts covered by referring expressly in the opinion to an existing list or a list prepared specifically for opinion purposes.

13. Such a description would not be required if the opinion preparers have conducted the inquiry described in the 1998 TriBar Report, *supra* note 3, at 618-19, 659, 664-65, or there otherwise is no risk of misunderstanding.

14. *See* TriBar Opinion Committee, *Opinions in the Bankruptcy Context: Rating Agency, Structured Financing, and Chapter 11 Transactions*, 46 Bus. Law. 717, 733 (1991); 1998 TriBar Report, *supra* note 3, at 607 n.37. Closing opinions may be different in this regard from tax opinions.

4.2 Outstanding Equity Securities

An opinion that all outstanding equity securities of the client are duly authorized, validly issued, fully-paid, and non-assessable can require an extensive legal and factual inquiry (for example, when the client has been in existence for a long time and has had many stock issuances). Consideration should be given to whether the benefit of the opinion to the opinion recipient justifies the cost and time required to support it.

4.3 Comprehensive Legal or Contractual Compliance

An opinion giver should not be asked for an opinion that its client possesses all necessary licenses and permits or has obtained all approvals and made all filings required for the conduct of the client's business. Similarly, an opinion giver should not be asked for an opinion that its client is not in violation of any applicable laws or regulations or that its client is not in default under any of the client's contractual obligations.[15] Neither a materiality exception nor a knowledge limitation makes these opinions appropriate.

4.4 Lack of Knowledge of Particular Factual Matters

An opinion giver normally should not be asked to state that it lacks knowledge of particular factual matters.[16] Matters such as the absence of prior security interests or the accuracy of the representations and warranties in an agreement or the information in a disclosure document (subject to section 4.5 below) do not require the exercise of professional judgment and are inappropriate subjects for a legal opinion even when the opinion is limited by a broadly worded disclaimer.

4.5 Negative Assurance

Opinion recipients sometimes seek negative assurance from the opinion giver regarding the adequacy of the disclosure in the prospectus or other disclosure documents furnished to investors in connection with a sale of securities. Such negative assurance is not an opinion in the traditional sense. Rather, the practice of providing negative assurance is unique to securities offerings and is intended to assist the opinion recipient in establishing a due diligence or similar defense. A request for negative assurance is appropriate only when it is requested for that purpose in connection with a registered securities offering or, depending on the nature of the disclosure document and the process by which it was prepared, an offering of securities exempt from registration.[17]

15. This *Guideline* is not intended to preclude a request for an opinion, otherwise appropriate, on a specific matter, for example, on whether specified activities of the client comply with the requirements of a specific statute.

16. The principal exception is the "confirmation" often included in closing opinions regarding the opinion giver's knowledge of legal proceedings to which the client is a party. *See supra* § 3.4.

17. A request for negative assurance will be appropriate, for example, in many Rule 144A and Regulation S offerings.

4.6 Fraudulent Transfer

An opinion on the enforceability of an agreement does not address the effect of fraudulent transfer laws on the other party's rights under the agreement.[18] Although a party to a transaction may be concerned about the effect of fraudulent transfer laws, an opinion giver could not render an opinion on those laws without relying heavily on assumed facts. Because opinions on the effect of fraudulent transfer laws are of limited value, they should not be requested absent a compelling justification.

4.7 Litigation Evaluation

The opinion giver ordinarily should not be asked to express an opinion on the expected outcome of pending or threatened litigation.[19]

4.8 Matters of Public Policy

Because public policy is a principal basis for invalidating contractual provisions, opinion givers should not qualify their opinions as a whole with a general exception for "matters of public policy."[20] When appropriate, however, an opinion giver may include an exception for matters of public policy with respect to a particular provision (such as a provision releasing the other party from liability without excluding liability for willful misconduct or fraud).

4.9 When Law Covered by Opinion and Law Selected to Govern Agreement are Different

When a closing opinion does not cover the law of a jurisdiction whose law is selected as the governing law in an agreement, the opinion giver should explore with counsel for the opinion recipient how best to respond to a request for an opinion on the agreement's enforceability. When an opinion of local counsel is not cost justified, an acceptable alternative may be an opinion of the opinion giver that is limited to the enforceability of the governing law clause under the law covered by the opinion. Another acceptable alternative (which might be combined with the first) may be an opinion that the entire agreement would be enforceable if the law covered by the opinion were to apply (notwithstanding the governing law clause).

18. The "bankruptcy exception" (which is implied even when not stated) excludes the effect of fraudulent transfer laws from the enforceability opinion. *See* 1998 TriBar Report, *supra* note 3, at 624.

19. *See generally* American Bar Association, *Statement of Policy Regarding Lawyers' Responses to Auditors' Requests for Information*, 31 Bus. Law. 1709 (1976).

20. *See supra* note 6.

APPENDIX

Legal Opinion Principles

*By The Committee on Legal Opinions**

In the Committee's 1991 *Third Party Legal Opinion Report*[1] the Committee undertook to monitor developments respecting the *Report* and the *Legal Opinion Accord* contained in the Report. It also undertook in due course to take such further action as might seem appropriate. These *Legal Opinion Principles* are a product of those undertakings.

The *Report* and the *Accord* have made an important contribution to the learning on legal opinions. While the *Accord* has not gained the national acceptance the Committee had hoped, the *Guidelines* in the *Report* are frequently looked to for guidance regarding customary legal opinion practice. In section 152 of the recently adopted *Restatement (Third) of the Law Governing Lawyers*, the American Law Institute affirmed the importance of customary practice in the preparation and interpretation of legal opinions. The Committee has prepared these Principles to provide further guidance regarding the application of customary practice to third-party "closing" opinions that do not adopt the *Accord*. The Committee hopes that these *Principles* will prove useful both to lawyers and their clients and to courts that from time to time are called upon to address legal opinion issues.

The Committee intends to consider the possible extension of these *Principles* to issues they do not now address. The Committee would welcome the assistance of all who are interested in participating in that effort.

I. General

A. At the closing of many business transactions legal counsel for one party delivers legal opinion letter(s) to one or more other parties. Those opinion letters, often referred to as third party opinion letters, are the subject of these *Legal Opinion Principles*.

B. The matters usually addressed in opinion letters, the meaning of the language normally used, and the scope and nature of the work counsel is expected to perform are based (whether or not so stated) on the customary practice of lawyers who regularly give, and lawyers who regularly advise opinion recipients regarding, opinions of the kind involved. These *Legal Opinion Principles* are intended to provide a ready reference to selected aspects of customary practice.

* Thomas L. Ambro, Chair. Donald W. Glazer and Steven O. Weise, Co-Reporters.

1. Committee on Legal Opinions, *Third-Party Legal Opinion Report, Including the Legal Opinion Accord, of the Section of Business Law, American Bar Association*, 47 Bus. Law. 167 (1991).

C. An opinion giver may vary the customary meaning of an opinion or the scope and nature of the work customarily required to support it by including an express statement in the opinion letter or by reaching an express understanding with the opinion recipient or its counsel.
D. The opinions contained in an opinion letter are expressions of professional judgment regarding the legal matters addressed and not guarantees that a court will reach any particular result.
E. In accepting an opinion letter, an opinion recipient ordinarily need not take any action to verify the opinions it contains.
F. The lawyer or lawyers preparing an opinion letter and the opinion recipient and its legal counsel are each entitled to assume that the others are acting in good faith with respect to the opinion letter.

II. Law

A. Opinion letters customarily specify the jurisdiction(s) whose law they are intended to cover and sometimes limit their coverage to specified statutes or regulations of the named jurisdiction(s). When that is done, an opinion letter should not be read to cover the substance or effect of the law of other Jurisdiction(s) or other statutes or regulations.
B. An opinion letter covers only law that a lawyer in the jurisdiction(s) whose law is being covered by the opinion letter[2] exercising customary professional diligence would reasonably be expected to recognize as being applicable to the entity, transaction, or agreement to which the opinion letter relates.
C. An opinion letter should not be read to cover municipal or other local laws unless it does so expressly.
D. Even when they are generally recognized as being directly applicable, some laws (such as securities, tax, and insolvency laws) are understood as a matter of customary practice to be covered only when an opinion refers to them expressly.

III. Facts

A. The lawyers who are responsible for preparing an opinion letter do not ordinarily have personal knowledge of all of the factual information needed to support the opinions it contains. Thus, those lawyers necessarily rely in large measure on factual information obtained from others, particularly company officials. Customary practice permits such reliance unless the factual information on which the lawyers preparing the opinion letter are relying appears irregular on its face or has been provided by an inappropriate source.
B. As a matter of customary practice the lawyers preparing an opinion letter are not expected to conduct a factual inquiry of the other lawyers in their firm or a review of the firm's files, except to the extent the lawyers preparing the opinion letter have identified a particular lawyer or file as being reasonably

2. *See* § II.A.

likely to have or contain information not otherwise known to them that they need to support an opinion.

C. An opinion should not be based on a factual representation that is tantamount to the legal conclusion being expressed. An opinion ordinarily may be based, however, on legal conclusions contained in a certificate of a government official.

D. Opinions customarily are based in part on factual assumptions. Some factual assumptions need to be stated expressly. Others ordinarily do not. Examples of factual assumptions that ordinarily do not need to be stated expressly are assumptions of general application that apply regardless of the type of transaction or the nature of the parties. These include assumptions that copies of documents are identical to the originals, signatures are genuine and the parties other than the opinion giver's client have the power to enter into the transaction.

IV. Date

An opinion letter speaks as of its date. An opinion giver has no obligation to update an opinion letter for subsequent events or legal developments.

Statement on the Role of Customary Practice in the Preparation and Understanding of Third-Party Legal Opinions*

At the closing of many business transactions, the lawyers for one party deliver to the other party a legal opinion letter covering matters the recipient has asked those lawyers to address. These opinion letters, also commonly known as closing or third-party legal opinions, are prepared and understood in accordance with the customary practice of lawyers who regularly give them and review them for clients.

Customary practice permits an opinion giver and an opinion recipient (directly or through its counsel) to have common understandings about an opinion without spelling them out. The use of customary practice does this in two principal ways:

1. It identifies the work (factual and legal) opinion givers are expected to perform to give opinions. Customary practice reflects a realistic assessment of the nature and scope of the opinions being given and the difficulty and extent of the work required to support them.
2. It provides guidance on how certain words and phrases commonly used in opinions should be understood. Customary practice may expand or limit the plain meaning of those words and phrases.

By providing content to abbreviated opinion language, customary practice permits the omission from an opinion letter of descriptions of the procedures that the opinion giver has performed and of many definitions, assumptions, limitations, and exceptions. Thus, it reduces the number of words needed to communicate complex thoughts. As a matter of customary practice, the explicit inclusion in an opinion letter of some but not all of these matters does not exclude others customarily understood to apply. A departure from customary practice is not implied and should not be inferred unless the departure is clear in the opinion letter.

The role of customary practice in third-party legal opinion practice is well established. The American Law Institute's *Restatement (Third) of the Law Governing Lawyers*** states:

> In giving "closing" opinions, lawyers typically use custom and practice to provide abbreviated opinions that facilitate the closing. Such opinions may not recite certain

* Editor's Note: This statement is published in the form approved by the authors, without any further editing by *The Business Lawyer*.

** The references to the *Restatement* in this statement are to Sections 51, 52, and 95 of the *Restatement*. The references also include the following Comments, Illustrations, and Notes to those sections: Section 51, Comment e; Section 52, Comment *b*, Comment *e*, Illustration 2; and Section 95, Reporter's

assumptions, limitations, and standards of diligence because they are understood between counsel.

The *Restatement* also refers to customary practice as an element in determining the "meaning of the opinion letter."

The *Restatement* identifies customary practice as a source of the criteria for determining whether the opinion giver has satisfied its obligations of competence and diligence. Under the *Restatement* the "professional community whose practices and standards are relevant" in making that determination is that of "lawyers undertaking similar matters." That professional community may vary based on, among other things, the subject of the opinion and the relevant jurisdiction.

The *Restatement* treats bar association reports on opinion practice as valuable sources of guidance on customary practice. Customary practice evolves to reflect changes in law and practice.

Some closing opinions refer to the application of customary practice. Others do not. Either way, customary practice applies.

* * * * *

This Statement is approved by the following bar and lawyer groups:

- Legal Opinions Committee of the Section of Business Law of the American Bar Association
- Legal Opinions in Real Estate Transactions Committee of the Real Property, Trust and Estate Law Section of the American Bar Association
- American College of Commercial Finance Lawyers
- American College of Mortgage Attorneys
- Attorneys Opinions Committee of the American College of Real Estate Lawyers
- Business and Finance Section of the Atlanta Bar Association
- Business Law Section of the Boston Bar Association
- Business Law Section of the California State Bar
- Commercial Law Section of the Delaware State Bar Association
- Real & Personal Property Section of the Delaware State Bar Association
- Corporate Law Committee of The Bar Association of the District of Columbia
- Business Law Section of The Florida Bar
- Real Property, Probate and Trust Law Section of The Florida Bar
- Real Property and Financial Services Section of the Hawaii State Bar Association
- Business Law Section of the Maryland State Bar Association
- Real Property Section of the Maryland State Bar Association
- State Bar of Michigan Business Law Section

Note to Comment *b*, Reporter's *Note* to Comment *c*. The *Restatement* sometimes refers to "custom and practice." The *Restatement* uses the phrases "custom and practice" and "customary practice" to mean the same thing.

- TriBar Opinion Committee (consisting of members of (i) the Special Committee on Legal Opinions in Commercial Transactions, New York County Lawyers' Association; (ii) the Corporation Law Committee, The Association of the Bar of the City of New York, (iii) the Special Committee on Legal Opinions of the Business Law Section, New York State Bar Association, and (iv) other state and local bar associations)
- Business Law Section of the North Carolina Bar Association
- Corporation Law Committee of the Ohio State Bar Association
- Business Law Section of the Oregon State Bar
- Business Law Section of the Pennsylvania Bar Association
- Business Law Section of the Philadelphia Bar Association
- Corporate, Banking and Securities Law Section of the South Carolina Bar
- Business Law Section of the State Bar of Texas
- Real Estate, Probate and Trust Law Section of the State Bar of Texas
- Business Law Section of the Washington State Bar Association
- Business Law Section of the State Bar of Wisconsin

SPECIAL REPORT

OF THE TRIBAR OPINION COMMITTEE

U.C.C. SECURITY INTEREST OPINIONS—REVISED ARTICLE 9

TABLE OF CONTENTS

Special Report of The TriBar Opinion Committee: U.C.C. Security Interest Opinions—Revised Article 9

*By The TriBar Opinion Committee**

1. Introduction

At the closing for a personal property secured transaction counsel for the borrower often delivers an opinion[1] to the lender concerning the security interests in the borrower's personal property the borrower has granted to the lender. The focus of this opinion is the Uniform Commercial Code (the "U.C.C."), particularly Article 9. In 1993 the Committee issued a *Report* (the "*1993 TriBar U.C.C. Report*")[2] on this subject. Since then substantial revisions to Article 9[3] have been adopted[4]

*The TriBar Opinion Committee (the "Committee" or "TriBar") includes members of the following organizations functioning as a single Committee: (i) Special Committee on Legal Opinions in Commercial Transactions, New York County Lawyers' Association; (ii) Corporation Law Committee, The Association of the Bar of the City of New York; and (iii) Special Committee on Legal Opinions of the Business Law Section, New York State Bar Association. Members of the Allegheny County (Pa.), Atlanta, Boston, Chicago, District of Columbia and Ontario Bar Associations and of the state bars of California, Delaware, North Carolina, and Texas are also members of the Committee. The members of the Committee and the Reporter and Editorial Group for this *Report* are listed in Appendix D. In addition to members of this Committee, drafts of this *Report* were provided to a small number of other lawyers with relevant expertise. The Reporter and the members of the Editorial Group express their sincere appreciation to those who provided comments on those drafts.

This *Report* has not been approved by the governing body or membership of any of the bar associations whose committees or members were involved in its preparation. Accordingly, the views expressed are solely those of TriBar. This *Report* states the consensus of the Committee. It does not, however, necessarily reflect the views of individual members or their firms, organizations, or associations on any particular point.

1. The opinion is normally one of several opinions included in a "closing opinion," that is an opinion letter given at the closing of a financial transaction to parties other than the opinion giver's client. *See generally* TriBar Opinion Committee, *Third-Party Closing Opinions,* 53 Bus. Law. 591 (1998) [hereinafter the "*1998 TriBar Report*"]. Unless otherwise specified, terms used in this *Report* have the meanings given to them in the *1998 TriBar Report. See generally 1998 TriBar Report*, art. I., at 595. The *1998 TriBar Report* has also been referred to as "TriBar II" because it supersedes the Committee's first report issued in 1979, as well as some of the Committee's other reports. *Id.* at 592. This *Report*, like the *1998 TriBar Report*, is substantially based on customary practice. *Id.* § 1.4, at 600–03.

2. *Special Report of the TriBar Opinion Committee: U.C.C. Security Interest Opinions*, 49 Bus. Law. 359 (1993) [hereinafter *1993 Security Interest Report*].

3. Unless otherwise indicated, references to the U.C.C. in this *Report* are to the 2002 Official Text of the U.C.C. (which includes revised Article 9). All emphasis is added, unless otherwise indicated.

4. In addition, Article 8 of the U.C.C. has been substantially revised since the *1993 TriBar U.C.C. Report*. The changes to Article 8: (i) moved most provisions concerning security interests in property subject to Article 8 from Article 8 to Article 9, and (ii) changed significantly the substance of those rules.

in each of the fifty states,[5] the District of Columbia, and the United States Virgin Islands. This *Report* discusses closing opinions under revised Article 9[6] and replaces the *1993 TriBar U.C.C. Report*. A summary of this *Report* is included as APPENDIX C.

While this *Report* provides a detailed discussion of Article 9 and opinions on security interests created under Article 9, opinion preparers who do not regularly work with Article 9 should consider whether to involve a lawyer familiar with Article 9 in the preparation of a U.C.C. security interest opinion.

Revised Article 9 has a broader scope than former Article 9, covering (i) sales[7] of accounts (which are defined more broadly under revised Article 9),[8] (ii) for the first time, sales of payment intangibles and promissory notes, and (iii) for the first time, security interests in deposit accounts. Revised Article 9 also significantly simplifies the process for filing a financing statement to perfect a security interest and contains numerous clarifications and other changes.

Opinions on security interests address the attachment (or creation[9]), the perfection, and on rare occasions the priority, of security interests in personal property. A security interest "attaches" (or is "created") when a debtor and a secured party satisfy the requirements of the U.C.C. for providing in favor of the secured

Revised Article 8 is in effect in all states, the District of Columbia, Puerto Rico, and the United States Virgin Islands. The changes to Article 8 are reflected in portions of this *Report*. *See* TriBar Opinion Committee, *An Addendum for Protected Purchasers—U.C.C. Security Interest Opinions*, 54 BUS. LAW. 1261 (1999). *See infra* § 8. Revisions to Article 1 of the U.C.C. were completed in 2001. As of July 25, 2003 the revised version of Article 1 has been adopted in Texas, the United States Virgin Islands, and Virginia.

5. Revised Article 9 broadly defines "state" to mean "a State of the United States, the District of Columbia, Puerto Rico, the United States Virgin Islands, or any territory or insular possession subject to the jurisdiction of the United States." U.C.C. § 9-102(a)(76). For convenience, the balance of this *Report* will use the word "state" as defined in Article 9 even though as of the date of this *Report* revised Article 9 has not yet been adopted in Puerto Rico or any of the territories or insular possessions included in the definition of "state."

6. State variations may affect the treatment of certain issues discussed in this *Report*. State variations are discussed in P. Christophorou et. al, *Under the Surface of Revised Article 9: Selected Variations in State Enactments from the Official Text of Revised Article 9*, 34 UCC L.J. 331 (Spring 2002)[hereinafter *Under the Surface*].

7. A "security interest" includes the interest of a *buyer* of accounts, chattel paper, payment intangibles, and promissory notes. U.C.C. §§ 1-201(37), 1-201(b)(37) (revised). U.C.C. § 9-109(d)(4)–(7) excludes some sales of these types of property from Article 9. Revised Article 9 classifies as a "debtor" a person who has an interest (other than a security interest) in the collateral, whether or not that person is an obligor. U.C.C. § 9-102(a)(28). A *seller* of accounts, chattel paper, payment intangibles, and promissory notes is also a "debtor." *Id.* § 9-102(a)(28). U.C.C. § 9-102(a)(72) defines who is a "secured party." *See infra* note 128. Article 9 clarifies that when a security interest has been granted to an agent for the benefit of others, the agent is the "secured party." *Id.* § 9-102(a)(72)(E). In addition, a buyer of accounts, chattel paper, payment intangibles, and promissory notes is a secured party. *Id.* § 9-102(a)(72)(D). If an obligation is secured by personal property, a person who is liable on the obligation, but is not the primary obligor, is a "secondary obligor" as to the obligation. *See id.* § 9-102(a)(71). If that person provides any collateral to secure its obligation, that person is a "debtor" as to that collateral. *See id.* § 9-102(a)(28), (59), cmt. 2.

8. Article 9 has always covered the sale of accounts. U.C.C. § 9-102(1)(b) (pre-revision). Revised Article 9 has a greatly expanded definition of accounts and as a result revised Article 9 covers a broader range of sales of payment rights. *See* U.C.C. § 9-102(a)(2). Article 9 continues to cover the sale of chattel paper. *Compare* U.C.C. § 9-102(1)(b) (pre-revision), *with* U.C.C. § 9-109(a)(3) (revised).

9. *See infra* § 3.

party a consensual[10] interest in personal property that secures payment or performance of an obligation.[11] "Perfection" affords the secured party statutory protections against the claims of most third parties[12] to the collateral. Usually, perfection results from actions taken (e.g., filing a financing statement in the proper office or taking possession of the collateral) that in legal effect give notice to third parties of the security interest of the secured party.[13] "Priority" is the ranking of the secured party's security interest in the collateral against competing claims to the same collateral.[14]

This *Report* addresses closing opinions on security interests covered by Article 9 of the U.C.C.[15] It also touches on the relationship of the U.C.C. to other law. The primary objective of this *Report* is to provide guidance on the customary[16]

10. Revised Article 9 does apply to one kind of non-consensual lien, referred to as an "agricultural lien." U.C.C. §§ 9-102(a)(5), 9-109(a)(2). Agricultural liens only arise in connection with "farm products" and are generally limited to goods, such as crops, owned by a person engaged in farming operations. *See id.* § 9-102(a)(34). This *Report* does not specifically address those liens.

11. A security interest also attaches in connection with the sale of most kinds of payment rights. *See supra* note 7.

12. Third parties may include other creditors (secured and unsecured), holders of judgment, tax, statutory, and other non-consensual liens, transferees of the collateral, and the debtor's trustee in bankruptcy. *See* U.C.C. § 9-317.

13. In some circumstances perfection is by control, which (depending on the method of control used) may not provide notice to third parties of the secured party's security interest in the collateral. U.C.C. § 9-314. In other circumstances perfection of a security interest is "automatic" or temporary and no notice is given to third parties. *Id.* §§ 9-308(d)–(g), 9-309, 9-312(e)–(g), and 9-315. *See infra* notes 93, 111–23 and accompanying text.

14. This *Report* addresses in a limited way the effect of the transition rules found in Part 7 of revised Article 9. *See infra* § 9. Part 7 of revised Article 9, in part, addresses (i) the effect of revised Article 9 on transactions closed under former Article 9 (or other applicable law) prior to the effective date of revised Article 9, and (ii) the effect of pre-effective date transactions on transactions closed after revised Article 9 became effective. The transition rules may have a limited effect on a security interest opinion concerning a new transaction entered into under revised Article 9.

15. Much has been written on security interest opinions. For a discussion of the effect of revised Article 9 on security interest opinions, see D. GLAZER, S. FITZGIBBON & S. WEISE, GLAZER AND FITZGIBBON ON LEGAL OPINIONS: DRAFTING, INTERPRETING AND SUPPORTING CLOSING OPINIONS IN BUSINESS TRANSACTIONS §§ 12.1–12.10 (2d ed. 2001 & Supp. 2002).

16. *See 1998 TriBar Report, supra* note 1, § 1.4, at 600–03. The *Legal Opinion Principles* (the "*Principles*") of the Committee on Legal Opinions of the American Bar Association's Section of Business Law also emphasize the role of customary practice in the giving of closing opinions. Committee on Legal Opinions, *Legal Opinion Principles*, 53 BUS. LAW. 831 (1998) [hereinafter *Principles*]. Section I.B. of the *Principles* states:

> [T]he scope and the nature of the work counsel is expected to perform are based (whether or not so stated) on the customary practice of lawyers who regularly give, and lawyers who regularly advise opinion recipients regarding, opinions of the kind involved.

Id. at 832.

The *Guidelines for the Preparation of Closing Opinions* (the "*Guidelines*") adopted by the American Bar Association's Section of Business Law, 57 BUS. LAW. 875 (2002), state in § 1.7:

> An opinion giver is entitled to assume, without so stating, that in relying on a closing opinion the opinion recipient (alone or with its counsel) is familiar with customary practice concerning the preparation and interpretation of closing opinions.

Id. at 876. [hereinafter *Guidelines*]; *see also 1998 TriBar Report, supra* note 1, at 601 n.24; RESTATEMENT (THIRD) OF THE LAW GOVERNING LAWYERS § 51(2) cmt. e, § 95 cmt. B (2000).

meaning and scope of U.C.C. security interest opinions,[17] and on the qualifications that are customarily understood to apply.[18] An *Illustrative Security Interest Opinion* is attached to this *Report* as APPENDIX A.

The main body of this *Report* discusses U.C.C. security interest opinions when the only law governing attachment (or creation), perfection, or, when addressed, priority of the security interest is the law covered generally by the opinion letter. APPENDIX B discusses opinions on perfection when the law of more than one state might be applicable.

Preparers of U.C.C. security interest opinions are subject to the same obligations they have in preparing any closing opinion: (i) not to give an opinion if they believe the opinion will, in the circumstance, mislead[19] the opinion

17. Practices under revised Article 9 are still developing. The Committee will monitor practice under revised Article 9 and consider supplements to this *Report* as appropriate.

18. As in the case of all closing opinions, U.C.C. security interest opinions are subject not only to applicable legal standards, but to relevant ethical standards as well. *See, e.g.*, N.Y. Jud. Law App. § 7-102(a)(5), (7); MODEL RULES OF PROF. CONDUCT R. 1.2(d), 2.3, 4.1, 8.4(c) (2003); *Guidelines, supra* note 16, § 2.3; GLAZER & FITZGIBBON, *supra* note 15, § 1.7. *See generally* RESTATEMENT (THIRD) OF THE LAW GOVERNING LAWYERS § 98.

19. The *1998 TriBar Report* describes the obligation as follows:

> Prior to the delivery of the opinion letter, the opinion preparers must ask themselves whether they believe that the opinions they intend to render will, under the circumstances, be misleading to the recipient. An opinion the opinion preparers believe to be misleading should not be delivered until *disclosures* are made to cure the problem . . . .
>
> When considering if an opinion to be given will mislead the opinion recipient, opinion preparers must think not only about the opinion itself but also about areas excluded from the opinion. Ordinarily, a non-standard exception indicates to the opinion recipient an area of concern. A non-standard exception is thus likely to be informative, rather than misleading. A stated assumption (other than one of general application—*see* Section 2.3(a)) may also alert the opinion recipient to a problem area.
>
> Common exceptions may mask problems that are different and more serious than the matters they are commonly understood to exclude . . . .
>
> Exclusions from opinions (whether understood without being stated, *e.g.*, insolvency law and local law, or stated in the opinion letter) relate to areas that are left by custom to the opinion recipient and its counsel. The opinion recipient should not assume that the opinion giver does not have significant information about these excluded areas. However, the opinion giver is not expected to disclose any such information to the opinion recipient. Only if the opinion preparers determine that the opinion will, under the circumstances, mislead the opinion recipient will the need for disclosure (or withholding the opinion) arise.
>
> In determining whether an opinion will mislead, the opinion preparers need only consider what the opinion letter (i) states and (ii) omits to state that is relevant to what is stated. Thus, the omission of information not relevant to the opinion given (*e.g.*, information relevant to litigation if no opinion is rendered with respect to the absence of litigation) does not mislead. The question the opinion preparers must consider is whether under the circumstances the opinion will cause the opinion recipient to misevaluate the specific opinion given.

1998 TriBar Report, *supra* note 1, § 1.4(d), at 602–03 (footnotes omitted). When considering the relevant circumstances, the opinion preparers may assume (without stating) that the opinion recipient (alone or with its counsel) is familiar with transactions of the type covered by the opinion. *See supra* note 16; *see also Guidelines*, *supra* note 16, § 1.5, stating, "An opinion giver should not render an opinion that the opinion giver recognizes will mislead the recipient with regard to the matters addressed by the opinions given." (footnote omitted).

recipient, and (ii) not to rely on unreliable[20] information.[21]

2. Preliminary Matters

2.1 Begin by Determining the Scope of the Security Interest Opinion

(a) Discussion between counsel

An initial and critical question in preparing a security interest opinion is its scope. What collateral will the opinion cover? What law will the opinion address? The opinion preparers[22] and the opinion recipient's counsel[23] should discuss these questions early in the opinion process.[24] The starting point for this discussion is the scope of the security interest opinion requested by the opinion recipient. In formulating a request, the opinion recipient should consider carefully the nature of the debtor's business, the nature of the collateral, and the size of the transaction.[25]

(b) Effect of limiting the security interest opinion to the U.C.C.

Lawyers often limit security interest opinions to the U.C.C. (or to Article 9 of the U.C.C.) of a specific jurisdiction. This *Report* refers to this limitation as a

20. The *1998 TriBar Report* indicates that an opinion giver may not rely on "unreliable" information:

> The opinion preparers may rely on information provided by an appropriate source . . . unless reliance is unreasonable under the circumstances in which the opinion is rendered or the information is known to the opinion preparers to be false (together "unreliable information"). Some information is false on its face . . . . Other information is so improbable . . . that it would be unreasonable for the opinion preparers to rely on it without further inquiry. Similarly, it would be unreasonable to rely on information that is inconsistent with a representation given in the same transaction or information known to the opinion preparers. If the opinion preparers identify information as "unreliable," they must find other information to establish the facts. Alternatively, they may include an express assumption regarding those facts in order to give the opinion. . . . In some cases disclosure may be required . . . .

1998 TriBar Report, supra note 1, § 2.1.4, at 610 (footnotes omitted).

21. The *1998 TriBar Report* also discusses the possibility that giving an opinion may give rise to liability under other laws, even if the opinion is not "misleading":

> OPINION GIVERS SHOULD CONSIDER WHETHER APART FROM THE OPINION LETTER THEY ARE EXPOSING THEMSELVES TO LIABILITY AS A RESULT OF THEIR INVOLVEMENT IN THE TRANSACTION UNDER THE ANTI-FRAUD RULES OF THE FEDERAL SECURITIES LAWS OR WHETHER CIVIL OR CRIMINAL FRAUD STANDARDS MAY BE APPLICABLE . . . .

1998 TriBar Report, supra note 1, § 1.4(d), at 603.

22. The "opinion giver" is the lawyer or law firm in whose name an opinion is given. *1998 TriBar Report, supra* note 1, § 1.9(e), at 606. The "opinion preparers" are the lawyers who prepare the opinion letter for the opinion giver. *Id.* § 1.8, at 605.

23. This *Report* assumes that the recipient of a security interest opinion will be advised by its own counsel, who is familiar with opinions of this type. *Guidelines, supra* note 16, § 1.7.

24. *Guidelines, supra* note 16, § 2.1.

25. *Id.* § 1.2; Restatement (Second) of the Law Governing Lawyers § 95, cmt. b.

"U.C.C. Scope Limitation."[26] U.C.C. Scope Limitations are common and as a general rule acceptable to opinion recipients. If, however, the opinion preparers believe that limiting an opinion to the U.C.C. will be misleading to the opinion recipient, they should consider making appropriate disclosures to the recipient or its counsel concerning the significance of the limitation.[27]

The U.C.C. Scope Limitation excludes from the coverage of the opinion other laws of the specified state and laws of other jurisdictions (including federal law) even if they have an effect on the creation, attachment, perfection, or priority (if covered) of a security interest. An opinion limited to the U.C.C. of a particular state customarily is understood to be subject to each of the following limitations:

(i) *The opinion covers only security interests created under Article 9 of the U.C.C.* The only law the opinion covers is Article 9[28] of the U.C.C.[29] of the specified state, even when the character of the collateral[30] or the identity of the debtor[31] indicate that non-U.C.C. laws may be relevant.[32]

26. The U.C.C. Scope Limitation applies to the U.C.C. of each jurisdiction whose U.C.C. is stated to be covered. For example, the U.C.C. of one state may apply to the attachment of the security interest, while the U.C.C. of a different state may apply to the perfection of the security interest. *See infra* § 3.2; *see also infra* APPENDIX B (discussing choice of law).

27. *See supra* note 19. For example, the opinion preparers may recognize that the opinion recipient and its counsel are unaware that substantially all the collateral is likely to be subject to the requirements for perfection of non-U.C.C. certificate-of-title laws. *See* U.C.C. § 9-303 cmt 3; *see also infra* note 33 and accompanying text.

28. Limiting a security interest opinion to Article 9 of the U.C.C. also eliminates consideration of the security interests created by operation of law under other articles of the U.C.C.: Article 2 (U.C.C. §§ 2-401, 2-505, 2-711(3)), 2A (U.C.C. § 2A-508(5)), Article 4 (U.C.C. § 4-210), and Article 5 (U.C.C. § 5-118).

29. The opinion does address other Articles of the U.C.C. to the extent Article 9 looks to those Articles for definitions, procedures, or rules. For example, an opinion containing a U.C.C. Scope Limitation that addresses the perfection of a security interest in securities might involve the definitions of "control" or "delivery" found in Article 8. *See* U.C.C. §§ 1-201(14), 8-102(a)(15), 8-106, 8-301, 9-106, 9-313, and 9-314; U.C.C. § 1-201(a)(14) (revised). Similarly, an opinion containing a U.C.C. Scope Limitation that addresses the rights of a holder of a security interest in securities might involve the definition of "protected purchaser" in Article 8 and the substantive rights of a protected purchaser under Article 8. U.C.C. §§ 8-303, 9-331(b); *see also infra* § 8. Under former Article 8 security interests in securities were created and perfected under that Article. Under revised Articles 8 and 9 those security interests are created and perfected under Article 9, with some references to Article 8. *See infra* § 8.

30. An FCC broadcast license and an account receivable due from the U. S. government are two examples of collateral in which the enforcement of the security interest is subject to some extent to other (non-U.C.C.) laws. *See, e.g.*, Communications Act of 1934, 47 U.S.C. § 310 (2000) (FCC broadcast license may not be held by a foreign government); New Bank of New England, N.A. v. Tak Communications, Inc. (*In re* Tak Communications), 138 B.R. 568, 17 U.C.C. Rep. Serv. 2d (Callaghan) 218 (Bankr. W. D. Wis. 1992), *aff'd*, 985 F.2d 916, 19 U.C.C. Rep. Serv. 2d (Callaghan) 869 (7th Cir. 1993) (holding enforcement of security interest in broadcasting license subject to limitations); MLQ Investors L.P. v. Pacific Quadracasting, Inc., 146 F.3d 746 (9th Cir. 1998) (holding security interest in FCC license may be created and perfected under the U.C.C.; enforcement subject to FCC review); *see also* Assignment of Claims Act of 1940, 41 U.S.C. § 15 (2000); 31 U.S.C. § 3727 (2000) (security interests in receivables subject to Assignment of Claims Act need not be recognized by the federal government in certain circumstances when the government is an account debtor).

31. For example, a security interest granted by an investment company or a public utility holding company may be void if the debtor has not complied with the Investment Company Act of 1940, 15 U.S.C. §§ 80a-1 to 80a-64, or the Public Utility Holding Company Act of 1935, 15 U.S.C. §§ 79 to 79z-6.

32. Article 9 sometimes expressly defers to the attachment, perfection, and priority rules of other

(ii) *The opinion covers only U.C.C. collateral or transactions.* Under Article 9 some types of collateral and some types of transactions are not subject to some or all of the rules of Article 9.[33] Security interest opinions limited to the U.C.C. of the specified state cover only that portion of the collateral or transaction that is subject to Article 9 of the U.C.C. in the specified state. Thus, the opinion does not cover collateral or transactions to the extent they are excluded from the scope of Article 9 by U.C.C. section 9-109(c) and (d).

(iii) *The opinion covers only U.C.C. perfection methods.* The opinion does not cover collateral or transactions to the extent a security interest in the collateral may be perfected under non-U.C.C. law.[34]

(c) Drafting U.C.C. Scope Limitations

Opinion givers express the U.C.C. Scope Limitation in various ways.[35] The *1993 Report* contained a detailed version[36] of the U.C.C. Scope Limitation. As a matter

law as well as the effect of other law on a transaction subject to Article 9. *See, e.g.*, U.C.C. §§ 9-109(c), 9-201(b), (d), 9-311, 9-333. Although the U.C.C. expressly refers to these other laws, they are excluded from the coverage of the opinion by the U.C.C. Scope Limitation.

33. *See generally* U.C.C. §9-109(c), (d). Among the categories of collateral or transactions partially or generally excluded from Article 9 are: (i) collateral *to the extent* subject to the preemptive effect of a federal statute (such as the Ship Mortgage Act, 46 U.S.C. §§ 31301–31343); (ii) landlords' liens; (iii) collateral subject to liens created by statute or other rule of law in favor of persons providing services or materials except as provided under U.C.C. section 9-333 with respect to priority of those liens; (iv) claims for compensation of an employee; (v) collateral owned by a governmental entity to the extent the security interest granted by the governmental entity is expressly governed by another statute; (vi) claims under and interests in insurance policies (other than as proceeds of other collateral and certain assignments of health-care-insurance receivables); (vii) rights represented by a judgment; (viii) rights of set-off or recoupment (other than with respect to a depositary bank and rights of account debtors); (ix) real estate (including a lease or rents thereunder) (other than fixtures); (x) tort claims (other than commercial tort claims and tort claims that are proceeds of other collateral); and (xi) in most cases, deposit accounts in a consumer transaction (other than as proceeds of other collateral). Variations in enactments of revised Article 9 may affect the kinds of property and transactions to which revised Article 9 applies. *See supra* note 6.

34. For example, the perfection of a security interest in a registered copyright appears to require a filing with the federal copyright office under federal law. Aerocon Eng'g, Inc. v. Silicon Valley Bank (*In re* World Auxiliary Power Co.), 303 F.3d 1120 (9th Cir. 2002) (dictum). Although Article 9 refers to filings under other laws, *see, e.g.*, U.C.C. § 9-311(a)(1), an opinion subject to a U.C.C. Scope Limitation would not cover the perfection of the security interest in a registered copyright unless it does so expressly. The opinion *would*, however, cover issues concerning the security interest in the copyright that are subject to the U.C.C. and not subject to federal law, such as the attachment of the security interest. A secured party may perfect a security interest in a patent or a trademark by the filing of a financing statement under the U.C.C. *See, e.g.*, *In re* Cybernetic Servs., 252 F.3d 1039 (9th Cir. 2001) (patents); Trimarchi v. Together Dev. Co., 255 B.R. 606 (D. Mass. 2000) (trademarks); *see also* U.C.C. § 9-311.

35. Examples are:

- "We express no opinion except to the extent that [Article 9 of] the Uniform Commercial Code in effect in the State of [New York] governs the creation or perfection of the security interests referred to in this opinion letter."
- "To the extent [Article 9 of] the [New York] U.C.C. is applicable, the security agreement creates in favor of the Secured Party a security interest in the collateral, and the security interest of the Secured Party in the collateral is a perfected security interest."

36. *1993 Security Interest Report*, *supra* note 2, § II.3, at 366–68.

of customary practice, any indication in the opinion letter that reasonably communicates to the opinion recipient that the opinion is limited to the U.C.C. or to Article 9 of the U.C.C. of a particular state[37] is understood to convey the U.C.C. Scope Limitation described above.

(d) No opinion given on law governing perfection or priority

Except to the extent it does so expressly, a security interest opinion does not address which state's law governs the perfection, the effect of perfection or non-perfection, or the priority of the security interest.[38]

2.2 Remedies Opinions Do Not Include Security Interest Opinions

By long-standing custom remedies opinions on security agreements and security interest opinions are set forth in separate paragraphs in an opinion letter and address different subjects.[39] Remedies opinions address the formation of a contract and the enforceability of the opinion giver's client's undertakings in that contract.[40] Security interest opinions address satisfaction of the U.C.C.'s require-

37. If the U.C.C. Scope Limitation does not refer to a particular state, it should be understood as referring to the law of the state or states whose law is generally covered by the opinion letter. *See infra* § 3.2.

38. When the debtor is a registered organization, in almost all cases the proper (and only) place to file a financing statement is the state of the debtor's organization. The local law of the physical location of certain types of real-estate-related collateral (such as a security interest in fixtures perfected by a fixture filing, as-extracted collateral, and timber to be cut) continues to govern the perfection, the effect of perfection or nonperfection, and the priority of a security interest in these types of collateral by the filing of a financing statement. Further, the local law of the physical location of certain types of tangible collateral (such as goods, instruments, tangible chattel paper, negotiable documents, and certificated securities) continues to govern the *perfection* of a security interest by possession or delivery (in the case of a certificated security). In addition, regardless of the method of perfection, the location of such tangible collateral governs the *effect* of perfection or nonperfection, and the priority of the security interest in such collateral. *See* U.C.C. §§ 9-301(2), (3)(C), (4); *see also infra* Appendix B (discussing the effect of the mandatory choice-of-law rules set forth in U.C.C. § 9-301 concerning perfection). The Committee expresses no view on whether it is appropriate to request, or whether an opinion giver should provide, a choice-of-law opinion in any of these circumstances. *See generally* Permanent Editorial Board for the Uniform Commercial Code, *PEB Report: Article 9 Perfection: Choice of Law Analysis Where Revised Article 9 is Not in Effect in All States by July 1, 2001*, 56 Bus. Law. 1725, 1728 n.8 [hereinafter the "*PEB Report*"].

39. *See 1998 TriBar Report, supra* note 1, § 3.5, at 627 (discussing the presumption against opinions by implication).

40. *1998 TriBar Report, supra* note 1, § 3.1, at 619–21. For example, if a contract containing a security agreement includes a debtor's waiver of notice of foreclosure, or a waiver of the right to pay the debt prior to foreclosure, the *remedies* opinion may have to be qualified on those matters. *See* U.C.C. §§ 9-602(7) (limitations on waiver of debtor's right to notice); 9-602(11) (limitations on waiver of debtor's right to redeem collateral). *See generally* U.C.C. §§ 1-103, 1-105, 1-301(revised), 1-302 (revised), 9-602, 9-603.

ments[41] for establishing and preserving the secured party's interest in the collateral.[42] Standard exceptions[43] to the remedies opinion are not required for security interest opinions.

When a contract includes a security agreement, a remedies opinion on the contract is understood as a matter of customary practice not to express any conclusion on the creation, attachment, perfection, or priority of the security interest purportedly created by the contract, whether the opinion letter contains a security interest opinion or not.[44]

2.3 Analysis of Bankruptcy and Equitable Principles is Not Within the Scope of Security Interest Opinions

Although a secured party understandably wants assurance that it will be treated as a secured party in the event of the debtor's bankruptcy, except to the extent stated in the following paragraph, a security interest opinion is not an opinion on the effect of bankruptcy, fraudulent transfer, or other insolvency laws.[45] Nor does a security interest opinion cover the effect of equitable principles.

Under U.C.C. section 9-317, a holder of a perfected security interest (but not most unperfected security interests) has a claim to the collateral that is superior

41. The remedies opinion covers the enforceability of the security agreement as a contract. It does not cover the creation or attachment of the security interest, its perfection, or its priority. The existence of an enforceable contract is necessary, but not sufficient, to create the security interest. U.C.C. §§ 1-201(3) (definition of "agreement"), 9-102(a)(73) (definition of "security agreement"); 9-203(b)(3) (requirement of "security agreement").

42. U.C.C. § 9-201 states that, except as otherwise provided in the U.C.C., "a security agreement is *effective* according to its terms between the parties, against purchasers of the collateral, and against creditors." In addition, U.C.C. § 9-203(a) and (b) use the word "enforceable" in describing when a security interest attaches to collateral. Use of the words "effective" and "enforceable" has led some to argue (incorrectly in the Committee's view) that the remedies opinion should be interpreted to cover the attachment of the security interest. U.C.C. §§ 9-201(a), (b), and 9-203 establish conditions for the effectiveness and enforceability *of a security interest*, not of the *security agreement* that creates that security interest. Under Article 9, the "security agreement" is only that term of an agreement that creates or provides for a security interest. *See id.* § 9-102(a)(73). Although lawyers often refer to the entire agreement as a "security agreement," (a convention generally followed in this Report), strictly speaking for purposes of Article 9 the term "security agreement" is limited to the relevant language creating or providing for the security interest. *Id.* § 9-102 cmt. 3(b). A contract that includes a security agreement may be effective as a contract although it fails to create a security interest, e.g., because its description of the collateral is insufficient under U.C.C. § 9-108. *See id.* § 9-201, cmt. 2. A "term" of an agreement is "that portion of an agreement which relates to a particular matter." *Id.* §§ 1-201(42), 1-201(b)(40) (revised).

43. "Exceptions" include limitations and exclusions. *1998 TriBar Report, supra* note 1, § 1.9(i), at 606.

44. An opinion recipient occasionally will request an opinion stating that a "valid and enforceable" security interest was created or perfected. This language blurs the distinction between a remedies opinion on a contract that includes a security agreement and a security interest opinion, and the Committee recommends that the words "valid an enforceable" not be used. Even when used, however, an opinion on security interests is not customarily understood to address the enforceability of the agreement, except to the extent necessary for the attachment of the security interest.

45. For example, insolvent banks are subject to state or federal receivership (or similar) laws and are not eligible for relief under the Bankruptcy Code. 11 U.S.C. § 109(b)(2), (d) (2000). The discussion in this *Report* about the effect of the Bankruptcy Code on a security interest opinion also applies generally to these other laws.

to the claim of a judgment lien creditor who becomes a lien creditor after the security interest is perfected or certain other acts are taken. A trustee in bankruptcy has the power, under Bankruptcy Code section 544(a),[46] to avoid a security interest in personal property that is voidable as of the commencement of the case by a judgment lien creditor. Thus the bankruptcy trustee may set aside under that section most unperfected security interests, but not a perfected security interest. An opinion that addresses perfection under the U.C.C. provides the recipient the basis it needs to conclude that its security interest in the collateral cannot be avoided by a bankruptcy trustee under Bankruptcy Code section 544(a).

The opinion, however does not itself address other aspects of the status of the secured party's security interest in bankruptcy.[47] Accordingly, limiting a security interest opinion with a bankruptcy qualification serves no purpose and has no effect on the meaning of the opinion.

Similarly, because security interest opinions address compliance only with the U.C.C., the possible effects of equitable principles do not affect security interest opinions. This is so notwithstanding that, under the doctrine of equitable subordination,[48] inequitable conduct by a secured party may result in the subordination of a security interest to the security interests of junior secured parties or even to claims of unsecured creditors. Hence, applying an equitable principles qualification to the security interest opinion also serves no purpose and has no effect on the meaning of the security interest opinion.

2.4 A Security Interest Opinion Does Not Substitute for Either a "No Breach or Default" Opinion or a "No Violation of Law" Opinion

The attachment or perfection of a security interest may violate applicable laws outside the U.C.C. or result in a breach of or default under another agreement that binds the debtor. A security interest opinion does not address these violations, breaches, or defaults. If a recipient is concerned that the grant of a security interest may violate a law or result in a breach of other contractual obligations of the

46. *Id.* § 544(a).

47. Although a perfected security interest is protected from attack under Bankruptcy Code § 544(a), bankruptcy law may still adversely affect a perfected security interest. For example, Bankruptcy Code section 362, provides for an automatic stay against enforcement of security interests; section 364 permits imposition of a super-priority lien on collateral; section 552 limits the effect of a security interest granted and perfected pre-petition in property or proceeds acquired by the debtor post-petition; section 547 provides avoiding powers relating to preferential transfers; sections 548 and 544(b) provide avoiding powers relating to fraudulent transfers; section 506(c) permits collateral to be invaded to pay certain expenses; section 363 permits the sale or use of collateral under certain circumstances; and section 1129(b) permits collateral to be affected in connection with reorganization plans confirmed pursuant to the "cram-down" powers. These consequences of bankruptcy may pertain to all security interests, including those that have been properly created and perfected under the U.C.C.

48. *See id.* § 510; *see also* U.C.C. §§ 1-103; 1-310 (revised).

debtor, such as a negative pledge covenant, the opinion recipient should request a specific opinion on these issues.[49]

3. Creation or Attachment of Security Interests

3.1 Introduction

An opinion on a security interest typically states that the security agreement "creates" a security interest in the collateral[50] in favor of the secured party or that a security interest has "attached"[51] to the collateral. U.C.C. section 9-203 uses the term "attachment" to describe the event that makes the security interest in collateral enforceable between the debtor and the secured party.[52]

Customarily, the creation or attachment opinion is stated separately from the opinion on the perfection of the security interest. The attachment of the security interest is a step necessary for the perfection of the security interest.[53] Addressing creation or attachment separately from perfection of the security interest provides comfort that the opinion preparers have considered the specific legal elements necessary for creation or attachment. In addition, in some circumstances, the U.C.C. governs the creation or attachment of the security interest, while law outside the U.C.C. governs perfection of the security interest.[54]

49. *See generally 1998 TriBar Report, supra* note 1, §§ 6.5–6.6, at 654–62. The UCC Scope Limitation does not apply to a no-violation-of-law opinion, if given.

50. U.C.C. § 9-102(a)(12) defines "collateral" as "the property subject to a security interest." Although the attachment opinion commonly uses the present tense, it ordinarily covers after-acquired collateral. *See infra* § 7.1.

51. U.C.C. § 9-102(a)(73) defines a "security agreement" as an agreement that "*creates* or provides for a security interest." The word "create" is also found in U.C.C. § 9-109(a)(1) in specifying those transactions to which Article 9 of the U.C.C. applies. Some lawyers believe that the "creation" of a security interest is a necessary, but not sufficient, step for a security interest to attach to collateral. Under that view, an opinion on the "creation" of a security interest covers only some of the steps required for a security interest to "attach to" collateral and an opinion on the "attachment" of a security interest covers all of the steps. Other lawyers believe that no distinction should be made between "creation" and "attachment" opinions. *See infra* § 3.3. Both sides agree that even if a "creation" opinion is narrower than an "attachment" opinion, the additional elements necessary for attachment are implicitly covered when, as is usually the case, a "perfection" opinion is also given in the opinion letter. *See infra* notes 53, 335. However, as noted in section 3.3 *infra,* as a matter of customary practice, a creation or attachment opinion, whether express, or, by virtue of the giving of a perfection opinion, implied, is understood not to cover the question of whether the debtor has rights or the power to transfer rights in the collateral. Some opinion givers do not use either "create" or "attach" but instead state that "the secured party has a security interest in the collateral." This formulation of the opinion is unobjectionable and is understood to mean that the security interest has attached to the collateral.

52. Attachment also makes the security interest enforceable against some third parties. *See* U.C.C. §§ 9-201, 9-317.

53. U.C.C. § 9-308(a). If the opinion includes a "perfection" opinion, but neither a "creation" nor an "attachment" opinion, creation and attachment are implicitly covered by the perfection opinion (unless the opinion expressly assumes "creation" or "attachment"). When an opinion includes a "perfection" opinion but not a "creation" or "attachment" opinion and the opinion expressly assumes either the "creation" or the "attachment" of the security interest, the perfection opinion customarily is understood not to cover any of the elements of creation or attachment.

54. *See supra* § 2.1(b).

3.2 Choice of Law—Creation or Attachment of the Security Interest

The security agreement usually contains a choice-of-law term that selects the law of a specified state as its governing law. If that choice-of-law term is enforceable, the chosen-state's law will govern the attachment, validity, and enforcement of the security interest, and the characterization of the transaction.[55] As discussed below, the parties generally do not have the power[56] to specify the law governing perfection, the effect of perfection or nonperfection, and the priority of a security interest.

A remedies opinion[57] on the security agreement covers the enforceability of the choice-of-law term in the security agreement. The opinion preparers should address the enforceability of a choice-of-law term in a security agreement as they would address a choice-of-law term in any other contract covered by a remedies opinion.[58] An opinion on the enforceability of a choice-of-law term in the security agreement does not address what law governs the perfection, the effect of perfection or non-perfection, or the priority of the security interest.[59]

3.3 Requirements For Attachment

The Article 9 requirements for attachment are:

(i) the debtor has authenticated a security agreement that provides a sufficient description of the collateral;[60]

55. U.C.C. § 9-301 cmt. 2. Generally, the parties are free to choose the law applicable to the attachment and enforcement of the security interest if the state whose law is chosen bears a "reasonable relation" to the transaction. *Id.* § 1-105(1). Even if a choice-of-law provision is enforceable between the parties to the security agreement, it may not bind third parties. *Id.* § 9-401 cmt. 3. Revised Article 1, completed in 2002, eliminates the "reasonable relation" requirement in a domestic transaction, giving effect to the law chosen by the parties to govern the attachment and enforcement of the security interest, unless doing so would violate a fundamental public policy of the state whose law would apply in the absence of a choice-of-law clause. *Id.* § 1-301(revised). *See generally* Restatement (Second) of Conflict of Laws § 187(2)(b). Some states have adopted statutes that permit the parties to certain transactions to choose that state's law as the applicable law even in the absence of a reasonable relation to the chosen state. *See, e.g.*, N. Y. Gen. Oblig. Law § 5-1401 (McKinney 2001); Cal. Civ. Code § 1646.5 (West 1997); 6 Del. Code Ann. tit. 6, § 2708 (1999). In general, such a statute will be applied only by the courts of the state that has adopted it.

56. Under limited circumstances, for example, the perfection of a security interest in a deposit account or a securities account by control, the parties (which must include the relevant depositary bank or securities intermediary) may, in effect, be able to agree on the law governing perfection or priority. *See* U.C.C. § 9-304, 9-305. This *Report* generally does not cover those circumstances.

57. *See supra* § 2.2.

58. *1998 TriBar Report, supra* note 1, §§ 4.3–.6, at 633–36; *Guidelines, supra* note 16, § 4.9. For example, the opinion preparers might (i) cover the choice-of-law term in the opinion, (ii) exclude the choice-of-law term from the remedies opinion, (iii) state that the opinion is given as if the security agreement were governed by the law covered by the opinion, or (iv) address the law specified in the security agreement. *See generally* Appendix B (choice of law).

59. *See* U.C.C. §§ 9-301 to -307; *see generally* Appendix B (choice of law).

60. U.C.C. § 9-203(b)(3)(A). This requirement may be satisfied without an authenticated agreement if (i) the collateral is in the possession of the secured party pursuant to the debtor's security agreement, (ii) the secured party has control of the collateral pursuant to the debtor's security agreement, or

(ii) value has been given;[61] *and*

(iii) the debtor has rights in the collateral *or* the power to transfer rights in the collateral to a secured party.[62]

The opinion preparers must consider each of these issues.

(a) Security agreement

An enforceable agreement. For a security interest to attach to collateral, the secured party needs a security agreement.[63] Usually, the security agreement will exist in an authenticated[64] record.[65]

To confirm that a security agreement has been properly authenticated, the opinion preparers need to determine, as they would for any other agreement,[66] that the debtor has the power to enter into the transaction and has duly authorized, authenticated,[67] and delivered the security agreement. These issues are ordinarily covered by the remedies opinion.[68] Alternatively, as appropriate, the opinion giver may rely on an express assumption to rely on or refer to the opinion of other counsel[69] on any or all of these matters.

Grant of security interest. A "security agreement" is an agreement that "creates or provides for a security interest."[70] The security interest generally will not attach unless the security agreement "provides a description of the collateral."[71] The

(iii) the secured party has taken delivery of a certificated security in registered form pursuant to the debtor's security agreement. *Id.* § 9-203(b)(3)(B)–(D). The "agreement" by which the secured party obtains possession (or control, or has taken delivery) of the collateral must be a "*security* agreement." If the secured party has possession (or control, or has taken delivery) under an "agreement" that does not include a "*security* agreement," the necessary "*security* agreement" does not exist. *Id.* § 9-203 cmts. 3, 4. For example, an owner of goods may give possession of the property to a creditor of the owner for the sole purpose of the creditor repairing the goods. In that case, possession would be pursuant to an "agreement," but would not be pursuant to a "*security* agreement." Opinions are rarely given based solely on a "security agreement" that is not stated in an authenticated record and this *Report* does not address opinions given in those circumstances. *See supra* note 51.

61. U.C.C. § 9-203(b)(1).

62. *Id.* § 9-203(b)(2).

63. A "security agreement" is an agreement that "creates or provides for a security interest." *Id.* § 9-102(a)(73). *See supra* notes 42, 60.

64. "'Authenticate' means . . . to execute or otherwise adopt a symbol . . . with the present intent . . . to . . . adopt or accept a record."), U.C.C. § 9-102(a)(7). "Authentication" does not require a manual signature.

65. Generally, a "record" is information that has been "stored" and "is retrievable in perceivable form." *Id.* § 9-102(a)(69).

66. *See 1998 TriBar Report, supra* note 1, § 2.3(a), at 615.

67. Authentication would not be required for a security agreement that is not contained in a record. *See supra* note 64.

68. *See supra* § 2.2.

69. See *1998 TriBar Report, supra* note 1, §§ 5.1–.4, 636–39.

70. U.C.C. § 9-102(a)(73).

71. *Id.* § 9-203(b)(3)(A). If a security interest is created without the authentication of a record, a formal description of the collateral is not required for the security interest to attach to the collateral. *See supra* note 60.

opinion preparers should review the security agreement to confirm that it contains a present[72] grant[73] of a security interest in favor of the secured party.[74]

Collateral description. A security interest generally will not attach to collateral unless a "security agreement" "provides a description of the collateral."[75] The opinion preparers should determine whether this description[76] is sufficient[77] satisfy U.C.C. requirements. This may require the opinion preparers to exclude from the attachment opinion particular items or types of collateral that are referred to in the granting clause of the security agreement but are not described in the security agreement in a manner that meets the requirements of Article 9 for the description of the collateral.[78] The opinion requires the opinion preparers to review the granting clause in the security agreement and confirm that the description of the col-

72. A security agreement that "expressly postpones" attachment will not result in the present attachment of the security interest. U.C.C. § 9-203(a). *See, e.g., In re* Dolly Madison Industries, Inc., 351 F. Supp. 1038 (E.D. Pa. 1972), *aff'd mem.*, 480 F.2d 917 (3d Cir. 1973) (express deferral of attachment of security interest).

73. A security agreement does not have to use the word "grant." For example a "lease" that is characterized as creating a "security interest," see U.C.C. § 1-201(37), inherently "creates or provides" for a security interest as a result of that characterization and no separate "granting" language is necessary. U.C.C. § 9-102 cmt. 3b. Article 9 applies to the sale of certain types of property. *See supra* note 7. The operative "sale" language in the agreement providing for the sale of the property functions as the "granting" language in those circumstances and no separate granting language is necessary.

74. Article 9 does not require that the security agreement specify the obligation secured by the security interest. Security agreements customarily do so. The definition of security interest includes "an interest in personal property . . . which secures payment or performance of an obligation." U.C.C. § 1-201(37), U.C.C. § 1-201(b)(35) (revised). Unless stated otherwise in the opinion, the creation or attachment opinion means that each obligation purported to be secured by the terms of the security agreement is secured. The security interest opinion does not address the enforceability of the secured obligation. The security interest opinion typically does cover (sometimes by express assumption) the giving of value by the secured party. *See infra* notes 81–83 and accompanying text.

75. *See* supra notes 60, 71.

76. Generally a description of collateral is sufficient if it "reasonably identifies what is described." U.C.C. § 9-108(a). U.C.C. section 9-108(e), however, specifies types of collateral (commercial tort claims and certain consumer-related collateral) requiring special collateral descriptions.

77. When determining the sufficiency of the description of collateral, the opinion preparers need only consider the words in the security agreement, i.e., whether the collateral description reasonably identifies the collateral in which the security agreement purports to create a security interest. The opinion preparers have no responsibility to state that the description of the collateral does not describe some types of collateral that could have been covered or that the secured party may have intended to cover. *See infra* note 78. Nor are the opinion preparers responsible for verifying the existence of the collateral. *See infra* note 79. As to after-acquired collateral, see *infra* § 7.1.

78. Revised Article 9 expressly provides that a description of collateral by a "type" of collateral defined in the U.C.C. (e.g., "equipment," "inventory," "accounts," "investment property," and "general intangibles") sufficiently describes any of the collateral that fits within that term. U.C.C. § 9-108(b)(3). When a security agreement describes collateral by Article 9 type, the opinion assumes, without stating, that those words have the meanings given to them in Article 9 definitions. Other specific types of legally sufficient descriptions are also provided. *Id.* § 9-108(b). An all-encompassing "supergeneric" description (e.g., "all assets") is not sufficient for a security agreement, although it is sufficient for a financing statement. *Compare* U.C.C. § 9-108(c), *with* § 9-504(2). Where a description of collateral in a security agreement contains both a description of collateral that satisfies Article 9 for purposes of a security agreement and a supergeneric or other insufficient description of collateral, the opinion does not have to indicate that the supergeneric or other insufficient portion of the description is not sufficient unless the opinion preparers believe that not to do so would be misleading to the opinion recipient. *See supra* note 19. Similarly, a supergeneric description of collateral may include collateral

lateral is *legally* sufficient.[79] Sometimes the opinion preparers find circular, ambiguous, or vague descriptions. In that case, the opinion preparers should work with counsel for the opinion recipient to have the description clarified.[80]

(b) Value

The secured party's security interest cannot attach until value,[81] as defined in the U.C.C., is given. The U.C.C. expansively defines "value," providing that even an existing claim or a commitment to lend in the future will ordinarily satisfy the requirement.[82] In most cases the question of value is straightforward. Typically, the opinion preparers can easily confirm the borrower's receipt of the loan funds or other value (such as a commitment to lend) at or before the closing.[83]

(c) Opinion does not cover debtor's rights in the collateral

A security interest cannot attach to collateral unless the debtor has "rights in the collateral or the power to transfer rights in the collateral."[84] A security interest ordinarily can be no better than the debtor's rights in the collateral and will attach

that is not subject to the U.C.C. *See supra* text accompanying note 33. The U.C.C. Scope Limitation would exclude that collateral from the coverage of the opinion.

79. The attachment opinion covers the *legal* sufficiency of the description of the collateral, but not its *factual* accuracy. The factual accuracy of the description is not covered by the opinion. The opinion preparers are expected to determine whether the description of the collateral is, as a matter of law, sufficient, but do not have to inspect the collateral to determine whether the description of collateral is factually correct or accurate. For example, a granting clause in a security agreement purporting to convey a security interest in "all of Farmer Brown's assets" would likely be legally inadequate because of its failure to identify with sufficient specificity the particular assets subject to the security interest. U.C.C. § 9-108(c). An opinion on the legal sufficiency of a collateral description that identifies the collateral as "all of Farmer Brown's Guernsey cows" is sufficient, even if it is later discovered that Farmer Brown owned Hereford bulls and not Guernsey cows. The defect in the description of Farmer Brown's livestock is a matter of factual accuracy, which is not covered by the opinion.

80. If that cannot be accomplished, the opinion preparers should consider taking an express exception identifying that portion of the collateral description that is suspect. For example, "We express no opinion whether the description [. . .] contained in § [ ] of the Security Agreement reasonably identifies the collateral for purposes of §§ 9-108 and 9-203 of the U.C.C." A similar exception may be necessary if the secured party expects to perfect its security interest by filing a financing statement. *See* U.C.C. § 9-504.

81. *Id.* §§ 1-201(44), 1-204 (revised).

82. *Id.* §§ 1-201(44)(a), (b), 1-204(1), (2) (revised). U.C.C. section 9-203(b)(1) requires that value be given, but actual receipt of the value by the person granting the security interest (the "debtor") is not required. Hence, the value requirement of U.C.C. section 9-203(b)(1) can be satisfied even if the person granting the security interest is not the person receiving the value (typically the loan funds). *See, e.g.*, Putnam Realty, Inc. v. Terminal Moving & Storage Co. (*In re* Terminal Moving & Storage Co.), 631 F.2d 547, 550–51, 29 U.C.C. Rep. Serv. (Callaghan) 679, 682–83 (8th Cir. 1980); RESTATEMENT (THIRD) SURETYSHIP AND GUARANTY § 9 (1996); RESTATEMENT (SECOND) CONTRACTS § 71(4) (1981). The security interest opinion does not address whether the transaction could be subject to avoidance as a fraudulent transfer (or as a preference). *See 1998 TriBar Report, supra* note 1, § 3.3.2, at 624; *Guidelines, supra* note 16, § 4.6; *see also supra* § 2.4.

83. Alternatively, the opinion giver may assume, without stating, that the secured party has complied (or will comply) with any contractual obligation to extend credit or otherwise give value. *See generally 1998 TriBar Report, supra* note 1, § 2.3(a), at 615. If it is unclear, however, that value has been given, the opinion preparers should consider taking an express exception.

84. U.C.C. § 9-203(b)(2). The U.C.C. does not define "rights in the collateral."

only to those rights.[85] Although the debtor's having rights, or the power to transfer rights, in the collateral is a statutory element of attachment, as a matter of customary practice a security interest opinion is understood as not covering whether the debtor has any rights, or the power to transfer any rights, in the collateral. This is because the existence and extent of those rights is primarily factual. An opinion on the debtor's rights in the collateral is normally impractical,[86] if not impossible, and should not be requested.[87]

Although the debtor's having rights in the collateral or the power to transfer rights in the collateral is not covered by the opinion, some opinion givers qualify their opinions by stating, for example, that no opinion is expressed with respect to the debtor's rights in the collateral[88] or, alternatively, by pointing out that any decrease in the debtor's rights may decrease the secured party's rights.[89] Other opinion givers expressly assume that the debtor has rights in the collateral or the power to transfer rights in the collateral to the secured party. These qualifications are not necessary. Although a debtor must have some rights, or have the power to transfer rights, in the collateral before a U.C.C. security interest can attach to the collateral, a security interest opinion does not cover[90] the nature or extent of those rights.[91]

85. *Id.* § 9-203(b)(2). *But see, e.g., id.* §§ 2-403, 3-302, 7-502, 8-303, 8-502, 8-510, 9-318, 9-330, 9-331, 9-332 under which a security interest in collateral in some circumstances is not limited to the debtor's rights in the collateral to the extent described in those sections. In addition, U.C.C. sections 9-406 to -408 override in some circumstances contractual and statutory limitations on the right to the creation, attachment, perfection, and enforcement of security interests in certain types of collateral.

86. Moreover, a lawyer's investigation of the title to property that is not a matter of public record is unlikely to be productive.

87. A request for an opinion that the debtor "owns the collateral free and clear of all adverse liens, claims or encumbrances," or that the secured party has priority over all other possible claimants (whether claiming through the debtor or another person), although more oblique than a request for an opinion as to "good and marketable title," is no less a request for a title opinion, and is equally inappropriate. *See Guidelines, supra* note 16, § 4.4; *1998 TriBar Report, supra* note 1, at 629–30.

88. One form of statement is: "We have assumed that each item of the collateral exists or will exist and that the debtor has sufficient rights in each such item for the security interest of the lender to attach, and we express no opinion concerning the nature or extent of the debtor's rights in, or title to, any portion of the collateral." Other forms specifically advise recipients that (i) no investigation has been made concerning the existence or ownership of collateral, (ii) the debtor may not have title, but only a leasehold, consignment, or bailment interest in collateral or, if title is involved, that title may be voidable, (iii) the rights of the debtor may be subject to a constructive trust, (iv) the collateral may be subject to rights of a seller thereof (including rights of reclamation or stoppage in transit), or (v) previous owners and creditors of previous owners of the collateral may have superior rights to it. None of these statements is necessary.

89. For example, the collateral may be diminished by an account debtor or a depositary bank exercising a right of set-off or recoupment, or by the rights of a securities intermediary with respect to securities accounts or security entitlements maintained with that intermediary. *See* U.C.C. §§ 9-328(3), 9-340, 9-404(a). Similarly, the debtor's rights under a contract may be subject to provisions in the contract or other laws that limit the debtor's ability to grant an effective security interest in those rights. *But see generally* U.C.C. §§ 9-406 to -409. Where collateral is held by a third person (e.g., a bailee, warehouse, securities intermediary, or agent), the insolvency of that third party may affect adversely the rights of a secured party. A security interest opinion does not cover these issues.

90. If the opinion preparers believe that the opinion will mislead the opinion recipient because the debtor does not have rights, or the power to transfer rights, in important collateral, the opinion preparers should make appropriate disclosure. *See supra* note 19.

91. Even if a title opinion could be given (e.g., where ownership of the collateral is evidenced by a certificate of title), such an opinion is not implied in a security interest opinion.

4. Perfection of Security Interests in Article 9 Collateral

4.1 Introduction

An opinion on the perfection of a security interest in Article 9 collateral expresses the opinion preparers' professional judgment that the steps required by the U.C.C. to give the secured party's security interest priority over the rights of a lien creditor[92] have been (or will be) accomplished. These steps[93] generally give the secured party protection under the U.C.C. against the claims of third parties.[94]

An opinion on perfection requires the opinion preparers to consider:[95]

(i) what law[96] governs perfection of the security interest in the collateral;
(ii) what requirements must be met to perfect the security interest under the governing law; and
(iii) whether those requirements have been satisfied.

4.2 Mandatory Choice-of-Law Rules Governing Perfection

U.C.C. sections 9-301–307 set out mandatory choice-of-law rules for perfection, the effect of perfection or nonperfection, and priority of a U.C.C. security interest:[97]

92. U.C.C.§ 9-102(a)(52) (definition of "lien creditor").

93. The U.C.C. provides that, in certain instances, perfection will occur upon attachment of the security interest without any further act ("automatic" perfection). Examples of automatic perfection are security interests created by assignments of beneficial interests in decedents' estates, U.C.C. § 9-309(13); purchase money security interests in consumer goods, *id.* § 9-309(l); non-significant assignments of accounts and payment intangibles, *id.* § 9-309(2); sales of payment intangibles and promissory notes, *id.* § 9-309(3), (4); security interests in deposit accounts in favor of the applicable depository bank, *id.* § 9-104(a)(1); security interests in investment property created by a broker or securities intermediary, *id.* § 9-309(10); security interests in security entitlements (or securities accounts) in favor of the applicable securities intermediary, *id.* § 8-106(e), 9-314; and, of course, proceeds, *id.* § 9-315(3); *see also id.* § 9-308(d)–(g). In addition, a security interest may be temporarily perfected in some circumstances. *Id.* § 9-312(e)–(h) (automatic perfection for a limited period in instruments, certificated securities, goods in possession of a bailee, and negotiable documents in the stated circumstances). *See also infra* text accompanying notes 111–23. Though lawyers should be aware of those circumstances in which temporary perfection can occur, those circumstances are beyond the scope of this *Report*.

94. *See infra* text accompanying note 159.

95. A security interest in collateral cannot be perfected unless it has also attached to that collateral. U.C.C. § 9-308(a). Hence, when giving an opinion on the perfection of a security interest in collateral, the opinion preparers must also determine (or, if appropriate, expressly assume) that the security interest has attached to that collateral. Even if the opinion does not contain an express opinion on the attachment of the security interest, the elements of the attachment opinion are covered by the perfection opinion (unless expressly assumed). *See supra* notes 51–53.

96. Unless expressly addressed in the opinion letter, no choice-of-law opinion is given on the law that governs perfection of the security interest. *See supra* text accompanying notes 38, 59; *see also* Appendix B (choice of law). In the absence of a choice-of-law opinion, the perfection opinion is given under the law covered generally by the opinion.

97. The governing law for perfection is not necessarily the governing law for the attachment or the enforcement of the security interest. The law governing perfection is determined by the mandatory

(i) *Filing*. When a security interest is perfected by filing a financing statement,[98] perfection[99] is generally[100] governed by the "local law"[101] of the jurisdiction where the *debtor* is located.[102] The U.C.C. contains rules for determining the debtor's "location."[103]

(ii) *Possession or delivery*. When a security interest is perfected by possession or delivery, perfection is governed by the local law of the jurisdiction where the *collateral* is located.[104]

(iii) *Control*. For most security interests perfected by control, e.g., security interests in deposit accounts, letter-of-credit rights, and certain forms of investment property, perfection is generally[105] governed by the local law of the jurisdiction of a third party.[106]

In formulating its opinion request under former Article 9, the opinion recipient needed to consider all of the states whose laws might govern perfection of the

rules of U.C.C. sections 9-301 to -307, which cannot be altered by agreement. *See* U.C.C. §§ 1-105(2), 1-301(g)(8) (revised). The law governing attachment and enforcement is generally chosen by the parties to the security agreement. See *1998 TriBar Report*, *supra* note 1, §§ 4.3–4.6, at 633–36, *Guidelines*, *supra* note 16, § 4.9. *See supra* § 3.2.

98. The location of the debtor also generally governs perfection when perfection is "automatic" or "temporary." U.C.C. §§ 9-301(1), 9-305(c)(2), (3); *see also id.* §§ 9-309, 9-312(e)–(h).

99. Even when perfection of a security interest is governed by the debtor's location, for negotiable documents, goods, instruments, money, tangible chattel paper, and certificated securities, the effect of perfection or nonperfection and the priority of the security interest is governed by the local law of the location of the collateral. U.C.C. §§ 9-301(3)(c), 9-305(a)(1).

100. The perfection of a security interest in fixtures by a fixture filing and the perfection of a security interest in as-extracted collateral and timber to be cut are governed by the local law of the physical location of the collateral. U.C.C. § 9-301(3)(A)–(B), (4); *see infra* note 109.

101. As used in revised Article 9 "local law" means the substantive law of a jurisdiction (without giving effect to the choice-of-law rules of that jurisdiction). *Compare* U.C.C. § 9-301 cmt. 3, *with* U.C.C. § 9-103(3) (pre-revision); *see also 1998 TriBar Report*, *supra* note 1, § 4.3, at 633 n.89 (choice-of-law provision in agreement refers only to the substantive law of the jurisdiction); RESTATEMENT (SECOND) OF CONFLICT OF LAWS § 8 (1971). The *1998 TriBar Report* uses the term "local law" to refer to law below the level of state law, e.g., municipal law. *1998 TriBar Report*, *supra* note 1, § 1.9(n), at 607. This *Report* uses the term "local law" in the Article 9 sense (as the law of a jurisdiction without giving effect to its choice-of-law rules).

102. U.C.C. §§ 9-301(1), 9-305(c)(1).

103. *Id.* § 9-307. For registered organizations organized under state law (generally, corporations, limited liability companies, and limited partnerships), this is generally the organization's state of formation. *See id.* §§ 9-102(a)(70), 9-307(e); *see also* APPENDIX B (choice of law). Section 9-307 also provides rules for determining the location of other types of debtors, including individuals, non-U.S. debtors, and registered organizations organized under U.S. federal law. Additional rules exist that address changes in the location of the debtor. U.C.C. § 9-316; *see also infra* text accompanying notes 196–97.

104. U.C.C. §§ 9-301(2), 9-305(a)(1).

105. U.C.C. §§ 9-304 to -306. However, perfection of a security interest in electronic chattel paper by control is governed by the law of the location of the debtor. *Id.* § 9-301(1) Perfection of a security interest in a security certificate by delivery or control is governed by the local law of the location of the certificated security. *Id.* § 9-305(a)(1).

106. For example, the depositary bank (deposit accounts), the issuing bank or the nominated party (letter-of-credit-rights), the securities intermediary (security entitlements and security accounts), or the issuer (uncertificated securities). U.C.C. §§ 8-106(f), 9-304, 9-305(a)(2), 9-305(a)(3), 9-305(a)(4), 9-305(b), 9-306; *see id.* §§ 5-116, 8-110(e).

security interest in any part of the collateral. If a transaction involved a wide range of collateral, a debtor with many places of business, or both, a perfection opinion could involve the laws of many states.[107] Unless the transaction warranted an opinion on the laws of all of the applicable states, the opinion recipient under former Article 9 typically had to choose the state(s) for which it would request opinion coverage. This decision ordinarily turned on the value of the collateral in each state.[108]

Revised Article 9 limits the number of states whose laws may govern perfection of a security interest by filing. In most cases the perfection of the security interest by filing will be governed by the law of a single state, determined by the debtor's location.[109] Except as otherwise noted, this *Report* assumes that the law designated for coverage in the opinion letter is also the law governing perfection. Unless it does so expressly, a security interest opinion does not address the question of which state's law governs perfection of the security interest. APPENDIX B discusses opinion issues that arise when the law governing perfection is not the law generally covered by the opinion letter.

4.3 METHODS OF PERFECTION

The following table sets forth the principal methods for perfecting a security interest under Article 9 in the listed types of personal property as original[110] collateral:

	Available methods of perfection			
Type of Collateral[111]	**Automatic or temporary**	**Possession**	**Control**	**Financing statement**
Money[112]		X		

107. U.C.C. § 9-103 (pre-revision).

108. *Guidelines, supra* note 16, § 1.2. Similar issues arise under revised Article 9 when the debtor or the collateral is located in a jurisdiction that has not adopted revised Article 9. *See generally* U.C.C. § 9-307(c) cmt. 3.

109. For certain forms of collateral that have a clear local nexus, e.g., as-extracted collateral, and timber to be cut, perfection is governed by the local law of the jurisdiction where the collateral (or, in the case of as-extracted collateral, the wellhead or minehead) is located. UCC § 9-301(3)(B), (4). Note that once timber to be cut has in fact been cut, it is no longer "timber *to be* cut" (and instead is normally "inventory" consisting of lumber) and perfection is governed by the local law of the location of the debtor. *Id.* § 9-301 cmt. 5c. In addition, for fixtures, the perfection of a security interest is governed by the local law of the location of the *debtor* when accomplished by the filing of a financing statement and by the local law of the location of the *fixtures* when the security interest is perfected by a financing statement filed as a "fixture filing." *Id.* §§ 9-301(3)(A) cmt. 5b; 9-502(b).

110. Although not defined or used in the U.C.C., the phrase "original collateral" is understood to refer to collateral (including after-acquired collateral) in which a secured party has a security interest other than as proceeds of other collateral, as a supporting obligation, or as collateral for an obligation that is collateral. *See* U.C.C. §§ 9-102(a)(64), (77), 9-203(f), (g), 9-308(d), (e). Unless otherwise indicated, where this *Report* discusses collateral, it refers to original collateral.

111. Terms used in this column are defined in U.C.C. section 9-102(a) unless otherwise specified.

112. *See id.* §§ 9-312(b)(3) and 9-313(a) (possession). "Money" is the actual medium of exchange (i.e., currency) and does not include, for example, ancient coins (which would be "goods"), funds in

	Available methods of perfection			
Type of Collateral	**Automatic or temporary**	**Possession**	**Control**	**Financing statement**
Accounts, general intangibles (except sales of payment intangibles), commercial tort claims[113]	X			X
Payment intangibles (sales)[114]	X			
Instruments (except sales of promissory notes)[115]	X	X		X
Promissory notes (sales)[116]	X			
Goods,[117] *negotiable documents,*[118]	X	X		X
Tangible chattel paper[119]		X		X
Electronic chattel paper[120]			X	X
Deposit accounts, letter-of-credit rights[121]			X	
Investment property			X	X
(other than certificated securities)[122]	X			
Certificated securities[123]	X	X	X	X

a deposit account, or funds credited to a securities account. *Id.* §§ 1-201(24), 1-201(b)(24) (revised). *See infra* note 153.

113. U.C.C. § 9-310(a). A security interest in health-care-insurance receivables is automatically perfected in connection with its assignment to the provider of the health-care goods or services. *Id.* § 9-309(5). In addition, certain non-significant assignments of accounts and payment intangibles are automatically perfected. *Id.* § 9-309(2).

114. *Id.* § 9-309(3).

115. *Id.* §§ 9-312(a) (filing), (e) (temporary), (g) (temporary), 9-313(a) (possession).

116. *Id.* § 9-309(4).

117. *Id.* §§ 9-309(1) (automatic for purchase-money security interest in consumer goods), 9-310(a) (filing), 9-312(f) (temporary), 9-313(a) (possession). A secured party cannot perfect its security interest in goods in possession of a bailee and covered by a *non-negotiable* document of title by possessing the non-negotiable document. *Id.* § 9-312(d). A security interest in goods covered by a non-negotiable document of title may be perfected by (i) issuance of a document in the name of the secured party, (ii) the bailee's receipt of notification of the security interest, or (iii) filing in the proper place (the location of the debtor) of an appropriate financing statement covering the goods covered by the non-negotiable document. *Id.*

118. *Id.* §§ 9-312(a) (filing), (e) (temporary), (f) (temporary), 9-313(a) (possession). "Document" is defined in U.C.C. section 9-102(a)(30).

119. *Id.* §§ 9-312(a) (filing), 9-313(a) (possession).

120. *Id.* §§ 9-312(a) (filing), 9-314(a) (control).

121. *Id.* §§ 9-312(b)(l), (2) (control).

122. *Id.* §§ 9-309(9), (10), (11) (automatic), 9-312(a) (filing), 9-314(a) (control). *See also id.* § 9-308(f), (g).

123. *Id.* §§ 9-309(10) (automatic), 9-312(a) (filing), (e) (temporary), (g) (temporary), 9-313(a) (delivery), 9-314(a) (control). Possession by the secured party (or certain other persons) in the case of a certificated security is referred to as "delivery" of the certificated security. *See id.* § 8-301 (definition of "delivery").

(a) Opinions on perfection by filing financing statements

To render an opinion that the filing of a financing statement will perfect the security interest, the opinion preparers must determine whether the requirements for perfection under applicable law have been satisfied.[124]

To be "sufficient" under U.C.C. section 9-502(a), a financing statement must contain only three[125] items of information:[126]

(i) the name of the debtor;[127]

(ii) the name of the secured party;[128] and

124. Unless expressly covered in the opinion letter, the opinion does not include a choice-of-law opinion on which state's law governs perfection by the filing of a financing statement (or any other method of perfection). This *Report* assumes that the opinion will be rendered under the law covered by the opinion generally. *See generally* APPENDIX B (choice of law).

125. U.C.C. section 9-502(b) requires additional information for a real-property-related financing statement to be sufficient. The requirements for such filings are not addressed in this *Report*.

126. U.C.C. section 9-516(b) requires the filing office to reject a financing statement if it does not contain certain additional information (such as a mailing address of the debtor). Revised Article 9, however, also provides that if the filing office does accept the filing (if it provides or indicates the three items of information required by U.C.C. section 9-502(a)), the financing statement is effective to perfect the security interest even if it lacks some or all of the additional information. *Id.* §§ 9-516 cmt. 3; 9-520(c). Thus, an opinion on the *perfection* of the security interest by the filing of a financing statement may be given if the financing statement contains the three required items of information *and* has been accepted for filing, even if it does *not* contain the additional information. If the financing statement has not yet been accepted for filing by the filing office, unless the financing statement on its face contains all of the additional information necessary to avoid the required rejection of the financing statement, an opinion on perfection by filing should *not* be based on an assumption that the financing statement will be filed and accepted by the filing office or on a statement that "upon filing" the security interest will be perfected. If the financing statement does contain all such information, such an opinion would be appropriate. Except to the extent discussed in this *Report* an opinion on perfection by filing does not cover the accuracy of the information in the financing statement.

127. U.C.C. sections 9-503(a), (b), (c) describe the requirements for providing the debtor's correct name on the financing statement. A financing statement that does not contain the *exact* name of the debtor as specified in U.C.C. section 9-503 will not be sufficient unless a search of the filing office records under the debtor's correct name and using the "standard" search logic of the filing office discloses the financing statement containing the incorrect name. *Id.* § 9-506(c). The International Association of Corporation Administrators has suggested "standard" search logic that many states are likely to adopt. *See* The International Association of Corporation Administrators Web site, *at* http://www.iaca.org.

For a registered organization the opinion preparers ordinarily should obtain a state-certified copy of the debtor's charter or other similar document to confirm that the name in the financing statement is the debtor's correct name. This would ordinarily be the same document used to support the corporate status opinion. *See 1998 TriBar Report, supra* note 1, § 6.1, at 641–45. For other types of debtors, such as an "organization" (defined in U.C.C. sections 1-201(28), 1-201(b)(28) (revised)), that is not a "registered organization," the opinion preparers should examine an appropriate document, such as a copy of a general partnership's partnership agreement certified by a partner. The opinion preparers ordinarily may rely on a certificate of an officer, partner, or other appropriate official in these circumstances. *See 1998 TriBar Report, supra* note 1, § 2.2.1, at 611.

128. When a security interest is granted in favor of an agent, the agent is the "secured party" and the agent's name should be used as the "secured party's" name on the financing statement. *See* U.C.C. § 9-102(a)(72)(E) cmt. 2b. Alternatively, the financing statement may provide the name of a representative of the secured party even if the representative is not the "secured party." *Id.* § 9-502(a)(2). The failure to indicate the representative capacity of a secured party or representative of a secured party does not affect the sufficiency of a financing statement. *Id.* § 9-503(d). Because searches are not made in the name of the secured party, a mistake in the secured party's name should never cause the financing statement to be seriously misleading. *Id.* § 9-506 cmt. 2. This test provides more leeway than does the "standard search logic" test for the debtor's name. *See supra* note 127. The secured party ordinarily prepares the financing statement and provides its own name. The opinion

(iii) an indication[129] of the collateral[130] covered by the financing statement.[131]

The opinion preparers should do at least one of the following:

(i) confirm that an effective filing[132] of the financing statement in the appropriate filing office[133] in the applicable state[134] has occurred or will occur prior to the delivery of the opinion;[135]

(ii) assume expressly that an effective filing of the financing statement has occurred or will occur in a proper manner; or

(iii) state that perfection will occur "upon" the effective filing of the financing statement in the specified filing office.[136]

preparers may assume, without stating, that the financing statement accurately sets forth the name of the "secured party."

129. Article 9 does not require that a financing statement "describe" the collateral (as it does for a security agreement), but only that the financing statement "indicate" the collateral. The more limited requirement is intended to give third parties "notice" that "a person may have a security interest in the collateral indicated." *Id.* §§ 9-108, 9-203(b)(3)(A), 9-502(a)(2) cmt. 2.

130. U.C.C. section 9-504 provides that for a financing statement an "all assets" ("supergeneric") indication or an indication meeting the requirements of U.C.C. section 9-108 is sufficient. A "supergeneric" description is not sufficient for the description of the collateral in a security agreement. *Id.* § 9-108(c); *see supra* text accompanying notes 76–80.

131. Revised Article 9 does not require (as did former Article 9) that the debtor sign the financing statement. *Id.* § 9-502 cmt. 3. A filed financing statement, however, even if it is otherwise sufficient under U.C.C. section 9-502(a), is ineffective unless it is filed by a person entitled to file it. *Id.* § 9-510(a); *see id.* § 9-502 cmt. 3. A person is entitled to file an initial financing statement only if the debtor has authorized the filing. *Id.* § 9-509(a). U.C.C. section 9-509(b) provides that a debtor's authentication of a security agreement automatically authorizes the filing of an initial financing statement covering the collateral described in the security agreement. Thus, in the situations covered by this *Report*, see *supra* note 60, the opinion preparers (once they have satisfied themselves that the debtor has authenticated a security agreement) normally will have no difficulty confirming that the filing of the financing statement has been authorized by the debtor.

132. *See infra* note 212. "Filing" occurs when either a sufficient financing statement (including all additional information necessary to avoid rejection) and applicable filing fee is tendered to the filing office or the filing office accepts a sufficient financing statement (whether or not it includes the additional information). U.C.C. §§ 9-502(a), 9-516(a); *see supra* note 126. A reference in an opinion to the "filing" of a financing statement includes the "acceptance" of the financing statement by the filing office.

133. In almost all cases filing will be in the central filing office. U.C.C. § 9-501. This *Report* does not cover collateral of a type described in § 9-501(a)(1) of the U.C.C., which provides for a local filing (i.e., timber to be cut, as-extracted collateral, fixtures perfected by a fixture filing). *See supra* note 109. Special rules also apply to the perfection of a security interest in the property of a transmitting utility. U.C.C. § 9-501(b). These types of collateral raise unique issues that are beyond the scope of this *Report*.

134. Unless it does so expressly, a perfection opinion does not cover which state's law governs perfection of the security interest. *See supra* text accompanying notes 38, 59 and 96; *see also supra* § 4.2. If the opinion does not otherwise state, the perfection opinion is given under the law covered generally by the opinion letter. *See generally* APPENDIX B (choice of law).

135. *See* U.C.C. § 9-516; *see also id.* § 9-502(d). If the filing has been accepted, *see supra* notes 126, 132, all that is necessary is that the opinion preparers obtain a time-stamped, or preferably an acknowledgement, copy of the financing statement from the filing office in the jurisdiction in which the filing was made. *See infra* note 209 and accompanying text with respect to time-stamped copies and acknowledgement copies.

136. Frequently, opinion letters are delivered before filing (or before evidence of acceptance of the filing can be obtained). In these cases the opinion should state that perfection will occur "upon the filing of the financing statement" or "when the financing statement is filed" in the stated office. *See* U.C.C. § 9-516(a). The reference to the "filing" of the financing statement includes the acceptance of

(b) Opinions on perfection by possession[137]

Sometimes a security interest is perfected by possession of the collateral.[138] Although under revised Article 9 perfection can almost always be accomplished by filing a financing statement,[139] in some cases the security interest in collateral will be perfected by possession (instead of or in addition to perfection by filing or by another method) and the opinion recipient may request an opinion as to perfection by possession.

When perfection is by possession, the opinion preparers should determine whether the secured party obtained possession (directly or through a third party[140]) in a manner that satisfies U.C.C. requirements. Frequently, the opinion preparers are not present when the secured party (or its agent[141] or other third party) obtains possession. In that circumstance they should include in the opinion an express assumption on this issue or state that perfection will occur, for example, "upon the secured party's obtaining possession of the collateral."[142]

If perfection is to be accomplished by possession through a third party (other than a third party that is the agent[143] of the secured party), the third party generally

the filing by the filing office. *See supra* note 132. These statements are not appropriate when the financing statement on its face does not contain sufficient information to require the filing office to accept the financing statement. *See supra* note 126, *infra* note 209. Revised Article 9 provides for the electronic filing of financing statements. U.C.C. § 9-101 cmt. 4h. It is expected that procedures will be developed for opinion preparers to confirm these filings, such as receipt of a confirmatory e-mail or other communication from the filing office. *See id.* § 9-102(a)(18).

137. The discussion in this section is also relevant to an opinion on a security interest in a certificated security perfected by "delivery." *Id.* § 9-313(a). It should be noted, however, that "delivery" of a certificated security does not necessarily mean that the secured party has "control" of the certificated security. *Id.* § 8-106(a), (b); *see infra* at note 268 and accompanying text.

"Delivery" of a certificated security does *not* require the indorsement of the certificated security to the secured party (whether the security is in bearer or registered form). U.C.C. § 8-301(a). An indorsement may be necessary, however, to give the secured party "control" of the certificated security (which is another method of perfection) and to establish its rights as a "protected purchaser," which could affect the rights of the secured party against the claims of other persons to the certificated security. *See infra* § 8.1(a).

138. *See supra* text at notes 111–23.

139. Money is the only type of collateral in which a security interest can be perfected by possession, but cannot also be perfected by the filing of a financing statement. U.C.C. § 9-312(b)(3). *See also supra* text accompanying notes 112, 115, 117, 118, 119, 123.

140. The debtor cannot qualify as an agent of the secured party or as a bailee for purposes of the secured party's taking possession of collateral. U.C.C. § 9-313 cmt. 3. If an agent or third party is "closely connected to or controlled by the debtor," the debtor may still have possession. *Id.* The opinion preparers may assume, without so stating, that an agent or third party is not closely connected with or controlled by the debtor, unless the assumption is unreliable. *See supra* note 20.

141. *See* U.C.C. § 9-313 cmt. 3.

142. When perfection occurs by possession, perfection is governed by the law of the state where the *collateral* is located. *Id.* § 9-301(c). Unless it otherwise states, an opinion on perfection by possession is given under the law covered by the opinion letter generally. *See supra* text accompanying notes 59, 96. *See generally* APPENDIX B (choice of law).

143. If the agent is not the agent solely of the secured party, the secured party may still be able to obtain possession through possession by a bailee. Possession of the collateral by a third party (such as an escrow holder) that acts as an agent for both the debtor and the secured party does not prevent the third party from possessing the collateral for the secured party (assuming the third party is not controlled by the debtor). *See id.* § 9-313 cmt. 3. When the secured party is perfecting a security interest in a certificated security by "delivery," Article 8 states its own rules for possession through a third person. *Id.* §§ 8-106 cmt. 7, 8-301(a)(2).

must acknowledge in an authenticated record that it holds the collateral for the secured party's benefit.[144] In this circumstance, the opinion preparers should confirm that the acknowledgement is in an authenticated record, that the form of acknowledgment satisfies the substantive requirements of the U.C.C.,[145] and that on its face the acknowledgement purports to have been properly authenticated by the third party.[146]

(c) Opinions on perfection by control

When the secured party perfects its security interest by control, in most circumstances perfection will be governed by the local law[147] of the "jurisdiction"[148] of a statutorily-designated third person.[149] Article 9 contains rules for determining the jurisdiction of the third person.[150]

If a security interest is perfected by control, the opinion preparers must determine that the method of control satisfies statutory requirements for the type of collateral that is the subject of the opinion.[151] For example, when a control agreement is used to perfect a security interest in a deposit account, the opinion preparers must confirm that the control agreement satisfies the requirements for a control agreement[152] for deposit accounts.[153]

144. *Id.* § 9-313(c). No acknowledgment is necessary when the person in possession is an appropriate agent of the secured party, when the bailee has issued a negotiable or nonnegotiable document covering goods, or in a mortgage warehousing or similar transactions. *Id.* §§ 9-312(d)(2), 9-313(h) & cmts. 3, 9. Possession by a third party connected with or controlled by the debtor may not be effective. *See supra* note 140.

145. *Id.* § 9-313(c).

146. The opinion preparers may assume, without stating, that the acknowledgement in fact has been properly authorized and authenticated by the bailee and that the bailee in fact has possession of the collateral.

147. *See supra* text accompanying note 101. Unless it does so expressly, the opinion does not cover the question of which state's U.C.C. governs perfection of the security interest. *See generally* Appendix B (choice of law). Instead, the opinion only covers requirements for perfection under the law of the state whose law is covered by the opinion letter generally. *See supra* text accompanying note 109.

148. In these circumstances, Article 9 refers to the "jurisdiction" of the relevant person and not its "location." U.C.C. §§ 9-304 to -306.

149. *Id.* §§ 9-304 to -306. *See supra* note 106. Unless expressly stated, the opinion does not cover which state's law governs the perfection of the security interest. *See supra* text at notes 59, 96; *see generally* APPENDIX B (choice of law).

150. *See supra* note 106.

151. *See* U.C.C. §§ 9-104 to -107, 9-314.

152. *Id.* § 9-104(a)(2). For example, the control agreement used to perfect a security interest in a deposit account must include an agreement by the depositary bank to "comply with instructions originated by the secured party directing disposition of the funds in the deposit account without further consent by the debtor." *Id.* § 9-104(a)(2). The opinion does not cover the authorization, execution, and delivery of the control agreement by parties other than the opinion giver's client. *1998 TriBar Report, supra* note 1, § 2.3(a), at 615. Perfection of a security interest by control, unlike perfection by possession, does not involve common law concepts of "possession." *See* U.C.C. § 8-106 cmt. 7.

153. The opinion preparers may assume, without stating, that an account characterized by the parties to the transaction as a "deposit account" or as a "securities account" is that type of account for purposes of the opinion. The two are sometimes difficult to distinguish. *Compare id.* § 8-501(a) (securities account), *with* 9-102(a)(29) (deposit account); *see also* U.C.C. Article 8, Prefatory Note, III.C.4. If the collateral is a "securities account," the security interest may also be perfected by the filing of a financing statement; if the collateral is a "deposit account," it may not. U.C.C. §§ 9-312(a), (b)(1). If

(d) Opinions on automatic perfection

Some security interests are "automatically" perfected upon attachment of the security interest.[154] For example, automatic perfection occurs upon the *sale* of a payment intangible or the *sale* of a promissory note.[155] The law of the location of the debtor governs the perfection of a security interest in this circumstance.[156] In a transaction characterized by the parties as a "sale" of these types of personal property, if a perfection opinion is given the opinion preparers are entitled to assume (without stating[157]) that the transaction is in fact a "sale."[158]

5. Article 9 Priority Opinions

5.1 Introduction

The U.C.C. security interest system ranks the rights of the secured party in the collateral as against third parties.[159] Opinions on that ranking—known as "priority opinions"—have long been the subject of intense debate. Those opposed to priority opinions argue that they provide nothing beyond what the recipient knows from its review of U.C.C. search reports. Proponents contend that priority opinions provide the recipient information necessary for a genuine understanding of its position as against other claimants to the collateral. Those who give priority opinions typically do so only after including numerous qualifications and assumptions, which by their nature greatly reduce the value of the opinion.

a bank's product otherwise similar to a deposit account is represented by a paper-based certificate of deposit that is an "instrument" for purposes of Article 9, the putative deposit account is classified as an "instrument" and not a "deposit account." *Id.* § 9-102(a)(29). If the collateral is a deposit account, the only method of perfection is "control." *Id.* § 9-312(b)(1). If the collateral is an "instrument," perfection by control is not available and the only methods of perfection are the filing of a financing statement or taking possession of the instrument. *Id.* §§ 9-312(a), 9-313(a); *see supra* note 115, 121. If the collateral is described as a "certificate of deposit," the opinion preparer may assume, without stating, that it is a "certificate of deposit."

154. U.C.C. § 9-309; *see supra* note 93. Opinions on automatic perfection are sometimes given in structured financings.

155. U.C.C. § 9-309(3), (4). Automatic perfection does not apply to the sale of other kinds of instruments. In addition, a security interest in a supporting obligation and in the debtor's interest in collateral that secures the primary collateral provided by the debtor is automatically perfected upon the perfection of a security interest in the supported obligation or the primary collateral. *Id.* § 9-308(d), (e).

156. *Id.* § 9-301(1); *see supra* text accompanying notes 102–03. Unless it does so expressly, the opinion does not cover the question of which state's law governs perfection of the security interest. *See generally* Appendix B (choice of law).

157. The opinion preparers, however, may not rely on this assumption if they believe the assumption is unreliable. *See supra* note 20. The opinion preparers have no obligation to analyze whether the transaction is in fact a "sale." Nor would a remedies opinion cover this issue. *1998 TriBar Report, supra* note 1, §3.1, at 619–21.

158. An opinion recipient who wants a "true sale" opinion should request one expressly.

159. In effect, the perfection opinion advises the secured party that its rights are "senior" to the rights of a trustee in bankruptcy. U.C.C. §§ 9-102(a)(52)(C), 9-301 cmt. 2, 9-317(a)(2). Part 4 of this *Report* addresses opinions on perfection. *See supra* text accompanying note 92. The security interest opinion does not address other bankruptcy issues. *See generally supra* note 47. An opinion on the "priority" of a security interest does not address any bankruptcy issues. *See generally* The TriBar Opinion Committee, *Opinions in the Bankruptcy Context: Rating Agency, Structured Financing, and Chapter 11 Transactions*, 46 Bus. Law. 717 (1991).

For collateral in which the security interest is perfected by filing, the Committee's *1993 TriBar U.C.C. Report* suggested a form of opinion that the Committee believed fairly addressed the concerns of the contending camps and that would be useful in many situations. This opinion is known as a "Filing Priority Opinion" and is the opinion generally given in those rare circumstances in which priority opinions are given for security interests perfected by filing a financing statement.[160]

5.2 Scope of Priority Opinion

(a) U.C.C. Priority Opinion

As stated elsewhere in this *Report*,[161] by adopting a U.C.C. Scope Limitation an opinion giver limits the security interest opinion, and therefore a priority opinion, to the rules (including the priority rules) contained in Article 9. A priority opinion that is limited by a U.C.C. Scope Limitation is referred to in this *Report* as a "U.C.C. Priority Opinion."[162] As noted below, even this form of priority opinion would require many qualifications.[163] In practice, these opinions often include long lists of qualifications that have no relevance to the transaction at hand while still omitting at least some qualifications that may be relevant. A priority opinion that restates at length the limits of the priority of Article 9 security interests is not useful to (and often not welcomed by) the opinion recipient. Because a U.C.C.

160. Due to the simplified perfection rules in revised Article 9 and the limited nature of priority opinions, at least one rating agency has concluded that, for most structured financings, it will rely on the debtor's representations as to the attachment, perfection, and priority of a security interest under Article 9, rather than on legal opinions. *See* http://www.standardandpoors.com/ResourceCenter/RatingsCriteria/StructuredFinance/articles/060601_article9.html (last visited July 19, 2003).

161. *See supra* § 2.1.

162. A U.C.C. Priority Opinion should be distinguished from priority opinions that are not limited to the U.C.C. Two examples are the "Title Opinion" and the "All Laws Priority Opinion." The Title Opinion considers priority against all possible claimants having any type of claim to the collateral (whether claiming through the debtor or through a prior owner of the collateral), including not only common law and statutory liens, but also, for example, lease and set-off rights. The All Laws Priority Opinion considers only claims (i) of other creditors of the debtor who claim an interest in the collateral arising from any law covered by the opinion, and (ii) of subsequent purchasers of the collateral from the debtor.

While it is theoretically possible to give Title Opinions for Article 9 collateral, lawyers rarely do so. That reluctance is rooted in the risks that flow from the many uncertainties that are likely to remain even after the exercise of extraordinary diligence. For these reasons, the Committee is of the view that in virtually no circumstances involving priority of security interests in personal property governed by Article 9 should a Title Opinion be requested or given.

Similarly, when an All Laws Priority Opinion is given, it generally resembles a treatise on liens. This is of limited value to the recipient and burdensome to the opinion giver, especially when measured against its cost. A listing of the possible qualifications would be extremely long. *See, e.g.*, Business Law Section of the State Bar of California, *Report Regarding Legal Opinions in Personal Property Secured Transactions*, 44 Bus. Law. 791, 820–22 nn. 157 & 158 (1989). Thus, although an All Laws Priority Opinion is also theoretically possible, its use is also strongly discouraged. The creation of a catalog of all of the obscure statutory liens that might apply in limited circumstances to the collateral is normally a practical impossibility. If the opinion recipient has concerns about the priority of a particular lien arising under a statute other than the U.C.C., it should request that a specific priority opinion address that particular lien. For example, lenders sometimes request specific opinions with respect to federal tax or ERISA liens.

163. *See supra* note 162.

Priority Opinion[164] requires a boilerplate list of qualifications that relate to theoretically possible, but rarely applicable, events, most opinion recipients have long since abandoned requests for these opinions.[165] Instead the diligence-based Filing Priority Opinion (described below) has become the form of opinion customarily used in the rare circumstances when an opinion is given on the priority of a security interest perfected by the filing of a financing statement.[166]

(b) Diligence-based opinion format—Filing Priority Opinions

In those rare transactions when an opinion is requested concerning the priority of a security interest that has been perfected by filing a financing statement, the opinion given today is usually a Filing Priority Opinion. This opinion focuses primarily on the opinion preparers' review of a U.C.C. search report, and unlike a U.C.C. Priority Opinion does not require a long list of qualifications.

When a Filing Priority Opinion is given, the opinion confirms that:

(i) a U.C.C. search report identifying the correct, current[167] name[168] of the debtor was obtained from the appropriate filing office;[169]

164. Notwithstanding the imprecision of "first priority," opinions sometimes state simply that the secured party has a "first priority" security interest in the collateral. This usage is undesirable because it does not clearly indicate the types of claims (e.g., security interests and judgment creditors) over which the security interest has priority. When an opinion is given on the priority of a security interest perfected by filing over other security interests perfected by filing, if the opinion uses the phrase "first priority" without further explanation and is subject to a U.C.C. Scope Limitation, the most sensible interpretation is that the priority opinion is a Filing Priority Opinion, unless the opinion contains the long list of qualifications that would be used with a U.C.C. Priority Opinion.

165. In limited circumstances, a form of priority opinion may be given on security interests perfected by delivery or control. *See* discussion *infra*, §§ 5.3, 8.2, 8.3, 8.4.

166. Except for the discussion at notes 162–65, this *Report*, unlike the *1993 TriBar U.C.C. Report*, does not further address the Title Opinion, the All Laws Priority Opinion, or the UCC Priority Opinion. *See 1993 TriBar U.C.C. Report, supra* note 1, §V.B., at 380–83. In the hope of reducing the cost of preparing these opinions, the *1993 TriBar U.C.C. Report* listed priority qualifications the opinion preparers should consider taking when giving a U.C.C. Priority Opinion. These opinions are now rarely, if ever, given, and, therefore, the Committee has not updated the list of qualifications for revised Article 9.

167. The effect of post-closing changes in the name or location of the debtor is discussed below. *See infra* § 5.4(a). If the opinion preparers believe that a search under only the debtor's current name would mislead the opinion recipient, the opinion preparers should make appropriate disclosures. For example, the opinion preparers may know that the debtor has just changed its name. *See supra* note 19.

168. *See supra* note 127 and accompanying text as to the importance under revised Article 9 of using the correct name of the debtor on the financing statement and the factual inquiry appropriate for determining that name. By its terms, the Filing Priority Opinion covers only the current name of the debtor. A security interest perfected by the filing of a financing statement filed against the current debtor under a former name of the debtor or filed against prior owners of the collateral could have priority over the filing that is the subject of the opinion, but would not be identified in the search report and is not covered by the opinion. U.C.C. §§ 9-325(a), 9-507(a), (c).

169. The opinion ordinarily does not cover the question of which state's law governs perfection by filing. *See generally* Appendix B (choice of law). The search report would be obtained from the state where the opinion recipient has decided to file the financing statement for the current transaction. *See supra* text accompanying notes 97–103. If the debtor has changed the jurisdiction of its location within the four months preceding the through date of the search report, a possibility exists that another secured party would have a perfected security interest based on a filing in the debtor's former juris-

(ii) the search report states that it shows financing statements on file in that office as of an identified date (and, if available, time of day);[170] and

(iii) based solely on their review of the search report,[171] the opinion preparers have determined that (a) no other still-effective financing statement naming the debtor under its current name remains on file in the filing office, (b) if a still-effective, previously-filed financing statement remains on file, then, subject to any specifically identified exceptions, the security interest perfected by the prior filing would not have priority over the security interest covered by the opinion, or (c) if a still-effective, previously-filed financing statement remains on file that would give the security interest perfected by the prior filing priority over the security interest covered by the opinion, no prior filer against the debtor has priority over the security interest covered by the opinion because appropriate releases, terminations, or subordinations have been obtained.[172]

To give the opinion recipient the best available information on these matters in the most practical way, the Committee recommends that a Filing Priority Opinion read substantially as follows:[173]

> The U.C.C. Search Report sets forth the proper filing office and the proper name of the debtor[174] necessary to identify those persons who under the

diction. U.C.C. § 9-316(a)(2). The opinion does not cover the possible existence of these other filings. The effect of the transition rules of Part 7 of revised Article 9 on determining where to conduct a search is discussed below. *See infra* § 9.

170. The "through date" (or "effective date") should be identified in the opinion letter. The recipient of a Filing Priority Opinion then would be in a position to determine whether the searches on which the opinion is based are as of an acceptable date. The opinion does not cover the period between the through date and the date of the opinion letter.

171. The opinion preparers' review of filings identified on the report as made before the effective date of revised Article 9 should be based on definitions of collateral used in both former Article 9 and revised Article 9. U.C.C. § 9-705, ex. 7.

172. Under Revised Article 9, a termination statement and a release of collateral is an "amendment" to the initial financing statement. U.C.C. § 9-512(a). Like an initial financing statement, an amendment to a financing statement (including a release or a termination) does not have to be signed or otherwise authenticated by the debtor or the secured party. *Id.* § 9-502 cmt. 3. If, however, the amendment adds another debtor or more collateral, releases collateral or terminates the financing statement, it must be authorized, depending on the kind of amendment, by the debtor or the secured party, *Id.* § 9-509(a), (d). The filing office must retain all financing statements and amendments for at least one year following the date the financing statement would have lapsed in the absence of termination. *Id.* §§ 9-519(g), 9-522(a). Thus, a search report will show financing statements and related releases, termination statements, and other amendments for at least six years after the original filing of the financing statement. The opinion preparers are entitled to assume, without stating, that the releases, termination statements, and other amendments obtained in the search were authorized and therefore validly filed. *Id.* § 9-509; *see 1998 TriBar Report, supra* note 1, § 2.2.1(a), at 611. Article 9 refers to the subordination of a security interest, but does not provide for any filing concerning the subordination of a security interest. U.C.C. § 9-339.

173. *See infra* § 6 regarding the extent of information that should be included in the opinion to identify adequately the Financing Statement and the U.C.C. Search Report.

174. The debtor's name on the search report should match the name of the debtor in the financing statement. *See supra* note 127. Since the search will be obtained using the filing office's standard search logic, the search report will identify only those financing statements that sufficiently provide the debtor's name. U.C.C. §§ 9-503(a), 9-506(b), (c).

[name of State][175] U.C.C. have, as of the Effective Date, financing statements on file against the [Debtor][176] indicating any of the Filing Collateral, as of the Effective Date. [Except for __________,] [T][t]he U.C.C. Search Report identifies no still-effective[177] financing statement naming [Debtor] as debtor and indicating any of the Filing Collateral filed in the Filing Office, prior to the [Effective Date] [filing in the Filing Office of the Financing Statement].[178]

Except for the obvious need to identify previously-filed financing statements indicating interests in the same collateral,[179] no priority qualifications to the Filing Priority Opinion are required because the opinion, by its terms, does not cover other competing interests. This eliminates the time-consuming and often expensive process of identifying theoretical bases from which an attack on priority could be launched.[180] The Filing Priority Opinion thus addresses an issue of significant

175. The state named should be the state where the financing statement has been or will be filed. *See supra* § 4.2.

176. The collateral may have been transferred to the debtor subject to a still-effective and perfected security interest created by the transferor in favor of a different security party and perfected by the filing of a financing statement naming the transferor as the debtor. U.C.C. §§ 9-315(a)(1), 9-316(a)(3), 9-507(a), 9-508(a). The opinion does not cover these other filings. *See infra* § 5.4(a).

177. A financing statement that has lapsed, or has been terminated, or that covered Filing Collateral that has been released, will nonetheless appear on the search report for at least one year following the date on which the financing statement would have lapsed in the absence of a termination. *See supra* note 172. That financing statement is no longer effective (as to the specified property in the case of a release) and need not be referred to if the Search Report identifying the financing statement (i) does not indicate that a continuation statement was timely filed, or (ii) also gives notice of the release or termination of the financing statement. The opinion preparers may rely on the information in the Search Report without any further investigation. *See supra* note 19. Financing statements generally are effective for a period of five years, and may be continued within six months prior to the expiration of the initial filing (and thereafter at five year intervals from the original expiration date). Financing statements filed with respect to certain types of debtors (i.e., transmitting utilities) or certain types of transactions (e.g., public finance and manufactured-home transactions) are effective for longer periods. U.C.C. § 9-515.

178. The first alternative bracketed words constituting the last phrase of this sentence would be appropriate if the Financing Statement was filed prior to the delivery of the opinion and if the U.C.C. Search Report lists the Financing Statement (i.e., if the financing statement was filed prior to the "through date" of the report). The second alternative would be appropriate if where the Financing Statement was not filed (or no evidence of the filing was obtained) prior to the opinion (or if it was filed after the "through date" of the Search Report), and thus the opinion refers to the date (and, if available, time of day) through which the Search Report discloses financing statements of record. In either event, the sentence contemplates an express listing of each prior filer whose still-effective financing statement indicates any of the Filing Collateral.

179. The opinion is limited to collateral "indicated" on the financing statement. *See* U.C.C. § 9-504. The opinion does not cover the possibility that the priority of a security interest in one type of collateral indicated in a financing statement identified in the search report may extend to another type of collateral *not* indicated in the financing statement as proceeds of the original collateral indicated in the financing statement. For example, a security interest in inventory, perfected by the filing of a financing statement, will have priority in accounts constituting proceeds of the inventory over a security interest in the accounts perfected by a later-filed financing statement. *See id.* § 9-322(b) cmt. 6.

180. A security interest in instruments, investment property, or chattel paper perfected solely by the filing of a financing statement will be junior in some circumstances to a security interest perfected by possession, control, or delivery of the collateral, as appropriate, even if the filing was made first. *Id.* §§ 9-328(1), (5), 9-330(a),(b), (d). The Filing Priority Opinion does not cover these issues. See generally *infra* sections 8.2, 8.3, 8.4 for a discussion of specific opinions that address some of these issues.

concern to the recipient: whether at the outset[181] of the transaction its security interest may be junior to the security interests of other Article 9 secured parties who have perfected their security interests in the same collateral by the filing of a financing statement in the same office.[182]

5.3 Priority Opinions When Perfection is Based on Possession or Control

A Filing Priority Opinion would, of course, be inappropriate when a security interest in the collateral may be perfected solely by possession or control.[183] Similarly, a Filing Priority Opinion would be of little value where perfection of a security interest in collateral can be by possession, delivery, or control, as well as by the filing of a financing statement. In many circumstances, a secured party that perfects its security interest by possession, delivery, or control of the collateral may have priority over another secured party that perfects solely by the filing of a financing statement.[184] When a security interest is perfected by possession, delivery, or control and the collateral is not an instrument, tangible chattel paper, or a certificated security, the qualifications that would be required are so extensive that a priority opinion would be of very limited value to the opinion recipient.

U.C.C. Priority Opinions with respect to instruments, chattel paper, or certificated securities in which a security interest is perfected by possession, delivery, or control also are of limited value, except in addressing the priority of a security interest perfected by possession, delivery, or control over a security interest perfected solely by another method.[185] Nevertheless, the Committee recognizes that in this situation a U.C.C. Priority Opinion may be given that sometimes will be

181. An opinion generally does not cover the effect of post-closing changes in facts. *See infra* § 5.4(a); *see also 1998 TriBar Report, supra* note 1, § 1.2(b), at 597; *Principles, supra* note 16, § IV.

182. Because a Filing Priority Opinion relates to specific financing statements and search reports, it is given as of the time through which those reports are complete.

183. For example, deposit accounts, letter-of-credit rights, and money. *See* U.C.C. §§ 9-312(b)(1), 9-312(b)(2), 9-312(b)(3).

184. *See id.*. §§ 3-303, 5-116, 7-502, 8-303, 8-502, 8-510, 9-328(1), (5), 9-329(1), 9-330(a), (b), (d), 9-331. Note that the perfection of a security interest in goods by possession does not give a secured party priority over a security interest in the goods perfected by the prior filing of a financing statement.

185. Under revised Article 9 the opinion preparers do not have to rely on the holder-in-due-course rules of Article 3, U.C.C. section 3-305 to give an opinion on the priority of a security interest in instruments perfected by possession over other security interests in the instruments perfected by a method other than possession. *See id.* § 9-330(d). The definition of "instrument" in Article 9 is broader than the definition in Article 3. *Compare id.* §§ 3-104(b), *with id.* 9-102(a)(47). This Article 9 priority opinion can be given concerning both negotiable and non-negotiable instruments. The opinion under Article 9 does not mean that the secured party's security interest in a negotiable instrument would be free of adverse claims. An opinion that a security interest in a negotiable instrument is free of claims to the instrument would be rendered under Article 3 and require that the secured party attain holder-in-due-course status. *See id.* § 3-305. *See generally infra* §§ 8.1, 8.3. For a discussion of priority opinions when the collateral is a certificated security, see *infra* §§ 8.2-.4.

useful to an opinion recipient.[186] Under revised Article 9, a secured party that takes possession of an instrument and satisfies certain other requirements has priority over a secured party that has perfected its security interest solely by a method other than possession.[187] To obtain priority, the secured party with possession must (i) give value, and (ii) take possession of the instrument in good faith without knowledge that the grant of the security interest violates the rights of a prior secured party. Value is rarely an issue.[188] As for the second requirement, the opinion preparers may assume, without stating, the absence of the required knowledge on the part of the opinion recipient. An assumption regarding the opinion recipient's good faith is implicit in all opinions.[189]

5.4 Inherent or Otherwise Unnecessary Qualifications to Perfection and Priority Opinions

(a) Subsequent events

Except to the extent discussed below[190] concerning after-acquired collateral and proceeds, opinion givers have no obligation when giving U.C.C. opinions to address the possible effect of subsequent changes in the facts.[191]

The passage of time and changes in facts after the date of a perfection opinion can result in the partial or complete loss of perfection unless additional steps are taken.[192] These steps include:

(i) filing of proper continuation statements;[193]
(ii) filings or other actions required with respect to proceeds of collateral;[194]
(iii) filings required within four months of the change of the name of the debtor;[195]
(iv) filings required within one year if the collateral is transferred to a person located in another jurisdiction;[196]
(v) filings required within four months if the debtor changes its location;[197] and

186. This discussion is applicable only in the context of an instrument. U.C.C. § 9-330(d). A similar analysis would apply to a possessory security interest in tangible chattel paper (U.C.C.§ 9-330(a), (b)) or to a certificated security that has been delivered to the secured party (U.C.C. § 9-328(1)). A U.C.C. Priority Opinion generally would require extensive qualifications and exceptions and would not be useful to the opinion recipient.
187. U.C.C. § 9-330(d).
188. *See supra* text accompanying § 3.3(b).
189. *1998 TriBar Report, supra* note 1, § 3.3.4, at 625 (assumption regarding opinion recipient's good faith). *See generally* U.C.C. § 9-331 cmt. 5.
190. *See infra* §§ 7.1, 7.2.
191. *See supra* note 181.
192. *See generally* Steven O. Weise & Susan R. Goldfarb, *The Dog Ate My Perfection—What Can Go Wrong Post-Closing*, 35 UCC L.J. 1 (Winter 2002–2003).
193. U.C.C. § 9-515(c).
194. U.C.C. § 9-315(d).
195. *Id.* § 9-507(c).
196. *Id.* § 9-316(a)(3).
197. *Id.* § 9-316(a)(2).

(vi) filings that may be required if the debtor transfers all or substantially all of its assets to another person or merges into or otherwise combines with another organization.[198]

Because these U.C.C. requirements for subsequent filings generally involve changes in facts that occur after the date of the opinion letter, the opinion does not cover them and express reference to them in the opinion letter is not necessary.

Changes in facts after the date of the opinion letter (e.g., failure of the secured party (directly or through a third party) to maintain possession of collateral (or the occurrence of events that cause collateral to cease to be subject to an effective control agreement) can also adversely affect perfection by possession or control. The opinion does not require an express assumption that no change will occur in the underlying factual basis for perfection by possession or control. Nor does the opinion have to state that:

(i) other creditors or purchasers might gain priority by subsequently obtaining possession, delivery, or control when the opinion recipient has perfected its security interest solely by the filing of a financing statement or by "automatic" perfection;[199] or
(ii) certain security interests subsequently perfected by filing (e.g. a purchase money security interest) may have priority.[200]

An opinion does not have to assume expressly that the factual requirements for continued perfection or priority will continue to be satisfied.[201]

(b) Other interests

A Filing Priority Opinion is limited to the priority of a security interest perfected by a secured party[202] only by the filing of a financing statement over other security interests perfected only by the filing of a financing statement. Hence, a Filing Priority Opinion does not require many of the qualifications that would be used in a U.C.C. Priority Opinion. The rules of priority contained in Article 9 that are based on information obtained from the Article 9 filing system cover *only* a "secured party." Thus, the opinion does not cover the interest of, and does not require

198. *Id.* § 9-508.

199. Persons who subsequently may obtain possession, delivery or control and thereby defeat the priority of the secured party if the secured party did not have possession, delivery or control include: (i) subsequent purchasers of chattel paper or instruments, U.C.C. § 9-330; (ii) holders in due course of instruments (as defined in Article 3, i.e, negotiable instruments) and protected purchasers of securities (as defined in Article 8), U.C.C. §§ 3-305, 8-303, 9-331; (iii) collecting banks, U.C.C. § 4-210; (iv) good faith purchasers of instruments for value without notice that the purchase violates the secured party's rights, U.C.C. § 9-330(d); (v) secured parties who take delivery of certificated securities, U.C.C. § 9-328(5); and (vi) secured parties who obtain control of investment property, U.C.C. § 9-328(1).

200. *Id.* § 9-324.

201. Proceeds of collateral and after-acquired property present special concerns. *See infra* §§ 7.1, 7.2.

202. A "secured party" generally is a person who holds a "security interest" that has been "created or provided for" under a security agreement. U.C.C. § 9-102(a)(72); *see also supra* note 7.

an exception for priority over the interest of, a person who is not a "secured party."[203] These other persons, who in some instances may have priority, include persons who:

(i) are neither creditors of the debtor nor subsequent buyers of the collateral from the debtor (except when Article 9 applies to a sale of collateral);[204] or
(ii) obtain superior rights under law other than the U.C.C.[205]

An exception is also unnecessary for persons who may obtain priority over a secured party based solely upon the secured party's agreement.[206] For example, if a secured party executes and delivers a subordination agreement or other intercreditor agreement (either before or after the delivery of the opinion), other persons may obtain rights in the collateral senior to the secured party's rights.[207]

6. References to Financing Statement and Search Reports in Opinion Letters

6.1 Description of Financing Statement

Because of the importance to a perfection opinion of the financing statement in favor of the secured party (where perfection is based on filing), opinion letters typically specify:

203. Some states provide for a filing in the filing office by a "lien creditor." *See, e.g.*, Cal. Civ. Proc. Code §§ 697.510–.670 (West 1987 & Supp. 2003); *see also* U.C.C. § 9-102(a)(52) (definition of lien creditor). If a Filing Priority Opinion is given and if those interests appear in the search report, the opinion giver should disclose these interests even though they are not "security interests." *See supra* note 19.

204. Persons who may obtain superior rights in the collateral, but whose rights are not within the scope of a priority opinion because they are neither creditors of the debtor nor subsequent purchasers of the collateral, include: (i) existing or future "true" lessees (in the ordinary course of business) of goods, U.C.C. § 9-321(c); (ii) existing or certain future (non-exclusive) licensees (in the ordinary course of business) of general intangibles, U.C.C. § 9-321(b); (iii) beneficiaries of implied or constructive trusts to the extent the collateral is (or is deemed to be) the property of those trusts; (iv) certain persons claiming rights of set-off or recoupment against certain types of collateral, U.C.C. §§ 9-340, 9-406(a); (v) persons whose liens or other interests (including ownership) were granted by persons other than the debtor (including prior owners of the collateral), U.C.C. § 9-325; (vi) certain statutory possessory liens, U.C.C. §§ 7-209, 9-333; and (vii) persons having rights of resale and stoppage with respect to goods under U.C.C. Article 2. U.C.C. §§ 2-403(1), 9-110 cmt. 5.

205. For example, unless otherwise separately addressed in the opinion letter, the opinion preparers need not identify other liens (whether common law or statutory, such as federal tax liens or ERISA liens) under which persons in some circumstances may take priority over a perfected U.C.C. security interest. For example, a federal tax lien filing will occur in the state of the debtor's principal executive office (for corporations and partnerships), which may not be the same state as the debtor's location for purposes of Article 9. I.R.C. § 6323(f)(2) (2003). In addition, when former Article 9 was in effect, courts found a federal tax lien filing effective even if it did not provide the debtor's exact name, if the name in the federal tax lien filing was not "seriously misleading" under rules similar to those applied under former U.C.C. section 9-402(8). *See, e.g.*, Allstate Financial Corp v. United States, 109 F.3d 1331 (8th Cir. 1997) (holding Federal tax lien filing was not seriously misleading).

206. *See* U.C.C. §§ 9-207 cmts. 5, 6, 9-315(a)(1) (secured party may authorize debtor to dispose of collateral free of the security interest); *Id.* § 9-339 (secured party may agree to subordinate its security interest in the collateral).

207. *Id.* § 9-339.

(i) the exact names of the debtor and secured party as they appear on the financing statement;[208]

(ii) the particular filing office where the financing statement is or will be filed; and

(iii) the filing status of the financing statement reviewed (e.g., unfiled, a timed-stamped copy, or a copy from the filing office acknowledging its acceptance of the filing).[209]

Sometimes an opinion letter does not refer to any particular financing statement or identify adequately the financing statement actually reviewed. In these situations the opinion recipient justifiably may assume that the opinion preparers reviewed[210] the financing statement used in the transaction. If the opinion letter does not identify the financing statement, the opinion recipient is entitled, absent knowledge to the contrary,[211] to assume that the opinion is based on the financing statement that is being used in the transaction and its filed or unfiled status as of the date of the opinion letter.[212]

208. Some opinions refer instead to a copy of the financing statement attached to the opinion letter.

209. U.C.C. § 9-516(a). If the opinion is based on an unfiled financing statement or a time-stamped financing statement, the opinion letter should make clear that an acknowledgement copy was not reviewed. That can be done by describing the U.C.C. financing statement as an "unfiled copy" or a "time-stamped copy" or, alternatively, by making express assumptions or stating conditions with respect to filing. For example, the perfection opinion could state: "Upon the filing of the Financing Statement in the Filing Office, the Secured Party will have a perfected security interest in . . . ." *See also supra* note 136 (as to when an opinion giver should *not* use language such as "upon filing" with respect to an unfiled financing statement.). *See also* note 134 on the meaning of "filing."

210. The review would confirm that the information in the financing statement is not substantively inconsistent with the corresponding information in the security agreement (e.g., the name of the debtor and the secured party, and the description of the collateral in the security agreement and the indication of the collateral in the financing statement). Secured parties sometimes draft the indication of collateral in the financing statement more broadly than the description in the security agreement. This does not expand the collateral to which the security interest attaches under the security agreement (and therefore the collateral in which the security interest can be perfected). For example, if the granting clause in the security agreement adequately identifies as collateral "copying machines and computers (each used in the debtor's business)," the indication of the collateral in a financing statement would be sufficient if it referred to "all equipment." U.C.C. §§ 9-102(a)(33), 9-108(b)(3), 9-504(1). A financing statement that indicates a broader set of collateral than that described in the security agreement is effective and perfects a security interest *to the extent* the collateral indicated in the financing statement is the same as the collateral described in the security agreement. *Id.* § 9-504 cmt. 2. The financing statement would not perfect a security interest in more than the copying machines and computers, even if the debtor authorized the filing with the broader description. Note that a secured party may file a financing statement indicating particular collateral only if the secured party has been "authorized" to do so. *Id.* §§9-509 cmt. 3, 9-510(a). Accordingly, if an indication of collateral in a financing statement includes collateral as to which the debtor did *not* authorize the secured party to file a financing statement, the financing statement is (to that extent) ineffective to perfect a security interest in that collateral. *Id.* § 9-510(a) cmt. 2, ex. 1.

211. *Principles, supra* note 16, § I.E, at 832.

212. If the financing statement is unfiled, the opinion recipient understandably may be concerned that the filing office may reject the financing statement. Filing officers may reject a financing statement that has the three items of information required by U.C.C. section 9-502(a) only for the limited reasons stated in U.C.C. section 9-516(b) and (d). If the only U.C.C. financing statement relied on is one that might be rejected later (i.e., it is unfiled or time-stamped), leaving the secured party to rely on U.C.C. section 9-516(d) to assert that the financing statement is "effective," prudence suggests that the status of the financing statement actually reviewed should be disclosed in the opinion letter. *See supra* note

6.2 Need to Identify Search Reports

Opinion letters that contain a Filing Priority Opinion typically describe the U.C.C. search reports that form the basis of the Filing Priority Opinion. Describing those reports is important because, as to factual matters, the opinion is limited by its terms to a review of *only* the information disclosed in them.

The description should specify:

(i) the person or entity conducting the search;[213]
(ii) the date of the report;[214]
(iii) the name of the debtor[215] identified in the report; and
(iv) the effective or "through date" (and, if available, time of day) of the search.[216]

6.3 No Need to State Qualifications as to Accuracy of Search Reports

Opinion givers have understandably been concerned that the U.C.C. search reports on which an opinion is based may be inaccurate, whether through mis-indexing or other mistake by the filing officer.[217] The opinion does not cover that risk.[218] Opinion preparers are entitled to rely, without verification, on the factual

126 A filer whose financing statement is wrongfully rejected has a perfected security interest under U.C.C. § 9-516(a), which provides in part as follows: "[C]ommunication of a record to the filing office and tender of the filing fee . . . constitutes filing [under Article 9 of the U.C.C.]." *Id.* § 9-516(a). The secured party will have a perfected security interest, but the filing office will not have a record of the financing statement in its records and the financing statement therefore will not appear on a U.C.C. search report. In this case, the secured party will not have priority against another, subsequent, secured party that obtains and perfects a security interest in the same collateral in reasonable reliance on the absence from the filing office records of the wrongfully-rejected financing statement. *Id.* § 9-516(d) cmt. 3. The opinion does not cover the accuracy of the information referred to in U.C.C. § 9-516(b)(5) nor does it cover the risk that any of this information in incorrect. *See supra* note 136.

213. In the illustrative language above, this would be included in the definition of U.C.C. Search Report.

214. In the illustrative language above, this would be included in the definition of U.C.C. Search Report.

215. *See supra* notes 127, 168.

216. In the Illustrative Security Interest Opinion, the search report is dated July 28 but refers only to financing statements on file in the particular filing office as of a stated time on July 1. If the opinion recipient did not file its financing statement until the date of the closing (August 1) and if a competing U.C.C. financing statement were filed during the thirty-one day "gap" between the effective date of the search ("effective date" or "through date") and the closing, the security interest of the competing creditor would rank prior to the security interest of the opinion recipient even if the opinion recipient closed its transaction first. U.C.C. § 9-322(a)(1), 9-322 cmt. 4, ex. 1. As a result, the through date is of great importance to the opinion recipient. A Filing Priority Opinion need not include a qualification with respect to possible "gap" filers because a Filing Priority Opinion is limited, by its terms, to secured parties identified in the search reports described in the opinion. *See supra* note 169.

217. A private person conducting the search may also make a mistake. *See* Puget Sound v. Unisearch, 47 P.3d 940 (Wash. 2002) (private search firm that reported incorrect information in a U.C.C. financing statement search report may enforce limitation-of-liability term of its agreement with its customer).

218. A secured party whose properly-filed financing statement is accepted, but mis-indexed, will have priority over a secured party that perfects its security interest by the subsequent filing of a financing statement unless the other secured party can establish its priority on a different basis. U.C.C. § 9-517.

accuracy of certificates of public officers, such as filing officers[219] and on written reports of third parties in the business of preparing U.C.C. search reports.[220]

A priority opinion based on search reports assumes, without stating,[221] the accuracy and completeness of those reports. Therefore, an opinion need not point out the possibility that prior security interests have erroneously been omitted from the search report, that mistakes were made by public filing officers, or that public records are incomplete.[222]

The opinion also need not identify priority risks arising from still-effective financing statements filed:

(i) using prior names of the debtor;[223]
(ii) when the debtor was located in a different jurisdiction;[224]
(iii) against a prior owner of collateral that has transferred the collateral to the debtor subject to a perfected security interest;[225] or
(iv) naming an "original debtor" for whose obligations the debtor, as a "new debtor," has become bound.[226]

219. *1998 TriBar Report, supra* note 1, § 2.2.1(a), at 611 & n. 43.

220. The filing office must make available to the public information on all records filed with the filing office. U.C.C. § 9-523(c).

221. Sometimes a member of the opinion giver's staff or a person who is not a search professional conducts a search (e.g., an on-line computer search of a data base) that does not use the filing office's standard search logic. An opinion letter should point out expressly if either of these types of searches forms the basis of a priority opinion, thus putting the opinion recipient on notice that the U.C.C. Search Report might not identify all filings that an official search might have identified.

222. This is so even though, under U.C.C. section 9-517, another secured creditor will have priority if its financing statement was accepted for filing by the filing officer, but was lost, never indexed, or improperly indexed by the filing officer and therefore did not appear on the search report. Under U.C.C. section 9-516(d), however, another secured creditor who presented a sufficient financing statement for filing and tendered the correct filing fee, but whose financing statement the filing office wrongfully refused to accept and thus does not appear on the search report, will be perfected, but junior to another secured party who reasonably relies on the absence of the wrongfully-rejected financing statement from the public record. *See supra* note 212.

223. Unless otherwise expressly stated, the priority opinion is based solely on a search under the debtor's current correct name, determined as provided in U.C.C. section 9-503(a), and does not need to exclude security interests perfected by the filing of a financing statement against the debtor using a name of the debtor other than the current correct name. When a debtor changes its name, a financing statement with the prior name remains effective to perfect a security interest in collateral in which the debtor had rights on the date of the name change and in collateral in which the debtor acquires rights within the following four months. U.C.C. § 9-507(c)(1). *See supra* note 167.

224. Filings made in the appropriate state under revised Article 9 on the basis of facts that were correct when the filing was made will remain effective for specified periods following a change in the applicable facts. U.C.C. section 9-316(a)(2) provides that a financing statement filed in the jurisdiction where the debtor was located at the time of the filing (see U.C.C. § 9-307) remains effective for up to four months after the change of the debtor's location to another jurisdiction (*e.g.*, a filing made in Pennsylvania against a general partnership with its chief executive office in Pennsylvania at the time of the filing will remain effective for up to four months after the partnership moves its chief executive office to New York). A debtor that is a registered organization is generally not able to change its location. A merger or other similar event is generally governed by the rules described in note 226.

225. A financing statement properly filed against a prior owner of collateral generally remains effective to perfect the security interest following the disposition. U.C.C. § 9-315(a)(1). There are exceptions to this rule. *See, e.g., id.* §§ 9-315(a)(1) (secured party authorizes disposition free of security interest), 9-316(a)(3) (transfer of collateral to a person located in another jurisdiction), 9-320 (transfer of goods to a buyer in ordinary course of business), 9-321 (non-exclusive license of general intangible and lease of goods in ordinary course of business).

226. If the debtor is a successor to a prior owner of collateral (e.g., a successor by merger, incor-

7. Property Not in Existence on the Date the Opinion is Delivered

Security agreements typically cover after-acquired property and proceeds—in both cases collateral not in existence on the date of the opinion is delivered.[227] Although an opinion ordinarily speaks only as of its date,[228] as a matter of customary practice the opinion is generally understood to cover after-acquired collateral and, to a limited extent, proceeds.

7.1 After-Acquired Property

(a) Attachment opinion is presumed given

The creation or attachment opinion is understood to cover after-acquired collateral[229] if after-acquired collateral is included[230] in the collateral description.[231]

poration of a sole proprietorship, or similar transaction), security interests created by the predecessor debtor in that collateral and perfected by the filing of a financing statement may continue to be perfected by filings made against the predecessor debtor. *Id.* §§ 9-203(d)–(e), 9-508. If a "new debtor," as defined in U.C.C. section 9-102(a)(56), "becomes bound" as debtor by a security agreement entered into by another person, the agreement generally will create a security interest with respect to existing and after-acquired property of the new debtor to the extent the property is described in the agreement and another agreement is not necessary to make a security interest in the property enforceable. *See id.* §§ 9-203(d)–(e), 9-203 cmt. 7, 9-508 cmts. 2, 3. Different rules apply to a secured party of a transferor whose transferee does not become bound by the transferor's security agreement. *See supra* note 224. U.C.C. § 9-508(a) provides that a filing against the original debtor, as defined in U.C.C. § 9-102(a)(60), generally is effective to perfect a security interest in collateral that the new debtor has at the time it becomes bound by the original debtor's security agreement and collateral that it acquires after the new debtor becomes bound. *See* U.C.C. §§ 9-316(a)(3) cmt. 2, ex. 5, 9-508 cmt. 4 . This general rule is subject to significant limitations. For example, if the original debtor and the new debtor are located in different jurisdictions, a filing against the original debtor would not be effective to perfect a security interest in collateral that the new debtor has acquired from a person other than the original debtor or acquires in the future, and the secured party must file a financing statement in the appropriate jurisdiction against the new debtor to perfect its security interest in that collateral. *See id.* § 9-508, cmt. 4. U.C.C. section 9-508 does not apply to collateral transferred by the original debtor to the new debtor. For that collateral the filing against the original debtor continues to be effective until it lapses or perfection is lost for another reason. *Id.* § 9-508(c) cmt. 5; *see id.* §§ 9-316, 9-507(a). In some circumstances, the entity formed under the law of one state may "convert" into an entity under the law of another state and continue to be the "same" entity. *See, e.g.*, Del. Code Ann. tit. 6, § 18-214(g) (1999); Cal. Corp. Code § 17540.9(a) (West). In that circumstance, the rules applicable to a debtor's change in location would apply because the debtor's identity has not changed. *See supra* note 224.

227. Because opinions often use terms defined in the security agreement, such as "Collateral," "Trust Estate," "Stock," or "Pledged Securities," opinion givers should be mindful that the defined terms may include after-acquired property or proceeds.

228. *See supra* § 5.4(a).

229. Article 9 expressly permits a security agreement to provide for a security interest in after-acquired collateral. U.C.C. § 9-204(a). Whether a security agreement covers after-acquired collateral is a matter of interpretation of the security agreement under contract law. *Id.* § 9-108 cmt. 3. A security interest cannot attach to after-acquired consumer goods in most circumstances and never attaches to an after-acquired commercial tort claim. *Id.* § 9-204(b). Bankruptcy can affect the attachment of a security interest to after-acquired property acquired after the commencement of the bankruptcy case. *See, e.g.*, Bankruptcy Code, 11 U.S.C. § 552 (2000). These limitations on attachment are not covered by the opinion.

230. The opinion does not cover whether a secured party should have included an after-acquired collateral clause in a security agreement.

231. A financing statement does not have to refer to after-acquired property of the type indicated in

It is understood that the security interest will not attach to the after-acquired collateral until the debtor has acquired rights or the power to transfer rights in the after-acquired collateral.[232]

(b) Perfection opinion and priority opinion (when given) are presumed given as to after-acquired collateral in which security interest is perfected by filing

For collateral in which a security interest is perfected by filing, if the security agreement refers to after-acquired collateral,[233] a filing perfection opinion is understood to cover not only collateral existing on the date of the opinion, but also the after-acquired collateral when the security interest later attaches to the collateral. This is so because the factual predicates for the perfection opinion on existing filing collateral—a properly-drafted and authenticated security agreement and properly-completed and filed U.C.C. financing statements—also provide the basis for an opinion on the creation, perfection, and, when given, priority of a security interest in after-acquired collateral of the same type perfected by the filing of the financing statement.[234] Immediately upon the acquisition by the debtor of "rights," or the "power to transfer rights," in the collateral, the security interest will attach to those interests in the collateral and will then be perfected.[235] If an opinion giver does not intend to provide an opinion on after-acquired property, the opinion giver should include an express statement to that effect in the opinion letter.[236]

When perfection occurs through the filing of a financing statement, the delay in attachment of the security interest to the after-acquired property generally has no effect on priority under Article 9,[237] even though attachment (and therefore perfection) will not occur until the debtor acquires rights in (or the power to transfer rights in) the after-acquired property.

Although often less than ideal from a grammatical standpoint, the filing perfection opinion is generally understood to cover after-acquired property whether the opinion speaks in the past, present, or future tense. For example, when the collat-

the financing statement to perfect a security interest in the after-acquired property of that type if the security agreement creates a security interest in the after-acquired property. U.C.C. § 9-502 cmt. 2.

232. The opinion need not state expressly that attachment cannot occur until the debtor acquires rights or the ability to transfer rights in the collateral. *See id.* § 9-203(b)(2); *see also supra* § 3.3(a).

233. If the security agreement does not create a security interest in after-acquired property, no security interest in the after-acquired property can be perfected. U.C.C. § 9-308(a).

234. *Id.* §§ 9-204(a) (creation), 9-308(a) (perfection), 9-322(a)(1) (priority). The same is true for certain security interests perfected by control. *Id.* §§ 9-203(b)(3)(D), 9-312(b)(1), (2), 9-314(a), 9-328(1). *See infra* § 8.

235. *See* U.C.C. §§ 9-203(b)(2) (requirement that debtor has rights in the collateral), 9-204(a) (creation of a security interest in after-acquired property), 9-308(a) (requirements for perfection).

236. A security interest does not attach to an after-acquired consumer goods or commercial tort claims, and the opinion does not cover that issue. *See supra* note 229.

237. *See* U.C.C. § 9-322(a)(1) (generally priority over other security interests dates from *earlier* of filing or perfection).

eral includes after-acquired property, an opinion that the security interest in the collateral "was perfected" upon the filing of a financing statement would be understood to cover the after-acquired property. To the extent the opinion expressly refers to, or is understood to cover, the after-acquired property, it means that the security interest will attach (and will be perfected) only when the debtor has acquired rights (or the power to transfer rights in) the after-acquired property.[238]

(c) No perfection opinion or priority opinion (when given) is presumed given as to after-acquired collateral in which security interest is perfected by possession

The result is different for an opinion based on perfection by possession of the collateral. Neither a perfection opinion nor a priority opinion addresses after-acquired property of this type because the predicate for perfection *and* priority—possession—does not exist on the date of the opinion.[239]

(d) Perfection opinion and priority opinion (when given) are presumed as to certain after-acquired collateral in which security interest is perfected by control

For a securities account (and for security entitlements with respect to financial assets credited to the securities account[240]) in which a secured party has perfected its security interest by obtaining "control,"[241] a secured party that "obtain[s] control" of a securities account before another secured party "obtain[s] control" has priority as to after-acquired, as well as existing, collateral.[242] When the debtor later obtains rights in the after-acquired collateral (i.e., security entitlements with respect to financial assets later credited to the securities account), the secured party's priority would ordinarily relate back to the completion of the appropriate acts necessary to "obtain control." Thus, when a secured party obtains control of a securities account and the debtor later acquires additional security entitlements

238. The opinion need not state expressly that attachment (and therefore perfection) cannot occur until the debtor acquires rights or the power to transfer rights, in the collateral. *See id.* § 9-203(b)(2); *see also supra* § 3.3(c).

239. Perfection as to after-acquired property would not occur until the debtor acquired rights in the property *and* the secured party (directly or through a third party) acquired possession. *Id.* § 9-308(a); *see supra* § 3.3 (c). Priority of a security interest perfected by possession would date from time of possession (assuming the security interest has attached to the collateral). *See* U.C.C. § 9-322(a)(1). The same is true for perfection of a security interest in a certificated security by delivery or control. *Id.* § 9-328(5). Because either means of perfection of a security interest in a certificated security requires delivery of the security, an opinion is not presumed given as to perfection by delivery or control as to after-acquired certificated securities. *See id.* § 8-106(a)–(b) (defining control of certificated security). A perfection opinion could be given in these circumstances by stating that "upon the secured party's [taking possession][obtaining delivery][obtaining control] of the [collateral], the security interest in the [collateral] will be perfected."

240. *See infra* note 296.

241. Priority is also based on obtaining control for certain types of collateral where control is a (or the only) method of perfecting a security interest. The method of obtaining control varies according to the type of collateral. *Id.* §§ 9-104 to -107.

242. *See id.* §§ 9-328 cmt. 5, ex. 6; 9-329(2). *But see infra* note 311.

based on the crediting of additional financial assets to the account,[243] the secured party's priority depends on when the secured party obtained control of the securities account. A perfection opinion as to a securities account in which a security interest is perfected by control is understood as a matter of customary practice to cover after-acquired collateral that consists of security entitlements relating to financial assets later credited to that securities account.[244]

7.2 Proceeds of Collateral

A security interest opinion typically covers proceeds only to a very limited extent. Proceeds do not exist on the date of the opinion. Under U.C.C. section 9-102(a)(64), "'[p]roceeds' . . . means (A) whatever is acquired upon the sale, lease, license, exchange, collection or other disposition of collateral. . . ." U.C.C. sections 9-203(f) and 9-315(a)(2) provide that a security interest in collateral attaches to identifiable proceeds[245] of the collateral. While those sections provide for the continued attachment of the security interest, U.C.C. section 9-315(c) provides further that the security interest in proceeds is perfected if the secured party's security interest in the original collateral was perfected. U.C.C. section 9-315(d), however, provides that perfection lapses after 20 days unless the proceeds are "identifiable" cash proceeds or certain other kinds of proceeds, although in some circumstances further action must be taken before the end of the 20 day period to maintain perfection.[246] While U.C.C. section 9-203 provides for the continuation of a security interest in identifiable proceeds, other provisions of U.C.C. section 9-315 place significant restrictions on this security interest, affecting nearly every aspect of the security interest opinion. Since the limitations imposed by section 9-315 are well understood, the security interest opinion does not cover and does not have to state that it is limited by U.C.C. section 9-315.

For proceeds, security interest opinions are interpreted as a matter of customary practice as follows:

(i) they do not cover the application of U.C.C. sections 9-203 and 9-315 (and, accordingly, do not address the requirement that such proceeds be identifiable);
(ii) if qualified by a U.C.C. Scope Limitation, they only cover proceeds subject to Article 9 of the U.C.C.; and
(iii) they only cover the perfection or priority of the secured party's interest in the proceeds, if (i) the perfection and priority sections of the opinion

243. *See* U.C.C. § 8-501(a) (defining securities account).

244. For other types of collateral in which a security interest may be perfected by control (such as deposit accounts), the opinion preparers should examine the relevant priority rules. *See id.* §§ 9-327 to -329.

245. Section 9-315(a)(2) establishes the limitation that a security interest continues only in "identifiable" proceeds, and § 9-315(b) addresses when commingled proceeds (including cash proceeds) will be identifiable.

246. U.C.C. § 9-315(a)(2), (c)–(e).

expressly refer to proceeds, or (ii) the proceeds are after-acquired property of the same type as original collateral[247] covered by the perfection opinion and any priority opinion.[248]

Sometimes a secured party requests an opinion that it will be in the same position as to proceeds regardless of whether the debtor sells, leases, licenses, exchanges, collects, or otherwise disposes of the original collateral. Such an opinion is inappropriate because it depends on facts—whether the proceeds will be "identifiable" or the security interest in the proceeds will be perfected or have first priority—that cannot be determined at the time the opinion is delivered. For example, if the proceeds are identifiable cash proceeds in the form of a check and the check is in the possession of a holder in due course under U.C.C. Article 3, the holder in due course will take free of the secured party's security interest in the check as proceeds.[249]

8. "Priority" Opinions on Certificated Securities, Security Entitlements, and Securities Accounts

When the collateral is investment property[250] additional statutory rules apply. Although investment property can take many forms,[251] this *Report* is limited to "priority" opinions relating to security interests in certificated securities, security entitlements, and securities accounts.[252] These rules are complex and (as discussed below) different sets of "priority" rules apply to:

(i) securities (whether certificated or uncertificated); and
(ii) security entitlements and security accounts.

247. *See supra* note 110 (as to the meaning of "original collateral").

248. Although a perfection or priority opinion typically covers "proceeds" in only a limited way, particular collateral that is "proceeds" of original collateral may be covered by the opinion because the collateral that is proceeds may also be after-acquired property that is described as original collateral, depending on the terms of the security agreement. If the security agreement and financing statement describe or indicate as original collateral the property that is the proceeds, the opinion covers that property in the sense that it is original collateral. For example, assume the collateral described in the security agreement and indicated in the financing statement includes all of Farmer Brown's now existing and after-acquired cows and chickens. The opinion giver delivers perfection opinions covering both cows and chickens based on the filing of a financing statement describing both "cows" and "chickens." The fact that Farmer Brown thereafter trades two cows for a truckload of chickens (and the chickens therefore are "proceeds" of the cows) does not mean that no opinion was given with respect to the perfection of the security interest in the newly-acquired chickens as original collateral. In this example, the chickens were not only "proceeds" of the cows, but also after-acquired property (because the security agreement described after-acquired "chickens" as original collateral). Although no opinion was given with respect to the perfection of the security interest in newly-acquired chickens as "proceeds," an opinion was given concerning the perfection of the security interest in newly-acquired chickens as after-acquired original collateral.

249. U.C.C. §§ 3-305, 3-306, 9-331(a). Other persons that take possession of the check may also have priority over the secured party. *Id.* § 9-330(d).

250. *See id.* § 9-102(a)(49) (definition of "investment property").

251. E.g., certificated securities, uncertificated securities, securities accounts, or security entitlements (including security entitlements with respect to federal book-entry securities).

252. The use of other kinds of investment property (such as commodity contracts and commodity accounts) as collateral is less common and beyond the scope of this *Report*.

8.1 ARTICLE 8 PROTECTED PURCHASER OPINIONS[253]

(a) Elements of protected purchaser opinions

Article 8 accords special status to a "protected purchaser" of a certificated[254] security.[255] An opinion on the protected purchaser status of a secured party under Article 8 is an alternative[256] to a "priority" opinion under Article 9.

The term "purchaser" includes a person who obtains a security interest in property.[257] Protected purchaser status is thus available to secured parties as well as to owners of securities. Pursuant to U.C.C. section 8-303, a protected purchaser of a certificated security "takes free"[258] of any "adverse claim"[259] with respect to the

253. A similar approach can be taken for a priority opinion involving a negotiable instrument based on the holder-in-due-course rules of Article 3. U.C.C. §§ 3-305, 9-331(a). *See supra* note 185.

254. The protected purchaser rules also apply to an uncertificated security. *Id.* § 8-303. The definition of "control" is different, however, for an uncertificated security. *Compare id.* § 8-106(a), (b), *with id.* § 8-106(c). The "protected purchaser" rules do not apply to a purchase of (including a security interest in) a *security entitlement*. Similar, but distinct, rules concerning adverse claims apply to some purchasers of security entitlements. *See id.* §§ 8-502, 8-510; *see infra* § 8.3.

255. "Certificated security" is defined in U.C.C. § 8-102(a)(4). The status of collateral as a "certificated security" may be addressed by examining the certificate and the organizational documents of the issuer to determine that the security is represented by the certificate. For example, the certificate may recite that it is issued to evidence an entry on the records of the issuer (and does not represent the security). The determination of whether an interest in an entity (whether or not certificated) is in fact a "security" for purposes of Articles 8 and 9 is often straightforward, but may involve a complex factual analysis that opinion preparers ordinarily cannot be expected to make. The analysis of whether an interest is a "security" under other law, such as federal securities law, is generally not relevant to the analysis for purposes of Article 8 and Article 9. *See generally* U.C.C. § 8-102(d). Ordinarily an interest in a limited liability company or a partnership is not a "security." *Id.* § 8-103(c). The opinion preparers may assume, without stating, that a document or interest that appears on its face to be a "security" is a "security." Under U.C.C. definitions, debt instruments may be "securities" or "instruments." *Id.* §§ 3-104, 8-102(b)(15) (definition of security), 9-102(a)(47) (definition of instrument). For purposes of Article 9, however, a debt instrument cannot be both. *Id.* § 9-102(a)(47).

256. The alternatives are not identical. *See infra* § 8.3.

257. U.C.C. §§ 1-201(33). *See also id.* § 1-201(b)(30) (revised). The definition of "purchaser" is based on the definition of "purchase" in U.C.C. §§ 1-201(32) and 1-201(b)(29) (revised).

258. Although U.C.C. section 8-303 speaks in terms of a "protected purchaser" (which may include a secured party) "taking free" of adverse claims to (including another security interest in the same security, a secured party that obtains "protected purchaser" status does not "take free" of a previously-acquired security interest in the security. Rather that secured party obtains only a senior security interest in the certificated or uncertificated security, the other security interest remains attached to the security with junior priority, and the other secured party retains its status as such. *Id.* § 9-331 cmt. 2. If the secured party later forecloses its security interest pursuant to part 6 of Article 9, the foreclosure sale may have the effect of discharging the junior security interest. *Id.* § 9-617(a)(3). The purchase of a security by a *buyer* of the security who qualifies as a protected purchaser would "cut off" the security interest of a secured party that has previously acquired a security interest in the security. *Id.* § 9-331 cmt. 2. The opinion preparers may assume, without stating, that the opinion recipient (with its counsel) understands these distinctions. *See Guidelines, supra* note 16, § 1.7.

259. An adverse claim is "a claim that a claimant has a property interest in a financial asset and that it is a violation of the rights of the claimant for another person to hold, transfer or deal with the financial asset." U.C.C. § 8-102(a)(1) & cmt. 1. "Financial asset" includes a security. *Id.* § 8-102(a)(9). An "adverse claim" includes a security interest in favor of another. *Id.* § 8-102 cmt. 1. A secured party that has possession or control of collateral may grant a security interest in the collateral. *See id.* § 9-207(c)(3) cmts. 5, 6. Unless a secured party has agreed with the debtor that the secured party

security, including a claim that another person is the owner or has a property interest (including a security interest) in the security. Article 9 recognizes and defers to the rights of a protected purchaser under Article 8.[260]

The requirements of U.C.C. section 8-303[261] for becoming a protected purchaser of a certificated security are straightforward. The purchaser must:

(i) obtain control[262] of the certificated security;
(ii) give value;[263] and
(iii) not, at the time[264] control is obtained and value given, have notice[265] of any adverse claim[266] to the certificated security.[267]

To obtain control, the secured party must:

(i) if the certificated security is in bearer form, take delivery[268] of the certificated security;[269] or
(ii) if the certificated security is in registered form, take delivery of the certificated security and have the security either (a) registered in the name of

will not grant a security interest in investment property collateral provided by the debtor, if the secured party grants to a third party a security interest in that collateral, the first debtor's rights of redemption in the collateral do not constitute "adverse" claims. The third party's knowledge of those rights thus would not prevent the third party's security interest in the investment property collateral from being senior to such rights.

260. U.C.C. § 9-331(a). A similar provision applies to security entitlements. *Id.* § 9-331(b).

261. *Id.* §§ 8-110(a)(5), (b)(4), and (c) establish choice-of-law rules with respect to the assertion of adverse claims. Unless it does so expressly, a perfection opinion does not cover which state's law governs perfection. *See supra* text accompanying notes 59, 96. *See generally* APPENDIX B (choice-of-law).

262. The "control" necessary to establish protected purchaser status is the same "control" that is one of the ways to perfect the security interest in the certificated security. U.C.C. §§ 8-106, 9-106, 9-314(a); *see also supra* text accompanying § 4.3(c).

263. The "value" required for protected purchaser status is the same "value" required for attachment of the security interest. *See supra* § 3.3(b); *see also* U.C.C. §§ 1-201(44), 8-303 cmt. 2, 9-203(b)(1).

264. *See id.* § 8-303 cmt. 2.

265. "Notice of an adverse claim" for this purpose is defined in U.C.C. section 8-105. *Compare id.* § 8-105, *with id.* § 1-201(26), (27).

266. Notice of *any* adverse claim to a certificated security will disqualify the purchaser from being a protected purchaser as to *all* adverse claims to a certificated security. *Id.* § 8-303. A different rule applies when the collateral is a security entitlement. *See infra* text accompanying notes 299–304.

267. The good faith component for "*bona fide* purchaser" status under the former version of Article 8 has been dropped. *See* U.C.C. § 8-303 cmt. 4; *see also id.* § 8-302 (pre-revision).

268. *Id.* § 8-301(a). "Delivery" of a certificated security requires that the person taking delivery have possession of the certificate representing the certificated security (directly or through an appropriate third party). "Delivery" of a certificated security is sufficient to perfect a security interest in the certificated security, but is only one of the elements required for a secured party to qualify as a protected purchaser. *Id.* §§ 8-106(a)–(c), 9-313(a); *see supra* note 137. A "protected purchaser" opinion is based on an unstated assumption that the secured party (or its agent) will maintain continuous possession of the certificate representing the security in the same manner and at the same location. *See supra* text accompanying notes 199–200. "Delivery" of the certificated security does not require that the debtor indorse the certificated security to the secured party. *See infra* note 284. An indorsement may be necessary, however, for the secured party to obtain "control" of a certificated security. *Compare* U.C.C. § 8-301, *with* § 8-106(b)(1); *see infra* notes 272–75 and accompanying text.

269. U.C.C. § 8-106(a).

the secured party,[270] or (b) indorsed[271] to the secured party or in blank by an effective[272] indorsement[273] of the security.[274]

The opinion preparers can address the delivery, registration, and indorsement requirements by attending the closing (or otherwise witnessing delivery to the secured party), obtaining appropriate certificates from the debtor or others, relying on appropriate express or implied assumptions, expressing a conditional opinion, or some combination.[275]

Value for purposes of a protected purchaser opinion under Article 8 has the same meaning as it does for purposes of an attachment opinion under Article 9.[276]

The final element, lack of notice of adverse claims, however, requires additional analysis.

(b) Assumptions regarding notice

The secured party's lack of notice of adverse claims[277] is basic to the protected purchaser opinion and normally cannot be verified by the opinion preparers.[278] Moreover, the secured party by definition will neither be, nor be acting on behalf of, the opinion preparers' client. The opinion preparers, therefore, are permitted to rely on assumptions, whether stated or not, concerning the secured party's lack of notice of an adverse claim.[279]

270. If the certificated security is in the possession of a securities intermediary and is indorsed to the securities intermediary or in blank, then the collateral is a "security entitlement" and not a "security." *Id.* § 8-301(a)(2) & cmt. 2; *see infra* note 296.

271. The indorsement of a certificated security may be on the security itself or on a separate document (e.g., a stock power). *See* U.C.C. § 8-102(a)(11).

272. *Id.* Article 8 separates the meaning of "indorsement" from the effectiveness of the indorsement. *Id.* § 8-102(a)(11) cmt. 11. The facts necessary for an "effective indorsement," such as the authority of the person making the indorsement, are not ordinarily readily accessible to the opinion preparers. Thus, when a "protected purchaser" opinion depends on the existence of an effective indoresement, the opinion is based on assumptions regarding those facts, whether or not stated, and any reference in the opinion to an indorsement is understood to assume the "effectiveness" of the indorsement.

273. *Id.* § 8-107; *see also id.* § 8-303 cmt. 3.

274. *Id.* § 8-106(b).

275. The technical "delivery" requirements for the type of transfer necessary to establish protected purchaser status are set forth in U.C.C. section 8-301; *see also id.* § 8-301 cmt. 2. If the additional requirements to qualify for protected purchaser status are not met, the only opinion that could be given on the priority of the security interest would be an opinion on priority under Article 9. *See infra* § 8.2.

276. U.C.C. §§ 1-201(44), 8-102(c), 8-303, cmt. 2, 9-102(c); *see supra* § 3.3(b).

277. U.C.C. section 8-105 establishes whether a person has notice of an adverse claim.

278. The opinion preparers are not expected, for example, to make inquiry of the Securities Information Center or to determine whether the secured party has made that inquiry. The Securities Information Center is a national data bank established by the Securities and Exchange Commission to process reports and inquiries pertaining to missing, lost, counterfeit or stolen securities. *See* 11 C.F.R. § 240.17f–1; *see also* First Nat'l Bank v. Lewco Sec. Corp., 860 F.2d 1407, 7 U.C.C. Rep. Serv. 2d (Callaghan) 10 (7th Cir. 1988); Hollywood Nat. Bank v. IBM Corp., 38 Cal.App. 3d 607 (Cal. Ct. App. 1974). The definition of notice of an adverse claim, as applied to certain types of purchasers, includes information the purchaser would have obtained by inquiring of these sources. *See* U.C.C. § 8-105 cmt. 5.

279. The opinion preparers may not rely on an unreliable assumption. *See supra* note 19. For example, if an inspection of the stock certificate reveals an adverse claim, reliance on the assumption would not be appropriate. Similarly, a review of a U.C.C. filing search may show a filing covering the

(c) Qualifications

If the secured party is a protected purchaser,[280] the opinion preparers may render an opinion that the secured party acquired its interest "free of adverse claims,"[281] and no qualifications are required.[282]

As with other U.C.C. opinions, the opinion need not state expressly that it does not generally cover proceeds of (including distributions on) securities.[283]

8.2 Article 9 Priority Opinions on Certificated Securities

When perfection is based on delivery or control of a certificated security, an opinion giver may provide a "priority" opinion under Article 9 instead of a "protected purchaser" opinion under Article 8. A priority opinion addresses only competing security interests under Article 9 and not "adverse claims" generally.[284]

securities and give notice of an adverse claim. The existence of a filed, but unreviewed, financing statement does not give notice. U.C.C. § 8-105(e). Although notice of an adverse claim would prevent the secured party from obtaining its security interest free of any adverse claim, notice of an adverse claim would not prevent the secured party from obtaining priority by obtaining control of the certificated security. *See infra* note 288. Note that a different rule may apply if the collateral is an "instrument." U.C.C. § 9-330(d); *see supra* notes 187–89 and accompanying text.

280. *See supra* note 258 and accompanying text.

281. Opinions are sometimes requested that the secured party will acquire its security interest "free *and clear* of adverse claims." The "and clear" language does not appear in Article 8 and does not have a generally accepted meaning. It should not be used. If used, it adds nothing to the "free of adverse claims" language. See *supra* note 258 as to the meaning of "free of" in this context. The "free of adverse claims" language is not appropriate for a purchaser obtaining an interest in a security entitlement. U.C.C. § 8-502. *See infra* text accompanying note 288.

282. An opinion that the secured party acquired its security interest "free of adverse claims" addresses the secured party's rights at a particular point in time (i.e., when the secured party gave value and obtained control). It does not address the interests of claimants whose rights, if any, could arise in the future. Hence, as noted above, the possibility of future interests does not require a qualification to a "free of adverse claims" opinion. By way of contrast, and opinion on "priority" under Article 9 does cover some of these issues. *See infra* § 8.2 (regarding an Article 9 priority opinion as to a certificated security). Some opinion givers prefer, when the secured party meets the requirements to be a protected purchaser, to give an opinion that the secured party is a protected purchaser, rather than an opinion that the secured party's security interest is "free of adverse claims." In the case of opinions subject to a U.C.C. Scope Limitation, the Committee believes that either form of opinion is acceptable. Note that, due to the U.C.C. Scope Limitation, neither form of opinion addresses the secured party's priority with respect to interests in, or claims to, the collateral that are not governed by the U.C.C. *See supra* § 2.1.

283. Distributions with respect to a security (or any other collateral) are "proceeds." U.C.C. § 9-102(a)(64)(B). This reverses the rule of some oft-criticized decisions under prior law. *See, e.g.*, FDIC v. Hastie, 2 F.3d 1042 (10th Cir. 1993) (ordinary dividends on common stock not proceeds, based on former U.C.C. § 9-306 definition of "proceeds" before 1994 modification to that definition as part of the 1994 revisions to Article 8); *In re* Mintz, 192 B.R. 313 (Bankr. D. Mass. 1996) (payments not "proceeds" of rights to distributions associated with a partnership interest); *see supra* § 7.2 (regarding opinions on proceeds).

284. Both the "protected purchaser" and "priority based on control" opinions require that the secured party have "control" of the security. In addition, a "protected purchaser" opinion (unlike a "priority-based-on-control" opinion under Article 9 (as described in this *Report*) requires that the secured party not have notice of an adverse claim. *See supra* notes 265–66 and accompanying text. Both opinions require that the secured party (i) receive delivery (acquire possession) of the security

In addition to filing a financing statement,[285] a secured party may perfect its security interest in a certificated security by taking delivery[286] or obtaining control of the certificated security.[287] A secured party that obtains control of a certificated security has priority over another secured party that has perfected only by filing a financing statement, or receiving delivery,[288] or both,[289] or that is subsequently perfected by control.[290]

Because perfection by control[291] of a certificated security requires physical possession of the security certificate,[292] generally only one secured interest at a time[293] will be perfected by this method.[294]

certificate (directly or through an appropriate third party), (ii) give value, and (iii) satisfy the other requirements of control (i.e., re-registration or indorsement). A "priority-based-on-delivery" opinion would require that the secured party (i) receive delivery (acquire possession) of the security certificate (directly or through an appropriate third party), and (ii) because only an attached security interest can be perfected, give value. *See supra* note 95. Neither the secured party's lack of notice of an adverse claim nor an indorsement or re-registration is required for the secured party to have perfected its security interest by delivery.

285. Priority opinions where the competing security interests are perfected only by the filing of a financing statement are addressed elsewhere in this *Report*. *See supra* § 5.2.

286. "Delivery" of a security certificate is generally equivalent to the secured party obtaining possession of other tangible collateral. U.C.C. §§ 8-301(a)(1), 9-313(a). "Delivery" of a security certificate does not require an indorsement of the security certificate (as does control in the case of a registered certificated security), except in limited circumstances. *See id.* § 8-301(a)(3).

287. *Id.* §§ 9-313(a), 9-314(a); *see supra* § 4.3(c).

288. A secured party that has perfected its security interest in a certificated security in registered form by taking delivery or obtaining control of the security certificate has priority over a secured party that has perfected its security interest by a method other than by taking delivery or obtaining control. U.C.C. § 9-328(5). Unlike the priority, under U.C.C. section 9-330(d), of a secured party that takes possession of instruments over a secured party that has perfected its security interest solely by the filing of a financing statement, the priority of a secured party that takes delivery of a certificated security over a secured party that has perfected its security interest solely by the filing of a financing statement is not dependent on the secured party's lack of knowledge that its transaction does not violate the rights of the other secured party. *See id.* § 9-328(5). A priority opinion based on delivery (as against a secured party that has perfected its security interest solely by the filing of a financing statement) would be similar to a priority opinion based on control. This section of this *Report* addresses only a priority opinion based on control.

289. *Id.* § 9-328(1).

290. *Id.* § 9-328(2)(A); *see supra* § 4.3(c).

291. *Id.* §§ 8-106(a), (b), 8-301, 9-106.

292. Control of a certificated security requires "delivery" of the security to the secured party. *Id.* §§ 8-106(a), (b). "Delivery" requires possession of the certificated security by the secured party (directly or through an appropriate third party). *Id.* § 8-301(a)(1), (2); *see supra* § 4.3(b).

293. More than one secured party may have control of the same certificated security. For example, a secured party could have possession on behalf of itself *and* another secured party or a third party could have possession for both secured parties and therefore the certificated security could have been "delivered" to both secured parties. U.C.C. §§ 8-301(a)(2), 9-313(c). In that case, the first secured party to have obtained control would have priority. *Id.* § 9-328(2)(A). The opinion preparers may assume (without so stating) that the secured party or third party in possession does not have possession on behalf of a person other than the secured party that is the opinion recipient. *See id.* § 9-328 cmt. 5, ex. 6.

294. As with other collateral, the opinion (i) covers proceeds only to a limited extent, and (ii) generally does not cover the effect of a change in the facts that would result in a loss of perfection. *See supra* §§5.4(a), 7.2.

8.3 Article 8 "No Adverse Claim" Opinions for A Security Entitlement

(a) Introduction

Article 8 does not provide for characterizing a purchaser (including a secured party[295]) of a security entitlement[296] as a "protected purchaser."[297] Instead, without using that label, U.C.C. section 8-502 provides a purchaser[298] of a security entitlement who becomes the entitlement holder[299] with respect to the security en-

295. *See supra* note 257 (definition of "purchaser" includes secured party).

296. A "security entitlement" consists of "the rights and property interest of an entitlement holder with respect to a financial asset specified in Part 5 [of Article 8]." U.C.C. § 8-102(a)(17). An "entitlement holder" is "a person identified in the records of a securities intermediary as the person having a security entitlement against the securities intermediary." *Id.* § 8-102(a)(7). A "securities account" is "an account to which a financial asset is . . . credited . . . ." *Id.* § 8-501(a). A "security entitlement" includes personal rights against the applicable securities intermediary and a co-property right (with other entitlement holders holding security entitlements in respect of fungible financial assets through securities accounts maintained with the same securities intermediary) in the interests in financial assets of the applicable type held by the securities intermediary. It does not include a specific property interest in a particular financial asset held by the securities intermediary. *See id.* §§ 8-102(a)(17) & cmt. 17, 8-503(b) & cmt. 1. "Financial assets" include (i) securities and certain other types of property held by a securities intermediary for another in a securities account, and (ii) other property that the securities intermediary and the entitlement holder have agreed will be treated as a "financial asset." *Id.* §§ 8-102(a)(9), 8-103. A description of collateral as a "securities account" includes all security entitlements carried in the account. *Id.* § 9-108(d) cmt. 4; *see id.* §§ 9-203(h) ("attachment of a security interest in a securities account is also attachment of a security interest in the security entitlements carried in the securities account"), 9-308(f) (same for perfection). The discussion of "security entitlements" in sections 8.3 and 8.4 of this *Report* applies to security interests in "securities accounts." *Id.* § 9-308(f). A reference in an opinion to a "securities account" includes all security entitlements with respect to financial assets credited to the account.

297. The concept of "protected purchaser" in U.C.C. section 8-303 applies only to direct holdings of certificated and uncertificated securities. The concept does not apply to persons having security entitlements, including security entitlements with respect to certificated and uncertificated securities. *See* U.C.C. § 8-502 cmt. 1.

298. A "purchaser" includes a secured party. *See supra* text accompanying note 257.

299. U.C.C. section 8-502 only applies when the purchaser becomes the "entitlement holder." One way a secured party can perfect a security interest in a security entitlement is to obtain "control" of the security entitlement. U.C.C. § 9-314(a). One of the ways to obtain "control" is for the secured party to become the "entitlement holder" with respect to the security entitlement. *Id.* §§ 8-106(d)(1), 9-106(a). Other methods of obtaining "control" of the security entitlement (such as entering into a control agreement among the debtor, the secured party, and the securities intermediary), will suffice to perfect the security interest and provide the secured party with priority over other secured parties that have been perfected by a method other than control. Those methods, however, will not provide the secured party with rights under U.C.C. section 8-502. *See id.* §§ 8-106, 9-106, 9-314. Thus, U.C.C. section 8-502 is relevant to an opinion concerning the priority of a security interest in investment property *only* when the secured party perfects a security interest in a security entitlement by becoming the entitlement holder and not when the secured party obtains control by another method or perfects its security interest by another method. U.C.C. section 8-510(c) addresses the relative rights under Article 8 of competing claims to a security entitlement where the debtor remains the entitlement holder. By its own terms, U.C.C. section 8-510(c) does *not* apply to a case "covered by the priority rules in Article 9." Thus, an opinion addressing the "priority" over other secured parties of a security interest in a security entitlement perfected by a method other than the secured party's becoming the entitlement holder (such as by obtaining control by another method) would be given under Article 9. *See supra* § 8.3(c). Even in that case, U.C.C. section 8-510 governs the rights of a secured party as against the adverse claims of persons not covered by Article 9's priority rules. U.C.C. § 8-510 cmt. 2, exs. 1, 2.

titlement with protection against the assertion of adverse claims[300] against the security entitlement if specified conditions are met. If a purchaser meets the requirements of U.C.C. section 8-502 with respect to "an" adverse claim,[301] then "the"[302] adverse claim[303] cannot be asserted against that purchaser with respect to the security entitlement. Article 9 recognizes and defers to the rights of the purchaser under U.C.C. section 8-502.[304]

(b) Elements of the "no assertion of adverse claim" opinion for a security entitlement

Under U.C.C. section 8-502, to be protected against the assertion of an adverse claim to a security entitlement, a purchaser of the security entitlement must:

(i) acquire the security entitlement by becoming the entitlement holder in accordance with U.C.C. section 8-501;[305]
(ii) give value;[306] and
(iii) not have notice[307] of the relevant adverse claim at the time of acquiring the security entitlement and giving value.

In general U.C.C. § 8-501 provides that a purchaser (including a secured party) acquires a security entitlement with respect to a financial asset when the securities intermediary credits[308] the financial asset to the securities account of the purchaser (secured party).

(c) Qualifications

As previously discussed,[309] a secured party with a security interest in a security entitlement perfected by the secured party's becoming the entitlement holder may

300. An "adverse claim" includes a claim that another person is the owner of or has an interest, including a security interest, in the security entitlement. *See supra* note 259.

301. *See* U.C.C. § 8-502. When U.C.C. section 8-510 is relevant, *see supra* note 299, the same rule applies.

302. A purchaser of a certificated or uncertificated security with notice of *any* adverse claim will take the security subject to *all* adverse claims. U.C.C. § 8-303(b). A purchaser of a security entitlement with notice of "an" adverse claim will take subject to *that* adverse claim, but not *other* adverse claims of which it does not have notice. *Id.* §§ 8-502, 8-510.

303. *Id.* § 8-102(a)(1). An "adverse claim" includes a security interest in favor of another secured party. *See supra* note 259.

304. U.C.C. § 9-331(b).

305. *See supra* note 296.

306. The "value" required under U.C.C. section 8-502 is the same as the "value" required for the attachment of the security interest under U.C.C. section 9-203(b)(1). *See supra* § 3.3(b).

307. The requirement of lack of notice of a relevant adverse claim has the same meaning as for the Article 8 protected purchaser opinion. *See supra* § 8.1(b).

308. The opinion assumes, without stating, that any relevant financial assets have been credited to the securities account of the secured party. U.C.C. § 8-501(a).

309. *See supra* text accompanying notes 299–304.

have rights similar to those of a protected purchaser of a certificated security. An opinion that an adverse claim cannot be asserted against a secured party does not require any qualifications[310] because under U.C.C. Section 8-502 an adverse claim to a security entitlement may not be asserted against the secured party.[311]

As with other U.C.C. opinions, the opinion need not state expressly that its coverage of proceeds of (including distributions on) the security entitlements is limited.[312] Likewise, the opinion is based on an unstated assumption that the secured party will continuously maintain its status as the entitlement holder of the security entitlement for purposes of U.C.C. sections 8-502 and 9-314.[313]

8.4 Article 9 Priority Opinions on Security Entitlements[314]

When perfection is based on control (whether through the secured party's becoming the entitlement holder or otherwise) of a security entitlement, a "priority" opinion based on Article 9[315] can be given instead of a "no assertion of adverse claims" opinion under U.C.C. section 8-502.[316] The priority opinion

310. *See supra* notes 280–82.

311. *See supra* notes 298–304. It should be noted, however, that while the secured party's security interest in the security entitlement is free from adverse claims, if the requirements of U.C.C. section 8-502 are met, the security entitlement itself includes a co-property interest in underlying financial assets of the applicable type that is shared with the other holders of security entitlements in identical financial assets. *See* U.C.C. §§ 8102(a)(17) & cmt. 17, 8-502 cmt. 1, 8-503(b) & cmt. 1; *see also supra* note 300. The security interest is also junior to the claims of creditors of the applicable securities intermediary that have control with respect to such financial assets. *See* U.C.C. § 8-511(b). The opinion does not cover these issues.

312. *See supra* § 7.2.

313. *See supra* text accompanying note 294.

314. The approach used for opinions on securities accounts and security entitlements may be adapted for an opinion on a security interest in a deposit account. U.C.C. §§ 9-104, 9-314; *see* Appendix A (Illustrative Opinion). A security interest in a deposit account as original collateral may be perfected only by the secured party's obtaining control of the deposit account. *Id.* § 9-312(b)(1). The requirements for "control" of a deposit account are similar to those for control of a securities account. *Id.* §§ 8-106, 9-104. A security interest in a deposit account perfected by control will have priority over a security interest perfected by another method (such as a security interest in proceeds perfected by the filing of a financing statement indicating other collateral as the original collateral). *Id.* § 9-327(1). If more than one security interest is perfected by control, the priority of the secured parties generally depends on the temporal order in which they "obtain[ed]" control. *Id.* § 9-327(2). A security interest in favor of the depositary bank where the deposit account is maintained has priority over a security interest in favor of another person, even if that security interest was perfected by control before the depositary institution obtained control, U.C.C. § 9-327(3), unless the other person has perfected by becoming a customer of the depositary bank. *Id.* §§ 9-104(a)(1), 9-327(4).

315. A Filing Priority Opinion could also be given if perfection is obtained by filing a financing statement. *See supra* § 5.2(b).

316. Both the "no-adverse-claim" and "priority-based-on-control" opinions require that the secured party have "control" of the security entitlement. In addition a "no adverse claim" opinion (unlike a "priority based on control" opinion under Article 9 (as described in this *Report*)) requires that the secured party not have notice of an adverse claim. *See supra* notes 264–66, 277–79 and accompanying text. Both opinions require that the secured party (i) obtain control and (ii) give value.

would address only competing security interests[317] under Article 9 and not "adverse claims" generally.[318]

9. Revised Article 9 Transition Rules

Part 7 of revised Article 9 provides rules concerning the transition from former Article 9 to revised Article 9.[319] These rules have no effect on the attachment or perfection of an Article 9 security interest for transactions first[320] closing[321] *on or after* the effective date of revised Article 9.[322]

The transition rules could, however, have an effect on the priority of an opinion recipient's security interest in a transaction closing on or after the effective date of revised Article 9. For example, under the transition rules, a financing statement filed and effective under former Article 9 remains effective under revised Article 9 for specified periods[323] and that financing statement might not be filed in the same state[324] as a financing statement filed under revised Article 9.[325] Thus, the financing statement filed under former Article 9 would not be identified in a search report obtained from the appropriate filing office in the appropriate state under revised Article 9, but may still establish priority in favor of another secured party under the revised Article 9 transition rules.[326]

A Filing Priority Opinion by definition would be based solely on a review of the search report identified in the opinion[327]—presumably a report from the state

317. A security interest in a security entitlement perfected by control will have priority over a security interest perfected by a method other than control. U.C.C. § 9-328(1). A security interest in a security entitlement perfected by control would be junior to a security interest held by a secured party who already has control and to a security interest in favor of the applicable securities intermediary (even if it attaches in the future), unless the secured party has perfected by becoming the entitlement holder. *Id.* § 9-328. The opinion preparers may assume, without stating, that no other secured party already has control. If the securities intermediary, in the control agreement (or another document), does not waive or agree to subordinate any security interest it may have, the opinion preparers should consider qualifying an Article 9 priority opinion to note the securities intermediary's possible priority.

318. *See supra* § 8.3.

319. U.C.C. §§ 9-701 to -709. For thorough discussions of the transition rules, see B. Smith, *New Article 9 Transition Rules*, 74 Chi. Kent L. Rev. 1339 (1999); H. Sigman & Edwin E. Smith, *Revised U.C.C. Article 9's Transition Rules: Insuring a Soft Landing*, 55 Bus. Law. (2000); *see also supra* note 14.

320. *See supra* § 7.1.

321. This assumes that perfection is not based on an effective financing statement filed under former Article 9. *See* U.C.C. § 9-705(c).

322. Opinions addressing the effect of revised Article 9 (including the transition rules) on transactions that closed *prior* to the effective date of revised Article 9 are beyond the scope of this *Report*. Similarly, the effect of the adoption of revised Article 9 with delayed effective dates in five jurisdictions (Alabama, Connecticut, Florida, Mississippi, and the U.S. Virgin Islands) and lack of adoption in some jurisdictions (including Puerto Rico) is beyond the scope of this *Report*. *See PEB Report, supra* note 38.

323. U.C.C. § 9-705(c).

324. In addition, the financing statement may not have been filed in the same office within the state where the financing statement would be filed under revised Article 9. *Compare* U.C.C. § 9-401 (pre-revision), *with* U.C.C. § 9-501 (revised).

325. U.C.C. §§ 9-103, 9-401 (pre-revision); *see generally* Appendix B (choice of law); U.C.C. §§ 9-301 to -307, 9-501.

326. U.C.C. § 9-709(a).

327. *See supra* text accompanying note 173.

where the secured party has filed or will file a financing statement under revised Article 9.[328] As such, unless the opinion expressly refers to a search report obtained from the filing office in the appropriate state(s) and office(s) for the filing of a financing statement under former Article 9, a Filing Priority Opinion inherently does not address filings made under former Article 9 and affecting priority under the transition rules.

In view of the potentially significant effect of a filing in another jurisdiction under former Article 9 and the significant departure in revised Article 9 from the place-of-filing rules of former Article 9, if the opinion preparers believe that a Filing Priority Opinion based solely on a search report from the state where the filing occurs under revised Article 9 will mislead[329] the opinion recipient, the opinion preparers should consider either:

(i) disclosing to the opinion recipient that a search report was not obtained from any state where a filing might have been appropriate under former Article 9; or

(ii) obtaining search reports in those states, identifying them in the Filing Priority Opinion, and covering them in the Filing Priority Opinion.[330]

10. Conclusion

This *Report* is intended to provide guidance to lawyers who are asked to give U.C.C. security interest opinions. Broad principles of general application overlay the giving of security interest opinions. Opinions under Article 9 also call for familiarity with Article 9. While this *Report* provides a detailed discussion of Article 9 and opinions on security interests created under Article 9, opinion preparers who do not regularly work with Article 9 should consider whether to involve a lawyer familiar with Article 9 in the preparation of a security interest opinion.

This *Report* continues the TriBar tradition of attempting to combine theory with practice. If it has succeeded, the process of crafting U.C.C. security interest opinions will be simpler and their scope and meaning will be clearer.

July 25, 2003
All Rights Reserved
TriBar Opinion Committee
Copyright © 2003
Reprinted with Permission

328. *See supra* note 169.

329. *See supra* note 19.

330. The determination of the state or states in which to search for a financing statement filed under former Article 9 would be based on assumptions stated in the opinion letter on the location of tangible collateral or the debtor as those terms were used under former Article 9 or on a determination by the opinion recipient. *See* U.C.C. § 9-103 (pre-revision). The opinion preparers are not obliged to give a choice-of-law opinion when deciding where to search. *See* text accompanying note 39. When reviewing financing statements filed under former Article 9, the opinion preparers should consider the effect of a change in the definition of terms in revised Article 9. *See* U.C.C. §§ 9-703 cmt. 3, 9-705 cmt. 6, ex. 7; *see generally* Appendix B (choice-of-law).

Appendix A

Illustrative Security Interest Opinion[331]

Law Offices
Wise, Safe & Solvent LLP
One Thousand Wall Street
New York, New York 10005

August 1, 2003

Careful Lending Bank
Two Thousand Wall Street
New York, New York 10005

Ladies and Gentlemen:

We have acted as counsel to Rock Solid Corporation ("Borrower"), a New York corporation, in connection with the preparation, execution, and delivery of, and borrowing under, the Credit Agreement, dated August 1, 2003, between you ("Secured Party") and Borrower (the "Credit Agreement"), the Security Agreement, dated August 1, 2003, between Secured Party and Borrower (the "Security Agreement"), and the other documents identified below. This opinion letter is delivered to you pursuant to Section [ ] of the Credit Agreement.

References in this opinion letter to the "New York U.C.C." are to the Uniform Commercial Code currently in effect in the State of New York. Capitalized terms used but not defined in this opinion letter have the meanings given to them in the Security Agreement. All terms in opinions 2-[12] that are defined in the New York U.C.C. and that are not capitalized have the meaning given to them in the New York U.C.C.

For purposes of this opinion letter, we have reviewed the following documents:

(a) [Insert in appropriate lettered items the documents reviewed for non-security interest opinions, such as a certified copy of articles or certificate of incorporation];
(b) the Credit Agreement;
(c) the Security Agreement;
(d) the Pledge Agreement, dated August 1, 2003 (the "Pledge Agreement"), between Secured Party and Borrower;[332]

331. This Illustrative Security Interest Opinion is only a suggested starting point. It is not intended to be prescriptive, but only to provide a context for the commentary in the Special Report. The hypothetical transaction addressed here is one in which the debtor, in order to secure both existing indebtedness and future advances, has granted to the secured party a security interest in all of the debtor's existing and after-acquired personal property. The collateral includes instruments, certificated securities, security entitlements, and deposit accounts. The debtor is incorporated in New York. The U.C.C. search report with respect to filings with the New York Secretary of State naming the debtor indicates only one other secured creditor—Due Diligence Factoring Company—that filed a financing statement that includes collateral in which a security interest is granted to Careful Lending Bank, the secured party.

332. If the security interest in any of the collateral is perfected through the possession of the collateral by a bailee, perfection may involve an acknowledgement from the bailee that it is holding the collateral for the benefit of the secured party. *See supra* note 144.

(e) the Securities Account Control Agreement (the "Securities Account Control Agreement"), dated August 1, 2003, among Secured Party, Borrower, and Good Advice Broker;

(f) the Deposit Account Control Agreement (the "Deposit Account Control Agreement"), dated August 1, 2003, among Secured Party, Borrower, and Safe Deposit Bank;

(g) an [acknowledgment] [time-stamped] [unfiled] copy of a financing statement (the "Financing Statement") naming the Borrower as debtor and the Secured Party as secured party, [filed] [to be filed] in the Office of the Secretary of State of the State of New York (the "Filing Office"); and

(h) the report of Prompt and Efficient Document Services Corp., dated July 28, 2003, as to U.C.C. financing statements naming the Borrower as debtor (the "U.C.C. Search Report") and on file in the Filing Office as of 5:00 p.m. on July 1, 2003 (the "Effective Date"[333]).

For purposes of this opinion letter we have also reviewed such additional documents, and made such other investigation as we have deemed appropriate.

Based on the foregoing and subject to the other paragraphs of this opinion letter, we express the following opinions:

1. [Insert in appropriately numbered paragraphs non-security interest opinions].[334]
2. *First Alternative:* The Security Agreement is effective to create[335] in favor of Secured Party [, as security for the Obligations,][336] a security interest (the "Article 9 Security Interest") in the collateral described in the Security Agreement[337] (the "Article 9 Collateral").[338]

333. The "Effective Date" includes the time of day (if given) of the search report.

334. *See, e.g., 1998 TriBar Report, supra* note 1, at 667–74 (providing examples of Illustrative Opinion Letters).

335. Some lawyers believe that a "creation" opinion is narrower than an "attachment" opinion, while others believe that there is no difference. Both sides agree that all of the elements of attachment must be satisfied for a security interest to be perfected. Accordingly, a perfection opinion requires the opinion preparers to satisfy themselves that all of the elements of attachment have been satisfactorily addressed. Nevertheless, as noted in section 3.3(c) *supra,* as a matter of customary practice, a creation or attachment opinion, whether express or, by virtue of the giving of a perfection opinion, implied, is understood not to cover the question of whether the debtor has rights or the power to transfer rights in the collateral. If, however, an opinion expressly assumes either "creation" or "attachment" of the security interest for purposes of giving a perfection opinion, the perfection opinion as a matter of customary practice is understood not to cover any of the elements of creation or attachment. *See supra* notes 51–53.

336. *See* note 74. This bracketed language would be implied in a creation opinion unless the opinion letter contains a contrary statement.

337. If the U.C.C. Scope Limitation set forth below (*see infra* text at note 368) is not used, language similar to the following should be included: "in which a security interest may be created under Article 9 of the [state] U.C.C."

338. The creation and attachment opinions in paragraph 2 define the broad term *Article 9 Collateral.* The perfection opinions in subsequent paragraphs divide the Article 9 Collateral into additional subcategories.

2. *Second Alternative:* A security interest (the "Article 9 Security Interest") in favor of Secured Party [, as security for the Obligations,][339] has attached[340] to the collateral described in the Security Agreement[341] (the "Article 9 Collateral").[342]
3. [Upon the filing[343] of the Financing Statement with the Filing Office,] [t][T]he Article 9 Security Interest in that portion of the Article 9 Collateral in which a security interest may be perfected by the filing of a financing statement under the New York U.C.C. (the "Filing Collateral") [will be] [is] perfected.[344]
4. The U.C.C. Search Report sets forth the proper filing office and the proper name of the debtor necessary to identify those persons who under the New York U.C.C. have, as of the Effective Date, financing statements on file against the Borrower indicating any of the Filing Collateral. Except for the financing statement naming Due Diligence Factoring Company as secured party, the U.C.C. Search Report identifies no still-effective financing statement naming Borrower as debtor and indicating any of the Filing Collateral filed in the Filing Office, prior to the [Effective Date] [filing in the Filing Office of the Financing Statement].[345]
5. The Article 9 Security Interest in that portion of the Article 9 Collateral consisting of the instruments[346] identified on Schedule 1 to the Security Agreement (the "Pledged Instruments") [is perfected by] [will be perfected upon] Secured Party taking possession[347] of the Pledged Instruments.[348]
6. The Article 9 Security Interest in the Pledged Instruments [is] [will be] prior to any other security interest created under Article 9.[349]

339. *See supra* note 74. This bracketed language would be implied in an attachment opinion unless the opinion letter contains a contrary statement.

340. *See supra* § 3.3.

341. If the U.C.C. Scope Limitation set forth below (*see infra* text at note 367) is not used, language similar to the following should be included: "in which a security interest may be created under Article 9 of the [state] U.C.C."

342. The creation and attachment opinions in paragraph 2 define the broad term *Article 9 Collateral*. The perfection opinions in subsequent paragraphs divide the Article 9 Collateral into additional subcategories.

343. "Filing" includes the "acceptance" of the financing statement by the filing office. *See supra* notes 132–36.

344. Because the hypothetical transaction that is the subject of this opinion letter involves a blanket security interest in all types of collateral including some (e.g., deposit accounts) in which a security interest may not be perfected by filing a financing statement, the opinion in this paragraph states that it is limited to collateral in which a security interest may be perfected by filing.

345. *See supra* § 6.2. If the financing statement has not yet been filed or was filed after the Effective Date, the first set of bracketed words (and not the second set) would be used. If the financing statement was filed and is identified in the U.C.C. Search Report, the second set of bracketed words (and not the first set) would be used.

346. For related assumptions (stated and unstated) and exceptions *see supra* § 4.3(b).

347. The opinion does not have to specify the state in which the secured party has taken possession. *See supra* note 142.

348. If the Pledged Instruments are indicated as collateral in the Financing Statement, the Financing Statement would also perfect a security interest in the Pledged Instruments and this paragraph may be omitted unless opinion number 6 is also being given.

349. This opinion should be given *only* if secured party has perfected by possession. *See supra* opinion number 5; *see also* notes 187–89 and accompanying text. Note that this opinion is based on an unstated assumption that Secured Party took possession of the instruments in good faith without

7. *First Alternative:* The Article 9 Security Interest[350] in that portion of the Article 9 Collateral consisting of the [shares of stock] [bonds] [other certificated securities] represented by the certificates identified on Schedule A to the Pledge Agreement (the "Pledged Securities") [is perfected by] [will be perfected upon] delivery of the certificates to the Secured Party.[351]
7. *Second Alternative:* The Article 9 Security Interest[352] in that portion of the Article 9 Collateral consisting of the [shares of stock] [bonds] [other certificated securities] represented by the certificates identified on Schedule A to the Pledge Agreement (the "Pledged Securities") [is perfected by] [will be perfected upon] indorsement and delivery of the certificates to Secured Party.[353]
8. *First Alternative:* Secured Party [acquired] [will acquire] the Article 9 Security Interest[354] in the Pledged Securities free of adverse claims.[355]
8. *Second Alternative:* The Article 9 Security Interest in the Pledged Securities [is] [will be] prior[356] to any other security interest created under Article 9.[357]

knowledge that the grant to it of the security interest in the instruments violates the rights of a prior secured party. For a discussion of this and other related assumptions (stated and unstated) and exceptions, see *supra* section 5.3. Note also that if the related perfection opinion is qualified by reference to Secured Party's "taking possession of the Pledged Instruments" (see opinion number 5), the qualification also applies equally to the opinion in this paragraph, which is understood as being similarly premised on Secured Party's taking possession.

350. This is an opinion on perfection based on Secured Party's receiving "delivery" of the Pledged Securities. For related assumptions (stated and unstated) and exceptions, *see supra* § 4.3(b).

351. If the Pledged Securities are indicated as collateral in the Financing Statement, the Financing Statement would also perfect a security interest in the Pledged Securities and this paragraph may be omitted unless the opinion in opinion number 8, *Second Alternative,* is being given.

352. This is an opinion on perfection based on Secured Party's obtaining "control" of the Pledged Securities. For related assumptions (stated and unstated) and exceptions, see *supra* § 4.3(c).

353. If the Pledged Securities are indicated as collateral in the Financing Statement, the Financing Statement would also perfect a security interest in the Pledged Securities and this paragraph could be omitted unless one of the opinions in opinion number 8 is being given.

354. For related assumptions (stated and unstated) and exceptions, *see supra* § 8.1. If the opinion preparers have not satisfied themselves that one or more of the following actions has occurred, the following assumptions should be set forth in the opinion: "Assuming that each Pledged Security either is in bearer form or, if in registered form, is registered in the name of Secured Party or is indorsed to Secured Party or in blank". The opinion preparers may assume, without stating, that the indorsement is effective. *See supra* note 272.

355. This opinion should be given only if Secured Party has perfected by obtaining control (see opinion number 7, *Second Alternative*) and the other elements for Secured Party to qualify as a protected purchaser have been met. U.C.C. § 8-303; *see supra* § 8.2. If this opinion is given, it requires that the opinion preparers satisfy themselves that Secured Party has obtained control of the Pledged Securities. Note that this opinion is based on an unstated assumption that Secured Party does not have notice of an adverse claim to the Pledged Securities. Sometimes an opinion giver will not give a "free-of-adverse-claims" opinion, but will give an opinion that Secured Party is a "protected purchaser," which is the predicate for the "free-of-adverse-claims" opinion. Note also that if the related perfection opinion is qualified by reference to the "delivery of the certificates to Security Party" (see opinion number 7, *First Alternative*), the qualification is understood to apply equally to the opinion in this paragraph.

356. *See supra* § 8.2.

357. For related assumptions (stated and unstated) and exceptions, *see supra* § 8.2. This opinion should be given only if Secured Party has perfected by delivery (see opinion number 7, *First Alternative*) or control (see opinion number 7, *Second Alternative*). *See supra* § 8.2 (priority of security interest perfected other than by delivery or control). Note also that if the related perfection opinion is qualified by reference to the "indorsement and delivery of the certificates to Secured Party" (see opinion number 7, *Second Alternative*), the qualification is understood to apply equally to the opinion in this paragraph.

9. The Article 9 Security Interest in the Securities Account[358] [is perfected by] [will be perfected upon] the execution and delivery[359] of the Securities Account Control Agreement.[360]
10. *First Alternative:* The Article 9 Security Interest in the Securities Account [is] [will be] prior[361] to any other security interest created under Article 9.[362]
10. *Second Alternative:* No action based on an adverse claim to a financial asset credited to the Securities Account[363] may be asserted against Secured Party.[364]
11. The Article 9 Security Interest in the Deposit Account[365] [is perfected by] [will be perfected upon] the execution and delivery of the Deposit Account Control Agreement.[366]

358. *See supra* note 296.

359. If Secured Party obtains control by becoming the entitlement holder, the Securities Account Control Agreement would not be necessary for Secured Party to obtain control. *See supra* note 299.

360. If the Securities Account is indicated as collateral in the Financing Statement, the Financing Statement would also perfect a security interest in the Securities Account (including any security entitlement with respect to financial assets credited to the Securities Account) and this paragraph could be omitted unless one of the opinions in opinion number 10 is being given..

361. Article 9 (and not Article 8) provides the priority rules. *See supra* § 8.3.

362. Note that this opinion is based on an assumption, which need not be stated, that Secured Party does not have notice of an adverse claim to the relevant financial asset. For a discussion of this and related assumptions (stated and unstated) and exceptions, see *supra* § 8.3. The opinion set forth in this paragraph should be given only when Secured Party has perfected its security interest in the Securities Account and related security entitlements by obtaining control (see opinion number 9). If (i) Secured Party has not obtained control by becoming the entitlement holder, and (ii) the securities intermediary has not waived any security interest that it has or may come to have in the securities account and related security entitlements or subordinated that security interest to the Secured Party's security interest (see U.C.C. § 9-328(3)), the opinion preparers should consider noting the security intermediary's possible priority under U.C.C. section 9-328(3) and the possible priority of security interest perfected by earlier-obtained control under U.C.C. section 9-328(2)(B)(ii). *See supra* note 319. Note also that if the related perfection opinion is qualified by reference to the "execution and delivery of the Securities Account Control Agreement" (see opinion number 9), the qualification is understood to apply equally to the opinion in this paragraph.

363. *See supra* § 8.3.

364. Note that this opinion is based on an assumption, which need not be stated, that Secured Party does not have notice of an adverse claim to the relevant financial assets. For a discussion of this and other relevant assumptions (stated and unstated) and exceptions, see *supra* § 8.3. The opinion set forth in this paragraph should be given only when Secured Party has perfected its security interest in the Securities Account and related security entitlements by obtaining control (see opinion number 9). The opinion in the *Second Alternative* is based on U.C.C. section 8-502, which applies only when Secured Party is the entitlement holder with respect to the Securities Account. *See supra* note 299. When Secured Party obtains control by the use of a control agreement, the opinion in the *Second Alternative* is not appropriate and a priority opinion, if given, should use the *First Alternative*. The opinion preparers should consider noting the security intermediary's possible priority under U.C.C. § 9-328(3). *See supra* note 360. When Secured Party obtains control by becoming the entitlement holder with respect to the Securities Account, the rules of U.C.C. § 8-502, as well as the rules of Article 9, may be relevant. *See supra* note 299.

365. *See supra* note 314. Note that, unlike security interests in instruments, certificated securities, and security entitlements, which can be perfected either by the filing of a financing statement or by possession, delivery, or control (as appropriate), security interests in deposit accounts can only be perfected by control. *See* U.C.C. § 9-312(b)(i); *supra* note 121 and accompanying text.

366. If Secured Party obtains control by becoming the customer of the depositary bank with respect to the Deposit Account, the Deposit Account Control Agreement would not be necessary for Secured Party to obtain control. *See supra* note 314.

12. The Article 9 Security Interest in the Deposit Account [is] [will be] prior[367] to any other security interest created under Article 9.[368]

Our opinions above are subject to the following additional exceptions, assumptions, limitations, and qualifications:

A. [*Insert assumptions and exceptions applicable to non-security interest opinions*].[369]

The opinions expressed in this opinion letter are limited to the federal law of the United States, and the law of the State of New York. Our opinions in paragraphs 2-[12] are limited to Article 9 of the New York U.C.C.[370]

This opinion letter is being delivered to you in connection with the above described transaction and may not be relied on by you for any other purpose. This opinion letter may not be relied on or furnished to any other person without our prior written consent.[371]

Very truly yours,[372]

367. For related assumptions (stated and unstated) and exceptions, see *supra* note 318; *see also supra* § 8.3.

368. If (i) Secured Party has not obtained control by becoming the customer of the depositary bank with respect to the Deposit Account, and (ii) the depositary bank has not waived or subordinated any security interest that it has or may come to have in the Deposit Account to Secured Party's security interest (see U.C.C. § 9-327(3)) the opinion preparers should consider noting the depositary bank's possible priority rights under U.C.C. section 9-327(3) and the possible priority of security interests perfected by earlier-obtained control under U.C.C. section 9-327(2). *See supra* note 314. Note also that if the related perfection opinion is qualified by reference to the "execution and delivery of the Securities Account Control Agreement" (see opinion number 11), the qualification is understood to apply equally to the opinion in this paragraph.

369. Note that the equitable principles limitation and bankruptcy exception should not be made applicable to security interest opinions. *See supra* § 2.3.

370. *See supra* § 2.1(b) (U.C.C. Scope Limitation).

371. *See Guidelines*, *supra* note 16, § 1.7.

372. Customarily, the opinion would be signed in the name of the opinion giver. 1998 *TriBar Report*, *supra* note 1, § 1.8, at 605.

APPENDIX B

PERFECTION OPINIONS UNDER THE LAW OF ANOTHER STATE[373]

GENERAL

The main body of this *Report* addresses U.C.C. opinions when the law applicable to the U.C.C. issues covered in the opinion is the same as the law generally covered by the opinion letter.[374] This APPENDIX B addresses opinions on:

(i) the perfection of a security interest when perfection is governed by the local[375] law of a state whose law is *not* covered generally by the opinion letter; and
(ii) what state's law governs the perfection, the effect of perfection or nonperfection, or the priority[376] of a security interest.

An opinion could be given that covers:

(i) neither set of issues;
(ii) the first set of issues and not the second set of issues;
(iii) the second set of issues and not the first set of issues; or
(iv) both sets of issues.

An opinion could also:

(i) assume conclusions concerning one or more of these issues, or
(ii) be phrased using a conditional statement of the applicable law[377] as discussed below.

The Committee takes no position on whether an opinion recipient should request these opinions or whether an opinion giver should be willing to provide them.[378]

LIMITED OPINIONS ON THE U.C.C. OF OTHER JURISDICTIONS ARE NOT INAPPROPRIATE WHEN GIVING A PERFECTION OPINION

The jurisdiction whose law governs the perfection of a security interest frequently is not the jurisdiction whose law is covered generally in the opinion letter.[379] Nonetheless, the opinion recipient and the opinion giver may agree that the opinion recipient should receive an opinion that the security interest has been perfected under the law of the state whose law governs perfection.[380] One alter-

373. This discussion would also apply to a priority opinion given under the law of another state.
374. *See supra* § 2.1(d).
375. *See supra* note 101 (meaning of "local law").
376. In some instances, the law of the state whose law governs the perfection of the security interest does not also govern the effect of the perfection of the security interest or the priority of the security interest. U.C.C. § 9-301(3)(c); *see supra* note 99.
377. For example, an opinion could state, "If the law of [state] governs the perfection of a security interest in the Filing Collateral by the filing of a financing statement . . . "
378. *See supra* § 3.2.
379. *See supra* § 4.2.
380. An opinion that an act (such as the filing of a financing statement) under the law of a designated state would be sufficient to perfect the security interest under the law of that state is *not* an opinion that the law of the identified state is the law that governs the perfection of the security interest. An opinion does not cover which state's law governs perfection unless it does so expressly. *See supra* § 4.2.

native would be to obtain this opinion from local counsel. For cost/benefit or other reasons, however, that may not be desirable.[381] Thus, counsel for the debtor may decide to give an opinion on the perfection of a security interest under the law of a state on which it would not generally render an opinion.[382] This departure from normal practice would be possible because the U.C.C. has been enacted in substantially similar form in all states.[383]

If given, the opinion should describe the limited extent of the opinion preparer's review of the law governing perfection (e.g., the review is limited to the text of U.C.C. as it appears in the official statutory compilation or a recognized reporting service).[384] By making clear that the opinion preparers have not conducted the same degree of review (for example reviewing case law) that lawyers who regularly render opinions on the law of the state in question would conduct[385] the opinion preparers, will be putting the recipient on notice that the opinion is not the equivalent of an opinion of local counsel.

Choice-of-Law Opinion For Security Interest Perfected by the Filing of a Financing Statement

The choice-of-law opinion, if given, would cover which state's law governs the perfection[386] of a security interest by the filing of a financing statement. If that opinion is given, the opinion preparers may have to review the law of two states:[387]

381. *See Guidelines, supra* note 16, § 2.2.

382. *See infra* text accompanying note 384.

383. *See Under the Surface, supra* note 6.

384. This approach is similar to that commonly taken when giving opinions on the client's compliance with corporate formalities under the law of a jurisdiction other than the jurisdiction covered generally by the opinion letter when the opinion giver has concluded that it is competent to provide the opinion. *See 1998 TriBar Report, supra* note 1, § 4.1, at 631. Unlike the corporate opinion, however, as a matter of customary practice, the opinion concerning the law of another jurisdiction would not be understood to cover the decisional law under the U.C.C. of the other jurisdiction nor any filing office rules of the other jurisdiction. *See* U.C.C. § 9-526. Because a U.C.C. opinion is narrower, is based on general U.C.C. expertise, and the U.C.C. has been adopted in a substantially uniform manner in all of the states, the opinion preparers often may reasonably conclude that they are competent to provide an opinion on these issues under the law of another state. The same would be true for a review of search reports when a Filing Priority Opinion is given. *See supra* text accompanying notes 168–84. The giving of an opinion on the law of a state where the opinion preparers are not licensed is not the "practice of law" in that state. Restatement (Third) of the Law Governing Lawyers § 3 cmt. e (2003); Model Rules of Prof'l Conduct, R. 5.5(c)(4) (multijurisdictional practice of law).

385. This discussion assumes that the opinion is subject to a U.C.C. Scope Limitation and, therefore, that the opinion preparers do not have to determine whether the collateral is subject to the U.C.C. as adopted in the state whose law governs perfection. *See supra* § 2.1(b).

386. Where the security interest is perfected by the filing of a financing statement, the law of the same state would also govern the *effect* of perfection or nonperfection of the security interest and the priority of the security interest (except where the collateral is negotiable documents, goods, instruments, tangible chattel paper, or investment property). U.C.C. § 9-301(3)(c).

387. Under former Article 9 opinion givers normally did not give opinions on which state's law governed the perfection of the security interest. This reflected the fact that under former Article 9 the law of many states could govern the perfection of the security interest, depending on the location of the debtor and the location of tangible collateral. U.C.C. § 9-103 (pre-revision). Under revised Article 9 the law of only one state governs the perfection of a security interest perfected by the filing of a financing statement. Although an opinion on which state's law governs perfection does not raise the same issues under revised Article 9 as it did under former Article 9, the Committee takes no position on whether an opinion on which state's law governs perfection should be requested or given.

1) the law of the state whose law is generally covered by the opinion letter; and
2) the law of the state of the "location" of the debtor, which is the law that governs perfection by the filing of a financing statement.[388]

The opinion expresses the opinion preparers' professional judgment only on how the highest court of the state whose law is covered by the opinion would rule on the issue.[389] A court making a choice-of-law analysis must begin[390] its analysis with the choice-of-law rules of the forum. Thus, the opinion preparers begin with the choice-of-law rule found in U.C.C. section 9-301[391] of the state whose law is covered generally by the opinion letter.[392] The opinion preparers do *not* begin with the law governing perfection because they have not yet reached that point in their legal analysis.[393]

The opinion preparers should use the following sequence of steps in making their choice-of-law analysis. First, they should determine the "location" of the debtor under the law generally covered by the opinion. That determination requires a determination of the type of "person"[394] the debtor is for purposes of revised Article 9, again under the law generally covered by the opinion. The determination of what type of "person" the debtor is under revised Article 9 is a necessary step in determining the "location" of the debtor.

If the debtor is a "registered organization" organized under state law (generally a corporation, limited liability company, or limited partnership[395]), the debtor is "located" in its state of organization and the perfection of a security interest by the filing of a financing statement is governed by the law of that state.[396] Other types of entities, such as business trusts and real estate investment trusts,[397] may

388. *See supra* § 4.2. The law of that state also governs perfection in the absence of any special rule providing that the law of another state governs perfection. U.C.C. § 9-301(1).

389. *1998 TriBar Report, supra* note 1, § 1.2(a), at 595–96.

390. A state court would of course apply its own state's choice of law rules. RESTATEMENT (SECOND) OF CONFLICT OF LAWS § 6(1) cmt. a. When applying state law, a federal court exercising diversity jurisdiction must apply the choice-of-law rules in effect in the forum state. *See generally*, Erie R.R. Co. v. Tompkins, 304 U.S. 64 (1938); Klaxon Co. v. Stentor Elec. Mfg. Co., 313 U.S. 487 (1941); Day & Zimmermann, Inc. v. Challoner, 423 U.S. 3 (1975). *Klaxon* also requires that a bankruptcy court exercising federal jurisdiction apply the choice-of-law rules of the forum state "where no significant federal policy, calling for the imposition of a federal conflicts rule, exists." Bianco v. Erkins (*In re* Gaston & Snow), 243 F.3d 599, 607 (2d Cir. 2001).

391. There are related definitions in U.C.C. section 9-102 and in Article 1.

392. Of course, litigation concerning the perfection of the security interest could occur in a different state. The opinion does not cover these matters. The highly uniform adoption of the relevant provisions of revised Article 9 means that a court of another state should make the same analysis and come to the same conclusion as to the location of the debtor and, thus, the same conclusion on which state's law governs perfection. *See supra* note 6.

393. *See generally* U.C.C. § 9-101 cmt. 4(c). Any litigation involving the perfection of the security interest could, of course, take place in yet another state. *See Under the Surface, supra* note 6. The opinion letter, as a result of its statement of the law covered by the opinion letter, does not cover that possibility.

394. U.C.C. §§ 1-201(30), 1-201(b)(27) (revised).

395. *Id.* § 9-307 cmt. 4.

396. *Id.* § 9-301(1).

397. *See id.* 9-503 cmt. 2.

also be registered organizations, depending on the law of the state where they were organized.

To determine if the debtor is a "registered organization" under the law of the state whose law is generally covered by the opinion letter, the opinion preparers must look to the law of the jurisdiction of organization of the debtor for certain information. A "registered organization" is "an organization organized solely under the law of a single state or the United States and as to which the state or the United States must maintain a public record showing the organization to have been organized."

The determination of whether the debtor can be organized under the law of more than one state[398] and whether the state must maintain the requisite public records would require a review of the law of the state of organization. Unlike Article 9 itself, these non-U.C.C. aspects of state law are not uniform. In some states these issues will not pose a problem.[399] In others, the opinion preparers may want to include in the opinion an express assumption (i) concerning the status of the debtor as a "registered organization" under the law of the state whose law is covered by the opinion, or (ii) regarding the relevant non-U.C.C. aspects of state law under the law of the state of organization.[400] If the opinion preparers determine that the debtor is a "registered organization," then, under the law generally covered by the opinion letter, the state of the debtor's organization is its "location."[401]

Determining the proper state in which to file a financing statement when the debtor is an organization other than a registered organization (e.g., a general partnership or common law trust) or an individual is less clear-cut. An organization other than a registered organization is generally located in the state of its chief executive office.[402] If a trustee of a common law trust[403] owns the collateral under applicable non-U.C.C. law,[404] the trustee is the "debtor"[405] and the rules applicable to the type of person the *trustee* is (e.g., individual, corporation) determine where to file a financing statement.[406] U.C.C. section 9-307(b)(1) provides that an individual debtor is generally "located at the individual's principal residence."

398. The opinion giver may assume, without so stating, that the debtor is not organized in more than one state.

399. U.C.C. § 9-102(a)(70), cmt. 11; *see, e.g.*, Revised Model Business Corporations Act §1.28 ("anyone" may obtain copy of certificate of existence); DEL. CODE ANN. tit. 7, § 103(c)(6) (1999) (expressly requiring that the state maintain the requisite public record).

400. For example, the opinion preparers will often expressly assume that the state of organization is required to maintain the requisite public record because the state may not have an express requirement.

401. Some opinion givers may be willing to give an opinion that the debtor is a "registered organization" under the U.C.C. of the state of its organization, but might not also give an opinion (based on that conclusion) under the law of the state whose law is generally covered by the opinion that the debtor is "located" in that state and therefore that the law of that state governs perfection.

402. U.C.C. § 9-307(b)(2), (3).

403. This may also apply to a business trust if the statute under which the statutory business trust is formed vests the property in the trustee.

404. Under non-U.C.C. choice-of-law rules, ordinarily this issue would be governed by the law that governs the trust. *See generally* RESTATEMENT (SECOND) OF CONFLICT OF LAWS §§ 267–75.

405. U.C.C. § 9-102(a)(28).

406. U.C.C. section 9-307. U.C.C. section 9-307 contains additional rules to determine the location

The determination of whether a debtor is a registered organization (and the related determination of the "location" of the debtor) is a legal issue that (subject to the considerations discussed above)[407] requires a review of statutes, organizational documents, and other public records. The determination of the location of other types of debtors is in part a factual issue that is customarily based on express assumptions or reliance on factual statements made by the debtor (e.g., the location of its chief executive office).

Perfection Opinion

Filing of financing statement. To give a perfection opinion under the law of the state where the debtor is located,[408] the opinion preparers must determine[409] whether:

(i) the state of the debtor's[410] location provides for the filing of a financing statement to perfect a security interest in collateral;[411]

(ii) the financing statement meets the requirements of U.C.C. section 9-502(a) as adopted in that state;[412]

(iii) on its face,[413] the financing statement includes the information listed in U.C.C. section 9-516(b)(5);[414] and

(iv) the financing statement has been properly filed[415] in that state (or is expected to be filed).[416]

These determinations would each be made under the law of the state of the *debtor's* "location." Unless the opinion expressly covers which state is the state of the debtor's location,[417] however, the perfection opinion would be given under

of additional entities, such as entities formed under federal law. *See, e.g.*, U.C.C. § 9-307(f). For a limited number of categories of collateral, the location of the debtor is not the place of filing. *See id.* § 9-301(3); *supra* notes 100, 109, 133.

407. *See supra* notes 394–401 and accompanying text.

408. A filing in another state may be required to the extent collateral includes fixtures that are the subject of a fixture filing, timber to be cut, or as-extracted collateral. U.C.C. § 9-301(3)(A), (B), (4); *see supra* notes 100, 109, 133. This *Report* does not address those filings.

409. As noted, one or more of these issues may be covered by the wording of the opinion, an assumption, or other exception. *See supra* notes 393–94 and accompanying text.

410. This opinion is *not* an opinion that the law of the state where the financing statement is being filed is the "location" of the debtor and that it therefore governs the perfection of the security interest by the filing of a financing statement.

411. U.C.C. § 9-307(c); *see supra* § 4.2. This assumes that the opinion is subject to a U.C.C. Scope Limitation and therefore, that the opinion preparers do not have to determine whether the collateral involved in the transaction is subject to the U.C.C. as adopted in the state where the debtor is located. *See supra* § 2.1(b).

412. *See supra* § 4.3(a).

413. This determination is not necessary if the financing statement has already been accepted by the filing office. *See supra* note 126 and accompany text.

414. *See supra* note 126 and accompanying text. If the financing statement has already been filed, this information would not be necessary.

415. *See supra* note 132 and accompanying text.

416. *See supra* note 136 and accompanying text.

417. *See supra* § 2.1(d).

the law of the state where the financing statement has been (or will be) filed. Once again, it is not inappropriate for the opinion giver to address the issue of perfection[418] of the security interest by filing of a financing statement in that state even though:

(i) it generally would be unwilling to render an opinion on that state's law; and
(ii) the opinion does not address the question whether the state where the filing has occurred is the correct state for the filing of a financing statement.[419]

Possession. When the secured party perfects its security interest by possession, the local law of the location of the *collateral* generally governs perfection.[420] If the collateral is located in a state other than a state whose law is generally covered by the opinion, to give an opinion on the perfection of a security interest by possession the opinion preparers must consider the U.C.C. of the state where the collateral is located.[421] It is not inappropriate for the opinion preparers to render an opinion on that state's U.C.C. even though they generally would be unwilling to render an opinion on the law of that state.[422]

The opinion preparers should satisfy themselves that:

(i) the relevant collateral is the kind of collateral in which a security interest may be perfected by possession under the Article 9 of the state where the collateral is physically located;[423] and
(ii) the secured party (directly or through a third party) has taken "possession" of the collateral as defined under Article 9 as adopted in the state where the collateral is located.[424]

Control. When the secured party perfects its security interest by control, a similar set of issues arises. As noted, perfection by control is governed by the "jurisdiction" of a specified third party for deposit accounts, securities accounts, se-

418. This opinion is not a choice-of-law opinion that the state where the financing statement was filed is the state of the "location" of the debtor and therefore the state whose law governs perfection of the security interest by the filing of a financing statement.

419. *See supra* § 2.1(d).

420. U.C.C. §§ 9-301(2), 9-305(a)(1). An opinion on the perfection of the security interest does not include an opinion on the law that governs the perfection of the security interest unless it does so expressly.

421. The opinion preparers have no obligation to determine the actual location of the collateral. They may assume, therefore, without stating, that the collateral is located in the state whose law is covered generally by the opinion. Some lawyers prefer to state this assumption expressly.

422. *See supra* note 384.

423. *See supra* § 4.3 (discussion of methods of perfection). As with other matters discussed in this Appendix B, one or more of the elements of this opinion may be assumed or otherwise excluded. *See supra* note 400 and accompanying text.

424. The opinion preparers do not, in fact, determine that the secured party has possession. *See supra* text accompanying note 146.

curity entitlements, uncertificated securities, and letter-of-credit rights.[425] If an opinion is given on perfection by control, the opinion preparers should consider whether the determination of the jurisdiction of the third party is a matter of the law of the state covered by the opinion.[426] The U.C.C. of the state whose law is covered generally by the opinion initially governs the question of the kind of collateral that is being considered for purposes of the application of that state's choice-of-law rules. The U.C.C. of the jurisdiction of the third party (i.e., the jurisdiction whose law governs perfection of the security interest by control pursuant to the choice-of-law rules of the state whose law is covered generally by the opinion) will also characterize the collateral to determine which of its local law substantive perfection rules will apply, whether it is the kind of collateral in which a security interest may be perfected by control and whether the requirements for control have been met. It is not inappropriate for opinion preparers to conduct that review even though they would not generally render an opinion on the law of that state.[427]

425. U.C.C. §§ 9-304, 9-305(a)(2), (3), 9-306; *see supra* notes 107, 151. Perfection by control of a certificated security is governed by the law of the jurisdiction where the security certificate is physically located. U.C.C. 9-305(a)(1).

426. *See supra* note 149 and accompanying text.

427. *See supra* note 384.

APPENDIX C

SUMMARY

General. This is a summary of some of the matters discussed in the 2003 TriBar Opinion Committee *Special Report on U.C.C. Security Interest Opinions—Revised Article 9*. This summary is qualified in its entirety by the more detailed discussion in the *Report*.

The *Report* provides guidance on closing opinions that address security interests covered by Article 9 of the U.C.C. The primary objective of the *Report* is to provide guidance on the customary meaning and scope of U.C.C. security interest opinions, and on the qualifications that are customarily understood to apply. An *Illustrative Security Interest Opinion* is attached to the *Report* as APPENDIX A. The main body of the *Report* discusses U.C.C. security interest opinions when the only law governing attachment (or creation), perfection, or, when addressed, priority of the security interest is the law covered generally by the opinion letter.

Preparers of U.C.C. security interest opinions are subject to the same obligations they have in preparing any closing opinion (i) not to give an opinion if they believe the opinion will, in the circumstances, mislead the opinion recipient, and (ii) not to rely on unreliable information.

Opinions under Article 9 call for familiarity with Article 9. While the *Report* provides a detailed discussion of Article 9 and opinions on security interests created under Article 9, opinion preparers who do not regularly work with Article 9 should consider whether to involve a lawyer familiar with Article 9 in the preparation of a U.C.C. security interest opinion.

Choice-of-Law. Except to the extent it does so expressly, a security interest opinion does not address which state's law governs the perfection of the security interest. APPENDIX B discusses issues that may arise when the law that governs the perfection of the security interest may not be the law covered generally by the opinion letter.

U.C.C. Scope Limitation. An opinion limited to the U.C.C. of a particular state customarily is understood to be subject to the following limitation, which the *Report* refers to as a "U.C.C. Scope Limitation:"

(i) The opinion covers only security interests created under Article 9 of the U.C.C.;
(ii) The opinion covers only U.C.C. collateral or transactions; and
(iii) The opinion covers only U.C.C. perfection methods.

As a matter of customary practice, any indication in the opinion letter that reasonably communicates to the opinion recipient that the opinion is limited to the U.C.C. or to Article 9 of the U.C.C. of a particular state is understood to convey the U.C.C. Scope Limitation.

Assumptions. Opinions on Article 9 security interests are based on many assumptions. Some assumptions must be stated. As a matter of customary practice, others do not need to be stated.

Remedies. Opinion letters typically contain separate security interest opinions and remedies opinions on security agreements (when a remedies opinion on the security agreement is given). Remedies opinions are understood not to cover security interest issues and security interest opinions are understood not to cover the matters addressed by a remedies opinion (except to the extent necessary to cover the effectiveness of the security agreement as a contract).

Attachment. Customarily the opinion on the creation or attachment of a security interest is stated separately from the opinion on the perfection of the security interest. The Article 9 requirements for attachment in most circumstances are:

(i) the debtor has authenticated a security agreement that provides a sufficient description of the collateral;
(ii) value has been given; *and*
(iii) the debtor has rights in the collateral *or* the power to transfer rights in the collateral to a secured party.

The opinion preparers should review the security agreement for compliance with the first requirement. They either may confirm satisfaction of the second requirement or assume it expressly. They may assume satisfaction of the third requirement without stating.

Perfection generally . An opinion on the perfection of a security interest in Article 9 collateral expresses the opinion preparers' professional judgment that the steps required by the U.C.C. to give the secured party's security interest priority over the rights of a lien creditor have been (or will be) accomplished.

Perfection by filing. The opinion preparers should review the completed financing statement to:

(i) confirm the accuracy of certain of the information in the financing statement; and
(ii) determine that the financing statement is complete.

The opinion preparers should then:

(i) confirm that an effective filing of the financing statement in the appropriate filing office in the applicable state has occurred or will occur prior to the delivery of the opinion;
(ii) assume expressly that an effective filing of the financing statement has occurred or will occur in a proper manner; or
(iii) state that perfection will occur "upon" the effective filing of the financing statement in the specified filing office.

Perfection by possession, delivery, or control. An opinion on these subjects requires attention to the special perfection rules for those methods of perfection.

Priority. In those rare transactions when an opinion is given concerning the priority of a security interest perfected by the filing of a financing statement, opinion givers and recipients generally use a Filing Priority Opinion, based on a review of a search report from the applicable U.C.C. filing office. For instruments, certificated securities, securities accounts, security entitlements, and deposit accounts, certain other kinds of "priority" opinions may be given in particular circumstances.

Inherent or Otherwise Unnecessary Qualifications to Perfection and Priority Opinions. Because as a matter of customary practice an opinion is understood not to cover changes in the facts following the closing of the transaction, opinion givers are not required in an opinion letter to describe how a post-closing change in the facts may affect the Secured Party's rights. Certain other matters also are customarily understood and need not be stated in the opinion letter.

Transition Rules. Part 7 of revised Article 9 provides rules concerning the transition from former Article 9 to revised Article 9. These rules have no effect on the attachment or perfection of an Article 9 security interest for a transaction first closing *on or after* the effective date of revised Article 9. They can, however, affect the priority of a security interest created or perfected under revised Article 9 as against a security interest created or perfected under former Article 9.

Appendix D

Members of TriBar Opinion Committee

New York County Lawyers Association

Donald S. Bernstein (Chair)
David L. Bleich
Slyvia Fung Chin
Sol Neil Corbin
Arthur Norman Field
Edward H. Fleischman
Joseph W. Halliday
Linda C. Hayman
A. Sidney Holderness, Jr.
Morton Moskin
Charles Niemeth
Sandra M. Rocks**
Myer (Mike) O. Sigal, Jr.
John B. Tehan
Judith R. Thoyer
Lawrence E. Wieman**

New York State Bar Association

Frederick G. Attea
Gerald S. Backman
J. Truman Bidwell, Jr.
Daniel Gersen
Joseph D. Hansen
Arthur J. Heath
Richard R. Howe
Christian G. Koelbl, III
Richard T. McDermott
Bernard W. Nimkin
Richard L. Veron

The Association of the Bar of the City of New York

Franci J. Blassberg
Rita M. Bolger
Edward H. Cohen
Philip E. Coviello
Jerome E. Hyman
Howard N. Lefkowitz
Vincent Monte-Sano
Joel I. Papernik
Robert Rosenman
Brian L. Schorr
Nancy Young

Boston Bar Association

Donald W. Glazer**
Professor Joseph Hinsey, IV
Stanley Keller

The State Bar of California

Steven O. Weise*

Chicago Bar Association

Robin Heiss

Delaware State Bar Association

Hon. Thomas L. Ambro***
James G. Leyden, Jr.

The District of Columbia Bar

Stephen Glover
James J. Rosenhauer

State Bar of Georgia

Jeffrey M. Stein

North Carolina Bar Association

A. Mark Adcock

Pennsylvania Bar Association

E. Carolan Berkley**
David A. Murdoch

Texas State Bar

Roderick A. Goyne

Ontario Bar

Wilfred M. Estey

*Reporter
**Member of Editorial Group
***Did not participate in the consideration and approval of the *Report*.

Special Report of the TriBar Opinion Committee: The Remedies Opinion—Deciding When to Include Exceptions and Assumptions

*By the TriBar Opinion Committee**

I. Introduction

The TriBar Opinion Committee's report on *Third-Party "Closing" Opinions*[1] (the "1998 TriBar Report") describes customary practice[2] in preparing and interpreting third-party closing opinions.[3] This Report augments the analysis of the remedies

*The TriBar Opinion Committee (the "Committee" or "TriBar") currently includes designees of the following organizations functioning as a single Committee: (i) Special Committee on Legal Opinions in Commercial Transactions, New York County Lawyers' Association; (ii) Corporation Law Committee, The Association of the Bar of the City of New York, and (iii) Special Committee on Legal Opinions of the Business Law Section, New York State Bar Association. Members of the Allegheny County (Pa.), Atlanta, Boston, Chicago, District of Columbia and Ontario Bar Associations and of the state bars of California, Delaware, Georgia, North Carolina, Pennsylvania, and Texas are also members of the Committee. The members of the Committee and the Reporter and Editorial Group for this Report are listed in Appendix A.

This Report has not been approved by the governing body or membership of any of the bar associations whose committees or members were involved in its preparation. Accordingly, the views expressed are solely those of TriBar. This Report reflects a consensus of the Committee. It does not, however, necessarily reflect the views of individual members or their firms, organizations, or associations on any particular point.

1. TriBar Opinion Committee, *Third-Party "Closing" Opinions: A Report of The Tribar Opinion Committee*, 53 Bus. Law. 591, 592 (1998). Terms used in this Report have the meanings given them in the 1998 TriBar Report. *See generally id.* Art. I, at 595–608. Like the 1998 TriBar Report, this Report refers to the lawyer or law firm rendering the closing opinion as the "opinion giver" and the lawyer or lawyers who prepare the opinion as the "opinion preparers."

2. *See* 1998 TriBar Report, *supra* note 1, § 1.4, at 600–03. *See also* Restatement (Third) of The Law Governing Lawyers §§ 51 cmt. e, 95(2) cmt. b (2000) [hereinafter Restatement of Law Governing Lawyers]; The Committee on Legal Opinions of the American Bar Association's Section of Business Law (the "ABA Section"), *Legal Opinion Principles*, 53 Bus. Law. 831, § I.B, at 832 (1998) [hereinafter ABA Principles] (stating "[T]he scope and nature of the work counsel is expected to perform are based (whether or not so stated) on the customary practice of lawyers who regularly give, and lawyers who regularly advise opinion recipients regarding, opinions of the kind involved."); The Committee on Legal Opinions of the American Bar Association's Section of Business Law, *Guidelines for the Preparation of Closing Opinions*, 57 Bus. Law. 875, § 1.7, at 876 (2002) [hereinafter ABA Guidelines] (stating "An opinion giver is entitled to assume, without so stating, that in relying on a closing opinion the opinion recipient (alone or with its counsel) is familiar with customary practice concerning the preparation and interpretation of closing opinions."); 1998 TriBar Report, *supra* note 1, §§ 1.4(a), 1.6, at 601 n.24, 604.

3. A third-party closing opinion (a "closing opinion") is an opinion letter delivered at the closing of a business transaction by counsel for one party to another party. In most jurisdictions, an opinion giver has the obligation to the opinion recipient to exercise care in preparing a closing opinion. An opinion giver, however, does not owe the recipient the broader responsibilities lawyers owe to their

opinion contained in that report.[4] The remedies opinion addresses the enforceability of each of the undertakings of the opinion giver's client (the "Company") in the agreement between the Company and the opinion recipient.[5] These undertakings include affirmative and negative covenants of the Company and the remedies specified in the agreement for breaches by the Company of its contractual obligations. They also include provisions for interpreting and administering the agreement and resolving disputes under it.[6]

The meaning of the remedies opinion is based on the customary practice of lawyers who regularly give, and lawyers who regularly advise clients regarding, opinions of the kind involved.[7] Customary practice allows the opinion to be expressed in only a few words and permits the opinion preparers to rely on many unstated exceptions, assumptions, and limitations.[8] By amplifying the meaning of abbreviated opinion language, customary practice provides the framework for preparing and interpreting the opinion, thus facilitating the process by which opinions are given and received and reducing cost.

Like other opinions typically included in a closing opinion, the remedies opinion requires the opinion preparers to make professional judgments regarding application of the law covered by the opinion to the provisions of the agreement.[9]

own clients. The responsibilities of an opinion giver in delivering a closing opinion are limited to the opinions rendered, as interpreted in accordance with customary practice. *See* 1998 TriBar Report, *supra* note 1, § 1.2(a), at 595–97. An opinion giver should not, however, render an opinion that it believes will be misleading to the recipient under the circumstances. *See id.* § 1.4(d), at 602–03.

4. The remedies opinion (also called the "enforceability opinion") is discussed in Article III of the 1998 TriBar Report. The following example of a remedies opinion is included in that Report: "The Agreement is a valid and binding obligation of the Company enforceable against the Company in accordance with its terms." *Id.* § 3.1, at 619.

5. *See id.* § 3.1, at 619–21. This Report assumes that the Company is a corporation; for its application to other entities, see *id.* § 1.2(g), at 599.

6. For a discussion of the categories of contractual undertakings addressed by the remedies opinion, see *id.* § 3.1, at 619–21.

7. *See supra* note 2. The customary practice relevant to any particular opinion is the customary practice applicable on the date of the opinion. Customary practice is described and discussed in the 1998 TriBar Report and other bar association reports and scholarly writings. *See, e.g.*, ABA Principles, *supra* note 2; ABA Guidelines, *supra* note 2. *See generally* DONALD W. GLAZER ET AL., GLAZER AND FITZGIBBON ON LEGAL OPINIONS: DRAFTING, INTERPRETING AND SUPPORTING CLOSING OPINIONS IN BUSINESS TRANSACTIONS (2d ed. 2001), which reproduces many of the bar association reports and includes a bibliography of scholarly writings. Customary practice is not static; rather, it changes over time as opinion practice evolves and new issues emerge and are addressed.

8. *See* 1998 TriBar Report, *supra* note 1, §§ 1.2(a), 1.4(a), at 595–97, 600–01. *See also* RESTATEMENT OF LAW GOVERNING LAWYERS, *supra* note 2, § 95, reporter's note to cmt. c, which states: "In giving 'closing' opinions, lawyers typically use custom and practice to provide abbreviated opinions that facilitate the closing. Such opinions may not recite certain assumptions, limitations, and standards of diligence because they are understood between counsel."

Like the law, closing opinions are the product not only of logic but of experience. *See generally* Oliver Wendell Holmes, Jr., THE COMMON LAW (Little, Brown and Co. 1963) (1881). The words of closing opinions, were they to be read literally and taken to their logical extreme, would not always square with the way they are understood in practice. Molded by experience, customary practice tempers logic with practicality, reflecting a realistic assessment of what lawyers can be expected to do, from the standpoint of expertise and cost, to support the opinions they render.

9. The opinion does not cover limitations on enforceability that arise under bodies of law that are excluded from the opinion either expressly by the coverage limitation (*see infra* note 25) or implicitly as a matter of customary practice. *See* ABA Principles, *supra* note 2, Part II: *Law*; 1998 TriBar Report,

That law includes both statutory law and case law. In the absence of statute or controlling precedent, opinion preparers look to general principles of contract law and, in particular, the principle that accords contracting parties broad latitude to order their affairs by agreement.[10]

The enforceability of contractual provisions is subject to the effect of bankruptcy and insolvency laws and the availability of equitable defenses. These matters are excluded from the opinion by the standard bankruptcy exception and equitable principles limitation which, although usually stated in the opinion, are understood to be applicable whether stated or not.[11] Furthermore, enforceability may depend on various factual matters that, as a matter of customary practice, are covered by assumptions of general application that apply even if not stated.[12] These include factual assumptions regarding the genuineness of signatures and conformity of copies with the originals.[13] They also include assumptions regarding good faith and the absence of fraud, coercion, duress, and similar inequitable conduct preventing formation of an agreement.[14]

Some matters that affect enforceability do not fit neatly within the limitations described above but nevertheless, as a matter of customary practice, are understood not to be covered by the opinion. This may be, for example, because of the practical inability of lawyers to make the necessary determination of the reasonableness of an economic remedy[15] or because of the discretion courts have under applicable law to decline to enforce an otherwise enforceable forum selection clause.[16] Customary practice as to such matters reflects a practical assessment of what opinion recipients can reasonably expect lawyers to do in preparing the opinion.

supra note 1, § 3.5.1, at 627–28 (stating that opinion covers only law that a lawyer would reasonably recognize as being applicable), and § 3.5.2, at 629–30 (stating that certain specific laws are understood not to be covered unless expressly identified).

10. *See* Restatement (Second) of Contracts ch. 8. introductory note (1981) [hereinafter Restatement of Contracts]. *See also* E. Allen Farnsworth, Contracts §§ 1.6, 1.7, and 5.1 (3d ed. 1999), which states:

> The principle of freedom of contract rests on the premise that it is in the public interest to accord individuals broad powers to order their affairs through legally enforceable agreements. In general, therefore, parties are free to make such agreements as they wish, and courts will enforce them without passing on their substance. Occasionally, however, a court will decide that this interest in party autonomy is outweighed by some other interest and will refuse to enforce the agreement or some part of it.

11. *See* 1998 TriBar Report, *supra* note 1, § 3.3, at 622–25.

12. *See id.* § 2.3(a), at 615. *See also id.* § 2.3, at 616 (stating "Opinion preparers should not rely on an unstated assumption if it is unreliable.").

13. *See id.* § 2.3(a), at 615.

14. *See id.* § 3.3.4, at 625 n.77.

15. *See infra* section III.B., "Economic Remedies Provisions," at notes 46–50. Although the Committee believes the preferred course is usually to deal with the issue of reasonableness explicitly in the opinion, many lawyers do not take an express exception unless they have serious doubts about the reasonableness of a particular economic remedy.

16. *See infra*, section III.F., "Forum Selection Clause," at notes 87–88. Although an express exception with regard to these matters is not required, some lawyers include one to avoid any risk of misunderstanding.

When an express exception or assumption[17] is included in an opinion, its purpose should be to highlight a legal issue that could affect enforceability.[18] Sometimes an express exception or assumption will be necessary for an opinion to be correct. At other times, it will be unnecessary but will help clarify how the opinion should be interpreted.

To maintain the opinion's effectiveness as a communication tool, the opinion preparers should consider, each time they give an opinion, which exceptions and assumptions are appropriate. The value of an opinion is undercut when the opinion preparers include exceptions and assumptions that relate to issues that are not covered by the opinion or that are not raised by the agreement.[19] The inclusion of such exceptions and assumptions burdens the opinion process, requiring often protracted discussion over the opinion's meaning and coverage and obscuring the issues the opinion is intended to bring to the recipient's attention.[20]

Part II of this Report describes a process for determining when the opinion preparers should include express exceptions or assumptions. Part III examines customary practice in giving opinions on the enforceability of several common contractual provisions.

II. Determining When to Include Express Exceptions or Assumptions

In determining when to include express exceptions or assumptions, opinion preparers may wish to ask themselves one or more of the following questions:[21]

Do any of the Company's undertakings raise legal issues of concern?

To determine whether any of the undertakings of the Company in the agreement raise legal issues that call into question their enforceability,[22] opin-

17. *See* 1998 TriBar Report, *supra* note 1, § 3.2, at 622. This Report uses the terms "express exception" to refer to any exception in an opinion other than the standard bankruptcy exception or equitable principles limitation, and "express assumption" to refer to any assumption set forth explicitly in an opinion other than an assumption of general application, which may be unstated. An express assumption may serve as a substitute for an express exception. *See id.* § 2.3, at 615–16. For example, when an agreement provides for a floating interest rate, the opinion preparers, rather than taking an exception for usury laws, might expressly assume that the interest rate will never exceed a specified level.

18. An opinion that is limited in a way that is not customary for transactions of the type involved is referred to as a "qualified opinion." *See id.* §§ 1.2(a), 1.9(i), at 595–97, 606–07. Sometimes opinion preparers conclude that an opinion can be given but should not be stated apart from its underlying reasoning. A reasoned (or explained) opinion may or may not be qualified. *See id. See also id.* § 1.6, at 604.

19. Nevertheless, when the size of the transaction or the significance of the issue does not justify the cost of fully researching the question, exceptions and assumptions that might have proven unnecessary after further inquiry are sometimes included and accepted by opinion recipients.

20. *See* ABA Guidelines, *supra* note 2, at 876 ("Closing opinions should not include assumptions, exceptions, and limitations that do not relate to the transaction and the opinions given.") *See also* Arthur Norman Field, *One Size Doesn't Fit All: Reject 'Kitchen-Sink' Responses in Opinion Letters*, Bus. Law Today, May/June 2002, at 61–62.

21. The questions do not have to be asked in any particular order. For example, some opinion preparers may begin their inquiry with the law covered by the opinion rather than legal issues generally.

22. *See* 1998 TriBar Report, *supra* note 1, § 3.1, at 619–21. The principal focus of the remedies opinion is the legal effect of the agreement's provisions as a matter of contract law. The opinion, however, also covers issues arising under some other bodies of law. For example, to give a remedies

ion preparers review the law of each jurisdiction (state or federal) whose law is applicable[23] and make a professional judgment[24] whether under that law the highest court of that jurisdiction would enforce those undertakings. For state law, that court will be the highest court of the state in question and, for federal law, the United States Supreme Court.

The opinion preparers normally will not have to conduct legal research on every contractual provision each time they render an opinion. For many common provisions, the opinion preparers' existing knowledge and experience typically will be sufficient without further research to permit them to address the legal issues presented.

Does the legal issue arise under the law covered by the opinion?

When they have identified a legal issue of concern, the opinion preparers should consider whether it arises under the law covered by the opinion.[25]

opinion, the opinion preparers normally need to satisfy themselves that the agreement has been properly authorized and executed, even if a separate opinion is not rendered on those matters. For a corporation, due authorization is a function of corporation law and due execution a function of corporation and agency law. Due authorization and due execution are sometimes dealt with by an express assumption or reliance on an opinion of local counsel—for example, when the opinion does not cover the corporation law of the state in which the Company was incorporated.

Due execution is also a matter of contract law. The contract law requirements governing due execution—such as those imposed by the Statute of Frauds or Sunday "blue laws"—normally will be those of the state whose law governs the agreement. *See generally* RESTATEMENT (SECOND) OF CONFLICT OF LAWS §§ 198–202 (1971) [hereinafter RESTATEMENT OF CONFLICTS].

23. This Report generally assumes that the opinion covers the law of the jurisdiction whose law governs the agreement.

24. RESTATEMENT OF LAW GOVERNING LAWYERS, *supra* note 2, § 95 cmt. c, states:

> [A] legal opinion . . . is based on legal research and analysis customary and reasonably appropriate in the circumstances and . . . states the lawyer's professional opinion as to how any legal question addressed in the opinion would be decided by the courts in the applicable jurisdiction on the date of the evaluation. The lawyer is not required to state reservations or doubts about legal issues unless they are of a nature that prevents the lawyer from reasonably concluding that the opinion reflects the result that would be reached by the highest court of the applicable jurisdiction.

The American Law Institute's former director, Herbert Wechsler, set forth the following "working formula" for the Institute's restatements of the law: "We should feel obliged in our deliberations to give due weight to all of the considerations that the courts, under a proper view of the judicial function, deem it right to weigh in theirs." President's Letter, 20 ALI Rep., Summer 1998, at 1, 3. In forming the professional judgments called for by an opinion, opinion preparers normally take similar considerations into account.

25. Closing opinions customarily state that their coverage is limited to the law of specific jurisdictions (the "coverage limitation"). *See* 1998 TriBar Report, *supra* note 1, § 4.1, at 631–32 (referring to the "laws covered limitation"). For example, if the agreement chooses New York law as the governing law and the Company is a Delaware corporation, many New York lawyers will limit the opinion's coverage to New York law, federal law, and the Delaware General Corporation Law. *See id.* § 4.1, at 631 n.85. The coverage limitation excludes from the opinion the law of other jurisdictions even though that law could affect the enforceability of the agreement. Depending on how it is drafted, the coverage limitation also may exclude areas of law within a specified jurisdiction. For example, opinions on Delaware corporations often are limited to the Delaware General Corporation Law, which is understood to include only the Delaware corporation statute, applicable provisions of the Delaware constitution, and reported judicial decisions interpreting that statute and those constitutional provisions.

Sometimes the opinion will cover the enforceability of several agreements, each of which is governed by the law of a different jurisdiction. Ideally, the coverage limitation should expressly limit the opinion on each agreement to the law governing that agreement. If, however, the coverage limitation simply

An express exception or assumption is not necessary if the legal issue arises under the law of a jurisdiction that is excluded from the opinion by the opinion's coverage limitation[26] or if the legal issue arises under certain laws, such as tax, antitrust, and securities laws, that, as a matter of customary practice, are understood to be excluded from the opinion.[27]

Is the legal issue covered by the opinion?

A legal issue that otherwise would require an express exception or assumption may already be addressed in some other way. For example, the bankruptcy exception excludes from the opinion the possibility that a covenant might not be enforced or a remedial provision might be stayed in bankruptcy. Similarly, the equitable principles limitation excludes the possibility that a court might decline to order specific performance of a particular contractual provision or to grant enforcement of contractual rights to a party with unclean hands.

A legal issue that otherwise would require an express exception or assumption also may be covered by an assumption of general application (which assumptions apply whether or not stated). Thus, the assumption regarding the genuineness of signatures (whether or not stated) excuses the opinion preparers from establishing that the agreement, in fact, was signed by the person who purported to sign it.

Finally, as discussed above, the issue might relate to a matter that is understood to be excluded from the opinion even if not expressly excluded.[28]

Can the legal issue be resolved by factual inquiry?

The enforceability of a contractual provision may depend on the facts. For example, whether a loan violates the applicable usury statute may depend on whether the charges imposed on the borrower by the lender in connection with the loan when added to the contractual interest rate cause that rate to exceed the usury limit. The opinion preparers may be able to avoid an express exception or assumption by additional inquiry into the relevant facts. Thus, in the foregoing example, they may be able to obtain a schedule quantifying all the charges the borrower is paying to the lender in connection with a loan.

recites that the law of each of the jurisdictions is covered, the remedies opinion as it applies to a particular agreement is, as a matter of customary practice, understood to cover only the law of the jurisdiction chosen in that agreement as its governing law.

26. The fact that an opinion giver has multiple offices does not change the effect of the coverage limitation. The opinion preparers are responsible only for the law designated in the opinion for coverage and are not required to check on the law of other jurisdictions with their firm's offices in those jurisdictions.

27. *See, e.g.*, 1998 TriBar Report, *supra* note 1, § 3.5.2(c), at 629–30. As indicated in that section, however, the Investment Company Act of 1940 may sometimes be covered. *Id.*

28. *See supra* notes 15 and 16 and accompanying text. *See also infra* note 62 (comity) and sentence in the text following note 69 in last paragraph of § III.E., "Chosen-Law Provision" (describing view of some lawyers).

Can the legal issue be avoided by restructuring the transaction or revising the agreement?

Sometimes, the transaction can be restructured or a contractual provision revised to avoid a legal issue. For example, if the agreement calls for a floating rate of interest (creating a risk that the interest rate could float above the applicable usury ceiling), that rate could be capped at the usury limit.

In deciding whether they need to include an express exception or assumption, opinion preparers need not ask all the questions outlined above or ask them in any particular order. Sometimes they will recognize immediately that an undertaking raises no legal issues or that a legal issue that otherwise would be of concern arises under laws that are not covered by the opinion. At other times, they will determine that a legal issue that initially concerned them is addressed by a standard exception or an unstated assumption or they will resolve it by further factual inquiry. In some cases, a potential legal issue will have been identified early on and avoided as an opinion issue in structuring the transaction.

When the opinion preparers conclude that an express exception or assumption should be included, they should promptly alert counsel for the opinion recipient.[29] Several alternatives might then be considered:

- Depending on the issues involved, the opinion recipient may decide to accept the opinion as qualified.[30] Exceptions to remedies opinions are often acceptable, especially when they relate to provisions that are generally recognized to raise concerns.
- The opinion preparers may be asked to look into the matter further. For example, additional legal research may reveal helpful authority or further factual inquiry may confirm that what initially appeared to be a problem in fact is not.
- The parties may agree to revise the agreement or the terms of the transaction to eliminate the problem. The agreement could be modified, for example, to make a provision waiving the Company's right to a jury trial sufficiently conspicuous to meet the applicable state's standard for enforceability.[31]

Which alternative the parties pursue will depend on various factors, including the nature of the legal issues involved and the expected cost of addressing them.

29. *See* 1998 TriBar Report, *supra* note 1, § 1.7, at 604–05 and ABA Guidelines, *supra* note 2, § 2.4, at 877–78, both discussing obligations under rules of professional conduct.

30. Another way used on occasion (e.g., in opinions on underwriting agreements in registered public offerings) to limit the opinion is to draft it to cover only matters of contract formation, such as due authorization, execution and delivery, and not enforceability.

31. *See infra* § III.C., "Waiver of the Right to a Jury Trial."

III. Applying the Process Described in Part II to Common Contractual Provisions

A. Interest on Overdue Interest

Loan agreements sometimes provide for the payment of interest on overdue interest.[32] Although the enforceability of an obligation to pay interest on overdue interest varies from state to state,[33] a provision requiring payment of interest on overdue interest is unenforceable in only a few states.[34] Some states have statutes validating provisions calling for the payment of interest on overdue interest.[35] Other states give effect to such provisions if specified requirements are met, such as a requirement that the intention to charge interest on overdue interest be clearly and prominently expressed in the agreement.[36]

In most states, therefore, interest on overdue interest does not present an enforceability issue or the issue can be avoided by satisfying specified requirements. When, however, a legal problem exists and it has not been cured, for example, by proper drafting, an express exception or assumption ordinarily will be necessary.

32. An example is a clause providing:

> Upon the occurrence and during the continuance of a default, the Company shall pay interest on the unpaid principal amount of the Note and on the unpaid amount of all interest payable hereunder that is not paid when due at a rate per annum equal to 2 percent above the rate otherwise required to then be paid on the Note.

Unlike other remedial provisions such as late charges and default rate interest on overdue principal, provisions for interest on overdue interest may, depending on the state, be unenforceable without regard to reasonableness. *See infra,* § III.B., "Economic Remedies Provisions."

33. *See generally* 45 Am. Jur. 2d *Interest and Usury* §§ 57–63 (1999); Annotation, *Validity of Agreement to Pay Interest on Interest*, 37 A.L.R. 325 (1925), supplemented in 76 A.L.R. 1484 (1932). Some states that generally enforce interest on overdue interest may have statutes prohibiting it in specified transactions, such as consumer loans. A requirement for interest on overdue interest may also violate a state's usury law. *See* 45 Am. Jur. 2d *Interest and Usury* § 176 (1999).

34. Interest on overdue interest should be distinguished from compound interest. In a number of states, compound interest may not be enforceable in some circumstances. *See* 15 Samuel Williston, A Treatise on the Law of Contracts § 1417 (3d ed. 1968); Annotation, *What is "Compound Interest" Within Meaning of Statutes Prohibiting Charging of Such Interest*, 10 A.L.R. 3d 421 (1966).

35. *See, e.g.*, N.Y. Gen. Oblig. Law § 5-527 (McKinney 2004) (applicable when original principal amount exceeds $250,000). Prior to enactment of the New York statute in 1989, contractual undertakings to pay interest on overdue interest were not enforceable in New York under a line of cases dating back to *Young v. Hill*, 67 N.Y. 162 (1871). Those cases necessitated exceptions to opinions on the enforceability under New York law of agreements containing interest on overdue interest provisions and may account for the continuing perception of some lawyers that such provisions are problematic. *See* Debentureholders Protective Comm. of Cont'l Inv. Corp. v. Cont'l Inv. Corp., 679 F.2d 264, 268, 271 (1st Cir. 1982), *cert. denied*, 459 U.S. 894 (1982) (upholding provision for interest on overdue interest in class of debentures governed by Massachusetts law but refusing to uphold provision in class governed by New York law as then in effect).

36. *See, e.g.*, Coupounas v. Madden, 514 N.E.2d 1316, 1322 (Mass. 1987); McConnell v. Merrill Lynch, Pierce, Fenner & Smith, Inc., 662 P.2d 916, 921 (Cal. 1983); Mountain States Broad. Co. v. Neale, 783 P.2d 511, 555 (Utah Ct. App. 1989).

B. Economic Remedies Provisions

Loan agreements often contain provisions that impose on the borrower a charge for late payments and a higher interest rate while the loan is in default.[37] As a matter of contract law, late charges and default interest rates typically are enforceable unless they are not reasonable in the circumstances and thus constitute a penalty.[38] The test for determining reasonableness varies from state to state, but generally a provision will be held to be reasonable if it bears a reasonable relationship to anticipated collection costs,[39] or, in some states in the case of a default interest rate, if it reflects the increased risk associated with the defaulted obligation.[40] Depending on the state, the courts also may consider whether an agreement relates to a commercial transaction and whether its terms were negotiated at arm's length by the parties or are consistent with industry practice.[41]

37. The agreements governing so-called A/B exchange transactions also usually include a provision increasing the interest rate if the securities are not registered under the Securities Act of 1933 by a specified date. In an A/B exchange, the registration covers the issuance of securities in exchange for like securities that were initially sold in an exempt offering. The higher interest rate is intended to reflect the increased risk to the holder associated with its inability to resell the securities publicly.

38. For cases applying a liquidated damages test to the determination of late charges as a penalty, *see, e.g.*, Collins v. Union Fed. Sav. and Loan Assoc., 662 P.2d 610, 618 (Nev. 1983); Krupp Realty Co. et al. v. Joel, 309 S.E.2d 641, 642 (Ga. Ct. App. 1983); and S.E. Land Fund v. Real Estate World, 227 S.E.2d 340, 342 (Ga. 1976). *See also* DeCordova v. Weeks, 140 N.E. 269 (Mass. 1923); A-Z Servicenter, Inc. v. Segall, 138 N.E.2d 266, 269 (Mass. 1956) (voiding the doubling of the interest rate and an acceleration of the interest to maturity as penalties). Some states also subject late charges and default interest rates to state usury laws. *See, e.g.*, Begelfer v. Najarian, 409 N.E.2d 167, 175 (Mass. 1980).

39. *See, e.g.*, Mack Fin. Corp. v. Ireson, 789 F.2d 1083, 1084 (4th Cir. 1986) (upholding late charges as reasonable); *In re* Egea, 167 B.R. 226, 231 (Bankr. D. Kan. 1994); *In re* Consolidated Prop. Ltd. P'ship, 152 B.R. 452 (Bankr. D. Md. 1993); *In re* Melbell Assoc, Inc., 99 B.R. 31, 34 (Bankr. E.D. Cal. 1989) (upholding a four percent late charge); *In the Matter of* Terry Ltd. P'ship, 27 F.3d 241, 244 (7th Cir. 1994) (three percent increase not unreasonable); Travelers Ins. Co. v. Corporex Properties, Inc., 798 F. Supp. 423, 427–28 (W.D. Ky. 1991) (four percent late charge not unreasonable); *In re* Gas Reclamation, Inc. Sec. Litig., 741 F. Supp. 1094, 1098 (S.D.N.Y. 1990) (three percent increase not unreasonable); Fleet Bank of Massachusetts, N.A. v. One-O-Six Realty, Inc., No. Civ. A. 94-3392-G, 1995 WL 389862, at *3 (Mass. Super. Jan. 17, 1995) (default interest rate of four percent over the contract rate reasonable, citing several federal courts that upheld an increased interest rate of three to four percent in the event of default).

The test for reasonableness cannot be applied mechanically because an economic remedy, such as a late fee or default interest rate, that has been found to be reasonable in one factual context may be found not to be reasonable in another. For example, the reasonableness of a particular percentage may depend on the amount involved and other factors. *See* Howard Johnson Int'l. Inc. v. HBS Family Inc., No. 96 CIV. 7687(SS), 1998 WL 411334, at *7 (S.D.N.Y. July 22, 1998) ("one size fits all" economic remedy not enforced on grounds that the same damage amount is not reasonable for all defaults).

40. *See, e.g.*, Dikeou v. Dikeou, 928 P.2d 1286, 1290 (Colo. 1997); Bloom v. Trepanal, 289 N.Y.S.2d 447 (N.Y. App. Div. 1968) and Union Estates Co. v. Adlon Constr. Co., 221 N.Y. 183, 184 (1917).

41. 24 Samuel Williston, A Treatise on the Law of Contracts § 65:13 (4th ed. 1997). *See* Metlife Capital Fin. Corp. v. Wash. Ave. Assocs., L.P., 732 A.2d 493 (N.J. 1999) (referring to industry practice in dealing with the reasonableness of a late fee of five percent and default interest rate of three percent above the stated rate). In upholding both a late fee and default interest rate, the court stated that "'[t]he overall single test of validity is whether the [stipulated damage] clause is reasonable under the totality of the circumstances'" and that "liquidated damages provisions in a commercial contract between sophisticated parties are presumptively reasonable and the party challenging the clause bears the burden of proving its unreasonableness." *Id.* at 499 (alterations in original) (internal citation omitted).

Some loan agreements require borrowers under specified circumstances to pay so-called "make-whole premiums" when repaying loans prior to maturity.[42] The enforceability of make-whole premiums also typically depends on their reasonableness.[43] Courts view favorably make-whole premiums expressed as a formula that discounts to present value the interest lost by a lender when a loan is discharged prior to its stated due date. Agreements often contain a formula that follows an approach approved by the courts.[44]

Liquidated damages, whether or not denominated as such, are also a type of economic remedy. Courts have adopted various tests for determining when a liquidated damages provision is enforceable.[45] In applying these tests to any particular provision, courts often rely on economic analysis and expert testimony.

In routine commercial transactions, lawyers may have little difficulty satisfying themselves that the economic remedies in the agreement—e.g., the late charge and default interest rate in a loan agreement—are reasonable under the law of the jurisdiction whose law is covered by the opinion. In other transactions, however, the opinion preparers may not be able to determine the reasonableness of an economic remedy. To do so may require knowledge of facts that are not ascertainable by the opinion preparers.[46] In addition, for many provisions, the case law, to the extent it exists, may be too particularized to provide meaningful guidance. When they conclude that the reasonableness of an economic remedy cannot be determined as a practical matter, some opinion preparers routinely include an express exception or assumption in their opinion.[47] Practice, however, is not universal. Other opinion preparers, in like circumstances, regard their inability to make a determination of reasonableness to be so well understood that they follow

42. Make-whole premiums often apply not only to voluntary repayments but also to early repayments necessitated by a default, change of control or failure to maintain a specified rating.

43. What is reasonable is usually a question of state law. In the case of secured claims, section 506(b) of the Bankruptcy Code could also apply. *See In re* Anchor Resolution Corp., 221 B.R. 330, 340 (Bankr. D. Del. 1998). However, the effect of section 506(b) is excluded from the opinion by the bankruptcy exception.

44. Courts have approved various formulas as reasonable. *See id. See generally* Chester L. Fisher III, *Make-Whole Prepayment Premiums Under Attack*, 45 Bus. Law. 15 (1989) and cases cited therein.

45. Most states look to whether the amount specified is a reasonable estimate of the damages that would be caused by a breach, determined at the time of contract. Some states apply a "second-look" test, which requires that the amount specified also be reasonably proportionate to the damages actually caused. *See* Kelly v. Marx, 705 N.E.2d 1114, 1115 (Mass. 1999) (upholding a liquidated damages provision and cataloging the various state law tests). *See also* BDO Seidman v. Hirshberg, 93 N.Y.2d 382, 396 (1999). In Brazen v. Bell Atlantic Corp., 695 A.2d 43, 48 (Del. 1997), the Delaware Supreme Court, in upholding a merger break-up fee denominated in the agreement as liquidated damages, stated that to be unenforceable "the amount at issue must be unconscionable or not rationally related to any measure of damages a party might conceivably sustain." *See also* Truck Rent-A-Center, Inc. v. Puritan Farms 2nd, Inc., 361 N.E.2d 1015 (N.Y. Ct. App. 1977).

For a provision to be enforceable many states also require that actual damages be uncertain or difficult to ascertain at the time of contract. *See* Restatement of Contracts, *supra* note 10, § 356 cmt. b. In many transactions, such as long-term leases and other complex financings, opinion preparers have no difficulty concluding that this requirement is satisfied.

46. For example, the relevant facts (such as the loss the opinion recipient expects to incur in the event of a default) may be known only to the opinion recipient.

47. These opinion preparers follow the practice of omitting an express exception or assumption only when they have satisfied themselves that the economic remedy is reasonable.

the practice—unless they have serious doubts about the reasonableness of a particular remedy[48]—of not taking an exception.[49] Although both practices are widely followed, the Committee believes that in most instances the preferred course is for the opinion preparers to deal with the issue of reasonableness explicitly in the opinion.[50]

C. Waiver of the Right to a Jury Trial

Agreements sometimes contain waivers by the parties of their right to trial by jury in the event of a dispute. Most jurisdictions permit such waivers.[51] In those

48. Serious doubt may exist, for example, because the amount involved greatly exceeds amounts that are customary or sanctioned by controlling precedent, or the methodology for calculation differs from the methodology used in cases in which a similar remedy was upheld by the courts.

49. Lawyers who follow this practice believe that, when an economic remedy is neither clearly reasonable nor clearly unreasonable, an opinion giver cannot be expected to consider and weigh all the factors a court would need to consider when deciding whether the remedy is enforceable. The analysis required to evaluate reasonableness in these circumstances is different, in kind, from the analysis an opinion giver would conduct when the possible future event under which the provision would be unenforceable is readily identifiable and a determination of the legal consequence of the event is straightforward. In the case of a floating interest rate, for example, opinion givers may, depending on the state, be required to take an exception if the rate could increase above the applicable usury rate ceiling because that future event is easy to identify and its legal consequences are clear. *See* 1998 TriBar Report, *supra* note 1, § 3.5.2(c), at 629–30. In contrast, opinion preparers, in evaluating the reasonableness of an economic remedy, may have to consider a variety of factors that are not readily identifiable and susceptible to straightforward analysis, such as the nature of likely future defaults, their possible timing, and the harm that the opinion recipient may foreseeably be expected to suffer.

50. Agreements in complex leasing and secured financing transactions often provide for economic remedies (such as liquidated damages), remedies against property (such as means of repossession or foreclosure), and remedial procedures (such as confessions of judgment) that may raise legal concerns. *See, e.g., In re* Trans World Airlines, Inc., 145 F.3d 124, 134 (3d Cir. 1998). *But see* Wilmington Trust Co. v. Aerovias de Mexico, 893 F. Supp. 215 (S.D.N.Y. 1995). Opinions in these transactions sometimes contain a "practical realization" exception. *See* 1998 TriBar Report, *supra* note 1, § 3.4, at 626–27. When they do, the enforceability opinion is understood not to cover the reasonableness of any particular remedial provision.

51. *See* Jay M. Zitter, Annotation, *Contractual Jury Waiver in State Civil Cases*, 42 A.L.R. 5th 53 §§ 2[a] & 3 (1996). *See also* Barclays Bank of New York v. Heady Elec. Co., 571 N.Y.S. 2d 650, 652 (N.Y. App. Div. 1991); Gunn v. Palmieri, 589 N.Y.S.2d 577, 577 (N.Y. App. Div. 1992); Palmer v. Lavers, 105 N.E. 1000, 1002 (Mass. 1914); Chase Commercial Corp. v. Owen, 588 N.E.2d 705, 708 (Mass. App. Ct. 1992). Georgia and North Carolina are exceptions to the general rule. *See* Bank S., N.A. v. Howard, 444 S.E.2d 799, 800 (Ga. 1994) (waiver of jury trial entered into independently of specific litigation not enforceable); N.C. Gen. Stat. § 22B-10 (2003) (waiver of jury trial void as contrary to public policy). California may also be an exception. *Compare* Grafton Partners L.P. v. Superior Court, 2004 Cal. App. LEXIS 153 (Cal. Ct. App. Feb. 6, 2004), *rev. granted*, *with* Trizec Properties, Inc. v. Superior Court, 229 Cal. App. 3d 1616 (1991). Even in jurisdictions where jury trial waivers are enforceable generally, such waivers may not be enforceable for certain types of claims. For example, in New York waivers of jury trial in leases of real property are ineffective as to claims for personal injury or property damages. N.Y. Real Prop. § 259-c (McKinney 2003). Many New York leases specifically exclude those claims from the waiver, thus eliminating the need for an opinion exception.

Although the effectiveness of a waiver of jury trial ultimately will be determined under the law of the forum in which the dispute is adjudicated, see *infra* note 62, unless an opinion otherwise states, it addresses enforcement of the waiver under the law of the jurisdiction whose law is covered by the opinion (and not under the law of other jurisdictions in which a dispute might, in fact, be adjudicated).

jurisdictions, no legal issue is presented, and an express exception or assumption is unnecessary.[52]

Some jurisdictions prohibit the parties to an agreement from waiving in advance their right to a jury trial or impose conditions on such a waiver. In those jurisdictions, an express exception or assumption would be necessary unless the conditions for enforceability of the waiver are satisfied or the legal bases for not enforcing the waiver are covered by a standard exception or unstated assumption.[53]

Often, when states impose conditions on enforcing a jury waiver, those conditions will not necessitate an exception. Some jurisdictions, for example, require that a waiver be sufficiently "conspicuous."[54] In those jurisdictions, if the waiver is not conspicuous initially, it ordinarily will be made conspicuous. Other jurisdictions require the waiver to be "knowing or intentional."[55] In those jurisdictions, the opinion preparers ordinarily will satisfy themselves that their client is aware of the waiver.

D. No Oral Modification Clause

Many agreements state that they may not be modified or their provisions waived except by a writing signed by the party against whom enforcement is sought. Some states have statutes validating no oral modification clauses.[56] In most other states, the parties to an agreement, as a matter of freedom of contract, may legally bind themselves to such a clause.[57]

In practice, however, courts often decline to enforce no oral modification clauses, even in states with statutes that expressly validate them.[58] The reason is that under the facts presented the party against whom enforcement is sought typically has relied on an oral modification to its detriment or has given additional

52. The Seventh Amendment to the U.S. Constitution does not preclude a party from agreeing to a waiver. *See* Melancon v. McKeithan 345 F. Supp. 1025, 1045 (E.D. La. 1972), *aff'd*, 409 U.S. 1098 (1973) (under Due Process Clause of Fourteenth Amendment, Seventh Amendment does not require states to provide jury trial in civil cases).

53. One basis some courts use to decline to enforce a jury trial waiver is the inequitable conduct of the party seeking enforcement in obtaining the waiver. *See* Rosenberg v. Merrill Lynch, 995 F. Supp. 190, 192 (D. Mass. 1998). An opinion is based on an unstated assumption regarding the absence of such conduct. *See* 1998 TriBar Report, *supra* note 1, § 3.3.4, at 625 n.77.

54. *See, e.g.*, Balram v. Etheridge, 449 N.Y.S.2d 389, 391 (1982) (holding clause in lease unenforceable because of failure to conform to minimum print size required by statute); Fairfield Leasing Corp. v. Technigraphics, Inc., 607 A.2d 703, 706 (N.J. Super. Ct. Law Div. 1997) (finding no waiver because clause was "utterly inconspicuous"); Colgate Constr. Corp. v. Hill, 334 N.Y.S.2d 1002, 1004 (1972) (finding waiver invalid because clause located inconspicuously on back of home improvement contract).

55. *See, e.g.*, Malan Realty Investors Inc. v. Harris, 953 S.W.2d 624, 627 (Mo. 1997) (requiring that waiver be knowing and voluntary); and Gaylord Dep't Stores, Inc. v. Stephens, 404 So. 2d 586, 588 (Ala. 1981) (finding waiver ineffective where not knowingly or intelligently made).

56. *See, e.g.*, N.Y. Gen. Oblig. Law § 15-301 (McKinney 2003). *See also* U.C.C. § 2-209(2) (2003).

57. For a contrary rule, *see* Son-Shine Grading, Inc. v. APC Constr. Co., 315 S.E.2d 346, 349 (N.C. Ct. App. 1984), *disc. rev. denied*, 321 S.E.2d 900 (N.C. 1984).

58. *See* 15 Samuel Williston, A Treatise on the Law of Contracts § 1828 (3d ed. 1968).

consideration for the modification.[59] These bases for refusing to enforce a no oral modification clause do not require an express exception or assumption. The first basis, detrimental reliance, is excluded from the opinion by the equitable principles limitation, which covers principles, such as equitable estoppel, that prevent a party making an oral modification from challenging the other party's reliance on it.[60] The second basis, additional consideration, is not covered by the opinion because the payment of additional consideration creates a new contract,[61] and only the existing contract and not the new contract is the subject of the opinion.

E. Chosen-Law Provision

The remedies opinion addresses the enforceability of the provision included in most agreements that chooses the law of a particular jurisdiction as the governing law.[62] Most states take one of two approaches to the enforceability of chosen-law provisions: the statutory approach or the Restatement approach.[63]

59. Thus, if a bank were to invoke a no oral modification clause and revoke an oral waiver by a bank officer, a court will decline to enforce the clause and will give effect to the waiver if the borrower has relied on the waiver to its detriment or given consideration for the waiver.

60. *See, e.g.*, Nassau Trust Co. v. Montrose Concrete Products Corp., 56 N.Y.2d 175, 183 (1982); Walter v. Hoffman, 267 N.Y. 365, 370 (1935) ("Even then, the question remains in each case whether a plaintiff has shown that a court should exercise its equitable power to prevent injustice."). *See also* Whittier v. Dana, 92 Mass. (10 Allen) 326 (1865); Stearns v. Hall, 63 Mass. (9 Cush.) 31 (1851); 1998 TriBar Report, *supra* note 1, § 3.3.4, at 625.

61. Referring to oral modifications to a written contract that expressly required any modifications to be in writing, Judge (later Justice) Holmes wrote in 1889 that "[a]ttempts of parties to tie up by contract their freedom of dealing with each other are futile." Bartlett v. Stanchfield, 148 Mass. 394, 395 (1889). Williston explains that an oral modification supported by sufficient consideration rescinds the no oral modification clause in the original contract. 15 Samuel Williston, A Treatise on the Law of Contracts § 1828, at 496 (3d ed. 1972). *See, e.g.*, First Pa. Mortgage Trust v. Dorchester Savs. Bank, 481 N.E.2d 1132, 1138–39 (Mass. 1985) (stating that, "[i]t is a settled principle that the mode of performance required by a written contract may be varied by a subsequent oral agreement based upon a valid consideration," and finding the oral exchange of promises by two banks in a loan participation arrangement to be valid consideration) (internal citations omitted).

62. Even if the law chosen in the agreement to govern is determined by a court to be the law generally governing the agreement, that law will not necessarily govern every aspect of the agreement. *See* 1998 TriBar Report, *supra* note 1, § 4.5, at 634. Some aspects of the agreement may be governed by mandatory choice of law rules. *Id.* For example, the effectiveness of a provision relating to conduct of a judicial proceeding, such as a waiver of jury trial, is governed by the law of the forum in which the dispute is adjudicated, whether or not that is the law chosen in the agreement. A remedies opinion does not require an exception for the possibility that the substantive law of a state whose law is excluded from the opinion by the coverage limitation might be applied to some aspects of the agreement as a result of a mandatory choice of law rule. If, however, the opinion preparers recognize that the law of another state would apply—such as they might in the case of a voting trust for a corporation's shares under the "internal affairs" doctrine—and believe that it would invalidate a provision of the agreement, the opinion preparers should consider whether giving the opinion, without bringing the issue to the attention of the opinion recipient, would be misleading. *See id.* § 1.4(d), at 602–03.

Under the principle of "comity," a court may give deference to an act of a foreign sovereign state whose law is not chosen to govern the agreement. Because application of the principle of comity is so well understood, it ordinarily does not require a further exception. *Id.* at § 3.1 n.71. Nevertheless, when the Company is a non-United States entity, some lawyers point out in their opinion that the enforceability of the agreement may be limited by the principle of comity. *See* Allied Bank International v. Banco Credito Agricolade Cartago, 757 F.2d 516, 522 (2d Cir. 1985).

63. Even if a state has a statute, it may follow the Restatement approach when the statute does not apply. This Report does not address opinions on chosen-law provisions whose enforceability is not governed by a statute or the Restatement approach.

Under the statutory approach, for commercial transactions involving more than a specified dollar amount, some states, including New York, Delaware, Illinois, and California, validate by statute contractual provisions selecting their law as the governing law regardless of whether the parties or transaction have a reasonable relation with their state.[64] Under the Restatement approach, states enforce chosen-law provisions unless (i) the jurisdiction whose law is the chosen law has no substantial or other reasonable relationship to the parties to the transaction or the transaction itself or (ii) application of the chosen law would be contrary to a fundamental policy of another jurisdiction that has a materially greater interest in the determination of the issue and that would be the jurisdiction whose law would apply in the absence of an effective chosen-law provision.[65]

In states that have adopted the statutory approach, opinion preparers typically have no difficulty concluding that an exception is not required. Thus, a New York opinion giver rendering an opinion on an agreement covered by the New York statute that chooses New York law as its governing law can render the opinion based solely on its determination that the requirements of the statute have been satisfied without concerning itself about contacts with New York.[66]

64. N.Y. Gen. Oblig. Law § 5-1401 (McKinney 2004); Del. Code Ann. tit. 6, § 2708 (2002); 735 Ill., Comp. Stat. § 105/5-5 (West 2004); Cal. Civ. Code § 1646.5 (West 2004).

65. Restatement of Conflicts, *supra* note 22, § 187(2) validates a chosen-law provision

> unless either (a) the chosen state has no substantial relationship to the parties or the transaction and there is no other reasonable basis for the parties' choice, or (b) application of the law of the chosen state would be contrary to a fundamental policy of a state which has a materially greater interest than the chosen state in the determination of the particular issue and which, under the rule of Section 188 [the state with the most significant relationship to the transaction and the parties], would be the state of the applicable law in the absence of an effective choice of law by the parties.

States may have fundamental policies, for example, with regard to non-competition provisions and distributorship arrangements.

If the Uniform Commercial Code applies, U.C.C. § 1-301 (2003) provides that, except as specified in other provisions of the Uniform Commercial Code, in commercial transactions the parties' choice of governing law is effective whether or not the transaction bears a relation to the state or country whose law is designated, except to the extent application of the chosen law would be contrary to a fundamental policy of the state or country whose law would govern in the absence of a choice of law by the parties.

66. Many opinion preparers in New York give the opinion in negotiated commercial transactions to which the New York statute applies even when the transaction and the parties have few, if any, contacts with New York beyond the contractual choice of New York law. Some opinion preparers, however, in that situation prefer to address the contacts issue explicitly in the opinion. Although not finding constitutionality to be an issue in the case before it, one federal court has observed that the courts have not considered whether the reach of the New York statute is subject to constitutional limitations. *See* Lehman Bros. Comm. Corp. v. Minmetals Int'l Non-Ferrous Metals Trading Co., 179 F. Supp. 2d 118, 137 (S.D.N.Y. 2000) (stating in dictum, "It remains to be seen, however, whether a state with *no* connection to either the parties or the transaction could apply its own law, consonant with the Full Faith and Credit Clause, when doing so would violate an important public policy of a more-interested state."). *See also* Int'l Indosuez Finance B.V. v. National Reserve Bank, No. 601467/99, 1999 N.Y. Misc. LEXIS 476 (N.Y. Sup. Ct. Oct. 22, 1999) (refusing to entertain constitutional challenge to the New York statute on the facts of that case, noting that "[t]he [t]ransactions bear a sufficient relationship to New York to support the application of New York law consistent with Due Process—wholly apart from GOL §5-1401. . . ."), *aff'd* on other grounds in Indosuez Int'l Finance B.V. v. National Reserve Bank, 720 N.Y.S. 2d 102 (App. Div. 2001), *aff'd* 98 N.Y.S. 2d 238 (2002); Allstate Ins. Co. v. Hague, 449 U.S. 302, 308 (1981).

In states that follow the Restatement approach, the analysis is more complex. In those states, the parties' choice of law will be given effect unless one of the two Restatement exceptions applies. The first exception applies when the chosen-law state has no substantial relationship with the transaction or the parties and no other reasonable basis exists for the parties' choice.[67] Whether a sufficient relationship exists depends on such factors as the jurisdictions in which the parties are organized, the parties' business locations, the place of negotiation and closing, the place where significant aspects of the agreement are to be performed (such as funding of loans, making of payments, delivery of goods, or performance of services), and the location of the subject matter of the contract or relevant bank accounts. The existence of one or more of these factors often permits the opinion preparers to make a professional judgment that the first of the Restatement's exceptions does not apply. When they cannot, the opinion preparers sometimes can arrange for a modification in the structure of the transaction to create the necessary contacts.

The second Restatement exception calls for application of the substantive law of a state other than the chosen-law state if (i) that other state has a materially greater interest in the determination of the particular issue and its law would be applied in the absence of an effective governing law clause, and (ii) application of the chosen-law state's law would be contrary to a fundamental policy of that other state.[68] This exception is not read to require opinion preparers to consider the possible application of the substantive law of a state whose law is not identified for coverage in the opinion's coverage limitation.[69] Some lawyers view this simply as an aspect of customary practice. Many others view the coverage limitation as excluding both the substantive law of states whose law is not expressly identified for coverage and the possible application of that law under choice-of-law principles. Thus, for example, when the state whose law is covered by the opinion and the chosen-law state are the same (e.g., they are both Massachusetts),[70] the

67. RESTATEMENT OF CONFLICTS, *supra* note 22, § 187, cmt. f. *See* Auten v. Auten, 308 N.Y. 155, 159–60 (1954) (applying choice-of-law principles to a contract in the absence of a chosen-law provision), which predates the New York statute. *See also* Allstate Ins. Co. v. Stolarz, 613 N.E.2d 936 (N.Y. 1993).

68. RESTATEMENT OF CONFLICTS, *supra* note 22, § 187(2)(b).

69. An opinion giver may not, however, knowingly mislead an opinion recipient with regard to matters covered by the opinion. *See* 1998 TriBar Report, *supra* note 1, § 1.4(d), at 602–03. Thus, if the opinion preparers recognize that a provision of the agreement is contrary to a fundamental policy of another state whose law would be applied by the chosen-law state in the absence of an effective governing law clause, they should consider whether giving an opinion that the chosen-law provision is enforceable, without bringing the issue to the attention of the opinion recipient, would be misleading.

70. When the law covered by the opinion is not the same as the law chosen in the agreement (e.g., a Massachusetts lawyer is asked to render an opinion on an agreement that chooses New York law), an opinion on the agreement might be limited to the enforceability of the chosen-law provision (i.e., whether a Massachusetts court, applying Massachusetts law, will give effect to the choice of New York law). *See id.* § 4.6, at 635–36. When it is so limited, this opinion often is accompanied by an opinion on the enforceability of the agreement if the substantive law of the state whose law is covered by the opinion (Massachusetts) were to apply. When both opinions are given, they are often combined by adding to the opinion on the enforceability of the chosen-law provision an opinion to the following effect: "but if the internal law of Massachusetts were nevertheless held to be applicable, the Agreement

opinion preparers are not required to point out in the opinion that they have only considered the chosen-law state's (Massachusetts') relationship to the parties or the transaction, and not the possibility that the substantive law of some other state might be relevant under the choice-of-law principles of the chosen-law state. Nevertheless, when another state has a significant relationship with the parties or the transaction, some lawyers choose to address the issue explicitly by including in their opinions an express assumption that the agreement does not violate the fundamental policies of other states or an express exception to like effect.

F. Forum Selection Clause

Commercial agreements often specify the forum where disputes between the parties are to be resolved.[71] Usually that forum is a court in the state whose law is chosen in the agreement as the governing law.[72]

Forum selection clauses may be either permissive or mandatory. A permissive clause authorizes the parties to a contract to bring suit in the specified jurisdiction but does not preclude a party from bringing suit elsewhere.[73] A mandatory clause

would constitute the Company's valid and binding obligation enforceable against it in accordance with its terms under Massachusetts law." This latter opinion has the same meaning as any other remedies opinion except that it does not address the enforceability of the chosen-law provision.

In a Restatement state (like Massachusetts), the opinion that the chosen-law provision selecting the law of another state (New York) will be given effect (under Massachusetts law) requires the opinion preparers to consider whether the "no substantial/reasonable relationship" exception to the Restatement's general approach to validating governing law provisions applies. If that exception does not apply (e.g., New York has a sufficient relationship to the parties or the transaction), the opinion requires the opinion preparers to determine whether the state whose law has been identified for coverage in the opinion (Massachusetts) has a fundamental policy that would be violated by the agreement. If they could render an unqualified opinion that the agreement would be enforceable if the law covered by the opinion (Massachusetts law) were to apply, they would not have to take an exception for violation of a fundamental policy of that state. If the agreement is enforceable under that state's law (Massachusetts law), that state (Massachusetts), by definition, would not have a fundamental policy against enforcement even if it were to have a materially greater interest in an issue. *See* Chase Manhattan Bank, N.A. v. Greenbrier North Section II, 835 S.W.2d 720, 725 (Tex. App. 1992). *See also* Guardian Sav. & Loan Assn. v. MD Assocs., 64 Cal. App. 4th 309, 322–23 (1998) (choice of Texas law given effect notwithstanding violation of California's fundamental policy against deficiencies in certain transactions because California did not have a materially greater interest in the issue than Texas).

71. A forum selection clause may designate the courts within a specific jurisdiction, for example, "the courts of the State of New York or a federal court located in New York." Sometimes it may designate a specific venue within the jurisdiction, such as "the courts of the State of New York located within New York County or the United States District Court for the Southern District of New York."

72. Because forum selection clauses normally designate the courts of the jurisdiction whose law is chosen as the governing law, this Report does not address opinions on clauses that designate the courts of other jurisdictions. *See supra* note 25. *See also* Cambridge Biotech Corp. v. Pasteur Sanofi Diagnostics, 740 N.E.2d 195, 201 (Mass. 2000), for an example of a clause selecting courts not located in the chosen-law jurisdiction. This Report generally assumes that the forum selection clause designates the courts located in a jurisdiction whose law is covered by the opinion.

73. An example of a permissive clause is: "The parties agree that any action involving a dispute under this agreement may be brought in the courts of the State of New York or a federal court located in New York, and they hereby submit to the jurisdiction of those courts."

requires the parties to bring suit only in the specified jurisdiction.[74] A forum selection clause is often accompanied by a consent by the parties to jurisdiction in the selected forum and may specify acceptable methods for service of process. Sometimes a permissive clause is accompanied by a waiver by the parties of their right to assert the doctrine of *forum non conveniens.*[75]

In determining whether they can render an opinion on a forum selection clause, the opinion preparers should consider the following:

Jurisdiction

Whether a clause is permissive or mandatory, a court will not give it effect unless the court has personal jurisdiction over the parties and subject matter jurisdiction over the issue in dispute.[76] Normally, inclusion of a forum selection clause in an agreement is itself sufficient to confer personal jurisdiction.[77] Similarly, selection of a court of general jurisdiction as the designated forum normally is sufficient to satisfy the requirement of subject matter jurisdiction.[78]

Applicable Legal Standard

Historically, most states took the position that, whatever an agreement might specify, courts should be free to determine for themselves whether to accept cases brought before them based on such factors as the sufficiency of contacts, the burden on the court, convenience, and the availability of other forums. When a forum selection clause is governed by the law of a state that

74. An example of a mandatory clause is: "The parties agree that any dispute involving this agreement shall be brought exclusively in the courts of the State of New York or a federal court located in New York, and they hereby submit to the jurisdiction of those courts."

75. *Forum non conveniens* is the doctrine under which a court may dismiss an action if, for the convenience of the parties, the witnesses, or the court, it decides that the action should proceed in another available forum in which the action might originally have been brought. *See* RESTATEMENT OF CONFLICTS, *supra* note 22, § 84.

In New York, by statute, parties to a qualifying contract are deemed to have waived their right to assert the doctrine of *forum non conveniens* even when they do not do so expressly. *See infra* note 91.

76. Opinion preparers address these jurisdictional requirements based on the facts as of the date of the opinion and need not point out that circumstances may change in the future.

77. Courts generally interpret a forum selection clause as a consent to personal jurisdiction in the designated forum. *See, e.g.*, Nat'l Union Fire Ins. Co., v. Williams, 637 N.Y.S.2d 36, 37, 39 (N.Y. App. Div. 1996) (addressing agreement not covered by the New York statute validating forum selection clauses). To be covered by the New York statute, N.Y. GEN. OBLIG. LAW § 5-1402 (McKinney 2004), an agreement must include an express consent to the jurisdiction of the New York courts.

78. Forum selection clauses normally do not specify a particular type of court. An exception is the selection of the Delaware Chancery Court as the venue to adjudicate disputes (as permitted by section 111 of the Delaware General Corporation Law). If a clause specifies a particular type of court, the opinion preparers must determine whether disputes under the agreement are within that court's subject matter jurisdiction. The parties cannot by contract confer subject matter jurisdiction on a court.

When a forum selection clause permits but does not require an action to be brought in federal court, many lawyers do not take an exception for the possible lack of federal subject matter jurisdiction. Some, however, do. Both practices are customary. If a clause designates the federal courts as the exclusive forum, the opinion preparers should consider whether a failure to refer in the opinion to limitations on federal jurisdiction would be misleading to the opinion recipient. *See* 1998 TriBar Report, *supra* note 1, § 1.4(d), at 602–03.

still takes that position, the opinion may require an express exception or assumption.

More recently, in recognition of the right of parties to order their affairs by contract, the courts of many states have abandoned old precedent and adopted the so-called "modern view," which gives forum selection clauses effect subject to some well-recognized exceptions.[79] Some states have enacted statutes that validate the enforceability of forum selection clauses in qualifying contracts.[80]

An opinion on a permissive clause without a waiver of *forum non conveniens* means that under the law chosen by the parties as the governing law the parties may bring an action in the designated forum.[81] Because a permissive clause, as interpreted by the courts, does not purport to foreclose a party from bringing an action in another state or, in the absence of a waiver, to prevent application of the doctrine of *forum non conveniens*,[82] the opinion does not mean that a party

79. *See* RESTATEMENT OF CONFLICTS, *supra* note 22, § 80; 7 SAMUEL WILLISTON, A TREATISE ON THE LAW OF CONTRACTS § 15:15 (4th ed. 1997) (citing cases that follow the modern trend of enforcing forum selection clauses); M/S Bremen v. Zapata Off-Shore Co., 407 U.S. 1 (1972); Carnival Cruise Lines v. Shute, 499 U.S. 585, 595 (1991); Jacobson v. Mailboxes Etc. U.S.A. Inc., 646 N.E.2d 741, 743 (Mass. 1995) ("We accept the modern view that forum selection clauses are to be enforced if it is fair and reasonable to do so."); Nat'l Union Fire Ins. Co. v. Worley, 690 N.Y.S.2d 57, 59 (N.Y. App. Div. 1999) (forum selection clause enforced even though New York statute did not apply).

Most states that follow the modern view will give effect to the selection by the parties of a particular venue within the state. *See* 7 WILLISTON ON CONTRACTS, § 15:15. In New York, by statute, a written agreement fixing the place of trial within the state, made before an action is commenced, will ordinarily be given effect. N.Y.C.P.L.R § 501 (McKinney 2004). In some states, even though a forum selection clause will be given effect, the selection of a specific venue may not be. *See, e.g.*, Alexander v. Super. Ct. (Brix Group), 114 Cal. App. 4th 723 (2003); Harry S. Peterson Co. v. Nat'l Union Fire Ins. Co., 434 S.E.2d 778 (Ga. Ct. App. 1993); Leonard v. Paxson, 654 S.W.2d 440 (Tex. 1983).

80. *See, e.g.*, N.Y. GEN. OBLIG. LAW § 5-1402 (McKinney 2004); 735 ILL. COMP. STAT. ANN. 105/5-5 (West 2004); CAL. CIV. PRO. CODE § 410.40 (West Supp. 2004); DEL. CODE ANN. tit. 6, § 2708 (2002).

Several states have statutes that render void as against public policy contractual provisions that require actions against parties within the state to be brought in a forum outside the state. *See, e.g.*, N.C. GEN. STAT. § 22B-3 (2003); IDAHO CODE § 29-110 (Michie 2004); MONT. CODE ANN. § 28-2-708 (2003); N.D. CENT. CODE § 9-08-05 (2003); OKLA. STAT. ANN. tit 15, § 216 (West 2004). Because the opinion typically covers the enforceability of a forum selection clause under the law of the jurisdiction whose law is chosen as the governing law and whose courts are selected as the forum, the opinion normally does not address the possible effect of a statute adopted by some other jurisdiction.

81. *See supra* note 73. As discussed above, the opinion also addresses the requirements for personal and subject matter jurisdiction.

82. In deciding whether to enforce a permissive clause, even in states that have adopted the modern view, courts normally regard themselves as free to apply the doctrine of *forum non conveniens* and dismiss an action when they perceive that litigating in another available forum will be more convenient for the parties, the witnesses, or the court itself. RESTATEMENT OF CONFLICTS, *supra* note 22, § 84. *See also* Argonaut P'ship, L.P. v. Bankers Trustee Co., No. 96 CIV.1970 (MBM), 1997 WL 45521, at *12 (S.D.N.Y. Feb. 4, 1997); Magellan Real Estate Inv. Trust v. Losch, 109 F. Supp. 2d 1144, 1162 (D. Ariz. 2000); Neo Sack, Ltd. v. Vinmar Impex, Inc., 810 F. Supp. 829 (S.D. Tex. 1993).

Sometimes courts appear to have stretched to interpret forum selection clauses as permissive so as to make it easier for them to approve maintenance of an action in another forum. *See* 7 WILLISTON ON CONTRACTS, § 15:15; Orix Credit Alliance, Inc. v. Mid-South Material Corp., 816 F. Supp. 230, 233 (S.D.N.Y. 1993); McDonnell Douglas Corp. v. Islamic Republic of Iran, 591 F. Supp. 293, 302–03 (E.D. Miss. 1984), *aff'd*, 758 F.2d 341 (8th Cir. 1985), *cert. denied*, 474 U.S. 948 (1985); Citro Florida, Inc. v. Citrovale, S.A., 760 F.2d 1231, 1232 (11th Cir. 1985).

may not bring an action outside the designated forum or that a court might not decline to entertain an action on the basis of the doctrine of *forum non conveniens.*[83] Although the doctrine of *forum non conveniens* is not covered, some lawyers nonetheless choose to point out its possible application in their opinions.

In deciding whether to enforce a mandatory clause (or a permissive clause with a waiver of *forum non conveniens*),[84] courts in a modern view state will not dismiss an action based on convenience but rather will give effect to the parties' choice of forum unless to do so would be "unfair or unreasonable." As interpreted by the courts, for enforcement to be unfair or unreasonable, a judicial determination is required that "enforcement of the clause would be so unreasonable and unjust as to make a trial in the selected forum 'so gravely difficult and inconvenient that the challenging party would, for all practical purposes, be deprived of his or her day in court.' "[85] The grounds for not enforcing a forum selection clause under this exception are much narrower than those required to invoke the doctrine of *forum non conveniens.* This exception is commonly referred to as the "Bremen" exception.[86]

In a modern view state, opinion givers rendering an opinion on a mandatory forum selection clause (or a permissive clause with a waiver of *forum non conveniens*) generally do not regard the possibility that a court might decline to enforce the clause by reason of the Bremen exception to require an opinion qualification.[87] This approach reflects the narrowness of the Bremen exception, the judicial discretion inherent in its application, and the inability of knowing in advance whether grounds for applying the Bremen exception will exist when an action is actually brought.[88] Nevertheless, the practice of not qualifying the opinion for this

83. The opinion also does not address whether a court in a jurisdiction that is not the selected forum and whose law is not covered by the opinion will dismiss a suit brought in that jurisdiction.

84. For purposes of determining whether to entertain an action in the designated forum and to decline to apply the doctrine of *forum non conveniens,* the courts treat a permissive clause with a waiver of *forum non conveniens* the same as a mandatory clause. *See* Blanco v. Banco Indus. de Venezuela, S.A., 997 F.2d 974, 979–80 (2d Cir. 1992); AAR Intern., Inc. v. Nimelias Enters. S.A., 250 F.3d 510, 525–26 (7th Cir. 2001). A permissive clause with a waiver, unlike a mandatory clause, however, does not seek to prevent a party from commencing an action elsewhere and does not constrain a court in the designated forum from dismissing an action for reasons other than *forum non conveniens* in favor of an action brought in another forum. *See* Fleet Capital Corp. v. Mullins, No. 03 CIV.6660(RJH)(KNF), 2004 WL 548240, at *5 (S.D.N.Y. Mar. 18, 2004) (action in designated forum dismissed in favor of prior pending action in another forum).

85. *See* Shah v. Shah, 626 N.Y.S. 2d 786, 788 (N.Y. App. Div. 1995) (citing, among others, M/S Bremen v. Zapata Off-Shore Co., 407 U.S. 1 (1972)); *see also* Roby v. Corp. of Lloyd's, 996 F.2d 1353, 1363 (2d Cir. 1993); Stamm v. Barclays Bank of N.Y., 960 F. Supp. 724, 729 (S.D.N.Y. 1997). Courts also decline to enforce the clause if it was obtained by fraud, duress or overreaching. A remedies opinion is based on an unstated assumption regarding the absence of such conduct. *See* 1998 TriBar Report, *supra* note 1, § 3.3.4, at 625 n.77.

86. *M/S Bremen*, 407 U.S. 1.

87. If the opinion preparers believe that, based on the circumstances existing on the date of the opinion, the *Bremen* exception would be applied, they should not render the opinion without taking an exception or otherwise bringing the issue to the attention of the opinion recipient. *See* 1998 TriBar Report, *supra* note 1, § 3.3.4, at 625 n.77.

88. Some lawyers believe that the equitable principles limitation encompasses the possibility that a court might apply the Bremen exception and decline to enforce a forum selection clause based on facts that exist when the action is brought. *See id.* § 3.3.4, at 625 (recognizing that the limits of the

issue is not universal, and some lawyers routinely point out the possible application of the Bremen exception in the opinion.[89]

In states that have enacted statutes, courts will generally enforce forum selection clauses when the criteria in the statute are met.[90] In New York, a statute enacted in 1984 expressly validates forum selection clauses in agreements relating to transactions involving not less than $1 million that select New York law as the governing law.[91] Accordingly, opinion preparers in New York typically give opinions without an exception on the enforceability of forum selection clauses (permissive or mandatory) selecting New York courts as the forum in agreements that qualify under the statute.[92]

IV. Conclusion

In the 1998 TriBar Report, the Committee observed that "at its best, the opinion preparation process can serve to clarify and improve transactions."[93] In this Re-

equitable principles limitation cannot be defined with precision but must remain flexible in view of the broad interest courts have to do justice).

89. A United States District Court also has discretion, under 28 U.S.C. § 1404(a), to transfer venue of a proceeding from one federal court to another. *See* Stewart Org., Inc. v. Ricoh Corp., 487 U.S. 22, 28–30 (1988). Federal courts have generally found §1404(a) to be applicable even to mandatory forum selection clauses but have not been uniform in the standards they have adopted for deciding whether to exercise the discretion granted by § 1404(a). *See* 17 James Wm. Moore et al., Moore's Federal Practice 111.04[2] (3d ed. 2004). Many federal courts have followed the admonition of the concurring opinion in *Stewart* that the statutory authority "should be exercised so that a valid forum-selection clause is given controlling weight in all but the most exceptional cases." *Stewart*, 489 U.S. at 33. *See, e.g.*, Falconwood Fin. Corp. v. Griffin, 838 F. Supp. 836, 840 (S.D.N.Y.1993); Jones v. Weibrecht, 901 F.2d 17, 19 (2d Cir. 1990); FUL Inc. v. Unified School Dist. No. 204, 839 F. Supp. 1307 (N.D. Ill. 1993); Medoil Corp. v. Citicorp, 729 F. Supp. 1456, 1459 (S.D.N.Y. 1990).

Other federal courts, however, have taken the position that the parties to a contract only have the power to limit a court's consideration of their convenience in determining whether to enforce a forum selection clause and not the convenience of witnesses or the interest of justice. *See, e.g.*, Capital Ventures International v. Network Commerce Inc., No. 01-CIV.4390(JSM), 2002 WL 417246, at *2 (S.D.N.Y. Mar. 15, 2002). As with the *Bremen* exception (and for similar reasons), many opinion preparers do not take an exception for § 1404(a) when rendering an opinion on a mandatory forum selection clause (or a permissive clause with a waiver of *forum non conveniens*) that includes the federal courts as a possible forum. Although unnecessary, some lawyers, however, to avoid uncertainty, do choose to point out the possible application of §1404(a) in the opinion.

90. *See supra* note 80.

91. N.Y. Gen. Oblig. Law § 5-1402 (McKinney 2004). N.Y.C.P.L.R. § 327(b) (McKinney 2004), a companion amendment to section 5-1402, provides that New York courts shall not stay or dismiss any action on the ground of inconvenient forum where section 5-1402 applies. The purpose of the statute was to assure the parties to an agreement that the courts would give effect to their choice of New York law as the governing law and their selection of the New York courts to resolve disputes. The trend for New York courts to recognize the parties' choice of forum was well under way in New York before enactment of the statute, *see, e.g.*, Arthur Young & Co. v. Leong, 383 N.Y.S.2d 618, 619 (N.Y. App. Div. 1976), and since the statute was enacted New York courts have followed the modern view even when the statute does not apply. *See, e.g.*, Roby v. Corp. of Lloyd's, 996 F.2d 1353, 1363 (2d Cir. 1993); Brooke Group Ltd. v. JCH Syndicate 488, 87 N.Y.2d 530, 534 (1996).

92. A New York court might still apply Bremen-like exceptions, but in view of the purpose of the statute to provide certainty to contracting parties, the grounds for departing from the statute, if a court were to do so, would presumably be limited to exceptional circumstances. Lawyers in New York do not routinely take an exception for such circumstances.

93. 1998 TriBar Report, *supra* note 1, at 665–66.

port, the Committee has described an approach for preparing the remedies opinion and determining when an express exception or assumption should be included, and has applied that approach to several common contractual provisions. The Committee believes that this approach, if broadly followed, will improve the opinion process and enhance the usefulness of the remedies opinion.[94]

August 2, 2004
All Rights Reserved
TriBar Opinion Committee
Copyright © 2004
Reprinted with Permission

94. As in the past we invite your comments on this Report. Address any comments to:

Chair, TriBar Opinion Committee
c/o New York County Lawyers' Association
14 Vesey Street
New York, NY 10007

APPENDIX A

Members of TriBar Opinion Committee

New York County Lawyers Association
Donald S. Bernstein (Chair) ***
David L. Bleich
Sylvia Fung Chin
Sol Neil Corbin
Arthur Norman Field ***
Edward H. Fleischman
Joseph W. Halliday ***
A. Sidney Holderness, Jr.
Morton Moskin ***
Charles Niemeth
Sandra M. Rocks
Myer (Mike) O. Sigal, Jr. ***
John B. Tehan
Judith R. Thoyer
Lawrence E. Wieman
Joel I. Papernik
Robert Rosenman
Brian L. Schorr
Nancy Young

New York State Bar Association
Frederick G. Attea
Gerald S. Backman
J. Truman Bidwell, Jr.
Daniel W. Gersen
Joseph D. Hansen
Arthur J. Heath
Professor Joseph Hinsey, IV
Richard R. Howe
Christina G. Koelbl, III
Richard T. McDermott
Bernard W. Nimkin
Richard L. Veron

The Association of the Bar of the City of New York
Franci J. Blassberg
Rita M. Bolger
Edward H. Cohen
Philip E. Coviello
Linda C. Hayman ***
Jerome E. Hyman ***
Howard N. Lefkowitz
Vincent Monte-Sano

Boston Bar Association
Donald W. Glazer **
Stanley Keller *

The State Bar of California
Steven O. Weise ***

Chicago Bar Association
Robin Heiss ***

Delaware State Bar Association
James G. Leyden, Jr.

The District of Columbia Bar
Stephen Glover
James J. Rosenhauer

Atlanta Bar Association
Jeffrey M. Stein

North Carolina Bar Association
A. Mark Adcock

Pennsylvania Bar Association
E. Carolan Berkley ***

Allegheny County (Pittsburgh) Bar Association
David A. Murdoch

Texas State Bar
Roderick A. Goyne

Ontario Bar
Wilfred M. Estey

Member Emeritus
Hon. Thomas L. Ambro ****

* Reporter
** Editor-in-Chief
*** Member of Editorial Group
**** Did not participate in the consideration and approval of the Report.

Third-Party Closing Opinions: Limited Liability Companies

*By the TriBar Opinion Committee**

The TriBar Opinion Committee's 1998 report, "Third-Party Closing Opinions," ("TriBar 1998 Report") addressed opinions commonly included in a standard closing opinion relating to corporations.[1] This report supplements the TriBar 1998 Report by addressing opinions on limited liability companies ("LLCs"),[2] specifically the opinions on status, power and action and, in a limited way, enforceability

---

* The TriBar Opinion Committee (the "Committee" or "TriBar") currently includes designees of the following organizations functioning as a single Committee: (i) Special Committee on Legal Opinions in Commercial Transactions, New York County Lawyers' Association; (ii) Corporation Law Committee, The Association of the Bar of the City of New York, and (iii) Special Committee on Legal Opinions of the Business Law Section, New York State Bar Association. Members of the Allegheny County (Pittsburgh, Pa.), Atlanta, Boston, Chicago, District of Columbia and Ontario Bar Associations and of the state bars of California, Delaware, Georgia, North Carolina, Pennsylvania, and Texas are also members of the Committee. The members of the Committee and the Co-Reporters and Advisers for this Report are listed in Appendix A.

This Report has not been approved by the governing body or membership of any of the bar associations whose committees or members were involved in its preparation. Accordingly, the views expressed are solely those of TriBar. This Report reflects a consensus of the Committee. It does not, however, necessarily reflect the views of individual members or their firms, organizations, or associations on any particular point.

1. *See* TriBar Opinion Committee, *Third-Party Closing Opinions: A Report of the TriBar Opinion Committee*, 53 BUS. LAW. 591, 599 (1998) [hereinafter "*TriBar 1998 Report*"] (suggesting that application of report to non-corporate entities could be derived by analogy to corporate model).

2. Although LLCs have come into general use only relatively recently, LLCs have become the vehicle of choice in many transactions. Indeed, the number of LLCs organized in Delaware now exceeds the number of Delaware corporations. The popularity of LLCs is attributable to the fact that, unlike limited partnerships and corporations, LLCs allow all their owners ("members," in LLC parlance) both limited liability and flow-through tax treatment.

LLCs are used in a wide variety of transactions, including (i) joint ventures and strategic alliances, (ii) international investment transactions, (iii) structured financings, and (iv) leveraged buyouts. LLCs serve as vehicles for conducting manufacturing and professional service businesses, for research and development, and for exploring for and mining natural resources. They also serve as general partners of limited partnerships; as special purpose finance vehicles; as vehicles for holding real property, investment securities and intellectual property; and as bankruptcy remote entities in structured financings.

Because of the widespread practice of organizing LLCs in Delaware rather than in the state where they principally do business, this report uses Delaware LLC law as a paradigm for its analysis and provides extensive citations to the Delaware Limited Liability Company Act, DEL. CODE ANN. tit. 6, §§ 18-101—18-1109 (2005) [hereinafter the "Delaware LLC Act"]. LLC statutes of other states often do not contain provisions comparable to those of the Delaware statute. Thus, lawyers giving opinions on LLCs organized in other states should always consult the LLC statute and relevant law of the state in which the LLC was organized.

of operating agreements.[3] Except as indicated, the terms used in this report have the same meanings as in the TriBar 1998 Report.

Like corporations and limited partnerships, LLCs are separate legal entities[4] that are creatures of statute. Today, every state has an LLC statute. Those statutes, however, are not uniform.[5] Some follow a corporation-law model, others a partnership-law model,[6] and still others a combination of the two.[7] Whatever model they follow, LLC statutes (like limited partnership statutes and unlike corporation statutes) typically provide an LLC's members broad contractual freedom[8] to determine how the LLC will be managed[9] and how the LLC's profits will be allocated and distributed. The contract governing the internal affairs of an LLC is commonly referred to as a limited liability company agreement or operating agreement ("operating agreement").[10] Although operating agreements may be oral,

3. Although this report addresses opinions on LLCs, it also may be relevant to opinions on other non-corporate entities, such as general and limited partnerships and statutory trusts.

4. *See* Delaware LLC Act § 18-201(b) *and* § 17-201(b) of the Delaware Revised Uniform Limited Partnership Act, DEL. CODE ANN. tit. 6, § 17-101—17-1111 (2005) [hereinafter the "Delaware LP Act"].

5. Unlike the Revised Uniform Limited Partnership Act, the Uniform Limited Liability Company Act has not been adopted in many states. Only eight states, of which the largest is Illinois, have modeled their LLC Acts on the Uniform Limited Liability Company Act (1996). *See* UNIF. LTD. LIAB. CO. ACT, 6A U.L.A. 95 (Supp. 2005).

6. For example, the Delaware LP Act and not the Delaware General Corporation Law, DEL. CODE ANN. tit. 8, § 101—398 (2001, Supp. 2004 & Supp. 2005) [hereinafter the "Delaware GCL"], served as the principal model for the Delaware LLC Act, and many of the section numbers of the Delaware LLC Act and Delaware LP Act correspond. The Delaware bar association committee that has responsibility for the Delaware LLC Act and its amendment also has responsibility for the Delaware statutes governing general and limited partnerships.

7. For a compilation of the various state LLC statutes and various governance models, *see* 3 LARRY E. RIBSTEIN & ROBERT R. KEATINGE, RIBSTEIN AND KEATINGE ON LIMITED LIABILITY COMPANIES, Appendices A and B (2d ed. 2005).

8. The principle of freedom of contract is a core feature of LLCs. *See, e.g.*, Delaware LLC Act § 18-1101(b) (policy is to give maximum effect to principle of freedom of contract and to enforceability of operating agreements). LLC statutes typically permit all but a handful of statutory provisions to be modified by the operating agreement. *See, e.g.*, 805 ILL. COMP. STAT. ANN.180/15-5 (West 2004); Elf Atochem, N. Am., Inc. v. Jaffari, 727 A.2d 286 (Del. 1999) (subject to a few non-waivable provisions, Delaware furnishes statutory answers only on matters not covered in an operating agreement).

9. Many LLC statutes, including Delaware's, permit LLCs to adopt virtually any management structure they desire. Some LLCs follow a corporate model under which management decisions are made by a board of managers subject to member approval for specified actions. Others follow a general or limited partnership model under which management decisions are made by the members or a designated manager (which may itself be an LLC or other entity). Many variations are possible—and common. Some states, including Delaware, expressly permit LLCs to delegate management rights to persons other than members and managers. *See* Delaware LLC Act § 18-407.

10. The Delaware LLC Act uses the term "limited liability company agreement." In Delaware that term means any agreement (whether referred to as a limited liability company agreement, operating agreement or otherwise), written or oral, of the member or members as to the affairs of the LLC and the conduct of its business. If written, the agreement may consist of a single document or multiple documents. *See* Delaware LLC Act § 18-101(7).

Operating agreements often address, *inter alia*: formation of the LLC; admission of members; appointment of managers (if any); purposes, powers and management structure; contributions by members; allocation of profits and losses; distributions to members; access to books and records and reporting requirements to members; fiduciary duties; related party transactions; exculpation; indemnification; assignment of membership interests; resignation and removal of members and managers; admission of substituted members and additional members; dissolution, winding up and termination;

opinion givers ordinarily insist that the operating agreement be reduced to writing before giving an opinion.[11]

When engaging in a business transaction with an LLC, the other party to the transaction often requests opinions on the LLC's status as an LLC (the "status" opinion); its power to enter into and perform its obligations under the transaction documents (the "power" opinion); and its authorization, execution and delivery of those documents (the "action" opinion). This report addresses those opinions at length. In addition, this report addresses in a limited fashion opinions on the enforceability of the operating agreement.[12]

The law of the state in which the LLC was formed governs the matters addressed by LLC status, power and action opinions.[13] Unless expressly excluded,[14] these opinions cover not only the applicable LLC statute but also applicable contract law and case law, including cases applying fiduciary duty concepts.[15]

1.0 Opinions on LLCs Organized in Delaware

LLCs, like corporations, often are organized in Delaware rather than in the state where they and their principal counsel are located. A question, therefore, arises as to what opinions their counsel can give when a transaction in which they are engaged calls for delivery of a closing opinion.

As non-Delaware lawyers often do when giving opinions on Delaware corporations,[16] lawyers who do not practice in Delaware routinely give status, power and action opinions on Delaware LLCs. As with Delaware corporations, they do so when in the specific circumstances of the transaction in question they regard themselves as competent to address the issues raised by those opinions.[17]

By analogy to opinion letters by non-Delaware lawyers on Delaware corporations, opinion letters by non-Delaware lawyers on Delaware LLCs often state that

---

amendment; and dispute resolution. When a matter is not addressed in an operating agreement, state LLC statutes typically provide default rules.

11. LLC statutes do not require the filing of operating agreements with the Secretary of State. Instead, LLC statutes ordinarily require the filing of a barebones document, often referred to as a certificate of formation, that does no more than provide notice to the public of the LLC's name and registered office and the name and address of its registered agent (and in some states (not Delaware) whether the LLC is member-managed or manager-managed).

12. Opinion recipients sometimes request opinions relating to the rights of equity holders, such as due admission of members, valid issuance of membership interests, and limited liability of members. These opinions are not addressed in this report.

13. For a discussion of opinions by non-Delaware lawyers on Delaware LLCs, see *infra* § 1.0.

14. For a discussion of the coverage of an opinion that states that it is limited to the Delaware LLC Act, see *infra* § 1.0.

15. For cases in Delaware applying fiduciary duty concepts, see *infra* note 64. Delaware case law on fiduciary duty draws on concepts developed not only in decisions on LLCs but also in decisions involving other entities, including corporations, partnerships and trusts. Coverage of fiduciary duties in LLC opinions is discussed in § 5.0, *infra*. Previous reports of the Committee have not addressed the contract law issues applicable to LLC status, power and action opinions. As indicated below, those issues often are not difficult.

16. *See TriBar 1998 Report*, *supra* note 1, § 4.1 n.85, at 631.

17. As discussed *infra*, opinions on an LLC's status, power and action cover not only the LLC statute and applicable case law but also, unless expressly excluded in the opinion letter, relevant Delaware contract law.

their coverage is limited to the Delaware LLC Act. When coverage is limited in that way, the question arises whether the opinions being given cover not only the statute but also applicable Delaware case law. Although the Delaware LLC Act is a relatively new statute and customary opinion practice is not as well established for opinions on Delaware LLCs as it is for opinions on Delaware corporations, the Committee believes that references to the Delaware LLC Act in opinion letters on LLCs, like references to the Delaware General Corporation Law in opinion letters on Delaware corporations, should be understood to encompass not only the Delaware statute but also relevant reported judicial decisions.[18]

Another question raised by a statement that coverage is limited to the Delaware LLC Act is whether it excludes from the status, power and action opinions issues of Delaware contract law that those opinions otherwise would cover. The Committee recognizes that a consensus currently does not exist on this question and that many lawyers may have read the statement as excluding those issues. The Committee believes, however, that a literal reading of the coverage limitation would be inconsistent with the approach taken in the LLC Act of relying heavily on the operating agreement, which is subject to contract law, for the matters addressed by the status, power and action opinions.[19] Thus, the Committee believes that a statement limiting coverage to the Delaware LLC Act should not be read to exclude from the coverage of the status, power and action opinions those Delaware contract law issues that are applicable to the matters covered by those opinions. The Committee notes, however, that the contract law issues applicable to those opinions ordinarily will not be difficult[20] and will not vary significantly from state to state. In the case of Delaware specifically, a knowledge of traditional contract law principles usually will be all that is required to give routine status, power and action opinions on Delaware LLCs.[21] Because of the uncertainty over

18. *See* TriBar Opinion Committee, *Special Report of the TriBar Opinion Committee: The Remedies Opinion—Deciding When to Include Exceptions and Assumptions*, 59 Bus. Law. 1483, 1487 n.25 (2004) [hereinafter "*TriBar 2004 Remedies Opinion Report*"]. If acceptable to the opinion recipient, an opinion giver might exclude coverage of relevant judicial decisions by so stating in the opinion letter or, alternatively, as is often done for UCC opinions, it may limit the cases covered by stating that it is only covering the cases summarized in a specified annotated version of the statute.

19. LLC statutes look to the operating agreement, a contract, to establish rules that in the case of a corporation often are provided by the statute. Thus, contract law bears on the formation of the operating agreement (*see infra* text accompanying notes 35–37) and on construction of provisions in the operating agreement relating to matters addressed by the status, power and action opinions, such as provisions limiting the LLC's power to engage in particular activities or requiring members' approval of transactions that fall within specified categories. As discussed in Section 4.0, *infra*, operating agreements (and not the LLC statute) often determine the steps required to authorize various transactions.

20. An exception, however, is the law relating to fiduciary duties. *See infra* § 5.0.

21. Section 18-1101(b) of the Delaware LLC Act gives maximum effect to the principle of freedom of contract and the enforceability of operating agreements. In addition, concerns about how particular terms may be construed are ameliorated by the deference Delaware courts pay to the language of a contract and the plain meaning of its terms. *See* Citadel Holding Corp. v. Roven, 603 A.2d 818, 822 (Del. 1992) ("It is an elementary canon of contract construction that the intent of the parties must be ascertained from the language of the contract."); Boesky v. CX Partners, L.P., No. Civ. A. 9739, Civ. A. 9794, Civ. A. 9748,1988 WL 42250, at *9 (Del. Ch. Apr. 28, 1988) ("There is great utility in the attempt by courts, when called upon to interpret . . . documents [drafted by sophisticated lawyers], to read the words used precisely."); Star Cellular Tel. Co. v. Baton Rouge CGSA, Inc., No. Civ. A.

whether a statement limiting an opinion to the Delaware LLC Act excludes applicable contract law, opinion recipients may properly ask opinion givers to confirm in their opinions that contract law, to the extent applicable, is being covered.

Section 6.0 of this report discusses in a limited way opinions on the enforceability of the operating agreement. Enforceability opinions are directed principally to issues of contract law. Thus, before giving an opinion on enforceability of the operating agreement of a Delaware LLC, non-Delaware lawyers need to ask themselves whether they have sufficient knowledge of Delaware contract law (as well as the LLC Act, including applicable case law) to address the issues raised by that agreement.[22] If the opinion preparers are not willing to address Delaware contract law generally, they should not give an opinion on the enforceability of the operating agreement.[23]

2.0 The Status Opinion: Formation and Existence

When engaging in a significant transaction with an LLC, the other party often requests an opinion from the LLC's counsel regarding its status as an LLC under the law of its state of formation. The LLC status opinion, like the corporate status opinion, appears as the first opinion in a typical closing opinion and serves as the cornerstone for many of the opinions that follow. The opinion customarily states that the LLC has been duly formed[24] and is validly existing as an LLC under the law of the state in which the LLC was formed. If the Secretary of State of that

12507,1993 WL 294847, at *4 (Del. Ch. Aug. 2, 1993) (if a term "has a plain or generally prevailing meaning . . . then no other evidence need be considered"), *aff'd*, 647 A.2d 382 (Del. 1994).

If a term is ambiguous, Delaware courts may consider other evidence and under some circumstances construe it against the drafter. Delaware courts, however, do not construe ambiguous terms against the drafter when a partnership agreement has been negotiated by sophisticated parties. *Compare* SI Mgmt, L.P. v. Wininger, 707 A.2d 37, 43 (Del. 1998) (court construed ambiguous terms against general partner who solicited investment by 1,850 investors who had no hand in drafting limited partnership agreement) *with* U.S. West, Inc. v. Time Warner, Inc., No. Civ. A. 14555, 1996 WL 307445 (Del. Ch. June 6, 1996) (court applied customary rules of contract interpretation where negotiations were between arm's-length bargainers of great sophistication). Delaware courts regularly apply to LLCs principles adopted in cases on limited partnerships. *See Elf Atochem, supra* note 8.

22. The contract law issues addressed by an opinion on the enforceability of an operating agreement often will be broader than the contract law issues addressed by the status, power and action opinions. Non-Delaware lawyers ordinarily are unwilling to give opinions on the enforceability under Delaware law of contracts that select Delaware law as their governing law. *Cf. TriBar 2004 Remedies Opinion Report, supra* note 18, at 1487 n. 25. *See generally infra* note 76.

23. An alternative ordinarily will not be to give an opinion "as if" the law of the opinion preparers' own state governed. In light of the internal affairs doctrine (see *infra* note 76), an "as if" opinion on the enforceability of an operating agreement is unlikely to be helpful in most circumstances. "As if" opinions are discussed in the *TriBar 2004 Remedies Opinion Report, supra* note 18, at 1497 n.70.

24. The Committee recommends use of the phrase "duly formed" (which is analogous to "duly incorporated" in opinions on corporations) in LLC status opinions because of uncertainty over the meaning of "duly organized." *See TriBar 1998 Report, supra* note 1, § 6.1.1, at 642–43. (As a matter of customary practice, an opinion on formation is understood to have the same meaning whether or not it uses the word "duly.")

state issues good standing certificates, the opinion might also cover good standing in that state.[25]

An opinion that an LLC has been duly formed means that the steps taken to create it satisfied statutory requirements in effect on the date of formation.[26] Those steps typically include (i) executing and filing a certificate of formation (referred to as a charter or articles of organization in some states) in a statutorily prescribed form and, if necessary, its acceptance by the Secretary of State, and (ii) adoption of an operating agreement by one or more members. In addition, in some states due formation of an LLC may be conditioned, among other things, on an LLC's having at least one member[27] who meets specified criteria.[28]

To support an opinion that an LLC has been "duly formed and is validly existing," the opinion preparers ordinarily should obtain a legal existence certificate from the Secretary of State[29] and copies certified by the Secretary of State of the

25. When the opinion covers "good standing," the phrase "in good standing" normally is added after the phrase "validly existing." The Committee's comments on "good standing" opinions on corporations apply with equal force to "good standing" opinions on LLCs. *See TriBar 1998 Report*, *supra* note 1, § 6.1.4, at 645–46 (noting that good standing opinions usually add little of value analytically because they normally are based entirely on a Secretary of State's certificate).

26. In giving this opinion, the opinion preparers are entitled to disregard defects in the formation process that the state of formation would deem inconsequential for determining LLC status. The Delaware LLC Act provides that an LLC is formed if there has been substantial compliance with the requirements of Section 18-201 of the Delaware LLC Act. As discussed in the text, an opinion that a Delaware LLC has been duly formed requires more than mere compliance with Section 18-201. The New York LLC Act does not contain a provision comparable to Section 18-201 of the Delaware LLC Act.

27. Although most states initially required at least two members, almost all states, including Delaware and New York, now permit LLCs to have only one member. *See* Delaware LLC Act § 18-101(7); N.Y. Ltd. Liab. Co. Law § 203(c) (McKinney 2006). *See generally* 1 Larry E. Ribstein & Robert R. Keatinge, Ribstein and Keatinge on Limited Liability Companies, § 4:3 at 4-4 & Appendix 4-2 (2d ed. 2005).

28. *See, e.g.*, Delaware LLC Act § 18-101 (11) and (12) (permitting natural persons and a broad range of associations, corporations, LLCs, partnerships, trusts and other legal entities to be members). The statute or operating agreement may specify when a person is admitted as a member and impose conditions on admission, for example, receipt by the LLC of a contribution in a specified amount. The Delaware LLC Act does not require that members make contributions unless the operating agreement, subscription agreement or similar agreement so provides. The Delaware LLC Act does specify that, in connection with the formation of an LLC, a person is admitted as a member of the LLC upon the later to occur of: (1) the formation of the LLC; or (2) the time provided in and upon compliance with the requirements of the operating agreement or, if the operating agreement does not so provide, when the person's admission is reflected in the records of the LLC (which records may include the operating agreement or a schedule or exhibit to the operating agreement). *See* Delaware LLC Act § 18-301.

Unless otherwise provided in the operating agreement, a person may be admitted as a member (including as sole member) of a Delaware LLC without acquiring an economic interest in the LLC. *See* Delaware LLC Act § 18-301(d). In structured finance and bankruptcy remote securitization transactions, operating agreements often provide for the admission of non-economic members as a mechanism for preventing an LLC from being inadvertently dissolved.

29. In Delaware, legal existence in the Secretary of State's Office normally is addressed in a Secretary of State's good standing certificate (even though an LLC may continue to exist while it is not in good standing). *See* Delaware LLC Act § 18-1107(h) and § 18-1108(a). Lawyers giving opinions on Delaware LLCs routinely obtain a good standing certificate to ascertain, among other things, that the certificate of formation for the LLC has not been cancelled for non-payment of annual taxes and penalties and interest or as a result of the resignation of the registered agent for non-payment of annual registered agent fees. If the Delaware Secretary of State cancels an LLC's certificate of formation for those reasons,

certificate of formation and all amendments, as well as copies of the operating agreement and all amendments.[30] The opinion preparers then should review the certificate of formation, as amended, to confirm that it satisfies statutory requirements[31] and does not contain an effective date that has not yet occurred.

If the state in which the LLC was formed requires as a condition of formation or existence that an LLC have a member within the meaning of the applicable LLC Act,[32] that it have an operating agreement,[33] or both, the opinion preparers should confirm that those requirements are satisfied. If the LLC has an operating agreement (as is required in Delaware), the opinion preparers should confirm compliance with any conditions in the operating agreement relating to the LLC's formation or continuing existence. The opinion preparers ordinarily will do this

---

the LLC will cease to exist as a separate legal entity unless and until the problem is rectified and the LLC is revived in the records of the Delaware Secretary of State. *See* Delaware LLC Act § 18-1109.

30. LLC statutes typically do not provide for the filing of operating agreements with the Secretary of State. Therefore, opinion preparers, when they are acting as principal counsel, ordinarily obtain from the person maintaining the LLC's records a copy of the LLC's operating agreement, often with a certificate confirming that the copy is accurate and complete. As with any information provided by an appropriate source, opinion preparers are entitled to rely on the copy of the operating agreement furnished to them unless reliance is unreasonable in the circumstances or they know it to be inaccurate or incomplete. *See TriBar 1998 Report, supra* note 1, § 2.1.4, at 610.

Some opinion preparers, particularly when they are not principal counsel, assume expressly in their opinions that the operating agreement furnished to them constitutes the entire agreement of the parties, that the operating agreement is in full force and effect, and that it has not been amended. Alternatively, they may state in their opinions that they have not reviewed any documents other than those listed, that they assume no provision or document exists that they have not reviewed that is inconsistent with the opinions they are giving, and that they have not conducted an independent factual investigation but have relied solely on the documents listed, all of which they assume to be true, complete and accurate in all material respects.

31. The duly formed opinion confirms compliance with the requirements in effect when the LLC was formed. The validly existing opinion confirms, *inter alia*, that no certificates have been filed terminating the LLC's existence.

32. Opinion givers are entitled to assume, without so stating and without further inquiry, that persons purporting to be members meet the requirements, if any, in the operating agreement and LLC law of the state in which the LLC was formed. For example, if a California corporation is listed as a member in the records of a Delaware LLC and executes the operating agreement as a member, the opinion preparers are not required to determine whether the California corporation is validly existing under California law. The opinion preparers only need to confirm that under the LLC law of Delaware and the LLC's operating agreement a California corporation is permitted to be a member.

If the operating agreement imposes any conditions on a person's becoming a member, the opinion also addresses satisfaction of those conditions by at least one member. Thus, if the operating agreement requires a person to make a contribution as a condition to being admitted as a member, the opinion preparers should confirm that the LLC has a member, for example, by obtaining a certificate from an appropriate person confirming that at least one member has met that condition, or they should expressly assume satisfaction of that condition.

33. *See* § 18-101(7) of the Delaware LLC Act and dicta in *Elf Atochem*, 727 A.2d at 291–93; CAP-ROC Manager, Inc. v. Policemen's & Firemen's Ret. Sys. of City of Pontiac, No. Civ. A. 1059-N, 2005 WL 937613, at *1 (Del. Ch. Apr. 18, 2005); Walker v. Resource Dev. Co. Ltd., L.L.C. (DE), 791 A.2d 799, 813 (Del. Ch. 2000). An opinion that a Delaware LLC has been duly formed or is validly existing requires that the opinion preparers confirm that the LLC has an operating agreement. That is so notwithstanding the use of the term "formed" in Section 18-201 of the Delaware LLC Act (discussed *supra* note 26). To avoid any question that an LLC has an operating agreement, opinion preparers often seek to have the operating agreement executed by all of an LLC's members and managers. *See infra* text accompanying notes 80–81.

In Delaware, a certificate of formation may be filed with the Secretary of State before an operating agreement is adopted. *See* Delaware LLC Act § 18-201(d).

by reviewing a copy of the operating agreement in effect at the time of formation and all amendments through the date of the opinion.[34] If formation and existence require compliance with other conditions, the opinion preparers also should confirm that those conditions have been satisfied.[35]

In states such as Delaware in which an opinion on formation and existence requires that an LLC have an operating agreement,[36] the opinion preparers must satisfy themselves or assume expressly that the prerequisites for creating an operating agreement in the state in which the LLC is formed have been met. The prerequisites for creating an operating agreement are based on, but may be less stringent than, the traditional prerequisites for forming a contract. In the case of a one-member LLC, for example, an operating agreement can be created by a single party. In the case of an LLC with more than one member, however, creation of an operating agreement, like the creation of a limited partnership agreement, may require an agreement of all the initial members.[37] Ordinarily, the prerequisites for creating an operating agreement will be easy to satisfy.

An opinion on an LLC's valid existence also confirms that the LLC's existence has not terminated. This aspect of the opinion can be more of a challenge than an opinion on the existence of a corporation because LLCs may cease to exist in many ways. Operating agreements, for example, sometimes specify a termination date or state that an LLC will dissolve upon the occurrence of a specified event, for example, resignation of a particular manager or failure to achieve specified financing goals by a certain date.[38] In addition, an LLC's existence may terminate by operation of law.[39] Thus, to give a valid existence opinion, the opinion pre-

---

34. *See supra* note 30.

35. In Delaware, the certificate of formation must be executed and filed with the Secretary of State by one or more authorized persons. Who constitutes an authorized person is frequently designated in the operating agreement. However, it need not be, and the person authorized to execute and file a certificate of formation may be designated in a separate writing or orally. Delaware requires that a certificate of formation state the name of the LLC, its address in Delaware, and the name and address of its registered agent for service of process in Delaware. *See* Delaware LLC Act § 18-201. Delaware also requires that the name of the LLC appropriately identify it as a limited liability company. *See* Delaware LLC Act § 18-102. Like many states, Delaware does not require that the certificate of formation disclose an LLC's members and managers, the amount of their investment, the nature of the LLC's business or its capital structure, or whether the LLC is managed by its members or managers. *See* Delaware LLC Act § 18-201.

36. *See supra* note 33. Meeting the prerequisites for creating an operating agreement does not mean that all of the terms of the operating agreement are enforceable. When an opinion recipient wants an opinion on the enforceability of an operating agreement (or particular terms of an operating agreement), it should ask for that opinion expressly.

37. Whether the initial members have effectively bound themselves is a matter of the contract law of the state where the LLC is formed, supplemented, as in Delaware, by provisions in the applicable LLC statute that may override requirements that otherwise would be applicable. *See* Delaware LLC Act § 18-101(7) (member need not execute operating agreement to be bound by it).

38. Unlike most corporations, many LLCs do not have perpetual existence. Instead, their operating agreements contain provisions stating that they will dissolve upon the occurrence of specified events or on a date certain.

39. An LLC may dissolve, for example, automatically when it ceases to have at least one member who meets specified criteria unless its existence is continued in a manner permitted in the applicable LLC statute or its operating agreement. *See* Delaware LLC Act § 18-801(a)(4). Thus, if membership interests have been transferred, the opinion preparers may need to confirm that the LLC continues to

parers must consider the various ways an LLC's existence may terminate under the statute under which it was formed and confirm (or expressly assume) that none have occurred. The opinion preparers also must review the certificate of formation and operating agreement to identify any provisions that could result in the LLC's termination and again confirm (or expressly assume) that those have not occurred.[40] Finally, the opinion preparers should confirm (or expressly assume) that the LLC has not taken any voluntary action to dissolve,[41] wind up or terminate or otherwise cease to exist, as it would have, for example, if it entered into a merger in which it was not the surviving party.

As in the case of a corporation, in some transactions opinion recipients are willing to accept an opinion that the LLC is "validly existing as an LLC" under the law of its state of formation without also receiving an opinion on the LLC's formation.[42] Unlike a "duly formed" opinion, this opinion does not require that the opinion preparers address compliance with the requirements for formation in effect when the LLC was formed.

The LLC status opinion addresses an LLC's status as an LLC. It does not address the liability of members for an LLC's obligations.

3.0 LLC Power to Enter into and Perform Its Obligations Under Transaction Documents

The opinion that an LLC has the power to execute and deliver, and to perform its obligations under, an agreement means that the LLC has that power under (i) the statute under which it was formed and (ii) its certificate of formation and operating agreement, each as amended through the date of the opinion. By analogy to the corporate power opinion, the opinion often is worded to refer to "limited liability company" or "LLC" power, but it is understood to mean the same thing whether those qualifiers are used or not.[43]

---

have at least one member because the mere assignment of LLC interests may not cause the assignees to be admitted as members. In Delaware, unless otherwise provided in an operating agreement, a member who assigns his entire LLC interest ceases to be a member, but the assignee is not admitted as a member without the consent of all members. *See* Delaware LLC Act §§ 18-301, 18-702, 18-704.

40. A Delaware LLC has perpetual existence if no time for dissolution is specified in its operating agreement. *See* Delaware LLC Act § 18-801(a)(1). However, a Delaware LLC that otherwise has perpetual existence may still be dissolved upon the occurrence of events specified in the operating agreement or the Delaware LLC Act. *See* Delaware LLC Act § 18-801.

41. An LLC may be dissolved and yet, so long as its certificate of formation has not been cancelled, still exist for purposes of winding up its affairs. *See* Delaware LLC Act §§ 18-201(b), 18-803 and 18-804. When giving an opinion on a dissolved LLC (for example, in a transaction in which the LLC is divesting itself of its remaining businesses), the opinion preparers should point out in the opinion letter that the LLC has been dissolved and exists solely for purposes of winding up its affairs. Note that a Delaware good standing certificate does not address dissolution because notice of dissolution is not required to be given to the Delaware Secretary of State when an LLC has dissolved.

42. *See TriBar 1998 Report*, *supra* note 1, at 644–45.

43. As with opinions on corporations, "full power" opinions should be avoided because of uncertainty regarding what "full power" might be interpreted to mean. *See TriBar 1998 Report*, *supra* note 1, § 6.3 n.138, at 652. "Full LLC power" opinions, however, are understood to have the same meaning as "LLC power" opinions.

Many LLC statutes permit LLCs to carry on any lawful business or purpose, subject to limited exceptions, and grant them broad powers to attain their purposes, subject to any limitations in their operating agreements.[44] The opinion means that the LLC has the power required, whether that power derives directly from the statute or, as permitted by the statute, from the operating agreement or some other document.

Even if the statute under which an LLC is formed grants it broad powers, the opinion preparers should confirm that neither the statute nor case law prohibits it from taking actions covered by the opinion.[45] In this regard, the considerations that come into play are the same as those for a corporate power opinion.[46]

Normally, certificates of formation do not address an LLC's powers.[47] Instead, those powers ordinarily are addressed in an LLC's operating agreement. Unlike corporations, LLCs often are formed for particular purposes and are limited by their operating agreements to the powers necessary to accomplish those purposes.[48] Thus, to give an LLC power opinion, the opinion preparers must carefully review the LLC's operating agreement.[49] When the opinion preparers identify a possible problem, they often resolve it by arranging for the operating agreement to be amended.[50]

Like an opinion on the power of a corporation, an opinion on the power of an LLC is understood as a matter of customary practice not to address restrictions on an LLC's power that do not derive from the statute under which the entity was formed (or its governing documents), such as laws requiring licenses or permits to engage in specified activities.

---

44. *See, e.g.*, Delaware LLC Act § 18-106(a) (permitting LLC to carry on any lawful business, purpose or activity, subject to some limited exceptions, and granting LLC broad powers to attain its purposes, subject to any limitations in its operating agreement).

45. In Delaware, for example, an LLC is not permitted to engage in the business of banking. *See* Delaware LLC Act § 18-106(a).

46. *See TriBar 1998 Report*, *supra* note 1, § 6.3, at 653.

47. Of course, if a certificate of formation sets forth an LLC's powers, the opinion preparers must take those powers and any limitations on them into account in giving the opinion. Delaware does not require that an LLC's powers be set forth in its certificate of formation. Indeed, in Delaware a limitation on an LLC's powers set forth in its certificate of formation may not be effective in limiting the LLC's exercise of those powers. *See* Delaware LLC Act §§ 18-201(a) and 18-207.

48. The limitation may be general, for example, limiting the LLC to the powers required to further its stated purpose. This type of limitation requires the opinion preparers to satisfy themselves that the transaction furthers the stated purpose. Alternatively, a limitation may be specific, for example, prohibiting the LLC from investing in anything other than government securities.

49. In some transactions, preparation of the opinion can require extensive analysis of the operating agreement and, if it is unclear, documents bearing on its interpretation. For example, the operating agreements of many investment LLCs specify the purposes of the LLC, such as to invest in particular businesses, and then enumerate limitations on the LLC's powers. Those limitations in turn may be waivable in specified ways, for example, by action of an advisory committee of non-managing members. In addition, the operating agreement may grant the LLC other powers—e.g., the power to make or withhold distributions, the power to merge, the power to sell assets to affiliates, the power to contract for services from affiliates—and subject them to various restrictions that similarly are waivable upon compliance with specified procedures.

50. In the course of that review, the opinion preparers should consider whether any relevant terms are susceptible to more than one interpretation. See *supra* note 21 for a description of cases in Delaware on construing agreements.

The opinion that an LLC has the power to enter into a transaction (and perform the obligations it is undertaking) is not an opinion that the LLC has taken the action required for it to exercise that power. That opinion is discussed in the following section.

4.0 Due Authorization, Execution and Delivery (the "Action Opinion")

The opinion that an agreement has been duly authorized, executed and delivered by an LLC means that the steps required by the LLC statute under which the LLC was formed and its operating agreement to approve the agreement were taken,[51] that the agreement was executed by persons with actual authority to act on the LLC's behalf, and that the agreement was delivered in accordance with applicable legal requirements.

Operating agreements take many different approaches to decision making. Some adopt a corporate model, requiring approval of both members and managers for major transactions and managers alone for other transactions and specifying the manner in which approval is to be obtained and the percentage of votes required. Others adopt a limited partnership model, in which a single individual or entity such as a managing member has sole and exclusive power on all matters, and still others adopt a general partnership model, in which each member is entitled to participate in the management of the LLC (except as provided in the operating agreement).[52] Often, in establishing the requirements for obtaining approvals, operating agreements permit less formality than corporation statutes.[53]

In confirming that an agreement has been duly authorized, the opinion preparers must ascertain what approvals the operating agreement requires for the LLC to enter into the agreement and satisfy themselves that the specified approvals meet statutory requirements.[54] They then should confirm that those approvals

51. LLC statutes typically contain default provisions that establish the approvals required when an operating agreement is silent on a question. In Delaware, for example, unless otherwise provided in an operating agreement, management decisions must be made by members having more than a 50% interest in the profits of the LLC. *See* Delaware LLC Act § 18-402.

52. Whatever the model, the opinion preparers may assume, without so stating, that when an approval is given by a member or manager that is not a natural person, the member or manager is the type of entity it purports to be, that it was authorized to approve the transaction, and that those acting on its behalf had the approvals they required. As with any unstated assumption, opinion givers may not rely on this assumption if reliance is unreasonable under the circumstances in which the opinion is given or they know it to be false. *See TriBar 1998 Report*, *supra* note 1, §§ 2.1.4, 2.3(c). To avoid any misunderstanding, some opinion givers choose to state the assumption expressly.

53. *See* Delaware LLC Act §§ 18-302, 18-404. The operating agreement, for example, might permit actions to be approved by a majority of the managers without a meeting or by a sole decision maker without formal action.

54. In some states, the statute may not permit decision-making authority to be given to certain classes of persons: for example, persons who are neither members nor managers. That is not the case in Delaware. *See* Delaware LLC Act § 18-407.

If the approval requirements in the operating agreement are unclear, the opinion preparers may require, as a condition to giving the opinion, that the operating agreement be amended to clarify the requirements or even to approve the transaction in question. If the LLC was formed in Delaware and the opinion preparers are not Delaware lawyers, they also may decide to consult with or obtain an opinion from Delaware counsel. *See supra* note 21.

For a discussion of the opinion's coverage of fiduciary duties, see *infra* § 5.0.

were obtained in the manner, if any, specified in the operating agreement. That can be done by obtaining a certificate from an appropriate person[55] detailing the action taken or, if the action requires a meeting or written consent, confirming the adoption of specified resolutions.[56] If the operating agreement or LLC statute permits a decision maker to approve a transaction without formal action, the opinion preparers may be able to infer approval from the decision maker's execution of the agreement. The opinion preparers also must confirm that those who executed the agreement on behalf of the LLC were authorized to do so.[57] Sometimes the operating agreement itself expressly authorizes the LLC to enter into specified agreements and particular persons to execute those agreements on behalf of the LLC. The due execution and delivery opinions relating to an LLC generally have the same meaning as the analogous opinions on corporations.[58]

5.0 Fiduciary Duties

When approving a transaction, the decision makers for an LLC are subject to fiduciary duties comparable to those applicable to directors of a corporation and general partners of a limited partnership.[59] Unlike corporations, however, LLCs in some states are permitted to include provisions in their operating agreements expanding or relaxing the fiduciary duties of their decision makers or even, in a few states such as Delaware, eliminating them (except for some fundamental duty such as, in Delaware, the implied contractual obligation of good faith and fair dealing).[60] Not all states permit LLCs that flexibility.[61]

---

55. The operating agreement may make clear who is an appropriate person by assigning a particular person, entity or designated official responsibility for the matter covered by the certificate. If the operating agreement does not, the opinion preparers will need to decide whom to look to for a certificate, for example, a manager or managing member. If the operating agreement provides for a secretary or similar recording officer, he or she normally will be an appropriate person. *See TriBar 1998 Report*, *supra* note 1, § 2.2.1, at 611–13.

56. Alternatively, in the case of a meeting, the opinion preparers could rely on a copy of the minutes.

57. The opinion preparers may, without so stating, rely on the assumptions described *supra* note 52 if the agreement was executed by a member or manager that is not a natural person.

58. *See TriBar 1998 Report*, *supra* note 1, § 6.4, at 653–54.

59. *See, e.g.*, Delaware LLC Act § 18-1101(c).

60. Delaware LLC Act § 18-1101(c) permits LLCs to expand, restrict or eliminate fiduciary duties of members and managers. It does not, however, permit LLCs to eliminate the implied contractual covenant of good faith and fair dealing. *See* Delaware LLC Act § 18-1101(c). The Delaware courts have articulated the conditions that must be met to restrict or eliminate fiduciary duties. One requirement is that a provision for that purpose be clear, express and unambiguous. *See* Miller v. American Real Estate Partners, L.P., No. Civ. A. 16788, 2001 WL 1045643, at *8 (Del. Ch. Sept. 6, 2001); Brickell Partners v. Wise, 794 A.2d 1, 3–4 (Del. Ch. 2001); Sonet v. Timber Co., L.P., 722 A.2d 319, 322 (Del. Ch. 1998).

61. For example, the Illinois Limited Liability Company Act provides that a member's fiduciary duties may not be eliminated or reduced. That Act, however, does permit an LLC in its operating agreement to "identify specific types or categories of activities that do not violate these duties, if not manifestly unreasonable . . . and . . . specify the number or percentage of members or disinterested managers that may authorize or ratify . . . a specific act or transaction that otherwise would violate these duties." It also provides that while the obligation of good faith and fair dealing may not be eliminated or reduced, "the operating agreement may determine the standards by which the performance of the obligation is to be measured, if the standards are not manifestly unreasonable." 805 Ill. Comp. Stat. Ann. 180/15-5(b)(6)(A)(B) and (7) (West 2004).

As they do when giving opinions on corporations,[62] opinion preparers ordinarily give opinions on LLCs without investigating whether decision makers violated their fiduciary duty in approving the transaction. Instead, they normally rely on an assumption, which ordinarily is unstated, regarding compliance with fiduciary duties.[63] If, however, the opinion preparers know of facts that in light of applicable case law cause them to question whether the assumption is reliable,[64] they are not permitted to rely on it without looking into the question further.[65]

Unless further inquiry satisfies the opinion preparers that their concerns are unfounded, they must consider what disclosures to make and, indeed, whether they should give the opinion at all. What they do will depend on the circumstances of the particular case. For example, if they know that giving the opinion would further wrongful conduct by their client[66] or would mislead the recipient with regard to its subject matter,[67] they should not deliver an opinion even if it is technically correct.

Even when LLC statutes permit operating agreements to relax or eliminate fiduciary duties to which decision makers otherwise would be subject,[68] they ordinarily do not, as noted above, allow LLCs to grant decision makers unbridled discretion. Instead, they require satisfaction of some minimum standard of conduct, such as the implied contractual obligation of good faith and fair dealing.

---

62. *See TriBar 1998 Report*, *supra* note 1, § 6.4, at 654.

63. The Committee believes that the absence of improper conduct of decision makers as among themselves during the course of their approving a transaction is covered by the unstated assumption regarding compliance with fiduciary duties (see *TriBar 1998 Report*, *supra* note 1, § 3.3.4, at 625 n.77) or, alternatively, by a similar unstated assumption directed specifically to that conduct. *See infra* text accompanying note 70. The analysis in the text assumes that the absence of such conduct is covered by an unstated assumption.

64. *See TriBar 1998 Report*, *supra* note 1, § 6.4, at 654. Facts that raise concerns include, for example, self-dealing by decision makers, disparate treatment of the LLC's members, or conduct by decision makers (as discussed in the final paragraphs of this section) that works to undermine the process by which the approval was obtained. In *Gelfman v. Weeden Investors, L.P.*, 859 A.2d 89 (Del. Ch. 2004), for example, the court found that while decision makers had authority to approve a series of steps (including an amendment to a partnership agreement) resulting in a repurchase of limited partnership interests at less than fair market value, the decision makers had a conflict of interest and under the entire fairness standard could not eliminate the limited partners' economic rights for less than fair market value. *See also* Solar Cells, Inc. v. True North Partners, LLC, No. Civ. A. 19477, 2002 WL 749163 (Del. Ch. Apr. 25, 2002) (applying similar principles to block a merger, notwithstanding provisions in an operating agreement purporting to waive conflicts of interest). The principle underlying these cases, as the Delaware Supreme Court has made clear, is that technical compliance with the law is not an unassailable defense. *See* Schnell v. Chris-Craft Indus. Inc., 285 A.2d 437, 439 (Del. 1971).

65. *TriBar 1998 Report*, *supra* note 1, § 2.3(c), at 616.

66. *See* MODEL RULES OF PROF'L CONDUCT R. 1.2(d), 1.13, 1.16(a), 4.1 (2002).

67. Opinion preparers are not permitted to give opinions, even if technically correct, that they recognize to be misleading to the recipient with regard to their subject matter. *See TriBar 1998 Report*, *supra* note 1, § 1.4(d), at 602–03.

68. *See, e.g.*, Delaware LLC Act § 18-1101(c) ("To the extent that, at law or in equity, a member or manager or other person has duties (including fiduciary duties) to a limited liability company or to another member or manager or to another person that is a party to or is otherwise bound by a limited liability company agreement, the member's or manager's or other person's duties may be expanded or restricted or eliminated by provisions in the limited liability company agreement; provided that the limited liability company agreement may not eliminate the implied contractual covenant of good faith and fair dealing.").

Further, for a provision restricting or eliminating fiduciary duties to be given effect, the courts may require it to be clear, express and unambiguous.[69]

When opinion preparers are concerned about the conduct of the decision makers, they should not automatically deliver an opinion in reliance on a provision in the operating agreement that by its terms permits that conduct. Rather, they should consider whether the courts will give the provision effect and, if so, who is affected by the conduct, whether disclosure of the issue in the opinion is sufficient to permit delivery of an opinion and, indeed, whether under the particular circumstances presented they should deliver an opinion at all.

In the case of both corporations and LLCs, the concept of fiduciary duty ordinarily is thought of as relating to the obligations of decision makers to the company and holders of equity interests in the company. A related basis for invalidating actions by decision makers, articulated in decisions in Delaware, involves trickery, other deceit or improper conduct by decision makers as among themselves in obtaining approval of a transaction.[70] If the opinion preparers know of conduct by decision makers that in light of applicable case law causes them to question the fairness of the decision makers' treatment of each other or the integrity of the process they have followed in approving a transaction,[71] the opinion preparers should not rely on an unstated assumption[72] but rather, as discussed above, should consider what disclosure to make and, depending on the circumstances, whether to deliver an opinion at all.

6.0 Enforceability of Operating Agreement

An opinion that the operating agreement is valid, binding and enforceable (commonly referred to as a "remedies opinion")[73] may be requested when the

69. *Miller*, 2001 WL 1045643, at *8; *Brickell Partners*, 794 A.2d at 3–4; *Sonet*, 722 A.2d at 322. *See supra* note 60.

70. *See* Adlerstein v. Wertheimer, No. Civ. A. 19101, 2002 WL 205684, at *11–12 (Del. Ch. Jan. 25, 2002) ("[The former director and controlling stockholder] was disadvantaged 'by the other directors' failure to communicate their plans to him.' Had he known beforehand that [other directors] intended to approve the . . . proposal and to remove him from office at the . . . meeting, he could have exercised his legal right to remove one or both of them and, thus, prevented the completion of those plans . . . Adlerstein had a right to . . . advance notice in order that he might have taken steps to protect his interests . . . For all the foregoing reasons . . . the actions taken at the . . . meeting must be undone."); VGS, Inc. v. Castiel, No. Civ. A. 17995, 2000 WL 1277372, at *1 (Del. Ch. Aug. 31, 2000) ("Because the two managers acted without notice to the third manager under circumstances where they knew that with notice that he could have acted to protect his majority interest, they breached their duty of loyalty to the original member and their fellow manager by failing to act in good faith. The purported merger must therefore be declared invalid."), *aff'd*, 781 A.2d 696 (Del. 2001) (table decision).

71. A question might arise, for example, if an operating agreement permits a manager to enter into related-party transactions approved by an Advisory Committee, and the manager makes incomplete disclosure or calls a meeting of the Advisory Committee when a transaction's most outspoken critics are known to be unavailable.

72. As noted in the second paragraph of this Section 5.0, the absence of such conduct ordinarily is the subject of an unstated assumption.

73. A remedies opinion on an LLC's operating agreement typically states that the operating agreement is a valid and binding agreement, enforceable against the LLC's members and managers in accordance with its terms. Less frequently, it also states that the operating agreement is enforceable

opinion recipient is acquiring a membership interest or when investment banking firms, lenders or rating agencies in structured finance transactions are concerned about the enforceability of covenants, restrictions and internal governance provisions in an operating agreement.[74] This opinion is often more difficult to give than the status, power and action opinions because it requires the opinion preparers to consider issues of state contract law that are not necessarily straightforward[75] and because it covers all the provisions in the operating agreement rather than simply those applicable to status, power and approval.[76]

The Committee discussed the remedies opinion in the *TriBar 1998 Report* and the *TriBar 2004 Remedies Opinion Report.*[77] The discussion in those reports applies to opinions on the enforceability of the operating agreement.[78] As indicated in those reports, the opinion addresses the legal effect of each of the contractual undertakings of the opinion preparers' client, subject to various assumptions and qualifications, express and implied. Two of the standard exceptions to the remedies opinion are the bankruptcy exception and equitable principles limitation.[79]

Whenever they give a remedies opinion, the opinion preparers must satisfy themselves that the client has taken the steps required to enter into the agreement[80] or they must assume expressly in the opinion that it took those steps. When giving a remedies opinion on an LLC's operating agreement, the opinion preparers usually will seek to have the LLC's members and managers execute the operating agreement, even though the applicable LLC statute may establish other

---

against the LLC itself. In Delaware, an LLC is bound by its operating agreement. *See* Delaware LLC Act § 18-101(7). *See also Elf Atochem, supra* note 8.

74. In structured financings, for example, enforceability opinions on the operating agreement address lenders' concerns that restrictions in the operating agreement on the purposes and powers of the LLC are valid; that provisions that require a lender's or independent manager's consent to dissolve, amend the operating agreement, or engage in material transactions such as a merger are enforceable against the members; and that the covenants necessary to support a nonconsolidation opinion are enforceable obligations of the members. Opinions on the enforceability of an operating agreement are less common in conventional financing transactions.

75. Issues of fiduciary duty can be particularly troublesome. For example, the enforceability of a provision reducing or eliminating fiduciary duties may be open to question. *See supra* notes 60 and 61.

76. The enforceability of an operating agreement, or at least those terms relating to an LLC's internal affairs, is governed by the law of the state in which the LLC was formed. *See, e.g.*, Delaware LLC Act § 18-901; Elf Atochem, N. Am., Inc. v. Jaffari, 727 A.2d 286 (Del. 1999). *See also* VantagePoint Venture Partners 1996 v. Examen, Inc., 871 A.2d 1108 (Del. 2005).

Because of the more complex contract law issues often presented, lawyers who are willing to give status, power and action opinions on an LLC formed in a jurisdiction in which they do not practice often are unwilling to give opinions on the enforceability of the LLC's operating agreement. That, however, is not always the case. Some lawyers who practice in a state other than the state of the LLC's formation may be willing to give an opinion on enforceability when they are confident that the operating agreement does not raise any issues under the law of the state of formation (entity law, contract law and relevant case law) that they are not comfortable addressing. To limit the breadth of the opinion, opinion givers sometimes cover the enforceability of only specified provisions in the operating agreement.

77. *See supra* notes 1 and 18.

78. An exception is the discussion of the benefits of giving the opinion as if the law of another jurisdiction applied. *See TriBar 1998 Report, supra* note 1, § 4.6, at 635 and *supra* note 23.

79. *See TriBar 1998 Report, supra* note 1, § 3.3, at 622.

80. Often, this issue is addressed expressly in a separate opinion or in a separate part of the opinion that states that the agreement has been duly authorized, executed and delivered.

ways for members and managers to be bound.[81] When a member or manager is a legal entity and not a natural person, the opinion preparers may assume without so stating that the member or manager is the type of entity it purports to be and that it was authorized, and obtained the approvals it needed, to enter into the operating agreement and to authorize the action of the persons who executed the operating agreement on its behalf.[82]

A remedies opinion on an operating agreement means that the rights and obligations of the LLC and its members and managers (or other equity holders or decision makers) set forth in the operating agreement, the provisions specifying a remedy in the event of a breach, and the provisions relating to governance and administration will be given legal effect, subject to the standard bankruptcy exception and equitable principles limitation and any other exceptions expressly stated or understood as a matter of customary practice to apply.[83] Thus, for provisions in an operating agreement that obligate members or managers to perform an affirmative act, such as making a capital contribution upon the occurrence of a specified event, but that do not specify a remedy for a failure to perform, the opinion is understood to mean that in the event of a breach, a court applying applicable law either will require the member to perform that act (subject to standard exceptions) or will grant money damages or some other remedy. For a provision that does specify a remedy, such as a reduction of a member's interest in the LLC if the member fails to make a contribution, the opinion is understood to mean that a court (again subject to standard exceptions) will give effect to the specified remedy as written. Operating agreements often contain detailed provisions on how the LLC is to be governed, how the operating agreement is to be amended, and how disputes, including interpretive questions, are to be resolved. The opinion on these provisions means that a court will require the LLC and its members and managers to abide by their terms as written (again subject to standard exceptions).

Conclusion

Opinions on LLCs are becoming increasingly common. To date, however, little guidance has been available on how they should be worded, what they mean or what work opinion preparers should do to support them. The Committee is hopeful that this Report will facilitate the giving of opinions on LLCs and thus improve

81. *See, e.g.*, Delaware LLC Act § 18-101(7) (stating that members, managers and assignees are bound by the operating agreement whether or not the member, manager or assignee executes the operating agreement).

82. When members or managers are natural persons, the opinion may be based on an assumption, which as a matter of customary practice need not be stated expressly, that they are competent to enter into the agreement. *See TriBar 1998 Report*, *supra* note 1, § 2.3(a), (c), at 615–16 (noting that opinion preparers may not rely on an unstated assumption if it is unreliable).

83. For a full discussion of the remedies opinion's coverage of various contractual provisions, see *TriBar 2004 Remedies Opinion Report*, *supra* note 18, § III and *TriBar 1998 Report*, *supra* note 1, § 3.1, at 619.

the opinion process. The Committee recognizes that custom is not a static concept and that customary practice with regard to LLC opinions is continuing to develop. Comments on this Report are welcome. Comments should be sent to Co-Chairs, TriBar Opinion Committee, c/o New York County Lawyers Association, 14 Vesey St., New York, NY 10007.

APPENDIX A

MEMBERS OF TRIBAR OPINION COMMITTEE

New York County Lawyers Association
Donald S. Bernstein
David L. Bleich
Sylvia Fung Chin
Sol Neil Corbin
Arthur Norman Field**
Edward H. Fleischman
Joseph W. Halliday
A. Sidney Holderness, Jr.
Lou Kling
Morton Moskin
Charles Niemeth
Sandra M. Rocks
Myer (Mike) O. Sigal, Jr.
John B. Tehan
Judith R. Thoyer
Lawrence E. Wieman
Nancy Young

New York State Bar Association
Frederick G. Attea
Gerald S. Backman
J. Truman Bidwell, Jr.
Gregory J. Blasi
Daniel W. Gersen
Joseph D. Hansen
Arthur J. Heath
Professor Joseph Hinsey, IV
Richard R. Howe
Christian G. Koelbl, III
Richard T. McDermott
Bernard W. Nimkin
Richard L. Veron

The Association of the Bar of the City of New York
Julie M. Allen
Franci J. Blassberg
Rita M. Bolger
Edward H. Cohen
Philip E. Coviello
Linda Hayman
Jerome E. Hyman
Rob (B. Robbins) Kiessling
Howard N. Lefkowitz**
Vincent Monte-Sano
Joel I. Papernik
Robert Rosenman
Brian L. Schorr
William C. Viets

Boston Bar Association
Donald W. Glazer*
Stanley Keller**

Delaware Bar Association
James G. Leyden, Jr.*

Chicago Bar Association
Robin Heiss

Toronto, Ontario Bar Association
Wilfred M. Estey

Atlanta Bar Association
Jeffrey M. Stein

Allegheny County (Pittsburgh) Bar Association
David A. Murdoch

State Bar of Texas, Business Law Section
Roderick A. Goyne

The District of Columbia Bar Association
Stephen Glover
James J. Rosenhauer

Pennsylvania Bar Association
E. Carolan Berkley**

State Bar of California
Steven O. Weise
Morris W. Hirsch
John B. Power

North Carolina State Bar Association
A. Mark Adcock

Georgia State Bar Association
Jeffrey M. Smith

Member Emeritus
Honorable Thomas L. Ambro***

*Co-Reporter
**Adviser
***Did not participate in the consideration and approval of the report.

Special Report of the TriBar Opinion Committee: Duly Authorized Opinions on Preferred Stock

*By the TriBar Opinion Committee**

Purchasers of newly-issued shares of preferred stock typically seek an opinion from the Company's counsel that the shares have been duly authorized and validly issued and are fully paid and nonassessable.[1] This report amplifies the discussion in § 6.2.1 of the 1998 TriBar Report of the meaning of the "duly authorized" part of this opinion when it is given on preferred stock.

An opinion that the shares of preferred stock have been "duly authorized" is understood as a matter of customary practice to mean that, in the professional judgment of the opinion giver:[2]

- the shares are part of a class or series of shares that the Company has the authority to issue—i.e., are part of the authorized capital stock of the Company;
- when the shares were issued, the Company had a sufficient number of authorized shares of that class or series available for issuance;[3]

---

* The TriBar Opinion Committee (the "Committee" or "TriBar") currently includes designees of the following organizations functioning as a single Committee: (i) Special Committee on Legal Opinions in Commercial Transactions, New York County Lawyers' Association; (ii) Corporation Law Committee, The Association of the Bar of the City of New York, and (iii) Special Committee on Legal Opinions of the Business Law Section, New York State Bar Association. Members of the state bars of California, Delaware, Georgia, North Carolina, Pennsylvania and Texas and of the Allegheny County (Pittsburgh, PA), Atlanta, Boston, Chicago, District of Columbia and Toronto, Ontario Bar Associations are also members of the Committee. The members of the Committee and the Reporter and Drafting Group for this Report are listed in Appendix A.

This Report has not been approved by the governing body or membership of any of the bar associations whose committees or members were involved in its preparation. Accordingly, the views expressed are solely those of TriBar. This Report reflects a consensus of the Committee. It does not, however, necessarily reflect the views of individual members or their firms, organizations, or associations on any particular point.

This Report is being published without further editing by *The Business Lawyer*.

1. This opinion also sometimes is given on previously issued shares of stock of the Company. For example, it may be given to underwriters in a Company's initial public offering or to stock exchanges in connection with listing the shares. *See* TriBar Opinion Committee, *Third-Party Closing Opinions: A Report of the TriBar Opinion Committee*, 53 Bus. Law. 591 (1998) ("1998 TriBar Report") § 6.2.5.

2. Certain of these conclusions also must be reached to give the "validly issued" part of the opinion and, thus, that opinion cannot be given if the "duly authorized" opinion cannot be given. When the preferred stock is convertible into other shares, such as common stock, the opinion recipient often will request an opinion on those shares as well.

3. In determining whether a sufficient number of authorized shares are available for issuance, the opinion preparers would have to take into account shares that have been "committed" to be issued

- the proper procedural steps were taken to create the class or series of shares,[4] including, if an amendment to the charter is required,[5] approval of the amendment by the board of directors and/or the stockholders by the requisite vote of each class or series entitled to vote,[6] as may be required by the applicable state corporation statute,[7] and the filing of the amendment in the proper form with appropriate state officials;[8]
- the Company's charter contains all the substantive terms, for example, par value, number of authorized shares and preferences, required by the applicable state corporation statute to create the class or series of preferred stock;[9] and

---

under a state corporation statute such as § 161 of the Delaware General Corporation Law ("DGCL"). That would include additional shares the issuer has become committed to issue as a result of triggering antidilution provisions in outstanding securities.

4. The Delaware Chancery Court has commented as follows on the importance of a corporation's observing the formalities for creating stock:

> Several policy reasons that justify the need for such formality readily come to mind.... Given the foundational importance of [corporate] securities in our economic system, it is critical that the validity of those securities, especially those that are widely traded, not be easily or capriciously called into question. Otherwise, the resulting economic uncertainty to investors and institutions that relied upon the integrity of those securities would be destabilizing. Accordingly, our statutory scheme, elucidated by case law, has developed a clear and easily followed legal roadmap for creating these valuable instruments that represent claims upon the enterprise's capital. Under that model, if that roadmap is followed, the investment community will be assured that the corporate securities created by that process will not be vulnerable to legal attack. If, on the other hand, it is not followed, then the securities will become subject to possible invalidation.

Kalageorgi v. Victor Kamkin, Inc., 750 A.2d 531, 538 (Del. Ch. 1999), *aff'd*, 748 A.2d 913 (Del. 2000) (TABLE); *see also Triplex Shoe Co. v. Rice & Hutchings*, 152 A. 342 (Del. 1930).

5. References to the charter mean the document that the applicable state corporation statute requires be filed with state authorities, typically the Secretary of State, to incorporate the corporation. It is called a certificate of incorporation in the DGCL and articles of incorporation in the Model Business Corporation Act.

6. Stockholder approval would not be necessary if the board, pursuant to a provision in the charter authorized by the state corporation statute, has so-called "blank check" authority to create the class or series of shares and establish its terms. When the director or shareholder actions being relied on took place some time ago, the opinion preparers may find the "presumption of regularity" helpful in giving the opinion. *See* 1998 TriBar Report § 2.4.

7. References to the applicable state corporation statute mean the statute as interpreted by the courts, as well as any applicable state constitutional provisions. For example, Delaware had a constitutional provision dealing with consideration to be received for par value stock before its repeal in 2004. *See* 1998 TriBar Report notes 126 and 137.

8. Ordinarily, if the board uses its blank check authority to create the class or series, a charter amendment, referred to as a certificate of designation in some states, must be filed with designated officials (typically the Secretary of State) and upon filing becomes part of the charter. *See Liebermann v. Frangiosa*, 844 A.2d 992 (Del. Ch. 2002). The requirements for a charter amendment to be "filed" are governed by the state corporation statute; for example, in some states filing does not occur until a document is accepted by the designated state official.

9. In some states, preferred stock must have a preference in liquidation or the payment of dividends or, depending on the statute, both. *See* § 501(b) of the New York Business Corporation Law; *Telvest, Inc. v. Olson*, 1979 Del. Ch. LEXIS 347 (Del. Ch. Mar. 8, 1979); *Starring v. American Hair & Felt Co.*, 191 A. 887 (Del. Ch. 1937); *see also Shintom Co. v. Audiovox Corp*, 2005 WL 1138740, at *3, n.7 (Del. Ch. May 4, 2005) ("the preferred stockholders must have some preferred right over the common, otherwise the stock is considered illusory"), *aff'd*, 888 A.2d 225 (Del. 2005).

- the Company has the power under the applicable state corporation statute and its charter to create stock having the rights, powers and preferences of the stock in question.[10]

The first four bullet points above are relatively straightforward. The fifth bullet point merits amplification because of uncertainty over whether the duly authorized opinion covers not only the issues addressed by the first four bullet points but also substantive issues addressed by the fifth bullet point.[11]

The starting point for the analysis called for by the fifth bullet point is the applicable state corporation statute.[12] Modern corporation statutes typically grant corporations the authority to create preferred stock having such terms as they may desire, subject only to compliance with the requirements of that statute[13] and the requirements, if any, of the corporation's charter. A duly authorized opinion is understood as a matter of customary practice to confirm that the Company has the power to create stock with the rights, powers and preferences of the preferred stock in question. Since most corporation statutes contain broad statutory authority to create and issue stock with whatever economic and other terms a corporation chooses,[14] an opinion preparer's inquiry regarding this point often

10. *See Waggoner v. Laster*, 581 A.2d 1127 (Del. 1990) (holding that stock created pursuant to the board's blank check authority was void because the blank check authority did not authorize the creation of preferred stock with supermajority voting rights).

11. This uncertainty may have existed because, when giving a due authorization opinion on an agreement, the opinion preparers principally focus on whether the agreement received all the necessary procedural approvals (although, as in the case of a contract to engage in an unlawful activity or an activity not within the company's corporate power, they also must consider whether the company has the power to enter into the agreement). Opinions on the due authorization of agreements are discussed in 1998 TriBar Report § 6.4.

12. The applicable state corporation statute may be the statute of the state in which the opinion preparers practice or it may be the statute of another state, such as Delaware. Non-Delaware lawyers are usually willing to give the duly authorized opinion on preferred stock issued by Delaware corporations when difficult issues are not presented. Ordinarily, opinions on Delaware corporate law given by non-Delaware lawyers are expressly limited to the DGCL. *See* note 7 *supra*.

In some states, regulated companies, such as public utilities, are incorporated under the general corporation statute but are subject to a separate regulatory statute of that state that limits the stock they may have or the terms of that stock or require that changes in the stock receive regulatory approval. In those limited cases, in giving the duly authorized opinion, the opinion preparers should consider the limitation or requirement for regulatory approval under the regulatory statute (even when the opinion is expressly limited to the applicable corporation statute) unless the regulatory statute is excluded from the opinion's coverage. *See* 1998 TriBar Report § 6.2.2 (indicating, in the context of the "validly issued" opinion, that these statutory provisions are treated, as a matter of customary usage, as though they appeared in the corporation statute).

13. The applicable corporation statute may require, for example, that all holders of shares of a class, if the class is not divided into series, and of a series if the class is so divided, have the same rights, powers and preferences.

14. In interpreting corporation statutes, courts usually are reluctant to impose limitations on a corporation's power that are not set forth expressly in the statute. *See, e.g., Unocal Corp. v. Mesa Petroleum Co.*, 493 A.2d 946, 957 (Del. 1985) ("[m]erely because the General Corporation Law is silent as to a specific matter does not mean that it is prohibited"); *Moran v. Household Int'l, Inc.*, 500 A.2d 1346 (Del. 1985) (holding in absence of affirmative evidence that the legislature intended to limit Section 157 of the DGCL to the issuance of rights for the purpose of a corporate financing, "we decline to impose such a limitation upon the section that the legislature has not"). *See also Hildreth v. Castle Dental Centers, Inc.*,

will be limited to whether any of the specified rights, powers or preferences of the preferred stock violate provisions of the corporation statute or the Company's charter.[15] Such a violation might exist, for example, if the preferred stock purports to deny holders voting rights, appraisal rights or inspection rights[16] mandated by the statute. Similarly, such a violation might exist if the preferred stock purports to deny holders voting rights when the charter prohibits non-voting stock or to grant a new class or series priority in liquidation over an existing class or series whose terms prohibit creation of stock with a higher priority. The economic terms of preferred stock, such as liquidation preferences or antidilution clauses, ordinarily do not violate the corporation statute and thus, as long as those terms do not violate the charter, usually do not require an exception.[17]

The duly authorized opinion does not address limitations that derive from sources other than the state corporation statute[18] or the Company's charter, such as other statutes and cases that do not arise under the corporation statute.[19]

Opinion recipients sometimes request that the opinion expressly confirm that the terms of the preferred stock do not violate the state corporation statute and the Company's charter. One formulation opinion preparers sometimes use for this confirmation is:

> The rights, powers and preferences of the preferred stock set forth in the [charter] do not violate [the applicable corporation statute] or the [charter].

The Committee believes, as indicated above, that this confirmation is already encompassed within the duly authorized opinion.[20]

---

939 A2d 1281 (Del. 2007) (rejecting claim that preferred stock was void because there was insufficient authorized common stock to permit exercise of conversion rights in full).

15. Although "no violation of law" and "no breach or default" opinions might cover the conclusions that the preferred stock provisions do not violate the corporation statute or the Company's charter (*see* 1998 TriBar Report §§ 6.5 and 6.6), the "duly authorized" opinion addresses those points directly.

16. *See Loew's Theatres, Inc. v. Commercial Credit Co.*, 243 A2d 78 (Del. 1968) (charter provision eliminating inspection rights was void).

17. Even if the opinion preparers are able to conclude that the board had the legal authority to create the stock in question, an issue could still exist as to whether the board, in exercising its authority, discharged its fiduciary duties. *Cf. Sample v. Morgan*, 914 A2d 647, 663–64 (Del. Ch. 2007) (distinguishing between board's having legal authority and its exercising that authority "consistently with equitable principles of fiduciary duty"). As a matter of customary practice, opinion preparers can assume without so stating that fiduciary duties have been satisfied unless under the circumstances that assumption is unreliable. *See* 1998 TriBar Report §§ 3.5.2(b) and 6.4. Compliance with fiduciary duties might, for example, be an issue, depending on the circumstances, when a corporation engages in a so-called "down round" financing in which the board of directors creates a new class or series of preferred stock for sale to investors that include affiliates of the directors at a price below that of the previous round. In those circumstances, the opinion preparers should consider the need to exclude compliance with fiduciary duties expressly from the opinion's coverage, assume such compliance expressly or, in some cases, decline to give the opinion at all.

18. *See* note 12 *supra* with respect to coverage of certain regulatory statutes.

19. Although limitations deriving from other sources are not covered by the duly authorized opinion, if the opinion preparers recognize that the creation of a class or series of stock would be prohibited by such a limitation, they should consider whether disclosure is required to avoid misleading the opinion recipient or, indeed, whether to deliver the opinion at all. *See* 1998 TriBar Report § 1.4(d).

20. A duly authorized opinion on preferred stock does not address provisions relating to the preferred stock that are contained in a separate agreement between the parties but that are not set forth in the charter, even if those provisions could have been included in the charter.

The duly authorized opinion does not cover a stockholder's ability to enforce the provisions of the preferred stock.[21] Rather, the opinion looks only to the Company's power under the applicable corporation statute and the Company's charter to create the class or series of preferred stock in question. Thus, like an opinion that a company has the corporate power to enter into and perform an agreement, an opinion that preferred stock has been duly authorized does not address the question whether the terms of the preferred stock (assuming the Company has the power to create them) will be given effect by the courts in a particular instance.[22]

Occasionally, an opinion recipient requests an opinion that the provisions of the preferred stock (or certain of the provisions) are "enforceable in accordance with their terms." Opinion givers normally are unwilling to give this opinion with respect to preferred stock, either generally or on specific provisions. This is because an opinion on the enforceability of an agreement addresses contract law concepts (and includes the standard exceptions[23]) and preferred stock provisions are not governed by contract law but rather by corporation law.[24] As one court has put it, unlike a holder of debt, a holder of preferred stock does not have "a legally enforceable right to payment."[25] Thus, the concepts underlying an enforceability opinion do not easily fit.

When preferred stock provisions are relatively straightforward, opinion preparers usually have little difficulty giving an unqualified duly authorized opinion. When preferred stock provisions are more complex (as they have become in recent years in some private transactions), opinion preparers may have more difficulty giving an unqualified opinion. If opinion preparers are unable to conclude

21. The Committee recommends that opinion givers avoid giving an opinion that "the rights, powers and preferences of the preferred stock are as set forth in the charter." Besides failing to cover rights granted by the applicable corporation statute, such an opinion might be read as confirming the enforceability of those rights, powers and preferences even though that may not be the intended meaning.

22. Nor, as noted in the 1998 TriBar Report § 6.2.1, does the duly authorized opinion cover compliance with disclosure requirements of state and federal securities laws in soliciting any required stockholder approval of the charter amendment creating the preferred stock.

23. The standard exceptions to a remedies opinion on an agreement are the bankruptcy exception and the equitable principles limitation, which are understood to be applicable whether stated or not. *See* 1998 TriBar Report § 3.3.

24. Corporation law limits the "promise" created by preferred stock. Thus preferred stock provisions cannot commit a corporation to pay amounts to preferred stockholders but can only set priorities on how any available funds may be distributed to stockholders. Dividend payments under a traditional "when, as and if declared" dividend provision are subject to the discretion of the board of directors exercising business judgment and such provision does not create an enforceable "promise." Even if dividends are styled as "mandatory," state corporation law generally requires that lawful funds be available (and imposes liability on directors for approving unlawful dividends) and that the dividends be declared by the board of directors (although a director may have liability for failing to declare a mandatory dividend when the corporation has lawful funds from which to pay it; *see Leibert v. Grinnell Corp.*, 194 A2d 846, 851 (Del. Ch. 1963) (observing in dicta that provision for mandatory dividends on stock is permissible if lawful funds are available from which to pay them)). Moreover, the rights of the preferred stock are subject to the rights of claimants with priority on the corporation's assets, such as creditors, regardless of the provisions of the preferred stock. In addition, the stated rights of the preferred stock can often be affected by various corporate actions, including a merger in which the preferred stock is exchanged for other securities or its provisions are modified.

25. *Harbinger Capital Master Fund I, Ltd. v. Granite Broadcasting Corporation*, 906 A2d 218, 225 (Del. Ch. 2006).

that the Company has the power to create a provision of the preferred stock under the state corporation statute or the Company's charter and the problem is not corrected, the opinion preparers should take an express exception for that provision or decline to give the opinion at all.[26] To illustrate, opinion preparers ordinarily would not be able to give an unqualified opinion if:

- the charter establishes a procedure for declaring dividends that contravenes the corporation statute, such as delegating authority to declare dividends to a third party or fixing the amount of the dividend by reference to an external source when the statute requires that the board of directors or a committee of the board have the authority to declare dividends or prohibits references to external sources in the charter;
- the charter eliminates statutory appraisal rights either by expressly denying those rights or by requiring all holders to vote in favor of a matter if a majority of the class or series so votes (a "drag-along") when under the applicable state corporation statute such a requirement constitutes an impermissible waiver of appraisal rights;[27]
- the charter provides for a lower percentage vote for approval of certain matters than the vote required by the statute;
- the charter gives holders of a class of stock the right to designate a member of a committee of the board when the statute authorizes only the directors to appoint members of committees of the board; or
- the board pursuant to blank check authority creates a class of stock that is non-voting when a provision in the charter only permits the creation of voting stock.

On the other hand, opinion preparers are not required to take an exception to the duly authorized opinion if the charter mandates redemption of the preferred stock upon the occurrence of a specified event or at the election of the holder even though the applicable corporation statute only permits redemption when the Company has sufficient lawful funds available to effect the redemption.[28] That is because corporation statutes usually do not deny corporations the power to create preferred stock with mandatory redemption provisions and, in fact, often expressly authorize creation of stock that is redeemable "at the option of the . . . shareholder . . . or upon the occurrence of a specified event."[29] The possibility that a particular provision of the stock, in this case the mandatory redemption

26. The decision whether to give an opinion at all will turn on the opinion preparers' judgment as to whether the provision would lead to invalidation of the preferred stock in its entirety. As discussed in the final paragraph of this report, an exception for a particular provision might not always be sufficient to address the issue.

27. *See* note 16 *supra* for a decision holding that a provision purporting to abrogate statutory inspection rights is invalid.

28. An exception would not be necessary whether or not the provision is qualified, as it often is, by the phrase "to the extent funds are lawfully available therefor" or the like. If it is not so qualified, however, the opinion preparers, to avoid misunderstanding, may want to consider pointing that limitation out to the opinion recipient.

29. Model Business Corporation Act, § 6.01(c)(2).

provision, might not be given effect in some circumstances is not, as noted above, covered by the duly authorized opinion.[30]

Depending on state law and the provision in question, a Company's lack of corporate power to create a provision of the preferred stock might give rise to a question regarding the validity of the preferred stock itself.[31] If it does and the provision is not eliminated or revised to remove the uncertainty regarding the Company's corporate power to create it, the opinion preparers may be unable to give a duly authorized opinion, even with an exception for the problematic provision, or they may be able to do so only by addressing in the opinion the possible effect of the provision on the validity of the preferred stock in its entirety.[32]

May 20, 2008

All Rights Reserved
TriBar Opinion Committee
Copyright © 2008
Reprinted with Permission

30. Unlike preferred stock, in some states common stock cannot be made redeemable. *See, e.g.*, Cal. Corp. Code § 402(c).

31. *See Waggoner v. STARR Surgical Co.*, 1990 WL 28979 at *5, n.7 (Del. Ch. March 15, 1990) (assumes preferred stock was invalid based on holding in *Waggoner v. Laster, supra* n.9). In *STARR Surgical Co. v. Waggoner*, 588 A.2d 1130 (Del. 1991), the court held that the invalidity of the preferred stock also could affect the validity of common stock issuable on conversion. *Compare Hildreth, supra* note 14 (contrasting *STARR* with the facts in that case and indicating that provisions of preferred stock could be severable.)

The reason for the provision's invalidity might affect the analysis. For example, if the board had the power to create the class of stock in question but not the particular provision, a court might hold the entire preferred stock invalid if the invalidity, in its view, constituted a "fundamental defect" as opposed to a "trivial technicality." *See Liebermann v. Frangiosa*, 844 A.2d at 1004.

32. Comments on this Report are welcome. Comments should be sent to Co-Chairs, TriBar Opinion Committee, c/o New York County Lawyers Association, 14 Vesey St., New York, NY 10007, or alternatively they can be e-mailed to the Reporter at *tribar@eapdlaw.com*.

Appendix A

Members of the TriBar Opinion Committee

New York County Lawyers' Association
Donald S. Bernstein (Co-Chair)
David L. Bleich
Sylvia Fung Chin
Sol Neil Corbin
Arthur Norman Field
Edward H. Fleischman
Nicolas Grabar
Joseph W. Halliday
A. Sidney Holderness, Jr.
Lou Kling
Morton Moskin
Charles Niemeth
Sandra M. Rocks
John B. Tehan
Judith R. Thoyer
Lawrence E. Wieman
Nancy Young

The Association of the Bar of the City of New York
Julie M. Allen**
Edward H. Cohen
Philip E. Coviello
Petrina R. Dawson
Linda Hayman
Jerome E. Hyman
Rob (B. Robbins) Kiessling
Vincent Monte-Sano
Joel I. Papernik
Robert Rosenman
Brian L. Schorr
William C. Viets

New York State Bar Association
Frederick G. Attea
Gerald S. Backman
J. Truman Bidwell, Jr.
Gregory J. Blasi
Ronald F. Daitz
Daniel W. Gersen
Joseph D. Hansen
Arthur J. Heath
Professor Joseph Hinsey, IV
Richard R. Howe**
Christian G. Koelbl, III
Richard T. McDermott
Bernard W. Nimkin
Richard L. Veron

State Bar of California
Steven O. Weise
Morris W. Hirsch
John B. Power

The District of Columbia Bar Association
Stephen Glover
James J. Rosenhauer
Arthur A. Cohen

Georgia State Bar Association
Jeffrey M. Smith

North Carolina State Bar Association
A. Mark Adcock

Pennsylvania Bar Association
E. Carolan Berkley

State Bar of Texas, Business Law Section
Roderick A. Goyne

Allegheny County (Pittsburgh) Bar Association
David A. Murdoch

Atlanta Bar Association
Jeffrey M. Stein

Boston Bar Association
Donald W. Glazer (Co-Chair)**
Stanley Keller*

Chicago Bar Association
Robin Heiss

Delaware Bar Association
James G. Leyden, Jr.

Toronto, Ontario Bar Association
Wilfred M. Estey

Member Emeritus
Honorable Thomas L. Ambro***

Special Adviser
Stephen C. Bigler**

* Reporter
** Member of Drafting Group
*** Did not participate in the consideration and approval of the report.

SPECIAL REPORT BY THE TRIBAR OPINION COMMITTEE

Opinions in the Bankruptcy Context: Rating Agency, Structured Financing, and Chapter 11 Transactions

TABLE OF CONTENTS

SPECIAL REPORT BY THE TRIBAR OPINION COMMITTEE

Opinions in the Bankruptcy Context: Rating Agency, Structured Financing, and Chapter 11 Transactions

*The Tribar Opinion Committee**

I. INTRODUCTION

Lawyers do not regularly issue formal written opinions on bankruptcy law issues to nonclient third parties. As indicated in the Committee's 1979 Report, *Legal Opinions to Third Parties: An Easier Path* ("1979 TriBar Report"), and in the vast majority of third party opinions given today, bankruptcy is generally *excepted* from the scope of the remedies opinion.[1]

In the late 1970s, however, requests for formal written legal opinions to nonclient third parties on bankruptcy law issues began to emerge in a limited range of financial and commercial transactions, principally third party credit supported financings and asset backed financings. This Special Report examines the opinions given in these special circumstances.

*The TriBar Opinion Committee ("Committee") consists of the following three groups, which have functioned as a single committee: (i) Special Committee on Legal Opinions in Commercial Transactions of the New York County Lawyers Association (Arthur Norman Field, Morton Moskin (Chairs), Donald S. Bernstein, David L. Bleich, Sol Neil Corbin, Stanley Garrett, Joseph W. Halliday, A. Sidney Holderness, Jr., Charles Niemeth, Mike Sigal, Roger M. Zaitzeff); (ii) Special Committee of the Corporation Law Committee of the Association of the Bar of the City of New York (Alan L. Beller, Franci J. Blassberg, Joel I. Greenberg, Arthur J. Heath, Karl B. Holtzschue, Jerome E. Hyman, Howard N. Lefkowitz, Vincent Monte-Sano, Joel I. Papernik); and (iii) Special Committee on Legal Opinions of the Business Law Section of the New York State Bar Association (Frederick G. Attea, J. Truman Bidwell, Ronald F. Daitz, Daniel Gersen, Sidney S. Goldstein, Joseph Hinsey IV, Richard R. Howe, Christian G. Koelbl III, B. W. Nimkin, John R. Tyler, Richard L. Veron). Thomas L. Ambro of the Delaware State Bar Association, Prof. Scott T. FitzGibbon, and Donald W. Glazer of the Boston Bar Association and Laurie G. Goldstein of the Chicago Bar Association are also members of the Committee.

Mike Sigal and Donald S. Bernstein acted as Co-Reporters for this Special Report.

The Committee intends to comment from time to time on current opinion questions. Readers of this Special Report are encouraged to send their comments, criticisms or suggestions to the TriBar Opinion Committee, c/o New York County Lawyers Association, 14 Vesey Street, New York, New York 10007.

This Special Report has not been approved by the governing board or membership of any of the bar associations whose committees were involved in this project. Accordingly, these conclusions represent only the views of the committees and their members.

Prior reports of the Committee are published at 34 Bus. Law. 1891 (1979); 36 Bus. Law. 429 (1981); and 44 Bus. Law. 563 (1989).

1. 34 Bus. Law. 1891, 1917, 1926 (1979).

Bankruptcy laws can impair contracts,[2] stay collection efforts, setoffs, and lien enforcement,[3] and cause the reversal of prepetition payments and other transfers of property.[4] Furthermore, bankruptcy courts are courts of equity,[5] with broad power to interpret the bankruptcy laws and to issue orders and injunctions in furtherance of the congressional goal of reorganization.[6] There has been surprisingly little appellate review of bankruptcy court decisions.[7]

The passage of the Bankruptcy Reform Act of 1978, which became effective on October 1, 1979,[8] caused lawyers, clients, and rating agencies[9] to focus on many bankruptcy law issues. Some of these issues were new[10] although many were present[11] under the predecessor bankruptcy law, the Bankruptcy Act of 1898, as amended, and the cases decided thereunder.[12]

Credit Supported and Structured Financings

The 1980s saw a dramatic increase in the use of new financing techniques to raise capital. Some were an effort to gain access to the capital markets or to

2. Hanover Nat'l Bank v. Moyses, 186 U.S. 181, 188 (1902); Kuehner v. Irving Trust Co., 299 U.S. 445, 451-52 (1937). *See, e.g.,* 11 U.S.C.A. §§ 727 and 1141(d) (West Supp. 1990) (relating to discharges); 11 U.S.C.A. § 365 (a), (e), and (f) (West Supp. 1990) (relating to executory contracts and unexpired leases, "ipso facto" clauses, and anti-assignment clauses); 11 U.S.C.A. § 502(b)(6) and (7) (West Supp. 1990) (relating to ceilings on damages); 11 U.S.C.A. § 552 (West Supp. 1990) (relating to after-acquired property clauses); 11 U.S.C.A. § 1111(b) (West 1979) (relating to nonrecourse clauses); 11 U.S.C.A. § 1129(b) (West 1979) (relating to approval of a plan of reorganization on a nonconsensual or "cram-down" basis).

3. 11 U.S.C.A. § 362(a) (West Supp. 1990).

4. 11 U.S.C.A. §§ 544, 547, 548, 550, and 553 (West Supp. 1990).

5. United States v. Energy Resources Co., 110 S. Ct. 2139, 2142 (1990) ("bankruptcy courts, as courts of equity, have broad authority to modify creditor-debtor relationships"); Bank of Marin v. England, 385 U.S. 99, 103 (1966); Sampsell v. Imperial Paper & Color Corp., 313 U.S. 215, 219 (1941); Pepper v. Litton, 308 U.S. 295, 307–08 (1939); 11 U.S.C.A. § 105(a) (West Supp. 1990). As courts of equity, bankruptcy courts employ equitable doctrines, such as substantive consolidation and equitable subordination, in administering bankruptcy cases.

6. Continental Ill. Nat'l Bank & Trust Co. v. Chicago, Rock Island & Pac. R.R. Co., 294 U.S. 648, 675–76 (1935); *In re* Ionosphere Clubs, Inc., 98 Bankr. 174, 176 (Bankr. S.D.N.Y. 1989) ("the paramount policy and goal of Chapter 11, to which all other bankruptcy policies are subordinated, is the rehabilitation of the debtor").

7. *See infra* section III. C.

8. This Act is codified as Title 11 of the United States Code and known as the Bankruptcy Code.

9. *See* Standard & Poor's Corporation, *S&P's Structured Finance Criteria* at 29–42 (1988) [hereinafter cited as "S&P's Criteria"]; Fitch Investors Service, Inc., *Fitch Rating Methodology for Pools of Secured Receivables* (1989) [hereinafter cited as "Fitch's Methodology"].

10. *E.g.*, the limitation on security interests in after-acquired property in 11 U.S.C.A. § 552 (West Supp. 1990); and the treatment, under some circumstances, of "nonrecourse" claims as having full recourse in Chapter 11 cases, in 11 U.S.C.A. § 1111(b) (West 1979).

11. *E.g.*, the equitable doctrines of substantive consolidation and equitable subordination; and the statutory power to avoid preferential transfers and fraudulent conveyances.

12. In the first addendum to the 1979 TriBar Report, the Committee concluded that the changes affected by the Bankruptcy Code were not sufficient to warrant a change in the opinion practices discussed in the 1979 Report. *An Addendum - Legal Opinions to Third Parties: An Easier Path,* 36 Bus. Law. 429 (1981) (hereinafter cited as "1981 TriBar Report").

reduce borrowing costs. Others resulted from the fact that, as borrowers' ratios of debt to capital increased, financers looked to the value of specific assets rather than the generalized credit of the borrowers.

Some of these new types of financing transactions are based upon an independent credit source (such as a bank or an insurance company),[13] which issues a letter of credit or surety bond in favor of the debt holders. Others are based upon a segregated defined pool of high quality assets.[14] Because the focus in these financings is on the credit of a third party or a specific asset pool, concern regarding the availability of remedies to reach that credit source or those assets if bankruptcy should ensue is heightened.

Rating Agency Opinions and the Timeliness Issue

Rating agencies, such as Standard & Poor's Corporation ("S&P"), Moody's Investors Service, Inc. ("Moody's"), and Fitch Investors Service, Inc. ("Fitch"), in determining whether to grant a rating based on the credit quality of the independent credit support or the segregated asset pool, analyze proposed financings in terms of both certainty of payment and timeliness of payment.[15] Since bankruptcy of the issuer (or an affiliated entity) can affect either the certainty or timeliness of payment, or both,[16] the rating agencies have begun in recent years to require opinions of counsel on bankruptcy issues in connection with the rating process.

Legal opinions, including bankruptcy law opinions, express a view on the ultimate outcome of the legal issue addressed. On the other hand, legal opinions (including those given to rating agencies) do not address whether a temporary restraining order, preliminary injunction or similar order pending determination on the merits would be issued. Legal opinions in the bankruptcy area, however, do address various legal issues relative to the structure of a transaction. It is from the opinion letters on these issues that the rating agencies purport to determine whether their criteria, including their criteria as to timeliness, have been met to their satisfaction.

How Broadly May Bankruptcy Opinions Be Read?

Bankruptcy opinions are troublesome. The problem is that they may be taken by some as meaning more than the opinion giver intends or could reasonably be expected to intend. Many lawyers are uncomfortable giving such opinions and others resist giving them.

13. Referred to hereinafter as "credit supported financing." *See* S&P's Criteria at 43–49.

14. Referred to hereinafter as "structured financing". *Id.* at 19–27.

15. Delay in payment of principal or interest will affect the value of the investment. *Id.* at 43.

16. Certainty of payment could be affected by, inter alia, factors such as preference recoveries, fraudulent conveyance recoveries or substantive consolidation. Timeliness of payment could be affected by, inter alia, factors such as an injunction against paying a letter of credit drawing, the bankruptcy filing by the issuer or the recharacterization of a "sale" to be a secured transaction, even though certainty of payment may not be necessarily affected.

This Special Report discusses various types of bankruptcy law opinions that are regularly given in financing and commercial transactions, principally letter of credit, insured and asset backed financings, and certain issues that are raised by virtually all opinions in the bankruptcy law area.[17] It suggests approaches to these opinions and the manner in which they may be fairly read by those who receive them.[18]

Bankruptcy Opinion Characteristics

The 1979 TriBar Report, which is the basis of most commercial transaction opinions used in practice today, dealt with the normal commercial transaction opinion. The form of opinion described in that Report was a "clean" opinion. A clean opinion is generally understood to be an opinion that does not contain any legal analysis in the opinion letter.

Most bankruptcy law opinions, by contrast, are "reasoned" opinions.[19] Reasoned opinions generally are understood to include opinions that are based on legal analysis discussed in the opinion letter. A reasoned opinion may reach either a qualified view or an unqualified view. In either case, the opinion is a "reasoned" one when, in the view of the opinion giver, its conclusions should not be stated apart from its underlying reasoning.[20] The use of a reasoned opinion is one method by which opining counsel communicates uncertainties and limitations to the recipient, even if opining counsel is able to reach an unqualified conclusion.

Accordingly, bankruptcy law opinions on certain issues have developed in reasoned form as a result of generally recognized limitations, discussed below, inherent in rendering opinions in the bankruptcy law area.[21]

17. This Special Report does not discuss the "remedies opinion"— the opinion that an agreement is a "legal, valid and binding obligation enforceable in accordance with its terms" and the related bankruptcy exception. These are discussed in the 1979 and 1981 TriBar Reports.

18. This Special Report is not intended to imply that it is appropriate to give a bankruptcy law opinion in any particular transaction or as to any particular issue. A number of factors (including legal uncertainties, the fact that many bankruptcy law issues are fact-driven, the sophistication of the recipient, the willingness of clients to bear the associated expenses, the opinion practices of counsel, and the custom of the community) bear on the appropriateness of giving a bankruptcy law opinion in a particular circumstance. This Special Report also does not take any position regarding the appropriate substantive law or public policy applicable to any particular bankruptcy law issue.

19. The primary exception is certain preference opinions. *See infra* section II. D.

20. If an opinion letter contains legal reasoning, it is understood that the legal opinion expressed therein is based on such reasoning whether or not explicitly prefaced by a phrase such as "based on the foregoing."

21. Reasoned opinions may be appropriate in a variety of circumstances. A lawyer normally will not give a clean opinion if he believes the opinion must be supported by reasoning. While the view of the recipient may not always coincide, as to bankruptcy law opinions, the reasoned form has general acceptance. It should be noted, however, that in some areas of bankruptcy law the statute or appellate case law is sufficiently clear in nondiscretionary areas to allow opining counsel to render clean opinions; the primary example of this is preference opinions discussed II. D.

Pervasive Equity Powers and Judicial Discretion

Bankruptcy courts are courts of equity and use their equity powers to further the congressional goal of promoting reorganizations, even to the extent of overriding what would otherwise appear to be absolute legal rights. For example, a bankruptcy principle as fundamental as equality of distribution to creditors of the same class may in some instances be overridden if a bankruptcy judge believes that it may be appropriate in order to promote a reorganization.[22]

Inherent in these equity powers is broad *discretion* that may be exercised on the basis of all facts and circumstances presented to the bankruptcy court. The breadth of this discretionary power is illustrated by a recent Supreme Court decision in which the Court determined that a bankruptcy court has the authority to order the IRS, a creditor, to treat payments under a Chapter 11 plan as payments of trust fund taxes.[23] The bankruptcy court had determined, in its discretion, that this provision was necessary for the success of the reorganization plan.[24] The Supreme Court held that this exercise of discretion was within the bankruptcy court's equity powers:

> The Bankruptcy Code does not explicitly authorize the bankruptcy courts to approve reorganization plans designating tax payments as either trust fund or nontrust fund. The Code, however, grants the bankruptcy courts residual authority to approve reorganization plans including "any . . . appropriate provision not inconsistent with the applicable provisions of this title." 11 U.S.C. §1123(b)(5); see also §1129. The Code also states that bankruptcy courts may "issue any order, process, or judgment that is necessary or appropriate to carry out the provisions" of the Act. §105. These statutory directives are consistent with the traditional understanding that bankruptcy courts, as courts of equity, have broad authority to modify creditor-debtor relationships.
>
> * * *

22. *See In re* Ionosphere Clubs, Inc., 98 Bankr. 174, 176 (Bankr. S.D.N.Y. 1989) and generally notes 5–6, *supra*.

23. United States v. Energy Resources Co., 110 S. Ct. 2139 (1990). This case involved so-called "trust fund" taxes, which are personal income taxes and social security taxes required to be withheld from employees. Under provisions of the Internal Revenue Code, if the employer fails to withhold and pay over these trust fund taxes, the Government may collect an equivalent sum from officers or other persons related to the employer who are responsible for collecting the tax. 26 U.S.C.A. § 6672 (West Supp. 1990). Under published IRS policy, payments with respect to taxes made under a Chapter 11 plan are deemed to be made first to nontrust fund taxes, thereby preserving to the Government the right to collect the trust fund taxes from the "responsible persons" if all taxes to be paid under the Chapter 11 plan are not made. The bankruptcy court had confirmed a reorganization plan providing that the payments under the plan (contrary to the published IRS policy) would be applied first to trust fund taxes.

24. A bankruptcy court's exercise of discretion, as long as it was within the powers committed to its discretion, is generally reviewable on appeal only under an abuse of discretion standard. *See* United States v. Lawless (*In re* Lawless), 79 Bankr. 850, 852 (Bankr. W.D. Mo. 1987) and cases cited therein. Also, the final order doctrine may preclude review, even under an abuse of discretion standard, of many bankruptcy court rulings. *See infra* section III. C.

> In this case, the Bankruptcy Court has not transgressed any limitation on its broad power.[25]

Given this equitable discretion and the possibility that facts and circumstances arising after the opining attorney delivers his opinion may be outcome-determinative[26] and given that many rulings of a bankruptcy judge, though of tremendous significance to the outcome of the bankruptcy case and the rights of parties, are not appealable as a practical matter,[27] lawyers experienced in the bankruptcy area are reluctant to render bankruptcy law opinions which may be viewed by the recipient as predictive of the outcome of a particular matter. When they do issue such opinion letters, they generally do so in reasoned form. The Committee believes that this use of reasoned opinions on bankruptcy law issues is sufficient to put the opinion recipient on notice as to these uncertainties and limitations.[28] Normally, the recipient will wish to consult with its own counsel to satisfy itself regarding the risks such limitations entail.

The Bankruptcy Process

Proceedings for reorganization under the Bankruptcy Code are complex multilateral negotiations against the backdrop of the threat of litigation before the bankruptcy court. Indeed, because the bankruptcy court is mandated to reduce all claimants to their lowest possible position (in an effort to maximize distributions to unsecured creditors and, in appropriate cases, to maintain equity values),[29] the threat of protracted litigation is a major factor in negotiations. This atmosphere in some instances is utilized by junior creditors and shareholders to induce compromise and settlement of a senior creditor's position.[30] The fact that a plan of reorganization normally involves a negotiated outcome in which the opinion recipient may feel constrained to compromise its

25. United States v. Energy Resources Co., 110 S. Ct. at 2142–43.

26. The issue of future-arising facts arises in other types of opinions such as the remedies opinion. This issue takes on special significance in the bankruptcy area, however, because of the broad discretionary powers granted to the bankruptcy courts and the possibility that future-arising facts could materially influence how a bankruptcy court exercises that discretion. By contrast, judicial discretion is excepted from the remedies opinion by the equitable principles exception. *See* TriBar Opinion Committee, *Legal Opinions to Third Parties: An Easier Path,* 34 Bus. Law. 1917–18 (1979) (hereinafter cited as "1979 TriBar Report").

27. *See infra* section III. C, regarding final orders in bankruptcy for purposes of appeal.

28. *See* 1979 TriBar Report, *supra* note 26, at 1895–96.

29. Through the use, among other things, of the avoidance powers and the equitable discretion described above.

30. For example, in the bankruptcy proceedings involving W.T. Grant Company, allegations by junior creditors that senior creditors should be equitably subordinated were settled for a significant sum. In the course of upholding the settlement, the United States Court of Appeals for the Second Circuit confirmed the relative lack of merit of these allegations. *See In re* W.T. Grant Co., 699 F.2d 599 (2d Cir. 1983).

position (or be forced to do so by the vote of other members of the recipient's class of claims)[31] cannot be addressed in a legal opinion.

Opining Counsel's Obligation

Although the factors discussed above are relevant to a sound evaluation of the bankruptcy risks in financial and commercial transactions,[32] bankruptcy law opinions are subject to the same general principles applicable to opinions on other legal issues. As with other opinions, the Committee believes that opining counsel's responsibility when rendering a bankruptcy opinion is limited to expressing an "opinion" on the legal question posed.[33] In rendering a third party opinion, opining counsel is not required, in the view of the Committee (i) to advise the opinion recipient as to the interplay of the issue opined on with the bankruptcy process or strategic factors or circumstances that might affect the outcome of the bankruptcy proceedings or (ii) to analyze the limitations of the opinion due to, among other things, reliance on assumptions or certificates. Rather, the Committee believes that bankruptcy law opinions, like other opinions to third parties, only express views on specific issues of law and do not impose an obligation of providing general advice to the recipient.[34]

II. SPECIFIC OPINIONS

Examples of bankruptcy law opinions given to rating agencies in credit supported and structured financing transactions and to acquirers and their financers in Chapter 11 transactions are discussed below. The first three opinions (substantive consolidation, asset transfers, and restrictions on access to bankruptcy) are frequently given in financings where a "special purpose" entity is utilized to segregate a group of high quality assets. The special purpose entity is used in an attempt to isolate those assets from the risks of bankruptcy normally attendant to even secured financings, including risks of timing of payment. The fourth opinion (preference) is used in financings based solely or primarily on credit support supplied by an unaffiliated third party, such as a bank or insurance company. The fifth opinion is given in the context of business divestitures by companies in bankruptcy.

The Committee has selected these types of opinions for analysis in this Special Report because (i) they are representative of commonly requested

31. *See* 11 U.S.C.A. § 1129(a)(8)(A) (West 1979), which provides that voting on reorganization plans is done by classes, and 11 U.S.C.A. § 1126(c) (West Supp. 1990), which permits a majority in number and two-thirds in amount to bind a class in a vote on a reorganization plan.

32. Because bankruptcy law opinions are most often requested by sophisticated institutions, the opinion recipient can be expected to consult with its own counsel or to have determined with the advice of its counsel that such consultation is not necessary under the circumstances.

33. An opinion is "a lawyer's informed judgment as to a specific question of law." 1979 TriBar Report at 1896.

34. *See* Model Code of Professional Responsibility DR 5-105 (1980). Of course, a lawyer cannot, in any circumstance, knowingly make a false statement of law or fact or knowingly assist a client in committing a fraud. *Id.* at DR 7–102(A)(5), (7).

opinions; (ii) they raise important and recurring issues that are present in most opinions in the bankruptcy law area; and (iii) they depict the unavoidable limitations inherent in opining in the bankruptcy area. The discussion below should be read with reference to the illustrative forms of opinions appended to this Special Report.[35]

A. SUBSTANTIVE CONSOLIDATION OPINIONS IN STRUCTURED FINANCINGS

Special Purpose Vehicle

In structured financings, securities are issued or debt is incurred by an entity that holds a defined group of high quality assets. These assets are the primary basis of the rating assigned by the rating agency or the credit decision in a nonrated transaction. The entity that issues the securities or incurs the debt is usually either a wholly-owned subsidiary or other affiliate of the company that receives the benefit of the financing or a trust or unaffiliated corporation established for the purposes of the financing. The entity is restricted in its activities to participation in the financing (thus, the term *special purpose entity*)[36] and is usually newly created for the purposes of the financing so that it has no pre-existing liabilities. The proceeds of the single purpose entity's sale of securities or incurrence of debt are transferred to the company for whose benefit the financing is arranged, usually as the purchase price for the assets if the assets are to be transferred to the single purpose entity to support the financing or as a dividend if the assets are already in the single purpose entity. In order for the transaction to achieve its purpose, it is necessary that the separateness of the single purpose entity be respected, even in the event of bankruptcy of the company that receives the benefit of the financing.[37]

The Substantive Consolidation Issue

Rating agencies are concerned that the special purpose entity could be affected by the bankruptcy of the company for whose benefit the financing is arranged. This is because part of a bankruptcy court's equitable powers include the power to substantively consolidate entities.[38] In a substantive consolidation,

35. An illustrative form of opinion letter relating to substantive consolidation, asset transfer, and advance restrictions on filing a petition in bankruptcy is appended as Exhibit A. An illustrative form of preference opinion in credit supported financings is appended as Exhibit B. An illustrative form of Chapter 11 business divestiture (sale of property) opinion is appended as Exhibit C. Neither the discussion in section II., nor the illustrative forms of opinions, are all-encompassing or applicable to all transactions of the type discussed. Any particular transaction may raise issues not discussed and each transaction must be analyzed on its particular facts.

36. Fitch's Methodology, *supra* note 9, at 7–8, 18.

37. *Id.* at 5.

38. *In re* Auto-Train Corp., 810 F.2d 270 (D.C. Cir. 1987); Chemical Bank New York Trust Co. v. Kheel, 369 F.2d 845 (2d Cir. 1966); Soviero v. Franklin Nat'l Bank, 328 F.2d 446 (2d Cir. 1964); Stone v. Eacho, 127 F.2d 284 (4th Cir. 1942); Fish v. East, 114 F.2d 177 (10th Cir. 1940).

the assets of two or more entities are pooled, intercompany claims are eliminated, and, with certain exceptions,[39] claims of outside creditors are treated as claims against the common fund.[40] Since substantive consolidation would defeat one of the major premises of the rating in a structured financing—that the holders of the rated securities can look to the segregated asset pool held by the special purpose entity without regard to the bankruptcy of the company that received the benefit of the financing—opinions as to substantive consolidation are regularly requested by the rating agencies in such financings.[41]

Some lawyers are concerned about giving a legal opinion as to what a court will find to be equitable at some future point in a bankruptcy proceeding. Not only is a discretionary judgment involved, at the time that judgment is made there may be relevant facts, circumstances, relationships, and other considerations that cannot be known by the opining lawyer when the opinion is given. While matters which cannot be known to the lawyer should not form a basis for liability, these lawyers are concerned that the opinion may prove to be "wrong."

Most lawyers are willing to give substantive consolidation opinions with respect to newly-created special purpose vehicles.[42] Many of these lawyers, however, are concerned about potential misunderstandings as to an opinion of this nature and, in order to fairly present the limitations implicit in such an opinion, have in the opinion letter outlined in great detail the factors considered by courts in determining whether substantive consolidation should be granted and, in addition, have:

(i) stated that substantive consolidation is an equitable doctrine, that relevant facts may arise in the future, and that courts have accorded different degrees of importance to different factual matters;

(ii) assumed that the entities involved will act in accordance with limitations designed to promote separateness drafted into the relevant documents;

(iii) assumed a number of objective facts which have been drafted into the documents to support separateness;

(iv) assumed certain subjective or conclusory facts, such as the newly-created entity has "sufficient employees" and will not be bound by business decisions of the parent without independent approval by the newly-created entity pursuant to its own corporate governance procedures;

39. Valid nonpreferential and nonfraudulent liens are not affected by substantive consolidation. *In re* Gulfco Invest. Corp., 593 F.2d 921, 926–27 (10th Cir. 1979). Other exceptions may exist in particular factual situations. However, even if a lien or other claim is excepted from substantive consolidation, substantive consolidation may affect the timeliness of payment.

40. *In re* Augie/Restivo Baking Co., 860 F.2d 515 (2d Cir. 1988).

41. It should be noted that other issues could also affect the basis of the rating. For example, if a sale of assets to the issuer is not considered to be a true sale under applicable law, the rating could be unavailable or based to some extent on the seller's credit.

42. Except in rare instances, lawyers resist giving substantive consolidation opinions in the case of a pre-existing corporation because of the virtual impossibility of isolating the present and historical facts to be considered.

(v) assumed the absence of any factors inconsistent with the other express assumptions; and

(vi) qualified the opinion by stating that there is no case directly on point and that there are uncertainties in rendering a substantive consolidation opinion.[43]

The rating agencies will normally require that assumptions relating to factual matters be supported by factual certificates or covenants in the transactional documents.

Even with these qualifications, some lawyers who give substantive consolidation opinions are concerned that the opinion recipient may believe that the opining lawyer is expressing a more definitive conclusion than the opining lawyer believes he is expressing, or can express, as to an equitable matter. This concern is based, in part, on the view that a substantive consolidation opinion is fundamentally different from the closing opinion normally delivered in a commercial transaction. In a remedies opinion delivered at a closing, the impact of equitable considerations is expressly excepted by the equitable principles limitation.[44] Substantive consolidation, on the other hand, involves an opinion as to a discretionary, equitable judgment to be made in the future, in the context of the congressional goal of promoting reorganizations, with respect to the interplay of facts, circumstances, relationships, and other considerations, some of which may exist at the time the opinion is rendered and some of which may arise in the future.

If despite these inherent limitations a reasoned substantive consolidation opinion is required in a structured financing or other special type of transaction, it should (without the need for express reference in the opinion letter) be understood to be subject to unavoidable uncertainties referred to in this Special Report because of the discretionary, equitable nature of the doctrine, as well as the impact of future-arising facts, circumstances, relationships, and other considerations, and also to be based upon the premise that the parties will act in accordance with the provisions of the relevant transactional documents. A form of reasoned opinion on substantive consolidation is included in the opinion letter appended as Exhibit A.

B. ASSET TRANSFER OPINIONS IN STRUCTURED FINANCINGS

As discussed above, in structured financings the rating or credit decision is largely dependent on the quality of a segregated asset pool. Normally, this asset pool is purchased by the special purpose entity with the proceeds of the financing. Sometimes, part of the asset pool is transferred to the special purpose

43. It is by no means clear that such detail is necessary. Although the illustrative forms of opinion appended to this Special Report eliminate much of this type of detail, as indicated in note 73, *infra*, the Committee does not take any position on the appropriateness of any particular form of opinion letter.

44. 1979 TriBar Report, *supra* note 26, at 1917–18.

entity as a capital contribution. If the transfer constituted a fraudulent conveyance, creditors of the parent (or its trustee in bankruptcy) could disregard the transfer, and the value of such assets would not be exclusively available to support the securities issued by the special purpose vehicle. Thus, in transactions of this nature, the rating agencies may require an opinion that the capital contribution to the special purpose entity (and, in some instances, also the purchase of assets by the special purpose entity) does not constitute a fraudulent conveyance.[45]

Fraudulent conveyance laws typically apply to two different types of transactions—those that are actually fraudulent and those that are defined to be constructively fraudulent.[46] Although state and federal fraudulent conveyance laws differ in certain particulars, constructively fraudulent transactions generally are based on: (i) the absence of fair consideration in circumstances where (ii) there also exist (a) certain economic predicates (such as insolvency or unreasonably small capital) or (b) certain subjective intent (such as intent to incur debts beyond ability to pay).

The elements of a constructive fraudulent conveyance are to a large degree factual. In order to give a fraudulent conveyance opinion with respect to a capital contribution in a structured financing, most lawyers rely on a certificate of an investment banking firm, or a valuation expert, for the existence of fair consideration from the perspective of the transferror.[47] If the certificate is incorrect, a fraudulent conveyance may exist.

Since any opinion that relies on assumed facts or certificates may not be correct if the underlying assumptions or certificates are not correct, many lawyers are uncomfortable with giving a fraudulent conveyance opinion. They are concerned that the opinion recipient may not appreciate how crucial to the view expressed are the underlying assumptions or certificates. This is further complicated in instances where (unlike most factual certificates that relate to relatively straightforward factual matters) the certificate itself is only an opinion —an opinion of an investment banking firm or valuation expert that "fair

45. The standard remedies opinion excepts out any opinion on the fraudulent conveyance laws by virtue of the standard bankruptcy exception. *See* TriBar Opinion Committee, Second Addendum to Legal Opinions to Third Parties: *An Easier Path,* 44 Bus. Law. *563, 569–72 (1989)* (hereinafter cited as "1989 TriBar Report"). In structured financings, however, there is a special request for a fraudulent conveyance opinion with respect to the assets contributed to the capital of the special purpose entity and in some instances with respect to the assets sold to the special purpose entity.

The importance of true sale treatment should also be noted. *See supra* note 41.

46. *See, e.g.,* 11 U.S.C.A. § 548 (West Supp. 1990); New York Debtor Creditor Law §§ 270–81. This Special Report does not discuss fraudulent conveyance opinions in the context of leveraged buy-outs, which topic is, inter alia, the subject of the 1989 TriBar Report, *supra* note 45.

47. Many lawyers also make an assumption as to the absence of actual fraud. Some lawyers only make an assumption as to actual fraud where their role in the transaction is a limited one, such as special counsel engaged to give an opinion under the laws of the state that has been chosen as the governing law under the transactional documents.

consideration" has been given—which in hindsight under judicial scrutiny, could be determined to be wrong.[48]

The Committee believes that the opining lawyer is under no obligation to provide generalized advice to the opinion recipient, such as advice as to the inherent limits of opinions of this nature. A form of reasoned opinion on this type of fraudulent conveyance issue is included in the opinion letter appended as Exhibit A.

C. OPINIONS REGARDING ADVANCE RESTRICTIONS ON ACCESS TO BANKRUPTCY IN STRUCTURED FINANCINGS

In certain types of structured financings, the special purpose vehicle that holds the segregated asset pool (a) is required to have independent, outside directors and/or (b) issues preferred stock to one or more unaffiliated third parties. The special purpose vehicle usually is a wholly-owned subsidiary of another company, and in order to make the special purpose vehicle "bankruptcy remote" (a rating agency term of art), the certificate of incorporation of the special purpose vehicle provides that an affirmative vote of a super-majority of the board of directors (including the required outside directors) and/or of the holders of the preferred stock must be obtained before it can file a voluntary bankruptcy case or amend these provisions. The rating agencies request an opinion on the validity of such provision because a bankruptcy of the issuer (which, absent such a voting requirement, could be caused solely by the parent) could jeopardize the timeliness of payment to the security holders.[49]

An opinion on this subject deals primarily with (a) the law relevant to the requisite authorization to file a voluntary petition for bankruptcy; (b) the

48. Practice has developed that the "fair consideration" issue is usually covered by a certificate, as opposed to an assumption. Sometimes certificates are given by a completely disinterested valuation expert. More frequently, certificates are given by an investment banking firm that is acting as underwriter or private placement agent for the securities being sold by the special purpose entity and/or receiving a substantial fee for advising the special purpose entity's parent in the transaction. Only on rare occasions are certificates of this nature given by officials of a company involved as a principal in the transaction, such as officials of the special purpose entity's parent. It is customary for opining counsel to identify the source of the certificate on which he is relying or to attach the actual certificate. Although it is not necessary, in the Committee's view, for the certificate to be attached to the opinion letter, the Committee believes that is the better practice. If the certificate is not attached, the Committee believes that, at a minimum, counsel should disclose the identity of the certifier. However, the Committee does not believe that it is the responsibility of opining counsel to pass on the qualifications or appropriate degree of disinterestedness of the certifier, except that counsel should not rely on a certificate if counsel knows, or has reason to believe, that the certifier is not qualified to express a view on the matter. *See* 1979 TriBar Report, *supra* note 26, at 1902. Rather, once disclosure is made (and subject to such exception), it is up to the opinion recipient to determine whether it is satisfied with the qualifications, status of disinterestedness, and other attributes of the certifier.

49. The rating agencies are generally not concerned about an involuntary filing because the special purpose entity has few, if any, consensual creditors who have not signed an agreement not to file an involuntary case against the special purpose entity (so called "no-petition" agreements).

possible recharacterization of the preferred stock as debt or otherwise ineligible to block the bankruptcy filing; and (c) the applicability of the public policy against advance restrictions on filing a petition for bankruptcy. The legal analyses in opinion letters on this subject vary in length although some go into detailed analysis in order to convey the novelty of the issue and the unavoidable uncertainties in opining on public policy issues in the bankruptcy area.[50]

The Committee believes that opinions regarding public policy are inherently limited because the opining lawyer can make only an informed judgment regarding how the public policy will be applied in a given case. The Committee believes that an opinion reasoned as to public policy issues is sufficient to put the opinion recipient on notice of the limitations inherent in opinions in the public policy area. A form of reasoned opinion on advance restrictions on access to bankruptcy is included in the opinion letter appended as Exhibit A.

D. PREFERENCE OPINIONS IN CREDIT SUPPORTED FINANCINGS

Numerous issuances of commercial paper, medium-term notes, and bonds are credit supported financings. In order to obtain a credit rating of the securities equal to that of the bank or other credit support provider, the rating agencies require an opinion to the effect that payments to the debt holders will not be preferential.[51]

50. The legal analysis underlying an opinion on this subject is based on the proposition that applicable nonbankruptcy law, as opposed to bankruptcy law, is the determining law as to the proper authorization for accessing bankruptcy. Price v. Gurney, 324 U.S. 100, 107 (1945); *In re* Eastern Bancorp., 23 Bankr. 474, 476 (Bankr. E.D. Pa. 1982). However, many lawyers are concerned that charter restrictions relative to filing bankruptcy might clash with the well-settled public policy against advance agreements with creditors not to file bankruptcy or not to invoke the rights and privileges afforded to a debtor. *See e.g.*, Federal Nat'l Bank v. Koppel, 253 Mass. 157, 159, 148 N.E. 379, 380 (1925); *In re* Weitzen, 3 F. Supp. 698 (S.D.N.Y. 1933); *In re* Markizer, 66 Bankr. 1014, 1018 (Bankr. S.D. Fla. 1986); *In re* Tru Block Concrete Products, 27 Bankr. 486, 492 (Bankr. S.D. Cal. 1983); *In re* George, 15 Bankr. 247, 248 (Bankr. N.D. Ohio 1981); *In re* Adana Mortgage Bankers, 12 Bankr. 989, 1009 (Bankr. N.D. Ga. 1980), *appeal dismissed per joint motion*, 687 F.2d 344 (11th Cir. 1982); *In re* Kriger, 2 Bankr. 19, 23 (Bankr. D. Or. 1979). In order to distinguish charter provisions requiring a preferred stockholder vote prior to filing a petition for bankruptcy from prohibited creditor veto provisions, some lawyers provide that the preferred stockholder vote on this issue is only operative while the special purpose entity is solvent and further provide, so as to help preclude a recharacterization of the preferred stock as debt; that the preferred stockholders only have normal preferred stock voting rights (such as the right to elect a majority of the board of directors if a dividend is missed or a redemption payment is not made); and expressly not the right to bring a lawsuit for the payment of money.

51. *See Moody's Approach to Rating Bank - Supported Debt Securities,* Moody's Bond Survey, 3979 (Jan. 3, 1983) (hereinafter cited as "Moody's Bond Survey"). However, where the credit support provider is an insurance company that will issue an insurance policy that specifically covers the preference risk, a legal opinion regarding preferences is normally not required.

A necessary element of a preference under the Bankruptcy Code, 11 U.S.C. section 547, is that it involves a transfer of property of the debtor. Generally,[52] a preference opinion in a credit supported financing focuses on the procedures by which moneys are transferred from the credit source to the debt holders so as to come to the conclusion that no preference exists because the debt holders are not being paid with property of the debtor. Preference opinions of this type generally appear to involve only opining counsel's view of substantive law, rather than equitable considerations or public policy, as applied to the procedures provided for in the transactional documents. These opinion letters are generally not based on assumptions or certificates as to facts although some opinion letters describe the procedures provided for in the transactional documents in detail and assume that the parties will act in accordance with the documents.[53] These opinions are usually "clean" as the opinion letters do not ordinarily contain legal reasoning.

The Committee believes that it is not necessary in the opinion letter to specify the procedures provided in the documents or to make an express assumption that the parties will act in accordance with the documents; the Committee believes that both matters are implicit in any opinion whether or not expressly stated. A form of opinion on preferences, which is a clean opinion, is appended as Exhibit B.

E. OPINIONS REGARDING COURT ORDER APPROVING SALE OF PROPERTY IN CHAPTER 11 CASES

Business divestitures by Chapter 11 debtors are increasingly prevalent. Often a sale of all or a substantial portion of the debtor's business or assets, either pursuant to court order or under a plan of reorganization, will maximize value for creditors and shareholders, and in some instances a sale of part of the business or assets will further the goals of reorganization by preserving the remaining business as a going concern.

Although there may be exceptions, these transactions are normally "friendly" (pursuant to contract), and the acquirer (and perhaps the lenders financing the acquirer) may require, as conditions to closing, opinions different in kind though serving the same purposes as legal opinions requested by acquirers in connection with divestitures outside of bankruptcy. For example, the acquirer may request an opinion to the effect that the order authorizing the contemplated

52. In certain commercial paper financings, some counsel will issue an opinion based on the exception from preference recovery for transfers "in the ordinary course" found in 11 U.S.C.A. § 547(c)(2) (West Supp. 1990). These are normally reasoned opinions.

53. Some lawyers utilize this detail as a precaution because a variance in the procedures provided for in the transactional documents could in some instances cause a payment to be preferential. As stated in the text, the Committee does not believe such detail is necessary. The illustrative form of preference opinion appended to this Special Report eliminates such detail as being unnecessary.

divestiture has been duly and validly entered by the court and is in full force and effect.

Unlike the normal out-of-court divestiture, debtors normally dispense with obtaining lien releases from creditors and waivers of covenant violations, relying instead on the power of the bankruptcy court to override such restrictions. However, prudent bankruptcy counsel normally will not give the foregoing opinions without qualification because the efficacy of the bankruptcy court's order may be limited if inadequate notice of the order has been given under the standards promulgated in *Mullane v. Central Hanover Bank & Trust Co.*, 339 U.S. 306 (1950). It is virtually impossible for the opining lawyer to be certain that proper notice has been given to every party entitled to receive it. Moreover, it may be possible for there to be appeals timely made and pending which have not been docketed in such a way that an opining lawyer can know of their existence at the time the opinion is rendered. For this reason, many opining lawyers in this area make assumptions regarding the adequacy of notice and the accuracy of the court's docket.[54] Others simply describe the notice procedures and the results of an inspection of the docket and refuse to give an opinion on this issue at all.

The Committee believes that such opinions may properly be qualified with respect to the adequacy of notice and the limitations inherent in the courts' record-keeping process. Further, the Committee believes that it should be the responsibility of the acquirer and his counsel to prenegotiate with the debtor and its counsel notice procedures that make them comfortable. A form of opinion addressing the bankruptcy court's order approving a sale of assets in Chapter 11 is appended as Exhibit C.

III. GENERAL ISSUES

In addition to the issues raised by the representative types of opinions discussed above, there are certain general issues, discussed below, that arise in most bankruptcy law opinions.

A. TEMPORARY RESTRAINT

In credit supported financings (discussed previously in section II. D), counsel for the bank or other credit support provider is usually required to give an opinion that the letter of credit or other credit support instrument is a valid and binding obligation enforceable in accordance with its terms, subject to the usual bankruptcy exception relating to insolvency laws applicable to the issuer of the credit support instrument.

Since the rating agencies have stated that timeliness of payment is an integral part of their rating criteria, many counsel state that they express no opinion as to whether a court, in the exercise of its equitable powers, may temporarily

54. As indicated in notes 43 and 53, *supra,* excessive detail is not necessary and is not utilized in the illustrative forms of opinions appended to this Special Report.

restrain payments under the support instrument. In any opinion context, there may be a restraining order or other delay. Third party legal opinions opine only as to the ultimate outcome. The Committee believes that the possibility of delay in a bankruptcy case should be understood whether or not expressly stated.

B. SHOULD/WOULD

The rating agencies have expressed the view that when a lawyer gives a "would" opinion he is giving a stronger opinion than when giving a "should" opinion.[55] Some lawyers also share the view that a "should" opinion does not go quite as far as a "would" opinion.

Many lawyers are uncomfortable with this distinction because they believe that a lawyer can only opine as to what a court should do when applying the applicable law to the relevant facts. Accordingly, some lawyers, when required to give a "would" opinion, have stated in the opinion letter that, in giving such an opinion, they are doing so on the understanding that the opinions expressed are not a prediction as to what a court would actually hold but an opinion as to the decision a court would reach if the issue were properly presented to it and the court followed existing legal precedents applicable to the subject matter of the opinion.

The Committee has found no case law or published secondary authority for the proposition that a stronger opinion is being expressed by the use of the word "would," in the context of a legal opinion, as opposed to the word "should."

As stated in the 1979 TriBar Report, "it should be understood that an opinion is not a guaranty, but merely a lawyer's informed judgment as to a specific question of law."[56] The Committee believes that this is true whether the opinion is phrased in terms of "would" or "should" and that both formulations convey the same informed judgment, and thus express the same opinion, as to a court's determination based upon existing legal precedents as applied to the facts on which the opinion is based. Accordingly, the Committee believes opining counsel can appropriately deliver "would" opinions in this area.

C. FINAL ORDER

Under 28 U.S.C. section 158(a), the district courts have jurisdiction to hear appeals from "final" orders of bankruptcy judges and, with leave of the district court, to hear appeals from interlocutory orders of bankruptcy judges.[57] The issue of what is a "final" order is not defined by statute and is not clearly defined by case law.[58]

55. S&P's Criteria, *supra* note 9, at 34, 39.

56. 1979 TriBar Report, *supra* note 26, at 1896.

57. Jurisdiction at the court of appeal level is limited solely to final orders. There is no court of appeal jurisdiction for interlocutory orders, even with leave of the court. 28 U.S.C.A. § 158(d) (West 1968 & Supp. 1990).

58. Developing case law in some circuits is tending to narrow the scope of what is a final order for appeal purposes. *See, e.g., In re* Phillips, 844 F.2d 230 (5th Cir. 1988) and cases cited therein.

Some lawyers are concerned that, if a bankruptcy judge were incorrectly to decide an issue in respect of which an opinion has been given, the opinion recipient may be saddled with the effects of the bankruptcy judge's ruling for a substantial period of time.[59] More importantly, the effects of such ruling may be carried forward into a plan of reorganization and, although an order confirming a reorganization plan is a final order for appeal purposes, the way the doctrine of mootness is developing in the bankruptcy area[60] may as a practical matter preclude effective appellate review of the bankruptcy judge's ruling (unless the opinion recipient can obtain a stay of the confirmation order which usually requires the posting of a substantial bond).

Given such circumstances, some counsel have begun to state in bankruptcy law opinions that they express no opinion as to whether a bankruptcy judge's ruling with respect to the subject matter of the opinion is a final order for purposes of appeal or whether the district court would exercise its discretion to grant leave to appeal. The Committee does not believe that such statements are necessary. The Committee believes that a lawyer giving a bankruptcy law opinion to a third party is not required to go beyond the specific legal question opined on and advise the opinion recipient as to the interplay of that question with the bankruptcy process. Advice of that nature, in the view of the Committee, should be obtained by the opinion recipient from its own counsel.[61]

D. UNQUALIFIED OPINIONS AND RISK

As indicated above, most opinions in the bankruptcy area are reasoned opinions.[62]

In 1983, Moody's published an article in *Moody's Bond Survey* in which it distinguished between "reasoned" opinions, on the one hand, and "unqualified" or "unequivocal" opinions, on the other hand, and asserted that if a lawyer gives an unqualified opinion the risk attendant to the issue opined on has in the opinion of such lawyer been "substantially eliminated."[63] In the Committee's view, to posit a dichotomy between reasoned opinions and unqualified opinions

59. Also, it should be noted that, on appeal, a bankruptcy judge's "[f]indings of fact, whether based on oral or documentary evidence, shall not be set aside unless clearly erroneous. . . ." Bankruptcy R. 8013.

60. *See In re* Crystal Oil Co., 854 F.2d 79 (5th Cir. 1988); Miami Center Ltd. Partnership v. Bank of New York, 838 F.2d 1547 (11th Cir. 1988); *In re* AOV Industries, 792 F.2d 1140 (D.C. Cir. 1986); *In re* Matos, 790 F.2d 864 (11th Cir. 1986); *In re* Roberts Farms, 652 F.2d 793 (9th Cir. 1981).

61. *See* notes 32–34 *supra* and accompanying text.

62. The only common exception is preference opinions, discussed *supra* in section II. D, that deal with the purely legal issue of whether property of the debtor has been transferred in a credit supported financing.

63. Moody's Bond Survey, *supra* note 51. In its article, Moody's seems to use the words "unqualified" and "unequivocal" interchangeably. Our Reports do not use the word "unequivocal." It is not a term used in case law and (except for Moody's 1983 article) secondary sources dealing with legal opinions. It is not a term generally used by lawyers with respect to legal opinions, and the Committee believes the use of such term would add confusion to the understanding of legal opinions.

as a basis for evaluating risk is unacceptably simplistic. Further, to use the distinction to support the assertion made as to the import of an unqualified opinion is simply wrong.

The division of all opinions into two categories—reasoned or unqualified/ "unequivocal"—is, as noted, too simplistic. A number of methods exist for an opinion giver to communicate uncertainties and limitations to the recipient. These methods include (i) clean opinions that express a qualified view or that exclude aspects of the subject of the opinion letter, and (ii) reasoned opinions. A reasoned opinion may reach a qualified or an unqualified conclusion,[64] but even if an unqualified conclusion is reached that ultimate opinion cannot be fairly separated from the totality of the opinion letter.[65]

Furthermore, there is no basis for the proposition that an unqualified/ "unequivocal" opinion, even in clean (as opposed to reasoned) form, means that all risks have been substantially eliminated. A lawyer is not an insurer or guarantor of opinions.[66] A lawyer is not liable for the "true state of the law," as long as the opinion is based on the reasonable exercise of informed judgment.[67] Moreover, all lawyers understand that the law is not changed by whether a lawyer's opinion is expressed as unqualified.[68]

Opinions have a predictive quality, but no third party opinion is ever so strong that the opinion recipient can fairly believe that risk has been eliminated. Our legal process in general, and the bankruptcy process in particular, does not allow for a risk-free environment with or without a legal opinion.

The Committee believes that the publicized statement of the rating agency equating an unqualified/"unequivocal" opinion with risk elimination is without analytical basis[69] and that it is inappropriate for any opinion recipient to

64. This Special Report does not take any position as to the various ways a qualified conclusion can be expressed.

65. In financial and commercial transactions, opinion recipients are normally represented by counsel (either inside counsel or outside counsel) and the recipient's counsel plays a role in the opinion process. "The parties to any transaction and their respective lawyers must ultimately determine for themselves the scope and content of an acceptable legal opinion for that transaction." 1979 TriBar Report, *supra* note 26, at 1896, n.2. Legal opinions necessarily contain technical, legal matters, and parties to financial commercial transactions that seek legal opinions normally are advised by counsel as to the scope and acceptability of those opinions. Opining counsel in appropriate cases may wish to (but is not obligated to) point this out to the recipient if it is obvious to opining counsel that the recipient is not represented by counsel.

66. Lucas v. Hamm, 56 Cal. 2d 583, 591, 364 P.2d 685, 689, 15 Cal. Rptr. 821 (1961); McCullough v. Sullivan, 102 N.J.L. 381, 384, 132 A. 102, 103 (1926); Practical Offset v. Davis, 83 Ill. App. 3d 566, 404 N.E.2d 516, 521 (1980); Prosser & Keeton, The Law of Torts 186 (5th ed. 1984).

67. Davis v. Damrell, 119 Cal. App. 3d 883, 887, 174 Cal. Rptr. 257, 259 (1981).

68. "An opinion cannot change the facts or the state of the law." 1979 TriBar Report, *supra* note 26, at 1895.

69. The traditional standard with respect to professional conduct is negligence. *See* Prosser & Keeton, *supra* note 66, at 186; DuPont v. Brady, 646 F. Supp. 1067, 1075–76 (S.D.N.Y. 1986), *remanded on other grounds,* 828 F.2d 75 (2d Cir. 1987); Marks Polarized Corp. v. Solinger & Gordon, 124 Misc. 2d 266, 476 N.Y.S.2d 743 (Sup. Ct. 1984). Equating an unqualified opinion with substantial risk elimination could be argued to impact on the standard of liability, by implying

believe, or advertise, that no risk exists in a transaction because an unqualified opinion has been received.

IV. CONCLUSIONS

The Committee believes that bankruptcy law opinions to nonclient third parties are governed by the same general legal principles that govern the commercial transactions opinions discussed in the 1979 TriBar Report: *to wit,* the opinion expresses an informed judgment as to the applicability of existing legal precedents to the facts on which the opinion is based; the opinion cannot change the law or the facts; and opining counsel is liable only for negligence.

The Committee also believes that opinions to nonclient third parties on bankruptcy law matters unavoidably have inherent limitations referred to above that generally do not exist in respect of the legal issues discussed in the 1979 TriBar Report. As discussed, these inherent limitations exist primarily because of: the pervasive equity powers of bankruptcy courts; the overriding goal of reorganization to which other legal rights and policies may be subordinated; the potential relevance to the exercise of judicial discretion of future-arising facts and circumstances; and the nature of the bankruptcy process. Furthermore, requests for third party opinions on bankruptcy law matters almost always arise in sophisticated financial and commercial transactions, and the Committee believes that when a reasoned opinion is received an analysis of the bankruptcy risks associated with the transaction is properly within the domain of the recipient, not the giver of the third party opinion.[70]

As applied to specific issues relative to bankruptcy law opinions to nonclient third parties, the Committee believes:

1. Bankruptcy law opinions, as other opinions, may appropriately be given as reasoned opinions, such as those appended to this Report. A reasoned opinion is sufficient to put the opinion recipient on notice as to the uncertainties and limitations, referred to above, inherent in opining on those bankruptcy law matters covered in the opinion, even where the ultimate judgment is expressed in unqualified terms.[71] A clean opinion is not properly understood to mean that all risks have been substantially eliminated.

2. Bankruptcy law opinions, as other opinions generally, speak only as to the ultimate outcome of issues as a legal matter and do not deal with issues such as temporary restraining orders, preliminary injunctions or

that something more akin to strict liability (rather than the traditional negligence standard) should be applicable when an unqualified opinion was given.

70. The rating agencies take the position that they are entitled to rely, without reinvestigation, on opinion letters provided to them and that they apply those opinions to the particular transaction at issue in arriving at a rating.

71. As discussed in section III. D, *supra,* a clean opinion that expresses a qualified view or that excludes aspects of the subject matter also puts the opinion recipient on notice as to uncertainties and limitations.

similar orders pending determination on the merits. The risk of delay in a bankruptcy case should be understood whether or not expressly stated.

3. Whether a legal opinion is expressed in terms of "would" or "should" does not affect the meaning of the legal opinion expressed. Both convey the same judgment as to the applicability of existing legal precedents to the facts upon which the opinion is based. No distinction should be drawn by either the opinion giver or recipient from the choice made between these two words as to the lawyer's level of confidence in the opinion expressed.

4. It is not necessary in an opinion letter to spell out procedures provided in the transactional documents or to make an express assumption that parties will act in accordance with the documents or to state that the opinion may not be correct if facts assumed or certificates relied upon are incorrect, as those matters are implicit in any opinion whether or not expressly stated.

5. Where an opinion letter states that a certificate is being relied on and the certificate is attached or the opinion letter discloses the identity of the certifier, it is the responsibility of the opinion recipient, and not opining counsel, to determine whether the certifier is satisfactory.[72]

6. Bankruptcy law opinions, as other third party opinions, are not required to go beyond the specific legal questions opined on and advise the opinion recipient as to the interplay of that issue with the bankruptcy process or as to the relationship of assumptions and certificates to the legal issue opined on or as to the limitations of the opinion.

In rendering opinions on bankruptcy law matters, counsel may wish to refer to this Special Report.[73] Such reference, in the Committee's view, would appropriately follow the tradition of its "easier path" philosophy by making counsel comfortable in eliminating detailed recitation of the uncertainties and limitations involved in bankruptcy law opinions.

June 1, 1990

All Rights Reserved
TriBar Opinion Committee
Copyright (c) 1990
Reprinted With Permission

72. This is of course subject to the exception stated in note 48, *supra,* if opining counsel knows, or has reason to believe, that the certifier is not qualified to express a view on the matter.

73. This Special Report does not take any position on the appropriateness of any opinion or any form of opinion letter in respect of any particular transaction. Those matters are determined in each instance by opining counsel, based on factors such as the facts of the particular transaction, custom as to the particular type of opinion, and counsel's individual opinion practices. Regardless of counsel's resolution of those matters, counsel may find it useful to refer to this Special Report. S & P and Fitch have indicated that such rating agencies will accept opinion letters that refer to this Special Report.

EXHIBIT A

ILLUSTRATIVE FORM OF OPINION FOR STRUCTURED FINANCING[1]

[Addressee[2]] [Date]

Dear Sirs:

We have acted as counsel to [name of issuer], a Delaware corporation[3] (the "Company"), a subsidiary of [name of parent company] ("Parent"), in connection with the proposed issuance by the Company of $__________ aggregate principal amount of its [title of security] (the "Bonds"). The Bonds will be issued pursuant to an Indenture dated as of [date] (the "Indenture") between the Company and [name of indenture trustee], as trustee (the "Trustee"). Unless otherwise defined herein, terms defined in the Indenture are used herein as therein defined.[4]

In connection with the proposed issuance and sale of the Bonds, you have requested our opinion:

> (i) whether, in the event of the insolvency of Parent, the Parent (as debtor-in-possession), or a creditor, trustee, [conservator[5]] or receiver of Parent [including the FDIC as conservator or receiver of Parent*], could cause a court lawfully to order the consolidation of the assets and liabilities of the Company with those of Parent;
>
> (ii) whether the transfers of assets by parent to the Company (the "Asset Transfers") described in items 2 and 3 under "Structure of the Transaction" below (the "Asset Transfers") constitute voidable fraudulent conveyances; and
>
> (iii) as to the validity of the provisions in the Certificate of Incorporation of the Company that requires the unanimous approval of the Company's Board of Directors [shareholders] for the voluntary commencement by the

1. This form of opinion is included for illustrative purposes only. The documentation used in transactions of this type will vary in form. As indicated in the accompanying Special Report, the appropriate application of substantive law to each opinion is a matter for the opining lawyer to establish. This shortened form of reasoned opinion has been prepared on the premise that the recipient has available the advice of counsel. See notes 32 and 65 in the accompanying Special Report. If it is obvious that such is not the case in a particular transaction, opining counsel may wish to (but is not obligated to) transmit a copy of the Special Report to the recipient unless the recipient is an institution such as a rating agency that is already aware of the Special Report.

2. Depending upon the circumstances, an opinion in this form may be addressed to the parent company of the issuer, the underwriters (if any), or a rating agency.

3. Delaware, often the state of incorporation of the issuing vehicle corporation, is used for illustrative purposes.

4. Because these opinions rely so heavily on specified assumptions of fact, references to opining counsel's investigations of fact are omitted.

5. Include if Parent is a bank or savings institution.

Company of any bankruptcy, insolvency or similar proceeding (the "Special Charter Provisions").

ASSUMPTIONS

We have assumed in rendering this opinion that the facts outlined below, which are provided for in the transactional documents or have been represented to us in certificates, are now and will at all relevant times[6] remain correct: [NOTE: THIS LIST DOES NOT REPRESENT THE FACTS OF EVERY TRANSACTION NOR IS THERE ANY SUGGESTION THAT THE ITEMS BELOW CONSTITUTE EITHER A NECESSARY OR SUFFICIENT LIST.]

A. STRUCTURE OF THE TRANSACTION.

1. The Company was incorporated in the State of Delaware on [date] and was formed for the limited purpose of issuing and selling the Bonds and in connection therewith managing the assets of the Company. The Certificate of Incorporation of the Company (the "Certificate") limits the Company's activities to (a) managing its assets, (b) issuing and paying the Bonds (and certain other debt), (c) paying dividends on its stock and (d) other lawful activities which are incidental to the foregoing.

2. The Company has been initially capitalized with a $_________ capital contribution by Parent in exchange for the issuance by the Company to Parent of ____ shares of common stock, par value $____ per share (the "Common Stock"). Parent is the sole owner of the Company's Common Stock.[7]

3. The Company will use the net proceeds from the sale of the Bonds to purchase assets constituting Eligible Assets[8] from Parent at their fair market value.

4. The Company will pledge all or substantially all assets of the Company to the Trustee as collateral to secure, among other things, the payment of principal and interest on the Bonds.

5. Subsequent to the issuance and sale of the Bonds, Parent may, but has no obligation to, make additional capital contributions to the Company.

6. Unlike more typical corporate opinions which are based upon facts that are ascertainable at the closing of the transactions in question, certain of the opinions expressed below depend largely upon facts which could arise in the future.

7. Alternate paragraph:

> 2. The Company has been initially capitalized with (i) a $_________ capital contribution by Parent in exchange for the issuance by the Company to Parent of ____ shares of common stock, par value $____ per share (the "Common Stock") and (ii) a $______ capital contribution by [name of unaffiliated investor] in exchange for the issuance by the Company to [name of unaffiliated investor] of ______ shares of Preferred Stock of the Company, par value $______ per share (the "Preferred Stock").

8. The term "Eligible Assets" would normally be defined in the indenture.

6. The Special Charter Provisions are set forth in Article [ ] of the Company's Certificate of Incorporation and provide that the Company shall not:

> "institute proceedings to be adjudicated a bankrupt or insolvent, or consent to the institution of bankruptcy or insolvency proceedings against it, or file a petition or consent to a petition seeking reorganization or relief under any applicable federal or state law relating to bankruptcy, or consent to the appointment of a receiver, liquidator, assignee, trustee, sequestrator (or other similar official) of the Corporation or a substantial part of its property, or make any assignment for the benefit of creditors, or, except as required by law, admit in writing its inability to pay its debts generally as they become due, or take any corporate action in furtherance of any such action, without, in each case, the unanimous [consent of the Board of Directors, which consent must include the consent of the independent director."[9]][10]

B. CORPORATE PROCEDURES.

The Company has taken, and so long as any Bond remains outstanding will take, the following steps to ensure that it operates and maintains its legal status as an independent corporation separate and distinct from Parent:

(i) The Company maintains and will maintain an office separate and apart from that of Parent through which the Company's business will be conducted;

(ii) at least one director and one executive officer (or one individual serving in both capacities) of the Company is not and will not be a director, officer, employee, or stockholder owning more than __%, of any Person owning beneficially, directly or indirectly, more than __% of the outstanding shares of the Company's Common Stock or a director, officer, employee, or a stockholder owing more than __%, of any such beneficial owner's parent, subsidiaries or Affiliates (other than the Company or another direct or indirect finance subsidiary of Parent);

9. Alternate:

"vote of all holders of Preferred Stock and Common Stock of the Corporation."

If this alternative is used, some Special Charter Provisions may also provide:

"In the event that (i) dividends are not timely paid on the shares of Preferred Stock or (ii) redemptions are not timely made of the shares of Preferred Stock, the exclusive remedy for holders of such shares against the Corporation shall be as set forth in this Certificate of Incorporation and in no event shall holders of such shares have any right to maintain a suit or proceeding against the Corporation in respect of such dividends or redemptions or damages for the failure to receive the same." [The exclusive remedy which is referred to above is the right to elect a majority of the Board of Directors.]

10. Some opining counsel also assume for purposes of the opinion that the Company will be solvent at all relevant times in order to eliminate uncertainty over whether normal corporate governance procedures continue to be fully enforceable after the Company becomes insolvent.

(iii) the Company maintains and will maintain its corporate records and books of account separate and apart from those of Parent;

(iv) the assets of the Company (including its funds) are not and will not be commingled with those of Parent;

(v) the Board of Directors of the Company has held and will hold all appropriate meetings to authorize all corporate actions by the Company—and regular meetings will be held at least quarterly;

(vi) the Company is and will be adequately capitalized in light of its contemplated business obligations;

(vii) the Company has provided and will provide for its operating expenses and liabilities from its own funds;

(viii) the Company will engage in transactions with Parent (x) only on terms and conditions comparable to transactions on an arms-length basis with unaffiliated Persons and (y) only with the prior approval of the Board of Directors including at least one of the independent directors;

(ix) although employees of the Company will participate in pension, insurance, and benefit plans maintained by the Parent, the Company will be charged its appropriate share of the cost thereof;

(x) except for the Parent's indemnification of certain obligations under the Underwriting Agreement, the Parent will not guarantee debts of the Company and the Company will not guarantee debts of the Parent;

(xi) the Company will not acquire obligations or securities of, or make loans or advances to, the Parent; and

(xii) the Company will have bills of sale (or similar instruments of assignment) and, if appropriate U.C.C.-1's, with respect to all assets purchased from the Parent.[11]

C. BUSINESS PURPOSE OF TRANSACTIONS.

The Board of Directors of Parent has adopted resolutions approving the creation of the Company in furtherance of a business plan to reduce interest rate risk and control credit risk. Such resolutions state that the Board of Directors has determined that the transactions contemplated by the proposed underwriting agreement (the "Underwriting Agreement") among the Company, Parent, and the underwriters providing for the sale of the Bonds are in the best interest of Parent and its creditors and that the transactions represent a practicable and reasonable course of action to improve the financial position of Parent. Such resolutions also provide that the proceeds of such transactions will be used to [add description of use].[12]

11. Other issues may arise in structuring a particular transaction, such as tax sharing arrangements and whether requirements should be imposed regarding the structure and frequency of directors' meetings. Counsel may treat these issues in various ways.

12. The use of the proceeds of the transaction could, in the view of some counsel, have an impact on the ability to render certain of the opinions set forth below.

D. FAIRNESS OF TRANSACTIONS.

The Company's title to the assets being transferred in connection with the Asset Transfers will be free and clear of all liens, claims, security interests or other encumbrances. Such transfers and other transactions between Parent and the Company have been and will be, in all instances, made in good faith and without intent to hinder, delay or defraud creditors of Parent.

On the date hereof, Parent will receive an opinion (upon which we are relying without independent investigation) from [name of investment bank or other valuation expert] to the effect that:

> (i) upon the date of original issuance of the Bonds, the value of the Company's Common Stock and the net proceeds from the sale of the Bonds transferred to the Parent represents a fair and reasonably equivalent consideration for the assets transferred by Parent to the Company; and
>
> (ii) the financing resulting from the issuance and sale of the Bonds constitutes a practicable and reasonable course of action designed to improve the financial position of Parent without impairing the rights of its creditors.

A copy of such opinion is annexed hereto as Exhibit __.

E. DISCLOSURE OF THE TRANSACTIONS.

The issuance and sale of the Bonds will be registered under and in compliance with the Securities Act of 1933, as amended (the "1933 Act"), on a Registration Statement on Form ____ (the "Registration Statement"). Parent will disclose all material transactions associated with the issuance of the Bonds in appropriate regulatory filings, [communications to depositors] and public announcements. The annual financial statements of Parent will disclose the effects of these transactions to the extent required by and in accordance with generally accepted accounting principles. In addition, the existence of the Company and its ownership of its assets by it will be disclosed in a note to such financial statements. The Indenture and other instruments underlying the subject transactions will be [filed with the SEC as an Exhibit to Parent's Annual Report on Form 10–K].[13]

DISCUSSION

A. CONSOLIDATION OF ASSETS AND LIABILITIES.

In order to satisfy the bankruptcy objectives of reorganization, equality of distribution, and equitable treatment of creditors, the bankruptcy courts have historically exercised their equitable powers in appropriate circumstances to treat separate and distinct entities as a single entity for bankruptcy purposes. Bankruptcy courts have broad discretion in the exercise of their equity powers.

13. Include where Parent is a reporting company. Alternatively, describe regulatory filings or availability of information to regulators.

In the course of applying these equitable powers under the rubric of "substantive consolidation," courts have looked at a number of factual indicia of separateness and the relative fairness of separate treatment of creditors of the entities.

[Counsel may, if desirable in counsel's judgment, insert additional analysis of the application of substantive consolidation principles to the facts of the transaction.]

Based on and subject to the foregoing [and while there is no case directly on point[14]] [and the issue is not free from doubt[15]], we are of the opinion that a court would not grant an order consolidating the assets and liabilities of the Company with those of Parent in a case involving the insolvency of Parent.

B. FRAUDULENT CONVEYANCE.

Resolving fraudulent conveyance issues, whether under state fraudulent conveyance law or the Bankruptcy Code, is more a factual inquiry than a legal inquiry. Parent has represented, and we have assumed for purposes of this opinion, that the Asset Transfers have been made in good faith and without intent to hinder, delay or defraud creditors of Parent. In addition, we have, without independent investigation, relied upon the determination of the Board of Directors of Parent that the transactions contemplated by the Underwriting Agreement represent a practicable and reasonable course of action to improve the financial position of Parent without impairing the rights of its creditors.

[Counsel may, if desirable in counsel's judgment, insert additional analysis of the application of the applicable fraudulent conveyance law to the facts of the transaction.]

Based on and subject to the foregoing, we are of the opinion that the Asset Transfers do not constitute voidable fraudulent conveyances.

C. THE SPECIAL CHARTER PROVISIONS.

The Special Charter Provisions raise issues under the corporate law of the State of Delaware and the public policy of the Bankruptcy Code against advance restrictions on commencement of voluntary bankruptcy proceedings. In addition, there is also an issue as to whether the Preferred Stock will be recognized as voting stock of the Company, rather than as debt.

[Counsel may, if desirable in counsel's judgment, insert additional analysis of the application of the foregoing considerations to the facts of the transaction.]

14. As indicated in the accompanying Special Report, the Committee takes no position on the substantive law applicable to any issue.

15. As indicated in the accompanying Special Report, the Committee takes no position on the appropriate application of substantive law.

Based on and subject to the foregoing [and while there is no case directly on point[16]] [and the issue is not free from doubt[17]], we are of the opinion that the Special Charter Provisions are valid, binding, and enforceable in accordance with their terms, except that no opinion is being expressed as to the availability of specific performance or other equitable remedies to persons seeking enforcement of the Special Charter Provisions.

* * *

We do not herein express any opinion as to any matters governed by any law other than the law of the State of [ ], the General Corporation Law of the State of Delaware and the Federal law of the United States. To the extent the foregoing opinions involve questions of Delaware law, we have relied upon the opinion of [ ], special Delaware counsel to the Company, dated today, a copy of which has been delivered to you.

We hereby consent to the filing of this opinion as an exhibit to the Registration Statement and to the reference to us under the caption "Legal Matters" in the Prospectus comprising a part of the Registration Statement without admitting we are "experts" within the meaning of the 1933 Act or the rules and regulations of the SEC issued thereunder with respect to any part of the Registration Statement.

This opinion should be interpreted in accordance with the Special Report by the TriBar Opinion Committee, *Opinions in the Bankruptcy Context: Rating Agency, Structured Financing and Chapter 11 Transactions,* 46 Bus. Law. ____ (1991).

Very truly yours,

16. See note 14, *supra*.
17. See note 15, *supra*.

EXHIBIT B

ILLUSTRATIVE FORM OF OPINION ON PREFERENCES IN CREDIT SUPPORTED FINANCINGS[1]

[Addressee] [Date]

Dear Sirs:

We have acted as counsel to [name of issuer], a [state of incorporation] corporation (the "Company"), in connection with the proposed issuance by the Company from time to time of up to $_________ of its commercial paper notes (each such commercial paper note having a maturity date not later than the 270th day next succeeding its date of issue, the "CP Notes"), to be issued pursuant to a Depositary Agreement dated as of [date] (the "Depositary Agreement") among the Company, [name of letter of credit bank] (the "Issuing Bank") and [name of depositary], as depositary (the "Depositary"). Unless otherwise defined herein, terms defined in the Depositary Agreement are used herein as therein defined.

CP NOTES

Payments of the face or principal amount of, and interest, if any, accrued to (but not including or after) the stated maturity date of, matured CP Notes are to be made by drawings by the Depositary under an irrevocable letter of credit (the "Letter of Credit") issued by the Issuing Bank in favor of the Depositary pursuant to the Letter of Credit and Reimbursement Agreement dated as of [date] (the "Letter of Credit Agreement") between the Company and the Issuing Bank. We understand that the CP Notes are to be offered in the U.S. domestic commercial paper market and will be sold principally on a discount basis although the Depositary Agreement and the Letter of Credit Agreement permit the offering or sale of CP Notes on an interest bearing basis. We also understand that the purchase of any CP Note will be made by the holder thereof for cash.

LETTER OF CREDIT

In connection with the issuance of the CP Notes, the Issuing Bank is issuing, at the request of the Company, the Letter of Credit in favor of the Depositary. The Letter of Credit permits the Depositary, subject to the terms and upon the

1. This form of opinion is included for illustrative purposes only. The documentation used in transactions of this type will vary in form. As indicated in the accompanying Special Report, the appropriate application of substantive law to each opinion is a matter for opining counsel to determine.

[Addressee] [Date]

conditions specified therein, to draw upon the Letter of Credit amounts to pay the face or principal amount of, and interest, if any, accrued to (but not including or after) the stated maturity date of, matured CP Notes. Under the terms of the Letter of Credit, payments are to be made directly to the Letter of Credit Account described below upon presentation to the Issuing Bank by the Depositary of a certificate in the form specified by the Letter of Credit. The Letter of Credit provides that the Issuing Bank is to pay all drawings made under and in conformity with the Letter of Credit with its own funds. The Letter of Credit also contains, in the required drawing certificate, a statement by the Depositary that such drawing is being made by the Depositary in its capacity as a fiduciary for the holders of the CP Notes.

[Counsel to Issuing Bank] has rendered a separate opinion to you of even date herewith to the effect that, except as described therein, the Letter of Credit is a valid and binding obligation of the Issuing Bank, enforceable against the Issuing Bank in accordance with its terms.

DEPOSITARY AND LETTER OF CREDIT AGREEMENTS

Under the Depositary Agreement, the Depositary is required to accept its appointment as a fiduciary for the holders of the CP Notes and is to maintain in its own name a trust account for the benefit of such holders (the "Letter of Credit Account"). Upon receipt of proceeds of a drawing under the Letter of Credit, the Depositary is to deposit such proceeds into the Letter of Credit Account. The Depositary is to pay the face or principal amount of, and interest, if any, accrued to (but not including or after) the stated maturity date of, matured CP Notes out of the Letter of Credit Account from the proceeds of drawings made under the Letter of Credit. The Depositary Agreement requires that moneys in the Letter of Credit Account not be commingled with moneys from any other source and contains other restrictions with respect to the Letter of Credit Account. The Letter of Credit Agreement provides that the Company [other parties] [is] [are] subject to certain limitations and restrictions in respect of reimbursement and other transfers of property to the Issuing Bank and the Depositary.

In connection with the [respective] rating[s] of the CP Notes by [name or names of rating agency], you have requested our opinion as to the legal issue addressed below.

Based on and subject to the foregoing and subject to the remaining paragraphs of this opinion letter, it is our opinion that payments by the Depositary of the face or principal amount of, and interest on, matured CP Notes from funds held by the Depositary in the Letter of Credit Account derived from drawings by the Depositary under the Letter of Credit will not constitute transfers of property of the Company voidable under Section 547 of the

[Addressee] [Date]

Bankruptcy Code (Title 11 of the United States Code) in the event that after such payments a voluntary or involuntary case under the Bankruptcy Code is commenced by or against the Company.

We note that because certain terms of the transaction described above change when the Letter of Credit expires by its terms or the Issuing Bank shall be in default under the Letter of Credit, the scope of the opinion expressed above is limited to payments occurring prior to the expiry of the Letter of Credit or the occurrence of a default by the Issuing Bank thereunder.

This opinion may be relied upon by [name or names of rating agency] solely in connection with its ratings of the CP Notes and may not be relied upon by any such entity in any other context. This opinion should be interpreted in accordance with the Special Report by The TriBar Opinion Committee, *Opinions in the Bankruptcy Context: Rating Agency, Structured Financing, and Chapter 11 Transactions,* 46 Bus. Law. ______ (1991).

Very truly yours,

EXHIBIT C

ILLUSTRATIVE FORM OF OPINION[1] REGARDING BANKRUPTCY COURT ORDER APPROVING SALE OF PROPERTY[2]

[Addressee] [Date]

Dear Sirs:

We have acted as special bankruptcy counsel to [name of debtor], a Delaware corporation (the "Debtor"), as debtor-in-possession in proceedings (the "Chapter 11 Proceedings") for reorganization under Chapter 11 of the Federal Bankruptcy Code, 11 U.S.C. section 101, et seq. (the "Bankruptcy Code") currently pending in the United States Bankruptcy Court for the [ ] District of [ ] (the "Bankruptcy Court"), and with respect to the motion of the Debtor (the "Sales Motion") seeking approval by the Bankruptcy Court, pursuant to section 363 of the Bankruptcy Code, of the transactions contemplated by the Purchase Agreement dated as of [date] between [name of purchaser] and the Debtor relating to the sale of [describe property being sold] (the "Property").

We have assumed that:

(i) each entity other than the Debtor's estate having an interest in the Property (or any portion thereof) has received due and sufficient notice of the Sales Motion and the Bankruptcy Court's hearing on the Sales Motion (the "Hearing"); and

(ii) the Order dated [date], a copy of which, [certified by the clerk of the Bankruptcy Court[3]], is annexed hereto as Exhibit A, was duly entered, is not subject to any request for rehearing, and has not been appealed or stayed.

With regard to the assumptions set forth in paragraph (ii) above, reference should be made to the copy of the Bankruptcy Court docket for the Chapter 11

1. This form of opinion is included for illustrative purposes only. The documentation used in transactions of this type will vary in form. As indicated in the accompanying Special Report, the appropriate application of substantive law to each opinion is a matter for the opining lawyer to establish.

2. This opinion would supplement routine opinions with respect to such matters as due authorization, validity, binding effect, and enforceability. In the context of Chapter 11 proceedings, counsel will often assume, for purposes of such opinions, that all necessary approvals have been obtained from the Bankruptcy Court and that a Bankruptcy Court order approving the transaction is in full force and effect. The form of opinion set forth below can be combined in a single opinion with routine nonbankruptcy opinions where corporate counsel and bankruptcy counsel are the same firm.

3. A copy of the order, certified by the clerk of the court, should be obtained if available.

Proceedings as of [date and time] annexed hereto as Exhibit B, showing entry of the Order on [date] and the absence of any subsequent request for rehearing, appeal, or order staying the effect of the Order. No such request for rehearing, appeal or stay has otherwise come to our attention. We note, however, that Bankruptcy Court docket cannot be taken as conclusive evidence of the absence of such a request, appeal, or stay.

Based on and subject to the foregoing and subject to the remaining paragraphs of this opinion letter, we are of the opinion that the Purchase Agreement has been duly authorized by all necessary action of the Bankruptcy Court and that the Order currently is in full force and effect.

In connection with the foregoing, we express no opinion regarding (a) the substantive effect of the Order, including, without limitation, whether the requirements for a sale of the Property free and clear of any interest therein of an entity other than the estate, as set forth in section 363(f) of the Bankruptcy Code, have been satisfied, and (b) whether the Order may be subject to alteration or revocation by the Bankruptcy Court or another court of competent jurisdiction subsequent to the date hereof.[4]

This opinion is limited to the federal bankruptcy laws and should be interpreted in accordance with the Special Report by The TriBar Opinion Committee, *Opinions in the Bankruptcy Context: Rating Agency, Structured Financing, and Chapter 11 Transactions,* 46 Bus. Law ______ (1991).

Very truly yours,

4. It is not unusual for transactions authorized after notice and hearing pursuant to section 363(b) of the Bankruptcy Code to close prior to expiration of the period for appeal if no stay of the Bankruptcy Court's order has been entered. *See* 11 U.S.C. § 363(m).

Closing Opinions of Inside Counsel

*By the Committee on Legal Opinions, ABA Section of Business Law**

I. Introduction

Although closing opinions often are rendered by inside counsel,[1] the literature on closing opinions[2] contains little specifically addressing opinions of inside counsel.[3] The subject of this report is inside counsel opinions.

Inside counsel is often in a position to render all or some of the opinions required as a condition to closing.[4] In appropriate circumstances, delivery of an opinion of inside counsel may reduce cost and avoid delay by eliminating the need for outside counsel to familiarize itself with matters already known to inside counsel or to duplicate work performed by inside counsel in the course of employment.[5]

II. Opinion Standards for Inside Counsel

A. General Principle: Duty of Care Applies to Inside as Well as Outside Counsel

Lawyers who deliver closing opinions, whether they are solo practitioners, members of a law firm or employees of a company, owe a duty of care to the

*Donald W. Glazer, Chair. E. Carolan Berkley and Seth Hoogasian, Co-Reporters. Linda C. Hayman served as a Co-Reporter for the initial draft of this report.

1. This report uses the term "closing opinion" to mean a written opinion letter delivered at the closing of a business transaction by counsel for one party to another party (or parties); the term "inside counsel" to mean a lawyer who is an employee of either the company for whom the opinion is delivered or an affiliated company; and the term "inside counsel opinion" to mean a closing opinion signed by inside counsel. Inside counsel, particularly those who also serve as officers of a company, may execute certificates in connection with the closing of a business transaction, and these certificates may contain legal conclusions. These certificates are not closing opinions as that term is used in this report.

2. *See* Restatement (Third) of The Law Governing Lawyers §§ 51, 52, 95 (2000 & Supp. 2001); TriBar Opinion Committee, *Third Party "Closing" Opinions: A Report of the TriBar Opinion Committee*, 53 Bus. Law. 592 (1998) [hereinafter *TriBar Report*]; Committee on Legal Opinions, *Legal Opinion Principles*, 53 Bus. Law. 831 (1998) [hereinafter *ABA Principles*]; Committee on Legal Opinions, *Guidelines for the Preparation of Closing Opinions*, 57 Bus. Law. 875 (2002) [hereinafter *ABA Guidelines*]; Donald W. Glazer, Scott FitzGibbon & Steven O. Weise, Glazer and FitzGibbon on Legal Opinions (2001) [hereinafter Glazer & FitzGibbon]; Darrel A. Rice, *Potential Liabilities for Legal Opinions in Securities Transactions*, 31 Rev. Sec. & Commodities Reg. 239, 242 (1998).

3. *See, e.g., TriBar Report*, *supra* note 2, at 592, 669; Glazer & FitzGibbon, *supra* note 2, at 24–25.

4. *See, e.g.*, Illustrative Opinion Letters of Inside Counsel attached as Appendices A-2 and B-2 to the *TriBar Report*, *supra* note 2, at 669–70, 673–74.

5. This report takes no position on when a recipient should accept an opinion of inside counsel or what matters such an opinion should cover.

recipient. That duty of care, as noted in Section 52 of the Restatement of the Law Governing Lawyers, is to "exercise the competence and diligence normally exercised by lawyers in similar circumstances."[6] The Restatement does not distinguish between inside counsel and outside counsel.[7]

B. Customary Practice as Starting Point

The scope and nature of the work that an opinion giver is expected to perform are based on customary practice.[8] This is so for opinions of inside counsel as well as outside counsel. As is true of outside counsel, inside counsel can limit or disclaim the obligation to exercise customary diligence.[9]

C. Who Owes the Duty of Care

The inside counsel who signs a closing opinion has personal responsibility for satisfying the duty of care owed to the recipient.[10] The other members of a law department, whether large or small, do not owe a duty of care to the recipient (unless they render an opinion and expressly permit reliance on it)[11] and are not vicariously liable to the recipient for violations of the duty of care by the signer of an opinion.[12]

D. Responsibility for Work of Others

Inside counsel who signs a closing opinion often is the head of the law department or, when a team of lawyers is working on a transaction, the senior member of the team. In many cases, the signer may not do all the work required to render the opinion but may need the assistance of others. Whether those other lawyers are subordinates or not, the signer of an inside counsel opinion is responsible for the care exercised by other lawyers who help prepare the opinion. The only exception is when the signer expressly relies on the opinion of another lawyer (whether inside or outside).[13]

6. Restatement (Third) of The Law Governing Lawyers § 52 (2000).

7. Generally, the *TriBar Report*, the *ABA Principles*, and the *ABA Guidelines* also do not distinguish between inside counsel and outside counsel. The *TriBar Report,* however, does contain two illustrative closing opinions of inside counsel, which are intended to provide context for that report. *See supra* note 4.

8. *See ABA Principles, supra* note 2, § I.B., at 832; *TriBar Report, supra* note 2, at 600–01; *see also ABA Guidelines, supra* note 2, at 876.

9. *See ABA Principles, supra* note 2, § I.C., at 832; *see also TriBar Report, supra* note 2, at 618–20.

10. Indemnification by the company for liability incurred by inside counsel in rendering a closing opinion may be available to inside counsel under the corporate law of the company's jurisdiction of incorporation, pursuant to the company's charter or bylaws, or under a contract with the company. Inside counsel may also be protected by insurance, such as directors and officers insurance or legal malpractice insurance. As a matter of customary practice, inside counsel opinions do not normally disclose whether indemnification or insurance is available to the signer. The steps inside counsel might take to protect against personal financial loss are beyond the scope of this report.

11. *See infra* note 15.

12. *See* Restatement (Third) of The Law Governing Lawyers § 58 cmt. C (2000) ("The lawyers of a corporate law department are not vicariously subject to each other's liabilities . . . .").

13. *See generally TriBar Report, supra* note 2, art. V, at 636–40.

By stating in a closing opinion that the signer is relying on the opinion of another lawyer, inside counsel, like outside counsel, may limit inside counsel's professional responsibility for the care exercised by the other lawyer in rendering that opinion.[14] In appropriate circumstances, the signer of an opinion may rely expressly on an opinion of another member of the law department, for example for legal matters arising under the law of a state or a specialized statute as to which the signer lacks the requisite competence.[15]

E. Investigation of Facts

The duty of inside counsel to investigate the facts supporting a closing opinion is the same as for outside counsel. Thus, inside counsel may properly look to (and may properly obtain) certificates from officers of the company with regard to the factual matters underlying particular opinions.[16]

F. Responsibility for Information Known to Others in Company

The signer of an inside counsel opinion is responsible for the knowledge of the lawyers who have participated in the preparation of the opinion (for factual matters relating to the opinions they have worked on). The signer also has responsibility to seek out others if the signer has identified others as having information not known to the signer that is needed to support particular opinions.[17] Otherwise, the signer of an inside counsel opinion is not responsible for information known to others in the company.

G. Inappropriate Opinion Requests

Opinion requests that the legal opinion literature characterizes as inappropriate should not be directed to inside counsel any more than they should be directed

14. By expressly relying on the opinion of another lawyer (e.g., local or specialized counsel), the signer of the opinion indicates that in the signer's professional judgment such reliance is reasonable. To establish that reasonableness, the signer must ascertain the reputation of the lawyer relied on for competence in matters of the kind involved. *Id.* at 638 (also pointing out that in expressly relying on the opinion of other counsel, an opinion giver is responsible for determining that the other opinion responds to the opinion giver's needs).

15. In the case of express reliance on another lawyer's opinion, the other lawyer should either address his or her opinion to the recipient of the principal opinion and grant the signer of the principal opinion permission to rely or address it to the signer and grant the recipient permission to rely. *Id.* at 639; *see* Glazer & FitzGibbon, *supra* note 2, § 5.3.1, at 135–38. Alternatively, the recipient might accept two separate opinion letters. *See TriBar Report, supra* note 2, at 636–38 (discussion of umbrella opinions and unbundled opinions).

16. *See ABA Principles, supra* note 2, § III.C., at 833; *TriBar Report, supra* note 2, art. II, at 608–19.

17. *See ABA Principles, supra* note 2, § III.A. & B., at 833. This responsibility derives from the signer's responsibility for the care exercised by lawyers who assist in preparing the opinion. The result is the same as for opinions of outside counsel: In each case the opinion giver is responsible for the knowledge of those who have participated in the preparation of the opinion. If other lawyers assist the signer in preparing the opinion, the signer is also responsible for those lawyers' seeking out others whom they have identified as having information needed to support the opinions on which they are working.

to outside counsel.[18] Thus, inside counsel, like outside counsel, should not be asked to evaluate the possible outcome of litigation (except in unusual circumstances)[19] or to deliver opinions that the company is qualified in each jurisdiction in which qualification is required,[20] is not in default of any contract, or is in compliance with all laws.[21]

III. Formalities

The lawyer who delivers an inside counsel opinion should sign the opinion in his or her own name and not in the name of the company or law department. This is because neither the company nor the law department is a lawyer or law firm and thus lacks the professional standing required to deliver a closing opinion.

Often, inside counsel opinions are delivered on company letterhead[22] and the signer's full corporate title (e.g., Vice President and General Counsel) appears below the signer's manual signature. Neither the use of company letterhead nor the indication of the signer's position with the company is understood as a matter of customary practice to change the signer's personal responsibility for an opinion.

In preparing a closing opinion, inside counsel should consider following the format for closing opinions recommended generally in the literature. That includes customary recitations and a statement that limits the law covered to that of a specific jurisdiction or jurisdictions.[23]

18. The presence or absence of indemnification or insurance does not affect the appropriateness of an opinion request.

19. *ABA Guidelines, supra* note 2, § 4.7, at 881.

20. *Id.* § 4.1, at 879.

21. *Id.* § 4.3, at 880.

22. Company letterhead is often personalized with the signer's name and position. Larger companies may have specialized letterhead for use by their law departments. Such personalized or specialized stationery has no legal significance. Indeed, it is not even necessary that the company for whom the opinion is delivered have its own separate stationery. In the case of affiliated companies, such letterhead may not exist.

23. Like outside counsel, inside counsel, in deciding what law to cover, should consider his or her competence in the applicable area of law. *See TriBar Report, supra* note 2, at 632.

Law Office Opinion Practices

*By the Committee on Legal Opinions, ABA Section of Business Law**

Analysis of a Survey

Every week hundreds, if not thousands, of third party legal opinions are delivered at closings for business transactions. What those opinions mean and the work lawyers are expected to do to support them has been the subject of numerous reports by this Committee, the TriBar Opinion Committee, and many state bar groups. Those reports, articles, and treatises on legal opinions have little to say about the practices law firms and law departments follow in discharging their responsibility to see that opinions are rendered (and received)[1] in a competent and ethical manner. This Report begins an inquiry into these matters.

Over the past thirty years, the giving and receiving of third party legal opinions has developed as a specialized area of practice. That practice is largely governed by custom.[2] Some transactional lawyers have developed substantial expertise in opinion practice; others have not. Thus, the Committee believes law firms and departments that deliver and receive closing opinions should periodically consider their policies and procedures for giving and receiving opinions in light of changes in their practice and personnel and developments in the law.

The Survey and Responses to It

In 2002, the Committee circulated a questionnaire to its more than 300 members regarding their firms' and departments' opinion policies[3] and procedures.[4] The questions[5] and a tabulation of responses are reproduced in the Appendix to

* Arthur Norman Field, Chair and Reporter. Donald W. Glazer and Carolan Berkley, Co-Reporters.

1. The "opinion recipient" is the other party to the transaction, not its legal counsel. The term "received" is used here to mean review of an opinion's acceptability by the opinion recipient's counsel. This review is different from the internal "review" of opinions that was the subject of the Committee Survey.

2. *See* Restatement (Third) of the Law Governing Lawyers §§ 51, 52, 95 (2000); The Committee on Legal Opinions, *Legal Opinion Principles*, 53 Bus. Law. 831 (1998); The Committee on Legal Opinions, *Guidelines for the Preparation of Closing Opinions*, 57 Bus. Law. 875 (2002); The Committee on Legal Opinions, *Third-Party Legal Opinion Report, Including the Legal Opinion Accord, of the Section of Business Law, American Bar Association*, 47 Bus. Law. 167 (1991) (providing an alternative approach that is in limited use).

3. E.g., Which Delaware opinions, if any, will a non-Delaware firm give?

4. E.g., Is the initial draft of an opinion required to be based on an office form? *See* Appendix, at [B 1–5]. References in this Report to specific survey questions are shown in brackets.

5. Changes have been made in a few questions for the sake of clarity.

this Report. The responses (which include comments in some cases) relate to business transactional law practice and not to other practice areas such as tax.[6]

Responses to the survey describe the practices of firms and departments that have representatives on the Committee and that returned completed surveys.[7] Thus, they are not necessarily representative of the practices followed by business lawyers generally.

The survey provides a starting point for developing policies and procedures and reviewing existing policies and procedures. The responses and comments show a wide range of approaches, reflecting the many factors that influence the choices law firms and departments make. Policies and procedures should not be adopted merely because they have been adopted by others, even many others.

Standard of Care; Customary Practice

The standard of care to which lawyers are subject is determined by the question: What would a lawyer of reasonable skill and knowledge and similarly situated have done under the circumstances?[8] An opinion giver thus has the responsibility to know customary practice—that is, of knowing the practice normally followed by lawyers who regularly give opinions and lawyers who regularly advise opinion recipients regarding opinions of the kind involved.[9]

Competence

Firms and departments that give or receive closing opinions have a responsibility to see that those involved in opinion practice are competent to engage in that practice and understand the ethical context in which third party opinions are given.[10] Competence requires not only familiarity with customary opinion practice but also relevant opinion literature, and the policies and procedures of their firm or department.[11] Firms and departments may or may not provide formal instruction regarding opinions and may or may not furnish to their lawyers forms and explanatory materials. The extent of formal education and written guidance appears to vary widely.[12]

6. Comments indicate that firms and departments sometimes follow different procedures when giving opinions outside the corporate transactional area (e.g., real estate, regulatory matters).

7. About 50 of the 250 surveys sent out were returned.

8. A lawyer who represents to a client that the lawyer has greater competence than normally demonstrated by lawyers who take on similar matters is held to the higher standard. Restatement (Second) of Torts § 299A cmt. d (1965); Restatement (Third) of the Law Governing Lawyers § 52 cmt. d (2000).

9. The Committee on Legal Opinions, *Legal Opinion Principles*, 53 Bus. Law. 831 (1998). A lawyer reviewing an opinion for the opinion recipient would likely have the same responsibility. Little has been written on this responsibility, and it has not been the focus of the Committee's discussions or this Report.

10. *See, e.g.*, The Lawyer's Code of Professional Responsibility NY DR 1-104C (2002); Model Rules of Prof'l Conduct R. 5.1 (2004).

11. Comments point out a need to keep Opinion Committee members informed of a broader range of matters than lawyers not on the Committee.

12. *See* Appendix, at [C (a)–(f)].

Some firms and departments require that the first draft of a closing opinion be based on a prescribed form.[13] Others require that the remedies opinion and the bankruptcy exception be stated in a particular way or that a provision defining the rights of recipients to rely be included.[14] This approach promotes uniformity and tends to discourage the rote copying of prior opinions. The danger of using a prior opinion (as opposed to a form) as a starting point is that the facts of the current and former transactions may vary in ways that are not obvious. Thus, modeling an opinion on a prior opinion creates the danger of giving an opinion whose implications are not fully understood.

Geography may be a factor. Those who practice outside the larger offices of the firm or department may find it more difficult to work in a system that relies on informal discussion. In some situations, the difficulty will be compounded by language and legal system differences from office to office. Specialization is also a factor. Those whose practice is highly specialized may be better able to distinguish between what is novel and what is merely beyond the experience of the particular lawyer. The availability of senior lawyers and their ability to teach can be significant. Those who have practiced together for a long time under consistent leadership will likely need less formal guidance as to opinion practice than those who have come together recently. The need for formal education, therefore, can vary from office to office within a firm as well as from one firm or department to another.

Consultation and the Consulting Lawyer's Responsibility

All lawyers recognize a need to consult when they reach the limits of their own experience. Sometimes the consultation is accomplished through review of treatises, articles, and opinions given or received in other transactions. More often it involves discussions with other lawyers in the firm or department. Consultation is a basic part of the culture of many firms and departments.[15] Some firms and departments require consultation before the giving of an opinion.[16] Others require consultation only in particular circumstances, for example, when an opinion raises difficult legal or factual issues or involves a new client. Sometimes the senior opinion preparer chooses the lawyer(s) who is consulted.[17] In other situations, the firm or department has a mechanism for assigning a second lawyer for con-

13. *See id.* at [E].

14. Comments on statements limiting reliance rights were extensive, reflecting the high level of concern opinion givers and recipients have in this subject. A number of firms and departments have adopted or amended policies in this area.

15. The variety of approaches to consultation (as to both the depth of involvement and the question of when it is required) described in the comments suggests that (when consultation is not required in all cases) firms and departments have made a "common-sense" effort to tailor the consultation requirement to situations in which they perceive themselves to have the greatest exposure.

16. *See* Appendix, at [D 1–3].

17. Comments indicate that in some specialized areas (e.g., Investment Company Act) consultation with lawyers other than the initial consulting lawyer may be required.

sultation. In some cases, malpractice insurers have encouraged use of some kind of formal consultation system.[18]

Sometimes the term "review" (as in "second partner review") is used instead of "consultation." This Report uses the term "consultation" rather than review. "Consultation" has different meanings in different contexts. To understand the role of the consulting lawyer, one needs to ask (among other things) which (if any) of the relevant documents the consultant is to read, whether consultation should extend to all opinions being given, and whether consultation should come early in the transaction or at a later stage.[19] The survey indicates that when unusual issues or problems are identified early in a transaction, consultation often begins at that time. Otherwise, consultation often begins later.

In some situations, the role of the consulting lawyer is informal; it is to respond to questions of the opinion preparers. Sometimes that role is broader, extending to the form of the opinion or even the conclusions being expressed. Comments indicate that the consultant's role may often be elastic, with consultants charged with determining the extent of their involvement. That determination may depend on the experience of the opinion preparers, the experience of the consultant, the novelty of the opinion, and other factors.[20] The role a consulting lawyer has played in the preparation of an opinion is confirmed in writing in some firms and departments, but in many others it is not.

Any internal consulting system assumes that the required expertise is available inside the organization. When it is not, experts outside the firm or department may be consulted, either formally or informally.

Opinion Committees and Their Functions

A high percentage of the firms and departments represented in responses to the survey have Opinion Committees.[21] The function of these Committees, however, varies widely. Many Committees meet only when required to set policy or to review recent developments. Informal interaction of members is often the norm.[22] Sometimes Committee members are on call to consult. In other situations, the Committee may oversee the formal or informal assignment of lawyers (whether or not members of the Committee) to consult.

Often education is a Committee function. Sometimes that involves administering continuing education programs; in other cases education is informal or is

18. Comments suggest that when the level of consultation is set at a very high level, the transaction itself, rather than merely the opinion, may be the subject of the review.

19. Often consultation is deferred until counsel has agreed on the opinions to be given. When that is done, the opportunity may be lost for the consulting lawyer to be involved in (i) discussions regarding which opinions to give and their wording, or (ii) structuring the transaction to avoid opinion questions.

20. *See* Appendix, at [D 1–2].

21. *See id.* at [B 1].

22. Comments indicate that some Opinion Committees seldom or never meet formally but decide issues informally (using telephone, e-mail, as well as in-person meetings) when the need arises. *See id.* at [C (a)–(f)].

conducted by outside providers. Comments indicate that some firms and departments have prepared forms, policy statements, and opinion manuals.

In some firms and departments, the Opinion Committee determines what opinion policies and procedures are to be followed. In others, those questions are handled by the leaders of practice areas alone or in consultation with the Opinion Committee.

All of the tasks performed by an Opinion Committee can be handled without an Opinion Committee (e.g., they may be handled by the management group of the firm or department or the leaders of the practice areas affected or some combination of them). In some firms and departments, Opinion Committees have a central role in determining how the opinion process works. That role may even extend to administering responses to annual auditor inquiries.[23]

Limits on Opinion Giving

A policy question for firms and departments is whether and how to limit the kind of opinions they are willing to give. Firms and departments often have a policy against giving opinions on the law of a state merely because one or more of its lawyers are admitted to the bar in that state. Admission to the bar does not equate to competence as to the subject matter of an opinion. Competence to give an opinion may exist without admission. Many firms and departments permit the giving of opinions on the law of states in which no one in the firm or department is admitted to practice.[24] One example is opinions on the Delaware General Corporation Law by lawyers not admitted to practice in Delaware. Another example is certain opinions under Article 9 of the Uniform Commercial Code.

Disclosure

Disclosure of interests that might influence the handling of an opinion (or in retrospect might be seen as an influence) raises difficult policy issues. A recipient of a closing opinion understands that an independent third party opinion giver is an oxymoron. This is because the opinion giver owes a duty to his client. Moreover, disclosure can be intrusive and would be difficult to administer.[25] What firm or department is in a position to identify all the personal entanglements between its lawyers and clients? Can a firm or department know whether stock of the client is held within a firm or company retirement fund?

Disclosure in an opinion of interests in and relationships with a client, therefore, is unusual. An exception is the status of a partner of the opinion giver (or law department member) as a director. Some opinion givers disclose that fact.

23. Comments and experience indicate that audit inquiry letters are often handled separately.
24. *See* Appendix, at [F 1–4].
25. *See id.* at [G 1–2].

Resources

The resources available to opinion givers and opinion recipients affect how they act.[26] For example, the survey indicates that law firms and departments make only modest efforts to maintain files of opinions given and received in a manner that facilitates later reference to them. Few firms and departments review opinions after they are given to see if policies were observed. Other areas more directly affected by ethical and legal requirements (e.g., conflicts, confidentiality) command greater resources.

Conclusion

Firms and departments have the responsibility to maintain the quality of the legal opinions they deliver and the quality of their review of those they receive. No one formula exists for maintaining quality. Comments indicate that differences in policies and procedures exist not only between firms and departments of similar size and with similar practices but also between practice areas within the same firms and departments. Indeed, some firms and departments (large and small) perceive that they have no need to establish opinion policies and procedures; in their environment, they see themselves as having sufficient informal education, supervision, and consultation to make formal policies and procedures unnecessary.

All firms and departments should periodically review their opinion practices in light of changes in the nature of their practice, their size, their culture, and the location of their offices. A thoughtful periodic review will help them maintain quality in their legal opinion practice.

26. *See id.* at [H 1–2].

APPENDIX

A. ABOUT YOU AND YOUR FIRM/DEPARTMENT

1) How many lawyers are in your firm/department?

1–5	0
6–25	4
25–100	8
over 100	38

2) How many lawyers in your firm/department are primarily engaged in a business law transactional practice?

1–5	0
6–25	6
25–100	20
over 100	24

3) How many offices (different cities) does your firm/department have?

1	10
2–5	18
over 5	22

4) Does your firm/department have non-U.S. offices?

Y	18
N	30

B. ABOUT THE COMMITTEE(S) IN YOUR FIRM/DEPARTMENT

1) Does your firm/department have an opinion committee(s)?

Y	34
N	10

2) If your firm/department has *more than* one opinion committee (or uses sub-committees), please describe by checking one or more choices below:

(a) separate committees for different geographic areas or offices	2
(b) separate committees for different practice areas *e.g.*, corporate, real estate, tax, intellectual property, bankruptcy	6
(c) separate committees for opinions to clients (rather than third party closing opinions)	1
(d) other (*please* describe)	5

3) The opinion committee(s) (or some "steering committee" of it) meets:

(a)	monthly	2
(b)	quarterly	1
(c)	at the call of the Chair	22
(d)	ordinarily by written consent to adopt policy	1
(e)	other (*please* describe)	14

4) How large is the opinion committee(s): (total on all committees)

(a)	5 or less	15
(b)	6–10	17
(c)	11–15	2
(d)	more than 15	6

5) Does the committee(s) keep minutes of meetings?

Y 4
N 34

NOTE: All questions that follow are about Opinion Committees.

C. FUNCTIONS OF THE COMMITTEE

1) Does the committee(s):

(a) circulate information about current cases and problems?
Y 26
N 13

(b) conduct educational programs on opinions?
Y 31
N 10

(c) provide written guidance about firm/departmental policies on opinion giving?
Y 36
N 4

(d) provide an opinion manual or other guide for opinion giving?
Y 25
N 16

(e) make materials available in the office/law department to lawyers who prepare opinions about opinion giving?
Y 36
N 5

(f) review opinions given (after the fact) as a quality control effort?

Y 6

N 35

D. CONSULTATION PRIOR TO GIVING OPINIONS

1) Does your firm/department require that:

(a) an opinion preparer routinely consult with an opinion committee member (or other designated lawyer) before giving any third party opinion?

Y 33

N 12

(b) an opinion preparer consult with an opinion member (or other designated lawyer) before giving any third party opinion that is novel or presents difficulty in any respect?

Y 29

N 13

(c) an opinion preparer consult with an opinion member (or other designated lawyer) before giving any third party opinion only if in the judgment of the opinion preparer that is advisable?

Y 9

N 31

2) When there is consultation with an opinion committee member (or other designated lawyer) about an opinion:

(a) the level of involvement of the consulting lawyer is determined on a case by case basis by the Committee, having in mind the subject matter of the opinion and its novelty

Y 22

N 15

(b) the level of involvement of the consulting lawyer covers the form of the opinion only

Y 6

N 29

(c) the level of involvement of the consulting lawyer is agreed upon by the opinion preparer and the consulting lawyer

Y 23

N 16

(d) the level of involvement of the consulting lawyer is determined by guidelines that have general application

Y 12

N 24

(e) other (*please* describe) 11

3) The consulting lawyer:

(a) becomes involved at the outset of the transaction

Y 3

N 32

(b) becomes involved when the need is perceived, ordinarily after the transaction documents have been circulated

Y 38

N 7

(c) other (*please* describe) 8

4) The consulting lawyer:

(a) is responsible to determine that the form of the opinion meets Committee (office) standards

Y 32

N 11

(b) is responsible to respond to questions of the opinion preparer and to raise matters that are apparent, but not to have overall responsibility for the opinion

Y 41

N 2

(c) is responsible only to determine whether the relationship between the opinion preparer and the client is such as to require special scrutiny, and if so, to provide such scrutiny based on the facts available

Y 1

N 39

(d) is responsible to "concur" in the opinion as if he or she had been the opinion preparer

Y 9

N 31

(e) has such responsibility as the opinion preparer and the consultant determine

Y 16

N 25

5) The relationship between the consulting lawyer and the opinion preparer:

(a) is formalized by the consulting lawyer signing the office copy of the opinion to indicate concurrence

Y 10

N 30

(b) is formalized by a memo for the opinion committee files

Y 5

N 34

(c) is formalized by a memo in the transaction files

Y 12

N 28

(d) is not formalized

Y 23

N 15

E. FORMAT FOR OPINIONS

1) Does your firm/department require that:

(a) opinions be in a designated form?

Y 21

N 27

(b) a supporting memo be prepared as to opinions to be given?

Y 9

N 37

F. LIMITS ON OPINION GIVING

1) Is there a firm/departmental policy or custom that precludes or limits giving opinions as to the law of a jurisdiction in which the firm/department has no office?

Y 36

N 13

If a limitation, what is it? 37

2) Is the giving of opinions under the Delaware General Corporation Law?

Y 42

N 6

3) Is there a firm/departmental policy or custom that precludes or limits giving opinions as to certain specialty areas (e.g., intellectual property, bankruptcy, tax).

Y 9

N 38

If so, describe which areas: 14

4) Does your firm/department permit the giving of opinions as to the law of jurisdictions in which the opinion preparer is not admitted?

Y 34

N 14

(a) as to the Delaware General Corporation Law?

Y	45
N	2

(b) as to Delaware LLCs?

Y	34
N	11

(c) as to the law of any state where a firm/department lawyer is admitted who reviews the opinion?

Y	17
N	29

5) Is there a firm/departmental policy or custom against the giving of opinions to third parties that are *not* closing opinions?

Y	7
N	38

G. OPINION LIBRARY

1) Does your firm/department collect opinions *given by* it in a manner that facilitates reference to them in giving other opinions

Y	17
N	31

2) Does your firm/department collect opinions *received from others* in a manner that facilitates reference to them in giving other opinions?

Y	6
N	42

H. DISCLOSURES IN OPINIONS

1) Does your firm/department have a policy or custom of disclosing any of the following in opinions:

(a) a partner is a director of the client

Y	17
N	17

(b) a partner is related by blood or marriage to a principal officer or controlling shareholder of the client

Y	9
N	20

(c) the firm or the opinion preparer has a significant investment in the client, any firm pension or profit sharing arrangement

Y	12
N	19

(d) one or more lawyers in the office (or immediate family members have a significant investment (directly or through a retirement plan) in the client

Y 7

N 19

(e) other (*please* describe) 11

2) If there is a disclosure policy, as to investments or relationships, how is the information to enable disclosure maintained on a current basis?

(a) periodic questionnaires?

Y 4

N 5

(b) requirement to periodically report?

Y 4

N 4

I. LIMITATIONS ON LIABILITY

1) Does your firm/department ordinarily include in third party opinion letters (or otherwise try to effect) a limitation on its liability for the opinion? If so, please describe:

Y 5

N 28

J. LIMITATION ON USE OF OPINION LETTER

1) Does your firm/department ordinarily include in third party opinion letters (or otherwise try to effect) a limitation on the assignability of the opinion letter? If so, please describe:

Y 47

N 1

2) Does your firm/department ordinarily include in third party opinion letters (or otherwise try to effect) a limitation on use of the letter in subsequent related or unrelated transactions?

Y 37

N 10

K. COMMENTS, QUESTIONS

3

Legal Opinions in SEC Filings

*Special Report of the Task Force on Securities Law Opinions, ABA Section of Business Law**

Introduction

Section 7(a) of the Securities Act of 1933 (the "Securities Act") requires a registration statement to contain the information specified in Schedule A to the Act.[1] Paragraph 29 of Schedule A requires the filing of "a copy of the opinion or opinions of counsel in respect to the legality of the issue."[2] The Securities and Exchange Commission (SEC) has addressed that requirement in Item 601 of Regulation S-K.[3] Under paragraph (b)(5) of Item 601, a registration statement must include as an exhibit "[a]n opinion of counsel as to the legality of the securities being registered, indicating whether they will, when sold, be legally issued, fully paid and non-assessable, and, if debt securities, whether they will be binding obligations of the registrant."[4] The opinion on legality appears as Exhibit 5 to a registration statement and is thus often referred to as an "Exhibit 5 opinion." This Report examines Exhibit 5 opinions.

Preliminary Matters

Neither the statute nor the SEC rules indicate to whom an Exhibit 5 opinion should be addressed. Customary practice is for the opinion to be addressed to the issuer. Counsel to the issuer—either inside counsel or outside counsel—renders the opinion.

An Exhibit 5 opinion need not be included as an exhibit to a registration statement as initially filed. The only requirement is that it be filed as an exhibit before the registration statement is declared effective. Thus, the opinion often is filed with an amendment to the registration statement.

The fact that the opinion must be filed before—and in the case of shelf registrations, often long before—the securities are actually sold gives rise to issues

*The Task Force is a joint effort of the Committee on Legal Opinions and the Subcommittee on Securities Law Opinions of the Committee on Federal Regulation of Securities of the American Bar Association, Section of Business Law. Keith F. Higgins served as reporter for this Report.

1. 15 U.S.C. § 77g(a) (2000).

2. *Id.* § 77aa(29).

3. 17 C.F.R. § 229.601 (2003). A similar requirement for small business issuers appears in Regulation S-B, and references in this Report to Item 601 of Regulation S-K also refer to the comparable provision of Regulation S-B. *Id.* § 228.601.

4. *Id.* § 229.601(b)(5).

about the appropriateness of assumptions that are included in the opinion. These assumptions are discussed below.

Rule 436 under the Securities Act requires that a written consent of counsel be filed as an exhibit to a registration statement, "[i]f any portion of the . . . opinion of . . . counsel is quoted or summarized as such in the registration statement or in a prospectus. . . ."[5] This requirement has led to speculation whether counsel rendering an Exhibit 5 opinion, whose name is included in the prospectus as having passed on the legality of the securities, is considered an expert for purposes of section 7 of the Securities Act. The statute itself refers to:

> any accountant, engineer, or appraiser, or any person whose profession gives authority to a statement made by him [who] is named as having prepared or certified any part of the registration statement, or is named as having prepared or certified a report or valuation for use in connection with the registration statement. . . ."[6]

The statute does not specifically refer to lawyers, an omission that may explain why Rule 436 refers to the consent of "an expert *or* counsel."[7] In any event, Rule 436 requires that a consent of counsel "be filed as an exhibit to the registration statement."[8] That consent is both to the filing of the opinion as an exhibit to the registration statement, and to the reference to counsel in the related prospectus. As a drafting matter, most lawyers include the consent in the opinion. Some also add a statement to the effect that the filing of the consent shall not be deemed an admission that counsel is an expert within the meaning of section 7 of the Securities Act. The SEC staff has not objected to "no admission" language. The SEC staff has objected, however, to language affirmatively denying that counsel is an expert within the meaning of the Securities Act. Whether counsel includes the "no admission" language or not should have no bearing on whether counsel is or is not an expert under section 7.

Rule 436(f) under the Securities Act specifies that, if an opinion filed as an exhibit relies on an opinion of another counsel, the consent of that other counsel need not be provided.[9] The SEC staff has taken the position, however, that a signed copy of the opinion relied on must be included as an exhibit to the registration statement.

Third party closing opinions often expressly limit their use. If an Exhibit 5 opinion were to state that it may be relied on only by the issuer, the SEC staff would almost certainly object, viewing such a limitation as being inconsistent with the purpose of paragraph 29 of Schedule A to the Securities Act.

5. *Id.* § 230.436(a).
6. 15 U.S.C. § 77g(a) (2000).
7. 17 C.F.R. § 230.436(a) (emphasis added).
8. *Id.*
9. *Id.* § 230.436(f).

Particular Classes of Securities

Equity Securities

Substantive Requirements

Item 601 of Regulation S-K requires that the opinion state that the securities, when sold, will be:

- Legally issued
- Fully paid, and
- Non-assessable.[10]

The phrase "legally issued," although taken directly from the language of the Securities Act, is not the language lawyers customarily use when rendering a third party closing opinion on equity securities. Thus, in Exhibit 5 opinions, many lawyers use the more customary formulation that the securities have been "duly authorized and, [when sold in accordance with the provisions of the applicable purchase agreement], will be validly issued, fully paid and nonassessable."[11]

The SEC staff does not insist on the "legally issued" language and many opinion givers use "duly authorized" and "validly issued" instead.[12] This is the language normally used in third party closing opinions, and its meaning (as well as the meaning of "fully paid and non-assessable") is the subject of numerous bar association reports.[13]

Because the Exhibit 5 opinion is delivered before the securities are sold, opinion givers often cast the opinion in the future tense, stating that the securities will be validly issued, fully paid, and non-assessable upon their sale in accordance with the applicable purchase agreement or governing document. Opinion givers also sometimes condition the opinion on further action by the board or a board committee. Opinion givers should be careful about the breadth of any such assumptions. Although an opinion giver may appropriately assume that the pricing committee of the board has taken the action necessary to set the sale price,[14] the SEC staff may object to an assumption that the board, or a pricing committee, has taken all required action prior to the issuance and sale of the securities. In general, assumptions should be limited to matters that structurally cannot be completed before effectiveness of the registration statement.

10. *Id.* § 229.601(b)(5).

11. Donald W. Glazer et al., Glazer and Fitzgibbon on Legal Opinions: Drafting, Interpreting and Supporting Closing Opinions in Business Transactions § 10.1, at 331–32 n.3 (2d ed. 2001) (indicating that counsel for the company normally renders an opinion that shares "have been duly authorized and validly issued and are fully paid and nonassessable.").

12. Due authorization is subsumed in validly issued even if not stated separately. *Id.* § 10.5. Thus, "validly issued" should be sufficient.

13. *See, e.g.*, TriBar Opinion Committee, *Third-Party "Closing" Opinions: A Report of the TriBar Opinion Committee*, 53 Bus. Law. 591, 648–50 (1998) [hereinafter TriBar 1998 Report] (discussing third party closing opinions). Many of the bar association reports describe opinion practice in particular states. By following the approach taken for third party closing opinions, opinion givers should be able to rely on the substantial body of literature describing customary practice regarding those opinions.

14. For example, this practice is usually followed when, in reliance on Rule 430A, the registration statement is declared effective before pricing occurs. *See* 17 C.F.R. § 230.430A(a) (2003) (indicating that a registration statement that omits the public offering price may be declared effective).

Opinions on Delaware Corporations by Counsel Not Admitted to Practice in Delaware

Counsel not admitted to practice in Delaware often render Exhibit 5 opinions on stock issued by Delaware corporations. Usually, they include in their opinions a so-called coverage limitation, limiting the scope of the opinions to the Delaware General Corporation Law. In the late 1990s, a question arose over the scope of the law covered by legality opinions on stock issued by Delaware corporations. In the registration review process, the SEC staff frequently commented that this limitation unacceptably limited the scope of the opinion because, on its face, it seemed to focus only on the Delaware corporation statute and not on the Delaware Constitution and judicial interpretations. That controversy has been largely resolved.

Representatives of the ABA Section of Business Law met with the staff and explained that the reference to the "Delaware General Corporation Law" was an opinion drafting convention, and that the practicing bar understood this phrase to cover the Delaware General Corporation Law, the applicable provisions of the Delaware Constitution, and reported judicial decisions interpreting these laws. Based on these discussions, the staff revised its procedures. These new procedures, which are described in the SEC Division of Corporation Finance's November 2000 *Current Issues and Rulemaking Projects* outline, are as follows:

- [The staff] will issue a comment asking counsel to confirm . . . in writing that it concurs with [the staff's] understanding that the reference and limitation to "Delaware General Corporate [sic] Law" includes the statutory provisions and also all applicable provisions of the Delaware Constitution and reported judicial decisions interpreting these laws. As part of this standard comment, [the staff] will ask that counsel file this written confirmation as correspondence on the EDGAR system. As such, it will be part of the Commission's official file regarding the related registration statement.
- Once [the staff has received] this written confirmation from counsel, [the staff] will not comment further on the inclusion of this language in the opinion for that registration statement.[15]

The revised procedure satisfies SEC staff concerns, although it creates what many view as the unnecessary step of having to confirm in writing to the SEC the customary meaning of opinion language. Many lawyers now include the required confirmation directly in their Exhibit 5 opinions.

Debt Securities

Binding Obligations

For debt securities, Item 601 of Regulation S-K requires the filing of an opinion that the securities will be "binding obligations of the registrant."[16] In practice, this

15. SEC Division of Corporate Finance, *Current Issues and Rulemaking Projects*, at 58 (Nov. 14, 2000), *available at* http://www.sec.gov/pdf/cfcr112k.pdf (last visited July 10, 2004).
16. 17 C.F.R. § 229.601(b)(5) (2003).

opinion, often referred to as the "remedies" or "enforceability" opinion, is stated in various ways. Perhaps the most common formulation is that the debt securities constitute valid and binding obligations of the issuer, enforceable against the issuer in accordance with their terms "except as may be limited by bankruptcy, insolvency or other similar laws affecting the rights and remedies of creditors generally and general principles of equity."[17] Minor differences in wording do not change the meaning of the opinion.[18]

Exhibit 5 opinions on debt securities typically refer to the debt instruments themselves rather than the indenture under which they are issued. An enforceability opinion on the debt securities covers those portions of the indenture that relate to the terms of the securities, including any terms in the indenture that further define terms in the securities, such as the terms for conversion.

Governing Law

Unlike the law governing the validity of equity securities (which is the entity law of the jurisdiction in which the issuer is organized), the law governing the enforceability of debt securities is generally the law chosen in the instrument under which the securities are issued. Often New York law is chosen to govern the obligations of the issuer in a registered debt offering. When counsel for the issuer is not in a position to render an opinion on New York contract law, underwriters may be willing to accept an opinion on the enforceability of the debt *as if* the law of counsel's home jurisdiction applied.[19] That practice is not acceptable to the SEC staff. The Securities Act requires an opinion on the legality of the issue, and the SEC staff takes the position that anything short of an opinion on the law that governs the enforceability of the debt securities will not suffice.[20]

Non-Standard Exceptions

Sometimes counsel includes exceptions, in addition to the standard bankruptcy exception and equitable principles limitation, to identify issues that affect the enforceability of particular provisions of the securities being registered. When including additional exceptions, counsel should consider whether they relate to issues requiring disclosure in the prospectus. In addition, counsel should be prepared for possible SEC staff comments.[21] If the exceptions simply make explicit what is understood as a matter of customary practice to be implicit or otherwise are not material, additional exceptions should not require prospectus disclosure.

17. TriBar 1998 Report, *supra* note 13, at 622–23 (noting the bankruptcy exception and equitable principles limitation to an "enforceability" opinion). The bankruptcy exception and equitable principles limitation are standard exceptions that are understood to apply even when not stated expressly. These exceptions do not require disclosure, and the SEC staff does not normally comment on them.

18. *Id.* at 619–20.

19. *Id.* at 635 n.98.

20. *See Current Issues and Rulemaking Projects*, *supra* note 15, at 58.

21. Counsel should keep in mind that "boilerplate" exceptions that do not relate to the securities being offered are likely to be questioned by the SEC staff.

Options, Warrants, and Rights

Rights to acquire securities, either equity or debt, are contractual rights. In that respect they are more like debt securities than equity securities.[22] In the case of warrants, for example, an opinion that a warrant is validly issued, fully paid, and non-assessable would be inapt because these concepts relate to stock—not contractual obligations.

An Exhibit 5 opinion on warrants should address their enforceability under the law chosen to govern the warrants. Typically, the offer and sale of the warrants and the securities underlying the warrants are registered at the same time. In that case, the Exhibit 5 opinion should state not only that the warrants are enforceable, but also that the underlying securities have been duly authorized and, upon delivery in accordance with the terms of the warrants, will be validly issued, fully paid, and non-assessable.

Particular Types of Offerings

Opinion practice varies, depending not only on the type of securities being offered, but also on the type of offering. The Exhibit 5 opinion—not simply the form of opinion—must be on file when the registration statement is declared effective. When a significant period elapses between effectiveness and the sale of the securities, special issues may arise.

Shelf Offerings

Shelf offerings under Rule 415 permit issuers to offer and sell securities long after a registration statement becomes effective.[23] Moreover, in the case of universal shelf registrations, the class or classes of securities to be offered and sold may not be known on the effective date. Exhibit 5 opinion practice has adjusted to accommodate shelf offerings.

Shelf Registrations for Specific Securities

When an issuer registers common stock to be issued from time to time in the future, the opinion should state that the shares have been duly authorized. The remainder of the opinion, however, often requires assumptions that various actions will be taken before the securities are issued. In addition to the assumptions that apply whenever shares are being issued in the future, such as the issuer's receipt of the required consideration, the opinion giver may need to assume expressly, among other matters, that:

- The board of directors adopts resolutions approving the issuance and sale of the common stock at a specified price or pursuant to a specified pricing mechanism.

22. This is the case even though an option, warrant, or right fits the definition of "equity security" in Rule 405 under the Securities Act. 17 C.F.R. § 230.405 (2003).

23. *Id.* § 230.415.

- If the issuer is in a regulated industry and requires regulatory approval pursuant to the law under which it was incorporated or a similar statute, it has obtained any necessary regulatory approvals.

These assumptions are perfectly appropriate, and the SEC staff has not objected to them before the shelf registration statement is declared effective.[24]

Most issuers filing a shelf registration statement for common stock register a specific number of shares rather than an aggregate dollar amount.[25] If the issuer decides to register an aggregate dollar amount of common stock, the opinion giver should assume that no more than a specified number of shares, based on the then current market price, will be issued and sold under the registration statement. That number should be available under the issuer's currently authorized common stock in its charter. If the issuer ultimately wishes to sell more shares than were covered by the original opinion, a new opinion should be filed, at the time of the takedown, covering the shares being issued.

Universal Shelf Registrations

Universal shelf registrations permit issuers to register an aggregate dollar amount of securities, designating by class the various types of securities (e.g., common stock, debt securities, convertible debt securities, preferred stock, and warrants) that may subsequently be issued, but not allocating the dollar amount among those classes of securities. A universal shelf registration statement thus requires more assumptions than even a shelf registration for a particular class of security. The board of directors will not have approved the terms of the debt securities or preferred stock at the time of effectiveness of the shelf registration statement. In the case of common stock, the issuer may not have sufficient authorized shares to permit an opinion that, were the issuer to elect to sell the entire aggregate dollar amount of securities registered as common stock at current market prices, the stock to be sold has been duly authorized.[26] Assumptions, therefore, are necessary, and the SEC staff has not objected to opinions that include reasonable assumptions.

Filing Updated Opinions

Shelf registration was not contemplated at the time Congress enacted the legality opinion requirement. Permitting assumptions in these opinions is necessary for the shelf registration process to work. Although the SEC has not adopted a rule that requires the filing of an updated opinion at the time of a shelf takedown,

24. *But see* the discussion *infra* entitled "Filing Updated Opinions."

25. Although an aggregate dollar amount of securities can be registered under Rule 457(o), 17 C.F.R. § 230.457(o) (2003), choosing that option would result in the issuer's being able to sell fewer shares if the price of the common stock increases from the price used to determine the registration fee.

26. This problem can be solved by assuming that, after the sale of shares of common stock under the registration statement, the total issued shares will not exceed the number authorized in the issuer's charter.

it has expressed the view that such an updated opinion is required. In note 47 of Release 33-6714, the SEC stated:

> Although certain qualified legality opinions may be filed as an exhibit to such a registration statement that is declared effective, after pricing and prior to sales an unqualified opinion (and consent) must be filed on Form 8-K [17 CFR 249.308] and thus incorporated by reference into the registration statement or must be contained in a post-effective amendment.[27]

The Division of Corporation Finance has affirmed this position in its *Manual of Publicly Available Telephone Interpretations*, in which it states that it will accept a "qualified opinion" at the time of effectiveness, "subject to the understanding that an unqualified opinion will be filed [before] any sales are made under the registration statement."[28]

In filing an updated opinion, an issuer can make an exhibit-only filing pursuant to Rule 462(d), which provides for the immediate effectiveness of post-effective amendments filed solely to include exhibits.[29] Alternatively, for shelf offerings conducted by an issuer under Rule 415(a)(1)(x), which must be registered under Forms S-3 or F-3, the opinion may be incorporated by reference into the registration statement through a Form 8-K or 6-K filing.[30]

Acquisitions and Exchange Offers

Acquisitions and exchange offers that involve the offer and sale of securities are registered on Form S-4. These registration statements require an Exhibit 5 opinion on the securities being issued in the acquisition. Often the issuance of the securities being registered requires the approval of shareholders. Such is the case in many stock-for-stock mergers, whether as a requirement of state corporation law or a securities exchange. Because an opinion must be on file before the registration statement is declared effective, as with shelf registrations, these opinions may be based on the express assumption that the required shareholder approval has been received.[31] The SEC staff does not require a new opinion following shareholder approval.

27. Elimination of Certain Pricing Amendments and Revision of Prospectus Filing Procedures, 52 Fed. Reg. 21,252, 21,255 n.47 (June 5, 1987).

28. SEC Division of Corporation Finance, *Manual of Publicly Available Telephone Interpretations*, at D.11 (1997), *available at* http://www.sec.gov/interps/telephone/1997manual.txt (last visited July 10, 2004).

29. 17 C.F.R. § 230.462(d) (2003).

30. *Id.* § 230.415(a)(1)(x).

31. An assumption may not be necessary, however, where the shareholder approval is obtained solely to satisfy listing requirements. Shares would still be validly issued even if a listing rule is violated.

No Registration Opinions

*Subcommittee on Securities Law Opinions, Committee on Federal Regulation of Securities, ABA Section of Business Law**

Introduction

The Securities Act of 1933 (the "Securities Act") makes it unlawful for any person to use jurisdictional means to sell any security unless a registration statement is in effect as to that security or an exemption from registration is available. One of the principal exemptions is Section 4(2) of the Securities Act, "transactions by an issuer not involving any public offering." These few words are the foundation for substantial transactions conducted every day, without any involvement of the Securities and Exchange Commission (the "SEC"), based on legal advice regarding the application of Section 4(2) and related SEC rules to a particular transaction. In many of these transactions lawyers deliver opinions to the effect that registration of the securities under the Securities Act is not required. This report discusses these opinions.

Two illustrative opinion letters are attached to this report, addressing typical transactions in which a no registration opinion is given. In the first, investors are purchasing shares of Common or Preferred Stock directly from the issuer in reliance on Section 4(2) or Regulation D and intend to hold the shares for some period of time. In the second, investment bankers, referred to as the "Initial Purchasers," are purchasing debt securities from the issuer and reselling them to "qualified institutional buyers" under Rule 144A and/or to offshore purchasers under Regulation S. In each case, the securities may be convertible into Common Stock. Each opinion letter is addressed to the purchasers of the securities from the issuer.

The illustrative opinion letters contain the types of opinions that are typically given and the kinds of express assumptions and qualifications that are commonly included. Each form may need to be tailored to fit a particular transaction.

Representations in Purchase Agreement

Each form is based on the assumption that the Purchase Agreement contains representations by the issuer relating to the offering of the securities, including

---

* Editor's Note: This report is published in the form approved by the Subcommittee on Securities Law Opinions without any further editing by *The Business Lawyer.*

the absence of "general solicitation" and "general advertising" and prior sales of similar securities that could be integrated with the offering covered by the opinion and, in the case of sales outside the United States in reliance on Regulation S, the absence of "directed selling efforts." Each form also assumes that the Purchase Agreement includes agreements by the issuer to limit future offers of the same or similar securities and, in certain cases, to provide information to holders of the securities.

The first opinion letter assumes that the purchasers are agreeing not to resell the securities except pursuant to an effective registration statement under the Securities Act or an exemption, such as Rule 144. The second opinion letter assumes that the Purchase Agreement requires the Initial Purchasers to sell the securities only to qualified institutional buyers or offshore purchasers who agree not to resell the securities except pursuant to an effective registration statement under the Securities Act or an exemption, such as Rule 144A or Regulation S.

The opinion giver of the first opinion letter must be satisfied as to the eligibility of the purchasers to acquire the securities pursuant to the exemption from registration being relied on. For example, an offering being made in reliance on Rule 506 of Regulation D may be structured so as to require all of the purchasers to be "accredited investors." The opinion giver may rely on representations in the Purchase Agreement, a placement agent's certificate, investor questionnaires or other procedures in confirming the eligibility of the purchasers.

Ordinarily, the text of the opinion letter itself will not refer to any of the above matters. Some lawyers expressly assume that the purchasers will comply with their agreements not to resell unless the securities are registered or an exemption is available, but many consider this unnecessary. Occasionally, lawyers expressly rely on a placement agent's certificate where the placement agent has undertaken to determine whether the purchasers meet specified eligibility criteria.

Covering Shares Issuable on Conversion or Exercise

In cases where the securities being sold are convertible into Common Stock or accompanied by warrants to purchase Common Stock, no registration opinions are sometimes given covering the issuance of the underlying Common Stock on conversion or exercise. In light of the added complexity in giving this opinion, many lawyers prefer not to include it and will do so only if requested. When the issuance of Common Stock on conversion is covered, some lawyers refer in the opinion letter to the conditions of the Section 3(a)(9) exemption from registration, for example by expressly assuming that no commission or other remuneration will be paid or given directly or indirectly for soliciting conversion. Others, regarding these conditions to be so well understood that they need not be stated or for other reasons, do not refer to these conditions.

In some cases, a no registration opinion may be given covering issuance of Common Stock on conversion only to the initial purchasers of the convertible securities but not to subsequent holders, who may not meet eligibility criteria.

Because the Section 3(a)(9) exemption does not extend to the issuance of Common Stock on exercise of warrants (except for "net" exercise as discussed below), no registration opinions covering the issuance of Common Stock on exercise of warrants, when given, are normally based on an express assumption or condition that on exercise the shares of Common Stock will be issued to the initial purchasers of the warrants who will continue to be eligible to purchase the Common Stock pursuant to the exemption from registration being relied on. The opinion also may be given based on "net" exercise (i.e., part of the Common Stock issuable on exercise is used to pay the exercise price) where net exercise is required by the terms of the warrants, or it is permitted and the opinion is limited to cases in which it is employed.

Excluding Coverage of Resales

Some lawyers include a sentence in the first form of opinion letter emphasizing that the opinion does not cover resales by the purchasers of the securities being purchased or of Common Stock issued on conversion. For example, "We express no opinion as to when or under what circumstances any [securities] purchased by you may be reoffered or resold, or any Common Stock of the Company issuable on conversion of the [securities] may be offered or sold." Other lawyers consider such a sentence unnecessary where the restrictions on resale are adequately disclosed in the offering materials, since the opinion as written does not purport to address resales by purchasers of the securities or offers or sales of the underlying Common Stock.

Information Provided by the Issuer

In offerings made in reliance on Rule 505 or 506 of Regulation D or on Rule 144A, specific requirements relating to information to be furnished by the issuer to the purchasers may have to be met. Where these requirements apply, many lawyers expressly assume that they have been satisfied. The statute itself (i.e., Section 4(2)) does not contain any information requirement, but even when no information requirement is applicable some lawyers nevertheless expressly assume the adequacy of the information disclosed to investors (whether by delivery or by access).[1] The concern giving rise to this assumption may derive from the decision of the Second Circuit Court of Appeals in *SEC v. Manor Nursing Centers, Inc.*, 458 F.2d 1082, 1098–1100 (2d Cir. 1972), which imposed "a mandate of truthfulness" on exempt offerings. Although the implications of this holding have been criticized for making every antifraud lawsuit under the securities laws relating to exempt offerings also a potential claim for violation of Section 5, and in the private placement context may have been substantially circumscribed by *Gustafson v. Alloyd Co.*, Inc., 513 U.S.

1. The assumption as to adequacy of the information may be included even in circumstances where the opinion giver is also providing negative assurance on the information being disclosed. See the Subcommittee's report, *Negative Assurance in Securities Offerings*, 59 Bus. Law. 1513 (August 2004).

561 (1995) (holding that the Section 12(a)(2) antifraud provision does not apply to exempt offerings), the holding of *Manor Nursing Centers* has never been specifically overruled in the Second Circuit. Other lawyers believe that the assumption is implicit and therefore unnecessary.

Short Positions

If the security being sold is Common Stock (or is convertible into or accompanied by warrants to purchase Common Stock) of a class that is publicly traded, and if the purchasers have or may create short positions in the Common Stock, issues concerning violation of Section 5 of the Securities Act could arise. Such issues are beyond the scope of this report. For example, use of the stock purchased in the exempt offering to cover the short position could result in a violation of Section 5. These issues can be addressed by representations or agreements in the Purchase Agreement, a certificate or in other ways. If a certificate is being relied on, the opinion letter may refer to it expressly.

ABA Principles

Some lawyers expressly refer to the ABA Legal Opinion Principles, which purport to apply to legal opinions whether or not expressly mentioned. *See* 53 Bus. Law. 831 (May 1998).

Conclusion

These illustrative opinion letters do not attempt to cover all situations in which no registration opinions are given, but they illustrate the form and substance of opinion letters customarily delivered.

Form of no registration opinion for common or convertible preferred stock sold directly to purchasers in reliance on Section 4(2) or Regulation D

[Letterhead of Law Firm]

[Date]

[To the purchasers]

____

____

____

Ladies and Gentlemen:

We have acted as counsel to ____________________, a ____________ corporation (the "Company"), in connection with the sale by the Company to you of _______ shares (the "Shares") of the Company's [Common] [Series __ Convertible Preferred] Stock, [par value $_____ per share] [without par value], pursuant to the Purchase Agreement, dated ________________, between the Company and you (the "Purchase Agreement"). This opinion letter is delivered to you pursuant to Section __ of the Purchase Agreement. Capitalized terms defined in the Purchase Agreement and not otherwise defined herein are used herein as defined in the Purchase Agreement.

We have examined such documents and made such investigation of law as we have deemed appropriate for purposes of the opinions set forth below. In giving these opinions, we have relied without independent verification on certificates of public officials and, as to matters of fact material to our opinions, on the representations, warranties and agreements of the Company in the Purchase Agreement and on certificates of officers of the Company [and others].[1]

Based on the foregoing and subject to the qualifications set forth below, we express the following opinions:

(__) [Opinions as to corporate status, validity of the Shares and any Common Stock into which the Shares are convertible, consents, authorizations and approvals and execution, delivery and enforceability of the Purchase Agreement omitted.]

(__) Assuming the accuracy of your representations and warranties and compliance with your agreements in the Purchase Agreement, the offer, sale and delivery of the Shares by the Company to you in accordance with the Purchase Agreement [, and the offer, sale and delivery of the Common Stock issuable on conversion of the Shares,][2] are not required to be registered under the Securities Act of 1933.

[In connection with our opinion set forth in paragraph (__) above, we have also relied, among other things, on your certificate dated the date hereof as to _______.][3]

---

1. If shares are being offered by a placement agent, reference should be made to a certificate or representations of the placement agent describing the manner in which it has offered the shares.
2. See "Covering Shares Issuable on Conversion or Exercise" in the accompanying Report.
3. See "Short Positions" in the accompanying Report.

The opinions expressed herein are limited to the federal law of the United States, the law of the State of __________ [and the Delaware General Corporation Law].

This opinion letter is being delivered to you in connection with the above described transaction and may not be relied on by you for any other purpose. This opinion letter may not be furnished to or relied on by any other person without our prior written consent.

Very truly yours,

Form of no registration opinion for debt securities sold to intermediaries for resale in reliance on Rule 144A or Regulation S

[Letterhead of Law Firm]

[Date]

[To the Initial Purchasers]

____
____
____

Ladies and Gentlemen:

We have acted as counsel to ____________________, a ____________ corporation (the "Company"), in connection with the offer and sale of $____________ aggregate principal amount of the Company's __________ Notes (the "Notes"), issued pursuant to the Indenture, dated as of __________________, between the Company and _____________________, as trustee (the "Trustee), which are being purchased by you (the "Initial Purchasers") pursuant to the Purchase Agreement, dated ______________, between the Company and the Initial Purchasers (the "Purchase Agreement").[1] This opinion letter is delivered to you pursuant to Section __ of the Purchase Agreement. Capitalized terms defined in the Purchase Agreement and not otherwise defined herein are used herein as defined in the Purchase Agreement.

We have examined such documents and made such investigation of law as we have deemed appropriate for purposes of the opinions set forth below. In giving these opinions, we have relied without independent verification on certificates of public officials and, as to matters of fact material to our opinions, on the representations, warranties and agreements of the Company in the Purchase Agreement and on certificates of officers of the Company [and others].

Based on the foregoing and subject to the qualifications set forth below, we express the following opinions:

(__) [Opinions as to corporate status, execution, delivery and enforceability of the Indenture, validity of the Notes (and any Common Stock issuable on conversion of the Notes), consents, authorizations and approvals and execution, delivery and enforceability of the Purchase Agreement omitted.]

(__) Assuming the accuracy of the representations and warranties and compliance with the agreements of the Initial Purchasers in the Purchase Agreement, the offer, sale and delivery of the Notes by the Company to the Initial Purchasers[,] [and][2] the initial offer, sale and delivery of the Notes by the Initial Purchasers [and the offer, sale and delivery of Common Stock on conversion of the Notes],[2] in each case in accordance with the arrangements relating to offers, sales and deliveries of

1. If the Notes are convertible into or accompanied by warrants to purchase Common Stock, add appropriate references.
2. See "Covering Shares Issuable on Conversion or Exercise" in the accompanying Report.

the Notes [and Common Stock][2] contemplated by the Purchase Agreement, the [Offering Circular] [other document(s)] and the Indenture, are not required to be registered under the Securities Act of 1933, and the Indenture is not required to be qualified under the Trust Indenture Act of 1939.

[In connection with our opinion set forth in paragraph (__) above, we have also relied, among other things, on certificates of [the Initial Purchasers] dated the date hereof as to ____________________.][3]

The opinions expressed herein are limited to the federal law of the United States, the law of the State of __________ [and the Delaware General Corporation Law].

This opinion letter is being delivered to you in connection with the above described transaction and may not be relied on by you for any other purpose. This opinion letter may not be relied on by or furnished to any other person without our prior written consent.

Very truly yours,

3. See "Short Positions" in the accompanying Report.

Negative Assurance in Securities Offerings (2008 Revision)

Report of the Subcommittee on Securities Law Opinions,
Committee on Federal Regulation of Securities,
ABA Section of Business Law

Introduction

In 2004, a report entitled *Negative Assurance in Securities Offerings* by the Task Force on Securities Law Opinions of the ABA Section of Business Law was published in *The Business Lawyer*.[1] The five-page report and accompanying three-paragraph "Illustrative Form of Negative Assurance" envisaged that a single disclosure document would contain all material information provided to prospective investors.

A year after the report was published, the U.S. Securities and Exchange Commission ("SEC") significantly altered the landscape for public offerings by adopting securities offering reform proposals.[2] The new rules codified the SEC's view that the potential liability of a seller of securities for deficiencies in disclosure is based on the information about the issuer and the offering conveyed to prospective investors at or before the time when the contract of sale is entered into, rather than the information in the prospectus sent with the confirmation of sale.[3] Moreover, the new rules permitted use of written communications other than the statutory prospectus, called "free writing prospectuses," to convey information to prospective investors,[4] and the requirement that the final prospectus be physically delivered to the purchasers was eliminated so long as the final prospectus is filed with the SEC and the purchasers receive notice that they have purchased

1. 59 Bus. Law. 1513 (2004). After the Task Force completed its negative assurance report in 2004, the Subcommittee, which was a part of the Task Force, continued to work in this area.

2. *See* Securities Offering Reform, Securities Act Release No. 33-8591, 70 Fed. Reg. 44722 (Aug. 3, 2005) (codified at 17 C.F.R. pts. 200, 228, 229, 230, 239, 240, 243, 249, and 274).

3. Under Rule 159, 17 C.F.R. § 230.159 (2008), information "conveyed" to the purchaser after the "time of sale (including, without limitation, a contract of sale)" is not taken into account in determining liability under sections 12(a)(2) and 17(a)(2) of the Securities Act of 1933, 15 U.S.C. §§ 77*l*(a)(2), 77q(a)(2) (2006). The final prospectus, if filed as required, is taken into account for purposes of liability under section 11, 15 U.S.C. § 77k (2006).

4. Rule 164, 17 C.F.R. § 230.164 (2008), permits use of a free writing prospectus by an eligible issuer if the conditions of Rule 433, 17 C.F.R. § 230.433 (2008), are met. These conditions relate to delivery or availability of the statutory prospectus, inclusion of information that does not conflict with the prospectus, legending, and filing.

securities in a registered offering.[5] In addition, the use of offering documents that incorporate by reference the issuer's reports filed pursuant to the Securities Exchange Act of 1934 ("Exchange Act") has continued to increase.

In light of these developments, the Subcommittee is updating the 2004 report and illustrative form of negative assurance to reflect current law and practice.[6]

History and Purpose

Under the Securities Act of 1933 ("Securities Act"), registered public offerings of securities are required to be made by means of a registration statement that includes a prospectus.[7] If any part of the registration statement, as of its effective date, contains a misstatement of a material fact or omits a material fact that is required to be included or necessary to make the statements therein not misleading, the purchasers have a cause of action under section 11 of the Securities Act against the issuer, its directors, and others, including the underwriters.[8] However, an underwriter is not liable under section 11 if it sustains the burden of proof that, after reasonable investigation, it had reasonable ground to believe, and did believe, that the statements were true and that the registration statement contained no such omission.[9]

To help them establish the statutory "due diligence" defense in registered offerings, underwriters have long followed the practice of requiring, as a condition to the closing, that counsel[10] participating in the preparation of the registration statement provide negative assurance regarding the disclosures in the registration statement and prospectus.[11] More recently, that practice has been extended to some unregistered offerings (e.g., under Rule 144A[12] or Regulation S[13]) in

5. Under Rule 174(b), 17 C.F.R. § 230.174(b) (2008), a prospectus need not be delivered if the issuer is a reporting company under the Securities Exchange Act of 1934, with specified exceptions. Rule 173(a), 17 C.F.R. § 230.173(a) (2008), requires only that a notice be given to each purchaser to the effect that the sale was made pursuant to a registration statement.

6. This Report supersedes the 2004 report.

7. Securities Act § 5(b)(2), 15 U.S.C. § 77e(b)(2) (2006).

8. *Id.* § 11, 15 U.S.C. § 77k (2006). In addition, section 12(a)(2) of the Securities Act, 15 U.S.C. § 77*l*(a)(2) (2006), provides a purchaser with a cause of action against a person who has offered or sold a security by means of a prospectus or oral communication that includes an untrue statement of a material fact or omits to state a material fact necessary in order to make the statements, in the light of the circumstances under which they were made, not misleading.

9. *See id.* § 11, 15 U.S.C. § 77k (2006). A similar defense is available under section 12(a)(2) of the Securities Act if an underwriter sustains the burden of proof that it did not know, and in the exercise of reasonable care could not have known, of the untruth or omission. 15 U.S.C. § 77*l*(a)(2) (2006). Other persons potentially liable under section 11, except the issuer, have similar defenses.

10. Both issuer's counsel and underwriter's counsel generally provide negative assurance and use forms of letters that in practice are essentially identical.

11. Receipt of negative assurance letters from counsel is only one part of an underwriter's "due diligence." It also includes, among other things, receipt of "comfort letters" from accountants, conversations with the issuer's management, representations from the issuer, certifications from the issuer's officers, and other procedures the underwriter considers appropriate under the circumstances.

12. 17 C.F.R. § 230.144A (2008).

13. *Id.* §§ 230.901–.905.

which an offering document comparable to the statutory prospectus in a registered offering is delivered and the process of preparing it is comparable to that followed in a registered offering.[14] Although sections 11 and 12(a)(2) of the Securities Act do not apply to unregistered offerings,[15] financial intermediaries and placement agents may request negative assurance to help them establish a defense to claims that might be brought pursuant to Rule 10b-5 under the Exchange Act.[16] The practice of requesting negative assurance has been further extended to some offerings outside the United States.[17]

Negative assurance is not a "legal opinion." Rather, it is a statement of belief, unique to securities offerings, based principally on counsel's participation in the process of preparing and discussing the registration statement or other offering document with the various participants in the process.[18]

This Report offers guidance on providing negative assurance in both registered and, where appropriate, unregistered securities offerings, and includes an illustrative form. The form does not address other matters that may be covered in negative assurance letters.[19]

---

14. In a Rule 144A offering, the issuer typically sells securities pursuant to the exemption from registration provided by section 4(2) of the Securities Act, 15 U.S.C. § 17d(2) (2006), to a limited number of financial intermediaries who promptly resell the securities to "qualified institutional buyers" pursuant to the resale exemption provided by Rule 144A. Regulation S provides an exemption for certain offshore offerings. Sometimes the issuer sells securities directly to ultimate purchasers solicited by financial intermediaries, who may agree to purchase any securities not sold.

Underwriters of municipal securities sold to the public but exempt from registration under section 3(a)(2) of the Securities Act, 15 U.S.C. § 77c(a)(2) (2006), often request negative assurance. Dealer-managers in exchange offers by companies offering to exchange their securities for securities of another company or another class of their own securities sometimes request negative assurance.

15. *See* Gustafson v. Alloyd Co., 513 U.S. 561, 581 (1995).

16. Rule 10b-5, 17 C.F.R. § 240.10b-5 (2008), requires "scienter," i.e., intent to deceive, manipulate, or defraud or similar reckless conduct. *See* Ernst & Ernst v. Hochfelder, 425 U.S. 185, 193 (1976). "Due diligence" as such is not a defense under Rule 10b-5, but, if established, it would help to demonstrate the absence of scienter.

17. Some underwriters ask for negative assurance letters in non-U.S. transactions not involving U.S. investors or U.S. law because they believe that their ability to demonstrate that they conducted the "due diligence" customary in U.S. offerings may be helpful in defending claims brought under foreign law. However, U.S. lawyers may be reluctant to provide negative assurance letters to help underwriters establish a defense against potential liability under foreign laws, even if those laws contemplate a "due diligence" type defense.

18. *See* "Procedures Undertaken by Counsel Providing Negative Assurance" and "Basis for Providing Negative Assurance" below. Giving a negative assurance letter does not imply that counsel has made an investigation of every statement in the offering document. It only confirms that the work that counsel did perform in connection with preparing and reviewing the offering document and other issuer documents did not cause counsel to believe that the offering document contained a misstatement or omission of material fact.

19. For example, a negative assurance letter in a registered offering or an accompanying opinion letter often contains statements to the effect that the registration statement and prospectus complied as to form in all material respects with the requirements of the Securities Act of 1933 and (where applicable) the Trust Indenture Act of 1939, 15 U.S.C. §§ 77aaa–77bbbb (2006), and the rules and regulations thereunder or, alternatively, that the registration statement and prospectus appeared on their face to be appropriately responsive in all material respects to those requirements. Lawyers generally view such

Recipients of Negative Assurance

The purpose of negative assurance is to assist the recipient in establishing a due diligence or similar defense. Therefore, negative assurance is customarily provided only to underwriters or other third parties that can avoid liability in a securities offering by establishing such a defense.[20] Ultimate purchasers of securities, unlike underwriters or other financial intermediaries, do not have liability under the securities laws and accordingly do not need a defense against liability. For this reason, requests for counsel to provide negative assurance to ultimate purchasers, or to issuers,[21] are not appropriate.[22]

Incorporation of Documents by Reference

Today, prospectuses used in almost all registered public offerings, except initial public offerings, and offering documents used in many unregistered offerings, incorporate by reference documents filed by the issuer under the Exchange Act that contain business information and financial statements.[23] The new form of negative assurance contemplates incorporation of documents by reference and defines the terms "Prospectus" and "Offering Document" as including the documents incorporated by reference.[24]

A registration statement on Form S-3 or F-3 must incorporate by reference the issuer's latest annual report on Form 10-K, 20-F, or 40-F, as applicable, and all reports on Form 10-Q or Form 8-K filed since the end of the fiscal year covered by the annual report.[25] The incorporated documents typically do not include

---

a "compliance as to form" statement as addressing only the apparent responsiveness of the relevant document to particular disclosure requirements and not as confirming that all applicable disclosure requirements have been satisfied or that the apparently responsive disclosure is accurate or complete. Because a "compliance as to form" statement does not address the substance of the information, it is usually given only as of a single relevant date.

20. In global offerings, underwriters sometimes also perform other roles, such as acting as "sponsor" or "listing agent" for a foreign stock exchange listing, for which they may be subject to potential liabilities under foreign law. However, lawyers may be reluctant to address negative assurance letters to underwriters acting in any capacity other than as underwriters, since their potential liabilities for other roles arise under foreign law that may not contemplate a "due diligence" defense.

21. Issuers have potential securities law liability, but no "due diligence" defense, under section 11 of the Securities Act, 15 U.S.C. § 77k (2006).

22. Although directors have a "due diligence" defense under section 11, negative assurance letters are usually not addressed to them. Directors usually have better access than outside lawyers to information that enables them to assess the accuracy and completeness of disclosure and generally establish their "due diligence" defense in other ways.

23. Incorporation by reference means that the document being given to investors is deemed to include the incorporated documents as if they had been physically attached in full text. The issuer usually undertakes to provide copies of the incorporated documents on request and without charge to any person who receives a prospectus, and the incorporated documents are generally available through the issuer's web site and other web sites such as the SEC's EDGAR system.

24. If documents are not incorporated by reference, references to them in the form may be deleted.

25. Registration statements on Form S-1 or F-1 for public offerings by reporting companies that are not eligible for Form S-3 or F-3 frequently incorporate the same documents by reference. Because Form 10-K either incorporates information from the issuer's proxy or information statement filed

information about the offering, such as the terms and price of the securities being offered. That information is included in the prospectus. Many offerings today are made by means of a "shelf" registration statement that covers multiple offerings of different kinds of securities and often becomes effective well before the issuer is ready to proceed with any particular securities offering.[26] When an offering does not occur immediately after the shelf registration statement becomes effective, any reports on Form 10-K (or 20-F or 40-F), 10-Q, or 8-K filed by the issuer after the effective date are deemed incorporated by reference in the registration statement so that, when the offering occurs, the registration statement includes the most recent information filed by the issuer concerning its business and the issuer's most recent financial statements.[27]

Liability under section 11 of the Securities Act is determined by reference to whether "any part of the registration statement, when such part became effective," contains a material misstatement or omission.[28] When an offering commences immediately after a registration statement becomes effective, liability under section 11 of the Securities Act will depend on the "total mix" of information in the registration statement and any documents incorporated by reference in it as of the effective date of the registration statement. However, after the 2005 rule revisions, a new effective date of the registration statement is deemed to be established when the issuer offers securities "off the shelf" pursuant to a new form of prospectus required to be filed with the SEC pursuant to Rule 424(b)(2), (b)(5), or (b)(7).[29] Under Rule 430B(f),[30] this effective date is the earlier of the date that the new form of prospectus is first used or the date and time of the first contract of sale of the securities to which it relates.[31] When more than one document is incorporated by reference in the prospectus, any statement contained in an earlier document is deemed modified or superseded to whatever extent it has been modified or

pursuant to Regulation 14A, 17 C.F.R. §§ 240.14a-1, 240.14b-2 (2008), or includes the information required by Regulation 14A, registration statements that incorporate Form 10-K reports also incorporate information filed by the issuer pursuant to section 14(a) of the Securities Exchange Act, 15 U.S.C. § 78n(a) (2006).

26. If the registration statement is on Form S-3 or F-3, Rule 415, 17 C.F.R. § 230.415 (2008), allows the securities to be offered on a delayed or continuous basis for a period of three years after its effective date.

27. This is not so, however, for information included in reports on Form 6-K subsequently submitted to the SEC by a foreign private issuer. That information is incorporated by reference only when the registration statement and Form 6-K expressly so provide. Offering documents used outside the United States may also incorporate documents filed by the issuer with an offshore regulatory authority or securities exchange.

28. 15 U.S.C. § 77k (2006).

29. *See* 17 C.F.R. § 230.424(b)(2), (b)(5), (b)(7) (2008). Occasionally, a negative assurance letter is given before a prospectus has been prepared for a particular offering. In such a case, the letter will address the registration statement as of its effective date or, if a document filed by the issuer after the effective date is incorporated by reference in the prospectus, it may refer to "each part of the registration statement, when such part became effective."

30. 17 C.F.R. § 230.430B(f) (2008).

31. This effective date relates to the issuer and the underwriters participating in the offering to which the prospectus relates, but not to accountants, other experts, directors, and signing officers, who are covered by other provisions of Rule 430B(f) that look to earlier dates.

replaced in a subsequent document, and the superseded information is no longer deemed to be included in the registration statement.[32]

In shelf offerings, the registration statement may describe multiple classes of securities that the issuer may offer, but when the issuer actually makes an offering, it may offer just one of the classes. The lawyers providing negative assurance may seek to narrow their review of the offering documents to the description of the class being offered and exclude the descriptions of the other classes.[33] In these circumstances lawyers may limit their negative assurance on the registration statement to apply only "insofar as it relates to the offering of the Securities." The new form of negative assurance includes optional language to that effect.[34]

Pricing Disclosure Package

Because Rule 159[35] provides that information conveyed to purchasers after the time of sale is not taken into account in determining liability under section 12(a)(2) of the Securities Act,[36] the new form focuses on the documents that are available to be conveyed to purchasers at or before the time of sale, which it refers to collectively as the "Pricing Disclosure Package." Different terms may be used in practice. The form provides for the documents in the Pricing Disclosure Package to be listed in Exhibit A to the letter. They would normally include a prospectus that is made available or distributed to investors before pricing (e.g., a preliminary prospectus or a base prospectus with one or more prospectus supplements), as well as certain other written documents ("free writing prospectuses") prepared at or before pricing that contain additional disclosures (e.g., a term sheet) and a description of any material information conveyed orally (e.g., the price in an initial public offering).[37]

32. *See* Rule 412, 17 C.F.R. § 230.412 (2008). The modifying or superseding statement need not state that it is modifying an earlier statement. This can result in difficult determinations regarding precisely what information is included in the "total mix" of the information in all the documents.

33. A similar circumstance can arise with respect to documents incorporated by reference, which may include information (e.g., some risk factors in Form 10-K reports, or certain Form 8-K reports) relating primarily to classes of securities that are not being offered.

34. This issue may also be addressed in some cases by defining the terms "Registration Statement" and "Prospectus" so as to include only the information relevant to the offering. In defining "Registration Statement" and "Prospectus," lawyers often refer specifically to particular amendments to the registration statement, base prospectuses, prospectus supplements, and other documents that have been filed with the SEC to make clear which ones are part of the "Registration Statement" and "Prospectus" for purposes of the letter.

35. 17 C.F.R. § 230.159 (2008).

36. *See supra* note 3.

37. The documents included in the Pricing Disclosure Package will vary depending on the circumstances of the offering. Drafts that are superseded by later drafts (e.g., preliminary prospectuses that are amended) and supplemental marketing materials (e.g., free writing prospectuses that are derived from the preliminary prospectus and do not contain additional material information) will not be included. In offerings of asset-backed securities, counsel may provide negative assurance only on a preliminary prospectus or a "virtual red" (a free writing prospectus containing substantially the same information as a preliminary prospectus) and not on other documents sent by underwriters or dealers to prospective investors prior to pricing.

Financial intermediaries in unregistered offerings often follow the practice of providing purchasers with a Pricing Disclosure Package.[38] The new form includes alternative language that may be used when this is done.

Time as of Which Negative Assurance Speaks

Because the purpose of negative assurance is to assist the recipients in establishing a due diligence defense, negative assurance letters in registered offerings address the documents on which liability may be based as of the date liability is determined under the Securities Act. Thus, for purposes of section 11 liability, the new form addresses the registration statement as of its effective date. Because of possible uncertainty as to what that date may be, some letters simply refer to "the effective date" or, in a shelf takedown, the "most recent effective date" of the registration statement. Other letters refer to a specific date, which is usually the same date as the prospectus but not identified as such. The new form allows for both alternatives.

Liability under section 12(a)(2) of the Securities Act is determined as of the date of the use or delivery of the allegedly misleading prospectus or oral communication.[39] The form addresses the prospectus as of its date and the Pricing Disclosure Package as of a precise time on a specified day, which is immediately before any sale has been made or contract of sale entered into and is generally the time when the offering price is fixed.[40] In the case of offerings exempt from Securities Act registration, the form addresses the offering document as of its date.

Manner of Expressing Negative Assurance

The illustrative form expresses negative assurance with the words "nothing came to our attention that caused us to believe." Alternative formulations are also common, such as "led us to conclude" in place of "caused us to believe," "no facts" in place of "nothing," and "nothing that came to our attention caused us to believe." These differences in formulation do not change the subjective nature of the negative assurance being given.

Procedures Undertaken by Counsel Providing Negative Assurance

Negative assurance letters generally state that counsel has read the registration statement or offering document and participated in discussions with representatives of the issuer and others but do not describe in detail all the work that counsel

38. This is true for domestic offerings. The documents used in offshore offerings by non-U.S. issuers, even when they include a Rule 144A component, are likely to be influenced by local market practices. If a Pricing Disclosure Package is used, it may include a preliminary prospectus that has been distributed to institutional investors before the prospectus to be used in the local market has been approved by the local regulator.

39. *See* 15 U.S.C. § 77*l*(a)(2) (2006).

40. Because counsel generally is not in a position to know when sales of securities actually began, the time described is usually a time that the underwriters have informed counsel preceded the first sale of the securities.

has done in connection with the offering.[41] Historically, counsel for the issuer in a securities offering gave a legal opinion on the validity of the securities being offered.[42] In addition, counsel participated in preparing the registration statement or other offering document, and this work provided the basis for giving negative assurance.

Today, however, the lawyers engaged to work on a securities offering may not have been involved in the preparation of the documents incorporated by reference.[43] In these circumstances, they may include additional language in the letter to emphasize the limited nature of the work they performed in connection with these documents. Some state that they did not participate in preparing the documents incorporated by reference.

Offerings using short-form registration statements and take-downs from shelf registration statements under Rule 415,[44] as well as comparable unregistered offerings, often take place within a short time—sometimes even overnight. In these offerings, lawyers customarily provide negative assurance based on their review, within the limited time available, of the offering document and the documents incorporated by reference, discussions with representatives of the issuer about these documents, and whatever knowledge they may have gained in prior representation of the issuer or participation in prior offerings by the issuer.[45]

Customary Qualifications

A lawyer is not an insurer of the adequacy of the disclosure in an offering document or a "reputational intermediary." Virtually all negative assurance letters state that counsel does not assume any responsibility for the accuracy, completeness, or fairness of the offering document, except to the extent that specific sections are addressed in a separate opinion or confirmation. Some letters refer to limitations on counsel's professional engagement and the fact that many of the disclosures in an offering document are of a non-legal character. Some state that counsel is relying on the judgment of management or others regarding the adequacy of disclosure. Many state that counsel has not undertaken to verify the facts contained in the disclosure document.

41. Unlike standard opinion letters, negative assurance letters typically do not state that in preparing the letter counsel has carried out such procedures as counsel has considered necessary or appropriate to provide negative assurance.

42. Schedule A to the Securities Act requires that "an opinion or opinions of counsel in respect to the legality of the issue" be filed with the registration statement. *See* 15 U.S.C. § 77aa(29). For a discussion of such opinions, see the article cited in *infra* note 55.

43. This is especially true in the case of underwriters' counsel, who may have had no prior contact with the issuer but is still expected to provide negative assurance.

44. 17 C.F.R. § 230.415 (2008).

45. When there is concern with the existing disclosure, the prospectus may be modified by means of a preliminary prospectus supplement or free writing prospectus or by a report filed on Form 8-K that has the effect of amending the prospectus through incorporation by reference.

Basis for Providing Negative Assurance

A statement of negative assurance by a law firm necessarily expresses only the actual subjective belief (i.e., conscious awareness) of those lawyers in the firm who have actively participated in the process of preparing the offering document.[46] That belief is subject to a good-faith standard and is based on their familiarity with the issuer and what they learned as a result of the procedures described in the negative assurance letter and their work in connection with the offering. When a law firm is acting as counsel to the issuer in an offering, the lawyers involved in the offering often consult with other lawyers in the firm who have performed other work for the issuer. When a law firm acts as counsel to the underwriters, the lawyers who work on the offering are likely to be the only lawyers in the firm who are knowledgeable about the issuer.[47]

Subjects Not Addressed

Negative assurance letters expressly exclude coverage of financial statements, as such, and this exclusion is understood to encompass the accountants' report, notes to the financial statements and financial statement schedules, whether or not expressly stated. Many negative assurance letters also expressly exclude financial, accounting, and/or statistical data[48] and assessments or reports on the effectiveness of internal control over financial reporting. In addition, many letters expressly exclude other "expertized" material, such as reserve information covered by an engineer's report and appraisals.

Underwriters may object to exclusions of matters that are not being covered by other participants in the offering process, such as accountants or other experts.[49] They reason that the letter is not only providing them negative assurance but is giving them the benefit of counsel's reading of the entire disclosure document. Accordingly, they may argue that the lawyers should suggest corrections to any

46. While some underwriters object to the inclusion in a negative assurance letter of "ring fencing" language to this effect, most lawyers believe that, based on custom and practice, the negative assurance statement should be understood by the recipient to be based solely on the knowledge of this limited group of lawyers. They believe that underwriters do not, and could not justifiably, believe that every lawyer in the firm would be consulted about every negative assurance letter. On occasion, underwriters have requested a statement that the belief expressed in the negative assurance encompasses all lawyers in the firm who have performed services for the client. Providing such a statement could require canvassing numerous lawyers in multiple offices who are not securities lawyers and have not devoted attention to the offering document. In addition, it would require those lawyers to make judgments beyond their expertise regarding the application of the federal securities laws to that document. Many lawyers would consider such an approach to be impractical and uneconomic.

47. Unlike counsel for the issuer, which is providing negative assurance to a third party, counsel for the underwriters is providing negative assurance to its clients, the underwriters.

48. Some lawyers refer to "information" instead of "data" or to data or information "derived from" the financial statements or the accounting records of the issuer. Even if statistical data or some financial information are not expressly excluded, underwriters understand that there are inherent limitations in the nature of a negative assurance letter insofar as it addresses disclosure outside the expertise of the lawyers providing it.

49. Accountants' comfort letters do not generally cover all financial or accounting data in the prospectus and never address non-financial statistical data.

perceived misstatements or omissions that the lawyers identify anywhere in the document, recognizing that lawyers will not necessarily have a full understanding of all matters. While in practice lawyers may suggest corrections throughout the document, many lawyers insist upon exclusions because they do not want to be perceived as providing even negative assurance on specialized information as to which other offering participants are more qualified to express a view.[50]

Addressing Disclosure as of the Closing Date

Recipients often request that negative assurance letters address the prospectus or offering document both as of its date and as of the closing date (i.e., the date of the negative assurance letter).[51] Many lawyers are willing to give negative assurance as of the closing date, even when it is unclear that the recipients' liability would be determined by reference to that date.[52] Lawyers who give negative assurance as of the closing date often perform additional procedures to update their work to the closing date and may describe such procedures in the letter.[53] The new form includes bracketed language in subparagraph (3) to be inserted when the letter covers the final offering document as of the closing date.

Role of Counsel

Negative assurance normally is provided only by counsel having overall responsibility for advising the issuer or underwriters (or other financial intermediaries) concerning the offering document. When other counsel has been retained to advise the issuer on a particular aspect of a transaction (e.g., tax, foreign law, intellectual property, or regulatory matters), such counsel usually addresses the portion of the offering document dealing with that matter by giving an opinion on the accuracy of the description rather than by providing negative assurance.[54]

50. Because a negative assurance letter is intended to be only one component of underwriters' "due diligence" and is informed by the other components, lawyers may decline to give negative assurance if other customary aspects of underwriters' "due diligence," such as receipt of accountants' comfort letters, are not contemplated.

51. Addressing the Pricing Disclosure Package as of the closing date is not appropriate since the Pricing Disclosure Package is superseded by the prospectus or final offering document shortly after the price and terms of the securities have been determined. Therefore, by the closing date the Pricing Disclosure Package, as such, is no longer being used.

52. Under the securities offering reform rules, the time of sale is the key reference point, but even when the underwriters have sold all the securities on the date of pricing and the closing date is three trading days later, underwriters may request that the negative assurance letter be updated to cover the final offering document as of the closing date.

53. A similar issue arises when counsel is asked to update negative assurance in connection with the closing of the underwriters' exercise of an overallotment option days or even weeks after the initial closing of an offering. Although the relevance of the subsequent closing date to the underwriters' potential liability is questionable (since the securities usually have been sold to purchasers long before the exercise of the overallotment option), many lawyers are willing to provide negative assurance at a subsequent closing, in which case they often perform additional procedures during the intervening period and describe those procedures in the letter.

54. Other counsel ordinarily should not be asked to provide negative assurance. However, such a request may be appropriate when such counsel has been retained specifically to advise the issuer

In some cases, such counsel may also provide an opinion to be filed with the registration statement.[55]

Conveyance Not Addressed

Some negative assurance letters state that counsel expresses no view on whether documents included in the Pricing Disclosure Package have been "conveyed" to purchasers by the underwriters. The new form does not include that disclaimer because in practice lawyers are not in a position to address conveyance, and the negative assurance given does not address it. Counsel cannot be expected to have knowledge of communications between the underwriters and the purchasers and, therefore, would have no basis for expressing a view.[56]

Location of Negative Assurance

Because negative assurance is not a legal opinion, it is generally provided in a separate letter[57] or in a separate unnumbered paragraph of a closing opinion. Either way, counsel's responsibility and the meaning of the negative assurance are the same.

IRS Circular 230

Some lawyers include a legend or paragraph referring to IRS Circular 230.[58] Many lawyers have concluded that a reference to IRS Circular 230 is unnecessary

---

regarding the disclosure in a particular area that is material to the issuer, such as patent or regulatory matters, is experienced in applicable securities law standards, and has had sufficient involvement with the disclosure document. When other counsel has been consulted with regard to particular matters, counsel principally involved in the preparation of the offering document may wish to indicate that, to the extent its negative assurance covers those matters, its belief is based on the advice of the other counsel. For example, in global offerings by foreign issuers, U.S. counsel may work closely with a local law firm regarding issues of foreign law or documentation in a language other than English and may seek to rely on that counsel in giving the negative assurance letter. Even in the absence of express reliance on other counsel, the recipient of a negative assurance letter should understand that the negative assurance it is receiving is necessarily based on the advice of the other counsel as part of the total mix of information.

55. Providing an opinion filed with the registration statement may result in an assertion of "expert's" liability under section 11(a)(4) of the Securities Act, 15 U.S.C. § 77k(a)(4) (2008), which imposes liability on persons whose profession gives authority to statements made by them that have been included in the registration statement with their consent. Legal opinions filed with registration statements sometimes state that counsel does not admit to being an "expert" within the meaning of the Securities Act. *See Special Report of the Task Force on Securities Law Opinions, ABA Section of Business Law, Legal Opinions in SEC Filings*, 59 Bus. Law. 1505, 1506 (2004).

56. If counsel representing the underwriters believes that the Pricing Disclosure Package has not in fact been conveyed to purchasers, counsel should consider whether to advise the underwriters separately of the potential consequences of non-conveyance.

57. The separate letter approach may help counsel limit the recipients of negative assurance to those for whom it is appropriate. As stated above under "Recipients of Negative Assurance," negative assurance is normally not directed to all the recipients of a closing opinion or all those identified as entitled to rely on it, such as trustees or transfer agents. Counsel providing negative assurance generally restricts distribution of copies of the letter, as discussed below.

58. 31 C.F.R. §§ 10.0–.93 (2008).

if the underlying disclosure document has been filed with the SEC or contains appropriate legends.[59]

Concluding Paragraph

Since the purpose of negative assurance is to assist the underwriters in establishing a "due diligence" defense, negative assurance letters normally include a paragraph similar to the concluding paragraph of the new form to emphasize that they are being furnished only to the underwriters (or other financial intermediaries) in their capacity as such and are not to be relied on by anyone else. Some letters state expressly that their purpose is to assist the recipient in establishing defenses under applicable securities laws.

59. IRS Circular 230 requires lawyers to include in documents they send to clients that contain any advice on taxes prominent legends stating that the advice cannot be used for the purpose of avoiding tax penalties that may be imposed and also requires lawyers to conform to specified standards if such advice is intended to be provided.

Illustrative Form of Negative Assurance[1]

Alternative First Paragraph—Registered Offering

Reference is made to the Registration Statement on Form [S/F]-[1/3] (File No. _______) (the "Registration Statement") and the Prospectus, dated ______, 20___ ([including the documents incorporated by reference therein, collectively,][2] the "Prospectus"),[3] relating to _________________ (the "Securities") of ___________ (the "Company"). As [counsel to the Company] [your counsel], we reviewed the Registration Statement and Prospectus together with the documents and information listed in Exhibit A hereto (such documents and information hereinafter referred to collectively as the "Pricing Disclosure Package")[4] and participated in discussions with your representatives and representatives of the Company, [its counsel,][5] [and] its independent registered public accounting firm [and your counsel][6] regarding such documents and information and related matters. [We did not participate in the preparation of the documents incorporated by reference in the Prospectus.][7]

* * * * *

Alternative First Paragraph—Unregistered Offering

Reference is made to the Offering Document,[8] dated ______, 20__ ([including the documents incorporated by reference therein, collectively,][2] the "Offering Document"), relating to _________________ (the "Securities") of ____________ (the "Company"). As [counsel to the Company] [your counsel], we reviewed the Offering Document [together with the documents and information listed in Exhibit A hereto (such documents and information hereinafter referred to collectively as the "Pricing Disclosure Package")][4] and participated in discussions with your representatives and representatives of the Company, [its counsel,][5] [and] its independent registered public accounting firm [and your counsel][6] regarding such documents and information and related matters. [We did not participate in the preparation of the documents incorporated by reference in the Offering Document.][7]

* * * * *

1. This form is included solely for illustrative purposes. The Subcommittee does not recommend any particular form of negative assurance.
2. See "Incorporation of Documents by Reference" in the Report.
3. See note 34 in the Report.
4. See "Pricing Disclosure Package" in the Report.
5. Insert where counsel providing negative assurance is representing the recipients.
6. Insert where counsel providing negative assurance is representing the Company.
7. See "Procedures Undertaken by Counsel Providing Negative Assurance" in the Report.
8. This form uses "Offering Document" for an unregistered offering. Change terminology to "Offering Memorandum," "Offering Circular," or other appropriate document as needed.

The purpose of our professional engagement was not to establish or to confirm factual matters set forth in the [Registration Statement, the Prospectus]—[Offering Document]—[or the Pricing Disclosure Package], and we have not undertaken to verify independently any of such factual matters. Moreover, many of the determinations required to be made in the preparation of the [Registration Statement, the Prospectus]—[Offering Document]—[and the Pricing Disclosure Package] involve matters of a non-legal nature.

Subject to the foregoing and on the basis of the information we gained in the course of performing the services referred to above, we confirm to you that nothing came to our attention that caused us to believe[9] that:

> [(1) the Registration Statement, as of [its [most recent] effective date]—[______, 20___],[10] [insofar as it relates to the offering of the Securities,][11] contained any untrue statement of a material fact or omitted to state any material fact required to be stated therein or necessary to make the statements therein not misleading, or][12]
>
> [(1)(2)] the Pricing Disclosure Package, as of __:__ _.m. on ________, 20__,[13] [insofar as it relates to the offering of the Securities,][11] contained any untrue statement of a material fact or omitted to state any material fact necessary in order to make the statements therein, in the light of the circumstances under which they were made, not misleading, or]
>
> [(1)(2)(3)] the [Prospectus]—[Offering Document], as of its date [and as of the date hereof],[14] [insofar as it relates to the offering of the Securities,][11] contained [or contains][14] any untrue statement of a material fact or omitted [or omits][14] to state any material fact necessary in order to make the statements therein, in the light of the circumstances under which they were made, not misleading;

provided, however, that we do not assume any responsibility for the accuracy, completeness or fairness of the statements contained in the [Registration Statement, the Prospectus]—[Offering Document]—[or the Pricing Disclosure Package] (except for ________),[15] and we do not express any belief with respect to the financial statements [or other financial[, statistical] or accounting data or information][16] or assessments of or reports on the effectiveness of internal control over financial reporting contained in[17] [the Registration Statement, the Prospectus]—[Offering Document]—[or the Pricing Disclosure Package].

---

9. See "Manner of Expressing Negative Assurance" and "Basis for Providing Negative Assurance" in the Report.
10. See "Time as of Which Negative Assurance Speaks" in the Report.
11. See "Incorporation of Documents by Reference" in the Report.
12. Include this subparagraph only in a registered offering.
13. See "Time as of Which Negative Assurance Speaks" in the Report.
14. See "Addressing Disclosure as of the Closing Date" in the Report.
15. Refer to any specific portions of the disclosure document—e.g., the description of a contract or a particular area of the law—when broader coverage is intended to be provided.
16. See "Subjects Not Addressed" in the Report.
17. Some lawyers add "or omitted from" to make explicit what is understood without that phrase.

This letter is being furnished by us only to you, is solely for your benefit in your capacity as [Underwriters][18] [to assist you in establishing defenses under applicable securities laws] and may not be used, quoted, relied upon or otherwise referred to for any other purpose or by any other person (including any person purchasing any of the Securities from you).[19]

18. In unregistered offerings, use term referring to financial intermediaries distributing the Securities.

19. See "Concluding Paragraph" in the Report.

Appendix A

Pricing Disclosure Package

1. [Prospectus or Offering Document]
2. [Free writing prospectus; term sheet]
3. [Description of any material information conveyed orally]

Statement on Effect of FIN 48 on Audit Response Letters*

By the Committee on Audit Responses, ABA Section of Business Law

On July 13, 2006, the Financial Accounting Standards Board ("FASB") issued Interpretation No. 48 ("FIN 48") on Accounting for Uncertainty in Income Taxes,[1] which is an interpretation of FASB Statement No. 109, Accounting for Income Taxes, issued in 1992.[2] FIN 48 applies to issues involving federal, state, local, or foreign income taxes. It is effective for public companies for fiscal years beginning after December 15, 2006,[3] and generally is effective for non-public companies for fiscal years beginning after December 15, 2007,[4] although the FASB has proposed a one-year deferral of the effective date for non-public companies.[5] FIN 48 provides that its guidance governs with respect to accounting for such tax contingencies in place of FASB Statement No. 5, Accounting for Contingencies ("FAS 5").[6] As discussed below, the Committee on Audit Responses of the American Bar Association's Section of Business Law ("the Committee") believes that the issuance of FIN 48 does not change the standards under which a lawyer should respond to an auditor's request for information regarding such contingencies. The Committee further believes that, although FIN 48 can affect the way a lawyer advises his or her client when income tax matters are involved, it does not alter the lawyer's professional responsibility to provide that advice when that is required within the scope of the lawyer's engagement.

---

* Editor's Note: This statement is published in the form approved by the Committee on Audit Responses on August 10, 2008. It has not been approved by formal action of the American Bar Association or the Council of the Section of Business Law, and it therefore does not constitute an official position by either. It does, however, represent the views of the Committee on Audit Responses.

1. Fin. Accounting Standards Bd., FASB Interpretation No. 48, Accounting for Uncertainty in Income Taxes (June 2006), *available at* http://www.fasb.org/pdf/fin%2048.pdf.

2. Fin. Accounting Standards Bd., Statement of Financial Accounting Standards No. 109, Accounting for Income Taxes (Feb. 1992), *available at* http://www.fasb.org/pdf/fas109.pdf.

3. FIN 48, *supra* note 1, at ¶ 22.

4. Fin. Accounting Standards Bd., FASB Staff Position FIN 48-2, Effective Date of FASB Interpretation No. 48 for Certain Nonpublic Enterprises (Feb. 1, 2008).

5. Fin. Accounting Standards Bd., FSP FIN 48-c, Proposed FASB Staff Position on Interpretation No. 48 (Nov. 4, 2008).

6. FIN 48, *supra* note 1, app. C, at ¶ C2.

HANDLING LOSS CONTINGENCIES UNDER THE TREATY

In 1975 the Board of Governors of the American Bar Association, following approval by the Section on Corporation, Banking and Business Law (now the Section of Business Law), approved a Statement of Policy Regarding Lawyers' Responses to Auditors' Requests for Information (the "ABA Statement")[7] that had been previously approved by the Auditing Standards Executive Committee of the American Institute of Certified Public Accountants ("AICPA"). The AICPA also approved in parallel Statement of Auditing Standards No. 12 recognizing the ABA Statement.[8] This so-called "Treaty" between the legal and accounting professions has operated successfully for over thirty years pursuant to the following ground rules:

- A lawyer will only furnish information in an audit response letter with respect to "loss contingencies" as defined in FAS 5 that may result in incurrence of a liability or impairment of an asset, if the lawyer has devoted substantive attention to and consulted with the client with respect to the following loss contingencies:
  - overtly threatened or pending litigation, whether or not specified by the client;
  - contractually assumed obligations that the client has specifically identified and upon which the client has specifically requested comment to the auditor; and
  - unasserted possible claims or assessments that the client has specifically identified and upon which the client has specifically requested comment to the auditor.
- A lawyer will not express any opinion in the audit response letter on the outcome of a loss contingency or the extent of possible exposure unless the lawyer concludes that liability is either probable or remote.
- A lawyer should not be requested to comment on unasserted claims unless the client has determined that it is probable (i.e., likely to occur) that a possible claim will be asserted, that there is a reasonable possibility that, if asserted, the outcome will be unfavorable, and that a resulting liability will be material to the financial condition of the client.
- A lawyer should confirm, as contemplated by the Treaty (see Paragraph 6 of the ABA Statement), that, when the lawyer, within the scope of his or her engagement, has formed a professional judgment that the client must disclose or consider disclosure of a possible claim in its financial statements, the lawyer will so advise the client and consult with the client regarding such disclosure. The auditor may assume that in these circumstances the lawyer has advised the client regarding disclosure of unasserted claims

7. 31 BUS. LAW. 1709 (1976). The ABA Statement and related relevant materials can be found in the *Auditor's Letter Handbook* published by the American Bar Association.

8. Am. Inst. of Certified Pub. Accountants, Statement of Auditing Standards No. 12, Inquiry of a Client's Lawyer Concerning Litigation, Claims, and Assessments (Jan. 7, 1976).

that may call for financial statement disclosure. If the lawyer's advice regarding disclosure is disregarded by the client, the lawyer, as a matter of professional responsibility, may need to consider withdrawal from the engagement or other remedial action.[9]

Just as a lawyer should be familiar with FAS 5 in responding to auditor's requests for information about loss contingencies and advising the client on its disclosure obligations, a lawyer should be familiar with FIN 48 when that is relevant to the lawyer's engagement.

The adoption of FIN 48 raises a number of issues with respect to audit response letters.

Dealing with FIN 48's "More Likely than Not" Requirement

FIN 48 requires the client to account in its financial statements for income tax loss contingencies (FIN 48 speaks in terms of "income tax uncertainties") based on the client's assessment under a two-step process: *first*, determining whether it is more likely than not that its position will be sustained upon examination, and *second*, if so, measuring and recognizing the largest amount of tax benefit that is greater than 50 percent likely of being realized upon ultimate settlement with a taxing authority that has full knowledge of all relevant information.[10] The unrecognized tax benefit is a liability and, if the client cannot reach the "more likely than not" conclusion, the entire tax liability must be recognized. In making the determinations under FIN 48, the client may choose to seek legal assistance regarding its tax position, but the required assessment and corresponding measurement is that of the client, as the Treaty specifically recognizes that a lawyer is not required to make determinations of what should be disclosed in financial statements.[11]

For purposes of preparing an audit response letter, a lawyer should continue to follow the usual practice under the Treaty regarding whether or not to comment on the expected outcome of asserted and unasserted claims disclosed in the audit response letter under the "probable" or "remote" standard, leaving it to the client to determine for financial reporting purposes whether its position will be sustained and the amount of the tax benefit, including whether the "more likely than not" determination can be made. Accordingly, because it would be a departure from the ABA Statement, a lawyer, if requested to do so, may appropriately decline to comment in the audit response letter on the determinations required to be made under FIN 48.

---

9. *See* ABA Statement, *supra* note 7, at 1714, 1724–25.

10. *See* FIN 48, *supra* note 1, at ¶¶ 6–8.

11. *See ABA Statement of Policy Regarding Lawyers' Responses to Auditors' Request for Information, Second Report of the Committee on Audit Inquiry Responses Regarding Initial Implementation*, 32 Bus. Law. 177, 183–84 (1976).

Dealing with Unasserted Income Tax Claims

Paragraph 38 of FAS 5 (which is quoted in the Commentary to the ABA Statement[12]) discusses when assertion of an unasserted claim is to be considered probable, and leaves to the client the determination of whether assertion of the claim is probable (i.e., likely to occur).[13] If the client determines that assertion is not probable, then no accrual or disclosure is required under FAS 5, and so long as the lawyer believes the client has a reasonable basis for its determination, the lawyer may deliver an audit response letter without the unasserted claim being disclosed.

FIN 48 has made Paragraph 38 of FAS 5 inapplicable to income taxes, and proceeds on the assumption that, in assessing whether the client satisfies the "more likely than not" criterion for success, it is to be presumed that the client's tax position will be examined by the relevant taxing authority that has full knowledge of all relevant information.[14] Thus, the client's judgment that a claim is not likely to be asserted by a taxing authority ceases to be applicable in determining what the client may need to disclose in the financial statements with respect to unasserted contingencies relating to income taxes. In cases where the lawyer has rendered substantive advice to the client with respect to a material unasserted contingent liability relating to income taxes, the lawyer, in responding to the auditor's request for information, should be aware of FIN 48, and if the lawyer has concluded that financial statement disclosure of the income tax contingency is required but is not satisfied that the auditor has been or will be made aware of the contingency, the lawyer should consider what action is appropriate as a matter of professional responsibility. Such action might include, depending on the circumstances, refraining from providing the audit response letter and possibly withdrawing from the engagement.

Addressing Asserted Income Tax Claims

Overtly threatened and pending income tax claims should continue to be handled in the audit response letter pursuant to the Treaty, as summarized above.

Effect of FIN 48's Amendment of FAS 5 on the Treaty

The last paragraph of the standard form of audit response letter included in the ABA Statement indicates that it is limited by, and in accordance with, the ABA Statement, and confirms that whenever a lawyer has formed a professional conclusion that the client must disclose or consider disclosure concerning an unasserted possible claim or assessment, the lawyer, as a matter of professional responsibility

12. *See* ABA Statement, *supra* note 7, at 1721.

13. *See* Fin. Accounting Standards Bd., FASB Interpretation No. 5, Accounting for Contingencies ¶ 38 (Mar. 1975).

14. *See* FIN 48, *supra* note 1, at ¶ 7a.

to the client, will so advise the client and will consult with the client concerning the question of such disclosure "and the applicable requirements of Statement of Financial Accounting Standards No. 5."[15] Notwithstanding that FIN 48 makes Paragraph 38 of FAS 5 inapplicable to unasserted claims for incomes taxes, the Committee believes, as indicated above, that this change to FAS 5 does not alter the professional responsibility of a lawyer to advise its client on financial statement disclosure with respect to income tax matters when that is required in connection with the lawyer's engagement.

15. *See* ABA Statement, *supra* note 7, at 1734, 1736.